EISENHOWER'S GUERRILLAS

BENJAMIN F. JONES

EISENHOWER'S GUERRILLAS

The Jedburghs, the *Maquis*, and the Liberation of France

OXFORD
UNIVERSITY PRESS

OXFORD
UNIVERSITY PRESS

Oxford University Press is a department of the University of Oxford.
It furthers the University's objective of excellence in research, scholarship,
and education by publishing worldwide. Oxford is a registered trade mark of
Oxford University Press in the UK and certain other countries.

Published in the United States of America by Oxford University Press
198 Madison Avenue, New York, NY 10016, United States of America

Library of Congress Cataloging-in-Publication Data
Jones, Benjamin F., 1966–
Eisenhower's guerrillas : the Jedburghs, the *Maquis*, and the liberation of
France / Benjamin F. Jones.
pages   cm
Includes bibliographical references and index.
ISBN 978-0-19-994208-4—ISBN 978-0-19-994209-1—ISBN 978-0-19-935183-1
1. World War, 1939–1945—Secret service—France.   2. World War, 1939–1945—Campaigns—France.
3. World War, 1939–1945—Underground movements—France.   4. Guerrillas—France—History—20th century.
5. Special forces (Military science)—France—History—20th century.   6. Special operations (Military science)—
France—History—20th century.   I. Title.   II. Title: Jedburghs, the Maquis, and the liberation of France.
D810.S7J46   2016
950.54'214—dc23   2015014744

1 3 5 7 9 8 6 4 2

Printed in the United States of America
on acid-free paper

Eisenhower's Guerrillas *is dedicated to the Jedburghs who were killed in action. They are:*

Lieutenant A. Bordes, French Army, Team Alec

Lieutenant A. Chaigneau, French Army, Team Aubrey

Major John Bonsall, US Army, Team Augustus

Captain J. Delwiche, French Army, Team Augustus

Technical Sergeant Roger Cote, US Army, Team Augustus

Captain J. F. D. Radice, British Army, Team Bunny

Captain Jean Roblot, French Army, Team Douglas II

First Lieutenant Lawrence Swank, US Army, Team Ephredine

Major Colin M. Ogden-Smith, British Army, Team Francis

First Sergeant Lewis Goddard, US Army, Team Ivor

Sergeant Lucien J. Bourgoin, US Army, Team Ian

Captain Victor Gough, British Army, Team Jacob

Lieutenant Maurice Boussarie, French Army, Team Jacob

Lieutenant Paul Angoulvent, French Army, Team Lee

Captain T. A. Mellows, British Army, Team Martin

Captain Gaston Vuchot, French Army, Team Veganin

Sergeant D. Gardner, British Army, Team Veganin

It is further dedicated to all those brave Free French and Maquis, *many who remain uncelebrated, who lost their lives in France's liberation. And to the memory of French Jedburgh Lieutenant Joe de Francesco and American Jedburgh Captain Bernard M. W. Knox. These two lived long past the war and they were instrumental in the making of not only this book, but of this historian.*

2 Corinthians 3:17

propter Gloriam Dei

CONTENTS

ACKNOWLEDGMENTS

In 1998, I began what I thought would be a simple historical project looking into how commandos fared when they parachuted into France to blow up bridges. What could be hard about that? But as Clausewitz tells us about war, "the simplest thing is difficult." Along the way I learned, and I hope the reader will learn, about war's complexity, diplomacy's impact on the soldier, and how much leadership matters.

Nothing like this gets done alone, and I had many supporters and a great deal of assistance. They include Mrs. Trish Young, who convinced the powers that be that I needed to do this and the Department of History at the Air Force Academy for asking me to join them—twice. To be asked even once is a rare privilege, and I feel blessed. Colonel Stephen Connelly, USAF Retired, suggested that I write about Second World War special ops. Thank you to the man who at one time commanded the finest outfit in the Air Force, the 352d SOG, and the best leader I've ever met.

Assistance came from great scholars, with John Sweets and Peter Maslowski leading the way. Their own scholarship served as my example, and I hope this is worthy of what they taught me. In meaningful ways I am also deeply grateful for the support and collaboration of Sir Robert Hickson, John Farquhar, Ted Wilson, Mike Neiberg, Roger Spiller, Samuel Lewis, Ed Kaplan, Colin Beavan, Troy Sacquety, Bob Wettemann, Mark Grotelueschen, Jim Layerzapf, Robert Clark, Eric Frith, Steven Kippax, Peter Lieb, Tom Laub, John Roche, James Quinn, Mac Knox, Charles Pinck, John Plating, Doug Kennedy, Jeanne Heidler, Dennis Showalter, Colin Burbidge, Patrice Berger, Mary and Van Kelly, Judy Paine, William Paine, Erin Greb, Susan Langner, Jenna Sorsen, Tom Jones, Randall Woods, and Jerry Sweeney. I've great appreciation for Tim Bent, Joellyn Ausanka, and Patterson Lamb at Oxford University Press for their hard work and patience with this rookie author. Thanks to my biggest cheerleader, my Dad, who sadly did not live see the end result; my greatest inspiration, my Mom; and the love of my life, my wife, Suzy, who endured more than fifteen years of Jedburgh and Eisenhower talk. It is done because of you, sweetie.

BFJ
Hartford, South Dakota
August 16, 2015

GLOSSARY

Allied Forces Headquarters (Mediterranean Theater) (AFHQ)

Allied invasion of Southern France (ANVIL)

Armée Secrète, French underground army or irregulars (AS)

Allied Military Government of Occupied Territory (AMGOT)

Bureau Central Rensiegnements et d'Action, or Free French Office of Intelligence and Action (BCRA)

Bureau de Rensiegnements et d'Action à Londres, or London Office of Intelligence and Action (BRAL)

Bureau d'Opérations Aériennes, or Office of Air Operations (BOA)

Airborne operation to be conducted by French Parachute forces (CAIMEN)

Comité départemental de Libération, or Departmental Committee of Liberation (CDL)

Comité français de la Libération nationale, or French Committee of National Liberation (CFLN)

Central Intelligence Agency (CIA)

Conseil nationale de la Résistance, or National Council of the Resistance (CNR)

Coordinator of Information (COI)

Comité d'action militaire, or Committee for Military Action (COMAC)

International communist organization, the COMINTERN

Chief of Staff to the Supreme Allied Commander (COSSAC)

Direction générale des services spéciales (DGSS)

Délégué Militaire National, or Military National Delegate (DMN)

Délégué Militaire Regionaux, or Military Regional Delegate (DMR)

Délégué Militaire de Zone, or Military Zonal Delegate (DMZ)

Initial operation for the invasion of southern France (DRAGOON)

Etat Major Forces Françaises de l'Intérieur, Headquarters of the FFI (EMFFI)

F SOE's "F Section" was for unilateral British activity

Fédération anarchiste ibérique, Iberian Anarchist Federation of Spain (FAI)

Federal Bureau of Investigation (FBI)

President Franklin D. Roosevelt (FDR)

Forces Françaises de l'Intérieur, or French Forces of the Interior (FFI)

Front national, Communist French resistance organization (FN)

Franc-Tireurs et Partisans Français Armed wing of the FN (FTPF or often simply the FTP)

First US Army Group (FUSAG)

Operations Director or Staff (G-3)

Gestapo Geheime Staatspolizei, German secret state police

Groupes mobile de reserve, Vichy paramilitary units (GMR)

Irish Republican Army (IRA)

Jedburgh, three-man Inter-Allied teams sent to operate behind enemy lines

Kommandeur der Sicherheitspolizei und des Sicherheitsdienst (KdS)

Maquis, colloquial term for French guerrillas

Military Assistance Command, Vietnam Studies and Observations Group (MACVSOG)

MilitärBefehlshaber im Frankreich, military commander in France (MBF)

Oberbefehlshaber West, German military commander for France and Belgium (OB West)

Operational Group, American special force teams (OG)

Oberkommando der Wehrmacht, German Armed Forces High Command (OKW)

Organisation de Résistance de l'armée, French regular army units in the resistance (ORA)

Office of Strategic Services, American central intelligence and special operations (OSS)

Office of Strategic Services/Special Operations (OSS/SO)

Allied plan to invade the continent of Europe set for 1944 (OVERLORD)

Parti Communist Français, French Communist Party (PCF)

Personnel, Individual Anti-Tank weapon used by the Americans and British (PIAT)

Political Warfare Executive British Cabinet officer (PWE)

Prisoner of war (POW)

RF Section coordinated British SOE activities with the Free French's Bureau

Royal Air Force (RAF)

Reserve Officer Training Corps officer training program at US universities (ROTC)

Secret Intelligence branch of the Office of Strategic Services, or SI

Secret Intelligence Service, British rival of the SOE (SIS)

Special Air Service British Army special forces (SAS)

Special Allied Airborne Reconnaissance Force (SAARF)

Sicherheitsdienst, German SS security service (SD)

Schutzstaffeln, German purely translated means Protection Squads, but by the war they were really main force combat units loyal to the Nazi party (SS)

Supreme Headquarters Allied Expeditionary Forces (SHAEF)

Société Nationale des Chemins de Fer, the French national rail service (SNCF)

Exercise and rehearsal for the Jedburgh Plan (SPARTAN)

Service du travail obligatoire, German labor draft of French workers (STO)

Special Operations Executive, British office for special operations and sabotage (SOE)

Special Projects Operations Centre Allied special operations headquarters, Algiers (SPOC)

Special Force Detachment American special forces liaison element (SF Det.)

Allied program that provided decoded German radio messages to senior officials (ULTRA)

Wireless transmitter (W/T)

United States Army Air Forces (USAAF)

US Joint Chiefs of Staff (JCS)

United States Marine Corps (USMC)

EISENHOWER'S GUERRILLAS

Jedburgh teams with approximate operating locations, June–September, 1944. (Erin Greb Cartography).

Eisenhower's Dilemma

Usually we pity the soldier of history that had to work with Allies.

—Dwight D. Eisenhower's private notes written while waiting for his first meeting with French commanders and marveling on how well the British and Americans were working together. (November 9, 1942)

I n the late spring of 1944, General Dwight D. Eisenhower was finalizing plans to liberate France from the Germans. Military preparations for the Allied invasion, code named Overlord, were materializing and the massive effort was about to begin. But preparing the combat forces was only the first condition necessary for a successful invasion. Eisenhower understood that he needed two more elements to be in place for the initial assault to succeed: a relatively effective and coherent French guerrilla force, and Allied support of that resistance. The first had been addressed by the time the coalition's forces were in their final training and assembly areas in England. French resistance, estimated by Allied intelligence to number over 100,000 combatants, had for some time agreed to recognize the authority of General Charles de Gaulle and was unified behind his leadership. The second element—American and British recognition of the Free French and General de Gaulle—was, however, another matter altogether. Without that diplomatic recognition, Eisenhower would be unable to effectively command the Free French.

By the time Eisenhower, the supreme commander of Allied Forces, was preparing the assault across the Channel, he had been the beneficiary of special operations planning and preparations that would not only enable him to conduct a large-scale amphibious attack but, almost as important, a coordinated guerrilla war that would support the troops once they had arrived. It would be the first campaign of its kind in the history of warfare. Largely inspired by T. E. Lawrence's effort to coordinate his Arab guerrilla warfare in concert with General Edmund Allenby's conventional forces campaigns during the First World War, this would be the first time the British and Americans would plan and organize a comprehensive insurgency in order to support a military campaign. Learning from Lawrence of Arabia, they also desired to take advantage of the technological innovations during the intervening years and use encrypted radio signals and heavy lift aircraft that would connect those behind the lines with Eisenhower's headquarters. By means of radio and the airplane, British and American and then later Eisenhower's coalition planners were able to maintain links to small Allied undercover and Free French networks behind enemy lines beginning in 1941. By May 1944, there were in place and ready to be deployed nearly one hundred teams, consisting of three men each and going under the code name "Jedburgh." These teams—consisting of a British or an American officer, a French officer, and a radioman of any one of the three nations—were to link up with the resistance fighters and then to serve as a liaison to them in order to effectively arm, train, and equip them. If necessary, they would provide leadership; but their primary mission was liaison. The Jedburgh teams had been ready to go a full month before D-Day, and the networks of French resistance, along with their British and American agents, were waiting impatiently for the invasion to begin.

However, the Jedburghs did not parachute into France prior to the June 6 invasion. This was due not to logistics but to politics, and this went to the heart of Eisenhower's dilemma, one over which he was powerless. It came from higher up the chain of command. Allied recognition of the French resistance, or lack of it, stemmed from the frosty relations between President Franklin D. Roosevelt (FDR) and Free French leader Charles de Gaulle, whose planners had been informally working with Eisenhower's staff in London to plan a post-invasion insurgency against the Germans. De Gaulle's provisional government, which largely grew out of his France Libre, or Free France, was by the time of Overlord in command of the Forces Françaises l'Intérieur, or the French Forces of the Interior (FFI), who were waiting for their chance to join in the Allied war effort. Roosevelt did not support General de Gaulle's provisional government because he was not convinced that it enjoyed the full support of the French people; it was, he felt, driven primarily by de Gaulle's personal ambitions. As a result, the Americans, and to some degree the British as well, did not offer unqualified support for the French resistance forces and could not tell them the timing, location, and other key details regarding Overlord. From Eisenhower's perspective, keeping the FFI in the dark was the largest stumbling block to freeing France from German control. He was well aware that de Gaulle and the FFI were determined to fight their war on their own terms and for French political objectives—rather than for American or British ones. Eisenhower's guerrillas, comprised of the Jedburghs and the French resistance forces often referred to as the Maquis, would fight on their own terms. And those terms were mainly de Gaulle's.

What follows is the story of the battle for France in the Second World War, a fight that from the French perspective was to be fought *with* the Allies militarily but *against* them politically. No resistance movement worked harder than the Free French to achieve victory, and Eisenhower could see that. His challenge was to get American political backing behind it despite the difference in political aims, for he knew that that would give the Allies greater combat effectiveness behind German lines. His efforts to connect the French resistance to his Allied command in the run-up to Overlord had been substantial. Assisting him was the British Special Operations Executive and the American Office of Strategic Services, which were able to coordinate to a limited degree with their French equivalent, the Bureau Central Renseignements d'Action (BCRA). These three organizations—each with its own particular history and agenda, and all of them incredibly secretive—were responsible for conjuring up the Jedburghs, whose mission was to link the Allied commander with the resistance groups in order to coordinate guerrilla operations with Eisenhower's overall plans for the liberation of France.

While partisan warfare occurred in nearly every theater of World War II—in China, Yugoslavia, and the Philippines—France was the only country in which large-scale plans to use it existed from the very start of military operations. But because Eisenhower knew that the insurgents would be French groups of marginally equipped and poorly trained paramilitary Maquis, it would be vital to have a French military commander in his headquarters coordinating matters and leading the Free French combat resistance groups. That commander would have to have the confidence of Eisenhower, General de Gaulle, and if at all possible, the Maquis themselves. But working with de Gaulle would require permission from his own political leadership—Roosevelt and Churchill. Understanding why such a foundational requirement proved nearly impossible to attain requires a brief look at each nation's fundamental aims and its perspective on Overlord's purpose.

In essence, British and American leaders, both civilian and military, viewed France as a military operation rather than a political objective. France, after all, lay between their armies and Berlin; it was less a country than territory on which to engage the enemy and, if possible, destroy it. The Germans had sixty combat divisions in France, approximately forty U-boats in French ports, more than 5,000 aircraft attempting to protect occupied French airspace, and an occupation civil-military force protecting and exploiting key resources.[1] In total, there were nearly a million Germans in France. Without them, Germany's war-making capacity would have been substantially weakened. The Allies therefore sought to destroy German forces in France while at the same time denying Germany French resources—labor, raw material, and manufacturing capacity.

The French viewed Overlord as a fundamentally different enterprise. For them, everything centered on regaining their independence as a nation.

Therefore, the entire Résistance, a term that includes all the political movements involved, whether de Gaulle's provisional government (originally founded in London and then formalized in liberated Algiers), the Maquis groups—"maquis" being a general term for a wide spectrum of underground para-military organizations fighting for de Gaulle, and taken from Corsican word for scrub brush—and the leadership of the several other resistance groups that had formed after the German occupation and formation of the Vichy government, such as the Armée Secrète, came together for one goal: the formation of a new France, one that embodied the revolutionary ideals of *liberté, egalité*, and *fraternité*.

The essence of their fight therefore was political; the military issues only supported the fundamental goals of political identity, one that continued after the fighting was over. As the writer and *résistant* Albert Camus put it in the underground newspaper *Combat* in March 1944, "our common hope is that when that day comes, [the Résistance] will retain enough momentum to inspire a new truth and a new France."[2] The French certainly agreed with the American and British aims as described in the Atlantic Charter of Self-Determination to which Roosevelt and Churchill agreed in the summer of 1941, months before the United States entered the war, as well as with their aim of a German "unconditional surrender," to which they agreed in January 1943. If the Résistance sought this, too, it was fundamentally driven by French independence, which would be achieved by means of three objectives: first, by ridding France of German forces; second, by punishing those French who had collaborated with the Germans; and last, by making sure that the Americans and British did not occupy France after the Germans were gone.[3]

Asserting French sovereignty was the ultimate aim, and that was precisely what had created Eisenhower's dilemma. Even as late as May 1944, Roosevelt and Churchill dismissed the role to be played by the French Resistance, de Gaulle, and the provisional government in Algiers. They planned to assume political power in France as the Germans were pushed out, with Eisenhower to be appointed the military governor of France.[4] Roosevelt's mistrust of the French governing elite had begun after the fall of France in 1940, when he and others had given up all hope of any French leader ever assembling a government that would independently fight the Germans. When the Allies invaded French North Africa in November 1942, Roosevelt pursued actions and spoke in ways that clearly demonstrated that the United States and the United Kingdom were the ruling authorities there rather than the French commanders or civil administrators. As the French resistance leaders coalesced around a provisional government in Algiers in June 1943, Roosevelt told Eisenhower that no such entity formed outside of France was legitimate. Roosevelt and de Gaulle had met for the first time the previous January, at the summit meeting in Casablanca. At that meeting de Gaulle very proudly told the president that France had been through hard times before, but that a strong French leader had always appeared and that France had not only recovered but thrived. As an example, he mentioned Joan of Arc. Roosevelt found de Gaulle's arrogance insufferable and their conversation (which was apparently poorly translated) colored his thinking.[5] Indeed, during the entirety of the war, FDR and de Gaulle never had a meeting at which each man could seem adequately to explain to the other his concerns and goals. The two meetings they did have, at Casablanca in January 1942 and later in July 1944 at the White House, were largely staged events with the private discussions obscured by each man's obdurate views about the other.

Ultimately as the Germans were being pushed out of France, however, the French exercised self-determination and united themselves on their own terms. Despite Roosevelt's and Churchill's wishes, Eisenhower never commanded France. Few were more grateful for that than Eisenhower himself. Not becoming the military governor of France meant he could focus instead on the fight to defeat Germany. When he took command at his Supreme Headquarters Allied Expeditionary Forces (SHAEF) in January 1944, Eisenhower not only accepted reality but understood that he would need the Maquis, the paramilitary combat arm of the Free French, to attack the interior German lines of communications and to impede German troops from making their way to the invasion area to mount an effective counterattack. However, perhaps the greatest service the Résistance or more precisely, de Gaulle's provisional government, could provide was administrative—seeing to local government functions, relieving Allied armies of this manpower-intensive task. Eisenhower and de Gaulle had a frank and constructive discussion in December 1943, just before Eisenhower took up his new command. Eisenhower soon after began planning with the French on all sorts of matters and sought proper authority from FDR and Churchill to do so in greater depth, meaning to plan out the occupation of France by Allied troops and to coordinate with the French on administrative matters. But Churchill allowed only a short leash, and Roosevelt's approval did not come until well after the Allied invasion.

These conditions meant that the Normandy invasion effectively took place in a kind of political void. The Jedburghs, once they were finally dispatched into France from the night of June 5 into late September 1944, therefore found themselves parachuting literally and figuratively into the void created by political mistrust at the highest levels. As a result they became involved in both military operations and diplomatic discussions—hence, the Jedburghs started with tactical intentions but many quickly found themselves dealing with the fallout of the diplomatic dispute among allies. The Jedburghs were designed to fight the Germans and to help the French fight the Germans but not to assist the French achieve their political aims—punishing the collaborators and setting up a government. Understanding this provides greater clarity as to why some Jedburgh teams succeeded and others failed. Generally, as we will see, when the local Maquis were well organized as well as closely linked with de Gaulle's Free French, a Jedburgh team succeeded at its objectives. When such was not the case, it did not.

The unresolved diplomatic and political issues—the void—initially left the Jedburgh teams ill fitted for their work. Permeating Allied planning for the Normandy invasion was the assumption that the French would not fight; therefore, devoting men, aircraft, and weapons as inducements would be a waste of precious resources. Had FDR and others perceived the Maquis as a viable and effective force, and had sufficient air drop missions been flown to arm groups well integrated into a strongly communicated plan with proper targets, the battle for France might have proven far less bloody for all concerned. Instead, when they did start setting up operations in France, the Jedburghs were stunned by the number of Maquis streaming into their camps, demanding weapons and the right to participate in liberating their country. When Eisenhower realized, as he did just days after D-Day, that the Maquis were rising all over France, overwhelming Allied abilities to arm, command, and control them, he had to direct them to stand down. As the campaign through France continued into the summer of 1944, he suspended air- lifting weapons to them in order to starve their combat operations. But for the Jedburghs, caught squarely in the middle, all this was not simply a theoretical debate about political control between generals and heads of governments; the results were playing out all around them, as more and more French proved themselves ready to turn on their German occupiers and—this is the critical point—to do so under Allied command. The Jedburghs' attempt to channel and control Maquis passion would prove to be their greatest challenge. They quickly understood that both they and the Maquis were Eisenhower's guerrillas.

This is not the first book on the Jedburghs—many fine ones have come before—but it is the first to examine their operations in light of the politics of the liberation of France. The Jedburghs provide a prism through which to view both Eisenhower's dilemma and the greater story of the liberation of France. In part this means looking at events from the Résistance's point of view. Most books on the Jedburghs have emphasized their heroic achievements. But the remaining question is what they might have accomplished had there been political agreement between the Allies and the French. By nature the Jedburghs were muddying distinctions between military and political considerations. That is why the Germans, who often described the Maquis as "*terroristen*," viewed the Jedburghs in the same way.

Most of all, this book will show how and why the first modern large-scale guerrilla campaign was meant to be conducted alongside the conventional campaign. The British were the original instigators of the Jedburgh plan and made the first efforts to create a guerrilla operation. The wider opening of the Special Operations Executive (SOE) records beginning earlier this century, along with their copies of the coded German battlefield messages and the release of SOE agents' personnel files in the custody of the Her Majesty's Government, make that clear. But the French role in the campaign and their crucial part lay in France in the Bureau Central Renseignements d'Action records. They are open but have remained largely ignored by English-speaking historians and authors. My own time with the BCRA records in Paris and the headquarters of the Forces Françaises de l'Intérieur records in the French Army Archives proved invaluable. English-language histories often imply that Maquis action resulted from the presence of the Allied and specifically the Jedburgh teams. Such was not the case. In fact, instead of assuming that everything the French Résistance accomplished in the fight for liberation was due only to British and American support, what follows is the narrative of how the French Résistance successfully achieved all its aims, often despite Britain and America.

As we will see, this does not diminish what the Jedburghs also accomplished, and a substantial part of this book will focus on their story. Time has taken many from us. When I started research on them in 1997, persistence and good fortune helped me locate several. The former French Jedburgh, Joe de Francesco, who by that time had become an American citizen and was living in South Carolina, proved a rich source of information. He had organized Jedburgh reunions and provided me with recent addresses and phone numbers. In the end, I was fortunate to glean evidence from thirteen American, French, and British Jedburghs. In 1943 and 1944, all of them had taken oaths not to talk "for 50 years," according to one. Nonetheless, a few details had started leaking into print.[6] Thomas Braden and Stewart Alsop's *Sub Rosa* appeared in 1946 and discussed the Office of Strategic Services (OSS) operations in World War II.[7] Alsop had been a Jedburgh and wrote vividly but generically about a team's operations. Another Jedburgh, William Dreux, published *No Bridges Blown,* his account of his recruitment into the OSS, as well as his training and experiences in France.[8] The title is telling: he expected to go into France and perform commando-style operations, blowing up bridges—but he did none of that. Few teams ever did.

The British Jedburghs have also, for the most part, kept their silence. However Lieutenant Colonel Sir James Hutchison published *That Drug Danger* in 1977.[9] Hutchison ran SOE's RF section, liaising with the Free French long before deploying to France, and therefore he had much more knowledge of the French networks and key players. A book by another former Jedburgh, M. G. M. "Bing" Crosby, *Irregular Soldier,* appeared in 1991 and recounts swashbuckling adventures.[10] Among the French, nearly all kept their silence—perhaps because France moved directly from World War II into brutal wars in Indo-China and Algeria, and both officers and noncommissioned officers (NCOs) maintained more of a wartime attitude about the nature of their work. While there were 104 French Jedburghs, more than from any other nationality, all but two—Paul Aussaresses and Jean Sassi—kept their silence.[11]

The men who put the Jedburghs into action and knew the most about the program took what they knew to their graves, leaving only the barest of descriptions. Brigadier Eric Mockler-Ferryman served as the SOE's Chief of Western Europe and also as the British senior officer in the British-American amalgamated Headquarters called Special Force Headquarters (SFHQ). He gave a few speeches after the war and may have written an unpublished memoir for his family, but in the end he left few details about the Jedburgh Plan. He passed away in 1978. His American counterpart, Colonel Joseph F. Haskell, never spoke publicly about his role as the American co-director of SFHQ, or about his time as director of OSS London, Special Operations office. He did speak to some historians and authors but provided only outlines of his work. He died in 1982, seemingly prouder of his time in the regular army and his service in the Battle of the Bulge. However, he did history one favor: he kept his papers, maps, photographs, and other items. After his death, his daughters wondered who might find them worth keeping. I did, and they rounded out other things I found in archives in the United States, Britain, and France. Mockler-Ferryman's and Haskell's French commander, General Pierre Koenig, also kept this effort secret. He was far more famous in France for other battles than for his experience as the commander of Eisenhower's guerrillas. Most of the French public preferred to hear about the open combat he conducted against the Germans and few realized his role with the Maquis for de Gaulle and Eisenhower. Had they known how hard he fought the Allied bureaucracy, with few aside from Eisenhower on his side, they might have appreciated him all the more. Koenig died in 1970, leaving very little behind but a stack of his official papers that today are housed in the French Army Archives in Vincennes, France.

Koenig and his chief of staff did, however, participate in a postwar US Army History Office project to detail the role of the French Maquis in the liberation of France. The British and Americans also participated in writing this historical work. All three countries classified the result, a manuscript of some 1,600 pages of narrative, maps, and original documents. As a result, it has languished in the French Army Archives, the US Army History Center at Carlisle Barracks, Pennsylvania, and in the SOE archives, nearly completely ignored since its declassification in the 1970s.[12] Nonetheless, it remains highly revealing, and perhaps better than most other histories on the topic lays out how the participants themselves viewed the role of the Résistance and how the Supreme Headquarters Allied Expeditionary Forces exploited it for Allied ends. For instance, it discusses the French regional differences and how the different Résistance groups and their para-military Maquis operated throughout the country, taking into account the various military and political roles the Résistance as a whole could and did play. Furthermore, it evokes the overall strategic aims and the various phases of combat in France during 1944. This book largely follows this first version of Jedburgh and resistance history organizationally, though it has also benefited from the work of numerous historians since, and a great deal of German Army contemporaneous evidence.

Concluded in November 1945, the History Office manuscript reports that in the end "the effort of the 'Resistants' is not capable of analysis in the form of a Balance Sheet." Guerrilla warfare does not by nature lend itself to precise numbers. "The essential thing is that the importance of their contribution to the operations for the Liberation of FRANCE did not escape their Allies. The praise...which American Generals, and particularly General Eisenhower, have rendered to the FFI, handsomely takes the place of missing statistics." The manuscript also quotes high-ranking German officers to buttress the argument that the Résistance and Maquis had a meaningful and important effect on the outcome of the liberation.[13]

Seventy years later, it is finally possible to produce a "Balance Sheet" to determine the effect of the Résistance by understanding Eisenhower's intent for his guerrillas. For too long the politics of the Résistance colored our historical understanding while our reading of the actions and daring of the Jedburgh teams left us shaking our heads in curiosity at their circumstances. *Eisenhower's Guerrillas* seeks to answer what was the nature of this warfare and why events transpired as they did. To use a phrase the novelist and Second World War SOE commando Evelyn Waugh repeats in his semi-autobiographical *Sword of Honour* trilogy, "quantitative judgments don't apply."[14] Indeed, measuring results of the Battle of France is impossible when the countries involved defined success so differently. Furthermore, our understanding of that history is largely from the Jedburghs and the Maquis themselves because Eisenhower, who sought to implement coalition political aims, never really explained his role and intentions. Therefore, previous histories are not the stories Eisenhower would have told, since his guerrillas, the Jedburghs and the Maquis, who did not fully understand it themselves, have been doing all the telling. But they did not know why events occurred as they did. All they knew was that they suffered for it.

Carl von Clausewitz argued, "The political object is the goal, war is the means of reaching it, and means can never be considered in isolation from their purpose."[15] The British, Americans, French, and of course the Germans all had their own objectives. The interplay between them is what makes this story so fascinating. The Jedburghs operated along the seams where these goals overlapped. My hope is that this book brings the Jedburghs and Maquis out of their obscurity and links them up with the main narrative of two truly great stories: the liberation of France, and guerrilla warfare in the twentieth century.

Guerrilla Warfare and the Design of the Jedburghs

The roots of guerrilla warfare reach back to ancient days. In fact, the Western world's first historian, Herodotus, wrote of the strange and exotic Scythians—strange in that they seemed unfettered by any link to specific territory; they could strike suddenly, hit hard, and then melt away quickly. In his terse reply in the year 508 BCE to Darius I, the Persian king with whom he was at war, the Scythian leader Idanthyrsus explained, "We Scythians have neither towns nor cultivated lands, which might induce us, through fear of their being taken or ravaged, to be in any hurry to fight with you."[1] Herodotus tells us that Darius, unable to make the Scythians stand and fight, was afraid of being cut off, feared cryptic threats, had grown weary of constant nightly ambushes, and was running low on supplies—and therefore he retreated. Herodotus believed that understanding how any polity waged its wars was a matter of understanding its underlying culture, which defines what it believes worthy of fighting for. The Scythians, like all wagers of partisan warfare, fought unconventionally—engaging in what we would call guerrilla warfare— because that was their only option if they were to defeat a much larger enemy.

More than one ancient text provides examples of guerrilla warfare. There are the Hebrews taking land from the Philistines in the Old Testament where the book of Judges shows time and again how a perceived weakness proves to be just the right strength; Xenophon and his Greek nationless mercenaries who marched through what is today Iraq and Turkey; Julius Caesar contending with marauding tribes in present-day Spain, France, and Germany; and Alexander the Great fighting and negotiating deals with Persians, Arabs, and Afghans fighting under emperors or as amorphous tribes in circumstances that might be reminiscent of United States Army operations against the Plains Indians in the nineteenth century. What confounded leaders and commanders from Darius to Lieutenant Colonel George A. Custer was that their foe could not be made to stand and fight for something that people such as Darius or Custer could recognize as a link to something politically vital or economically valuable.

Indeed, what all guerrillas have in common is that not only do they employ ambush tactics and fight in small amorphous groups, but they also display little or no recognizable link to anything. Clausewitz might call such a link a "center of gravity" upon which all things for waging their war would depend. Of course, every culture or society has a center of gravity, something important enough that they would fight to defend it, and as Idanthrysus explained later to Darius, the Scythians' center of gravity was the threat of losing their ancestors' graves. Custer's commander in 1876, General Philip Sheridan, recognized what the center of gravity was for the Lakota as he remarked that the westward movement of American settlers had "destroyed their commissary," the buffalo herds on which they were so dependent. The near extinction of the buffalo forced them to capitulate for lack of food and clothing. Sheridan, a man who made his name by conducting cavalry raids on Confederate supplies and communications, expressed things in ways familiar to him, as vague and clumsy as they may be to describe thousands of buffalo roaming the northern plains. Sitting Bull would not have recognized a commissary's management or sources while he certainly could recognize a buffalo's purpose in sustaining his people. Commissaries were the product of a society operated by people with defined societal roles, and that specialization could lead to extremely efficient use of human talent, skill, and labor, with more and more specialized tasks organized under law for a functionally literate people.

The guerrilla, then, is not a new phenomenon in modern times but the product of conditions and not a result of some kind of progress of humanity or history. Guerrilla fighters are, by definition, "irregulars" as they are not organized by a formal government; instead they are everyday men and women who, for whatever reason, have chosen to take up arms to fight their enemies. So the conditions require that there be no government, at least not one the guerrillas, or irregular forces, recognize as legitimate.

"Irregulars" are now defined as the opposite of a "regular" soldier, but regulars require the modern state. Formal and highly professional armies are the product of the modern state that evolved in the West with the end of the Thirty Years' War in 1648. As European armies marched and fought, laying waste much of central Europe and killing thousands, the major powers of the European continent fought brutal campaigns contending for land, influence, and secure borders. One result was the concentration of political power, gathered by kings over time, which meant that these royal families could put in place the necessary bureaucracy, raise revenue, and organize their society for a centralized purpose. It was men like Louis XIV of France, Charles V of Spain, and Frederick the Great of Prussia who created the modern European state. England and later Great Britain followed a slightly different path as it spent most of this era embroiled internally in religious debates and legal and political arguments between Parliament and the English kings that erupted in violence in the 1640s and again in 1689, with Parliament coming out slightly on top—a condition that did not happen often on the continent of Europe. Then, through slow consolidation of various powers, the beginning of popular politics and mass media, and steady reform, the British Parliament slowly, but clearly, became dominant by the early twentieth century. All this is important because when the state collapses, and it always does, and the conditions that created and sustain regulars are gone, the irregulars, or guerrillas return to assert authority. History suggests that ultimately, the ability to take armed action rests with the individual, not with a government, particularly when a legitimate government doesn't exist.

So where does the word "guerrilla" come from? It's a slang term, an implied put-down, that British field commander Lord Wellington used to describe the armed bands of Spanish nationalist forces fighting Napoleon's French armies in the Peninsular War of 1807–1814. In Spanish it means "little warriors," or "those fighting the small war." The British government sent Wellington and around 15,000 British soldiers to fight the French in Spain during the height of the Napoleonic Wars. Wellington sought to work with the Spanish guerrillas in order to overthrow the French-imposed Spanish government, thus weakening Napoleon. He was sporadically successful at linking his efforts to the guerrillas, but he could not sufficiently influence them, and communication with them was maddening. He made use of the Spanish translation of the term guerrilla, or "small war," which was in his time a military term that described small groups of organized troops who raided the enemy's interior supply lines and sought intelligence on the enemy's movements. But of course for these Spanish civilians now turned irregulars, it was not a small affair at all, but a fight that meant everything to them; it meant they could get their Spain back and define it themselves without foreign intervention from the French. The term "guerrilla" stuck in the English-speaking world and now has become synonymous with warfare conducted by those without a recognized government and animated by a kaleidoscopic command structure understood only by the fighters.

Relatively speaking, by the early and mid-twentieth century, the British had fought in more guerrilla or partisan campaigns than any other world power.[2] As the British Empire was growing quickly from South Asia to North America to Africa and the Middle East, the British found themselves confronted more and more with these partisans, irregulars, or guerrillas, as Wellington eventually called them. In fact, the British were involved with and against American Indian tribes fighting with or against the French and the Spanish in North America from the seventeenth century to the time the American "rebels" organized an army and colonial state militias began conducting armed actions against the British in 1775. Maddeningly resilient and impossible to completely eradicate, the Continental Army and their ephemeral cohorts in the newborn state militias were deemed by the British to be a rebel force. The guerrilla war experiences would not stop with the end of the

American Revolution. Other British wars include aspects of the Napoleonic Wars such as the Peninsular War, the War of 1812, the Anglo-Afghan War of 1832–1834, the Indian Mutiny in 1857, the Second Anglo-Afghan War in the 1880s, the Boer War in 1899–1902, "The Troubles" in Ireland and the persistent Irish Republican efforts to form their own state, British support to the Arab Revolt during the First World War, and the Third Anglo-Afghan War in 1919. These wars were fought to protect British trade, expand British influence, or punish unruly neighbors, but from the British point of view, the enemies were all employing small war, or guerrilla tactics, that the British often viewed as illegal if not immoral. But the British also exploited this style of warfare and supported or instigated guerrilla warfare when it suited them, such as during the Arab Revolt. But few in the British Army and police learned from these experiences in order to get better at countering it or exploiting it for British purposes. Even fewer politicians did.

None become more famous, for learning and explaining guerrilla warfare, than Thomas E. Lawrence. Lawrence of Arabia, as he came to be known, was a junior intelligence officer bored out of his wits in the British Army headquarters in Cairo when given an offhand opportunity to go into the Arabian desert, find a British liaison officer who was working with the Arabs, and assist him in getting Arab support for a rebellion against their Turkish masters in the Ottoman Empire. But he was not a typical junior officer. Prior to the war, Lawrence had studied ancient languages; gone on archaeological digs in what is today Israel, Jordan, Turkey, and Syria; and had produced maps and scholarly studies on the sites that the medieval Europeans had left in the Arab dust from the Crusades. Such work and experiences gave him an appreciation for topography, military campaign planning, the nature of offensive and defensive operations, and logistics. But he also reveled in learning as much as he could about the Arabs' culture, traditions and how they exercised authority. His sophisticated cultural understanding of the Arabs and the Europeans, his ability to speak Arabic, and his astonishing capacity to deal with physical pain provided the British an imaginative and energetic officer who could discern the Arab center of gravity, the Turkish Army's center of gravity, and capitalize on British strengths to match these against enemy weaknesses.[3]

But for all Lawrence's stamina, hard work, thoughtful understanding of the Arab culture, classical education, and sober sweat-drenched courage, British efforts would have been for naught had Lawrence not successfully partnered the Arab Revolt and its guerrilla campaign with the British conventional forces in such a winning way. The campaign succeeded because of the ready use the British conventional field commander, General Sir Edmund Allenby, made of Lawrence's efforts with the Arabs. Allenby understood that by linking his operations up the coast through Gaza then toward Jerusalem, and finally on to Damascus, he could hit Turkish forces weakened by Arab operations behind their lines, disrupting their logistics and keeping them off balance. The Turks constantly had to guess how to array their forces— whether they would concentrate them to fend off a regular force attack from General Allenby or disperse them to chase after Arab bands coming from the Ottoman's own territory; often they made the wrong choice.

Lawrence's partisan warfare often masked the overall British First World War strategic aim to maintain and defend what they had in Asia and Africa. In fact, the British and French aims for the Middle East, that Lawrence discerned only by watching the actions of his government as the war coalesced around the military victory he helped provide, deeply disappointed him and his Arab brothers in arms. British and French power was greater than Arab power, and the Europeans would decide the Arab fate at Versailles in 1919. Lawrence later reflected about how the older heads of governments and diplomats used this power to take away the very thing he and the young Arab guerrillas had fought to win, specifically, their best cities and their unambiguous independence from foreign powers. He wrote,

> The moral freshness of the world-to-be intoxicated us. We lived many lives in those whirling campaigns, never sparing ourselves: yet when we achieved and the new world dawned, the old men came out again and took our victory to re-make in the likeness of the former world they knew. Youth could win [the war], but had not learned to keep: and was pitiable weak against age. We stammered that we had worked for a new heaven and a new earth, and they thanked us kindly and made their peace.[4]

Lawrence's deep disappointment in the political misuse of his guerrilla war's victory did not resonate with most of his readers. Instead, his derring-do captured the headlines and filled people's imaginations. But Lawrence's words describe what the French resistance feared and sought to avoid when Eisenhower's campaign began twenty-five years later, for Frenchmen as different in temperament and beliefs as Albert Camus and Charles de Gaulle could agree on one big thing: France would not allow an Allied military victory to succeed, only to lose their French peace.

Nevertheless, because most of the British countering of irregular war occurred beyond its shores, guerrilla warfare came to be understood through the words of men like Rudyard Kipling and Winston Churchill. A professional writer who spent his life in south Asia, Kipling's eye for capturing cultural truths and the exotic Indian culture sold thousands of books in his lifetime. His influence on the English language persists to this day, but it pales in comparison to Churchill's influence not only on the political decisions of his time but also on his era's thinking on guerrilla war. As a Sandhurst-trained officer, Churchill was a romantic when it came to guerrilla warfare, often exaggerating the effectiveness of partisans fighting on their own, sometimes failing to fully recognize the relationship between conventional units and partisan bands working together to fight a common enemy. His experience with guerrilla warfare, intelligence, spies, and espionage were amplified by his lively imagination and wide-ranging intellect. As a young army officer and war correspondent at the turn of the century, he had fought in Africa against the Sudanese tribes and the Boers. In the 1890s he had covered American actions in Cuba, and British combat in Afghanistan, Egypt, and again back in Sudan, honing his writing skills on these experiences, publishing thousands of words. *The River War*, his 1899 account of his involvement as a young British Army officer in the Mahdist War in Sudan, is still highly regarded among military circles. Politically, Churchill had grown more conservative, and as he became a more senior member of Parliament with portfolios of War and later Colonial Minister in the 1920s, he grew especially concerned about the Bolshevik movement in Britain after the Russian Revolution and developed his own intelligence apparatus to keep tabs on it. He also struggled to come to terms with the

Irish Republican Army (IRA). After the violence of the Easter Uprising in 1916 and the "Bloody Sunday" assassinations in 1920, organized by the IRA intelligence chief Michael Collins, Churchill proved a key negotiator in the settlement that granted some concessions for Irish Home Rule. In the 1930s, while out of the government, Churchill developed a reliable intelligence network that kept him apprised of the growing German military capability. Whether in or out of government, his love for all aspects of such partisan warfare, intelligence, revolution, and revolt was undiminished and served as a driving force behind much that he did as prime minister.[5]

These experiences sold Churchill on guerrilla warfare's methods due to its relatively cheap cost, its lack of bloody engagements between large forces, and the clear political nature and influence such irregular forces could have. As one of Churchill's contemporary military strategists defined it, "Guerrilla warfare must always be dynamic and must maintain momentum."[6] Basing these opinions largely on the writings and experiences of Lawrence in the Arab Revolt, Basil H. Liddell Hart went on to say, "Static defense has no part in guerrilla action." In other words, the nature of guerrilla warfare is inherently offensive. That attribute, combined with the specter in British memory of First World War casualties despite monumental national efforts, made British leaders loath, throughout the entirety of the Second World War, to open up another western front for fear of the same costly futility. Therefore, when the French fell to the Germans in the dark days of June 1940, and indeed even after America's entry into the war, when hopes of victory brightened, the indirect quality of partisan warfare seemed a method Britain could use, along with strategic bombing, as they both offered an offensive action against the enemy while avoiding British fears of First World War–like stagnation and death.

Unlike the Americans, the British had contemplated many of these issues in the summer and fall of 1940 when they expected the Germans to follow up their successful invasion of France by landing in Britain next. They drew up contingency plans to fight "on the beaches,"[7] as expressed in Winston Churchill's famous speech, but they did more than talk and plan for it. The Royal Air Force fought a fierce battle against the Luftwaffe while the Royal Navy defended the sea approaches. The army, what remained of it after escaping destruction in northern France in 1940, also reorganized a Home Guard. The Home Guard included a closely guarded secret around a concept seeking to prepare for guerrilla warfare against the occupying Germans with what the British called Auxiliary Units. Should the Germans defeat and occupy Britain, these Auxiliary Units would then continue the fight using guerrilla warfare inside Britain.[8] The thinking and planning for these Auxiliary Units later led to the idea of forming their equivalent elsewhere in German-occupied Europe once invasion fears receded.

Germany's invasion of Poland on September 1, 1939, provoked the British government to declare war and Prime Minister Neville Chamberlain to ask Churchill to leave the backbenches of Parliament and join the government. Now Churchill was back in his element. In mid-August, the British Army dispatched a small military advisory mission to Poland and with them some intelligence service operatives. Their presence was indeed fortunate, for while the Polish were quickly defeated, these operatives managed to spirit out of Poland the German Army's encryption and cipher device known as the ENIGMA machine. Back in England, the British began to use it to decrypt German army dispatches and, as the war progressed, other kinds of coded radio traffic as well. Almost miraculously, the Germans maintained their confidence in their secure radio communications during the entire war, giving the Allies no end of extremely useful intelligence and arming Churchill, who delighted in what he called his "golden eggs."[9]

One of the British Army's intelligence officers in the Polish expedition was Colonel Colin Gubbins. A World War I veteran, Gubbins had also served in Ireland, where he soon found that he was, as he later wrote, "being shot at from behind hedges by men in trilbys and mackintoshes and not allowed to shoot back!"[10] Additionally he had served in the British Expeditionary forces in Murmansk when they had attempted to fight the Bolsheviks during the Russian Revolution. A man of considerable intellect who handled new languages easily, Gubbins was asked by the British Army to help with its 1939 instruction on subversive warfare. The effort resulted in the *Partisan Leaders' Handbook*. Initially the *Handbook* emphasized tactical issues, such as organizing ambushes and killing enemy informers. But Gubbins's thoughts matured, and the following year he began to see partisan warfare in a different light. He now believed that "if guerrilla warfare is co-ordinated and also related to main operations, it should, in favourable circumstances, cause such a diversion of enemy strength as eventually to present decisive opportunities to the main forces." Historian David Stafford asserted that whether they knew it, the British were "often following techniques that had been pioneered in Ireland by Michael Collins."[11] But certainly Gubbins and other British Army officers were seeing the world of the 1920s and '30s and learning their lessons. They read T. E. Lawrence's works or even knew him personally. They fought against Collins and the IRA, and observed and pondered the meaning of the "Fifth Column" activities in the Spanish Civil War, where radio propaganda warned of popular revolts behind the lines in Madrid while four columns of professional Spanish soldiers surrounded the city. They all realized that pairing the two—conventional forces with guerrillas—was a different method, one that might prove useful and even critically important in the war against Germany.

Gubbins and the rest of the unit, known as the No. 4 Military Mission, had arrived in Poland on September 1, 1939, the day the Germans invaded. As they appeared, they were greeted by a great outpouring of gratitude by Poles who met them. But when the German advance destroyed the Polish Air Force in the campaign's opening hours, and the Polish General Staff could not maintain a picture of what was happening, the Staff left Warsaw and moved south. Number 4 Military Mission left with them. What had been intended as a prudent action to set up a command element removed from threat turned into a full-scale escape from the chaos the German advance created each new day. The British mission wound up evacuating on the choked and confused roads moving south out of Poland into Romania and then via sea to Egypt. Near the Romanian border, Gubbins was discussing the situation with a Polish commander when they heard the news that the Soviets had invaded Poland from the east. All was going to be lost within hours, Gubbins believed, and he was frustrated that Britain's dithering with Hitler since 1938 had resulted in nothing beneficial for the Poles.[12]

With him was Captain Peter Wilkinson. A graduate of Cambridge, Wilkinson was a regular army officer and the son of an Indian Army officer killed in the Great War. Gubbins thought enough of Wilkinson to ask that he be named his liaison officer back in London, while Gubbins took

No. 4 Military Mission to Paris in early 1940. Their mission was to liaise and cooperate with the French in preparing their defenses against the Germans while maintaining their links inside Poland and in the Balkans. Wilkinson and Gubbins's efforts in France ended just a few months later when the Germans invaded France in May 1940. French forces fell back and the British Expeditionary Force, having fled northwest across Belgium and Holland, was forced to evacuate from Dunkirk across the English Channel, in a pell-mell flurry of activity from the end of May until early June. Gubbins found Wilkinson—who had flown from Paris—in London and asked him to come to work with him on yet another assignment: to help set up a resistance movement inside Britain, "in the event, which now seemed likely, that the Germans invaded the British Isles."[13] Gubbins and many in the British Army were convinced that they would have to press the fight, as Churchill now exhorted all Britons to do, and with any available means. They would become partisans in their own country and put to use the methods learned from Michael Collins, the Soviets, Lawrence, and the fighters in the Spanish Civil War.

Churchill, who became prime minister when the Germans invaded France, now faced the daunting challenge of defending a demoralized nation with an army in a state of great confusion. With France's capitulation, Britain now had no solid ally on the continent of Europe. British policy had assumed that France would maintain its own defense and provide a bulwark, keeping the German Wehrmacht from reaching the English Channel. In a somber cable to President Roosevelt late in the evening of June 12, 1940, he wrote that the new undersecretary of state for National Defense, "a young General de Gaulle," was for fighting on but he feared that "the aged Marshal Pétain who was none too good in April and July of 1918 is I fear ready to lend his name and prestige to a treaty of peace for France." Churchill pressed Roosevelt to help him stiffen French resolve, relating to the American ambassador Joseph Kennedy that he had emphasized to the French that Germany would ultimately lose the war and that Britain would continue to fight on, alone, if necessary.[14]

Churchill's cable to Roosevelt frames the issues as well as the people who would be involved in the eventual liberation of France. Both Britain and France had leaders who believed in the possibility of defeating

Germany, but Britain's greatest believer was able to maintain British will to fight, while de Gaulle was still a junior general and, according to his memoirs, unwilling to think of things outside his military role. De Gaulle's entreaties to senior French generals fell on deaf ears or were met with scorn.[15] Pondering the direness of their fate, and inspired by Churchill's determination to fight on, British authorities, military and civil, believed that subversive warfare within occupied Europe would be key. Furthermore, of course, they had to create the capability within Britain to wage an insurgency should the Germans defeat and occupy the country. The difficulty lay in how to organize such an office. Should it be military or civilian? Should it report directly to the Cabinet or be a part of it? And who should lead it? Furthermore, what would its overall objective be?

In deliberations within a closed and senior circle of British Army, Secret Intelligence Service (SIS), and Cabinet officials in June and early July of 1940, Churchill determined that the office should be headed by a civilian and that it would report to the Cabinet through the minister for Economic Warfare. Churchill appointed Hugh Dalton, a veteran of the French and Italian theaters in the First World War and a well-respected Labour Member of Parliament (MP), to be minister of Economic Warfare, overseeing all efforts to strangle Germany's economy. The newly formed Special Operations Executive (SOE)—the office under discussion—would reside inside this new ministry and coordinate its activities with only the most senior leadership within existing British military and intelligence organizations. In this way, the British Army generals and intelligence officials believed, SOE activities would be closely tied and coordinated with British political aims. In June and July of 1940, while Pétain was establishing his armistice with the Germans and his government in the spa town of Vichy, Churchill approved Dalton's proposal to collect and provide him with intelligence from the War Office, the Foreign Office, and the Secret Intelligence Service. More important, Churchill approved Dalton's authority to create his own staff and add new capabilities as he saw fit.[16] Such authority proved valuable to Dalton as the politics involved in establishing a new organization and taking pieces out of other well-entrenched parts of the government would be bruising and persistent.

Dalton proved up to the task and understood the basic issue that subversion and sabotage had to be linked to political aims. His successor, a conservative MP named Rondell Cecil Palmer, Third Earl of Selbourne, became head of SOE on February 22, 1942, and maintained its existence by working diligently to keep his agents' actions within the bounds of British policy so as not to be at cross purposes with the Foreign Office and theater commanders. Colin Gubbins had been brought into SOE at its inception, since his military staff that had gone to Poland and France was subsumed into the new Special Operations Executive. At first he was placed in charge of organizing what were called the Auxiliary Units, which would conduct resistance against the Germans should they succeed in their invasion of Britain.[17] Later, he took on training, linking SOE efforts with the Joint Planning Staff—the British equivalent of the planning offices of the Joint Chiefs of Staff—and ensuring that SOE procedures linked smoothly with the Royal Air Force (RAF) and the British Navy. He performed these functions exceedingly well, organizing the establishment of more than fifty secret training facilities. Gubbins's reputation for working well with other parts of the government enabled him to be named the executive of SOE in September 1943,[18] after the theater commander in the Balkans complained about SOE operations, forcing the issue to Churchill. Lord Selbourne fired the executive then in charge of SOE, Charles Hambro, and promoted Gubbins, now a major general, to the position. Selbourne maintained his position as Cabinet member responsible for Political Warfare while Gubbins directed SOE. His role then became mainly one of training saboteurs, providing them with effective equipment, disguises, and cover stories, and then making them available to theater commanders for operations against Germany and Japan. Within the war's various theaters of operation, SOE would then be working for the British theater commander, making Gubbins's saboteurs subject to a wide array of commanders, driving up or down SOE's impact in the campaign.

The SOE's stature in the war effort was both elevated and solidified when on September 30, 1943, the American-British planning staff responsible for designing the invasion of northwest Europe assumed control of their theater's SOE for the purposes of linking partisan action with their conventional efforts for operations on the Continent.[19] A military man running

SOE at the very time the Allied level of effort began to be concentrated on the invasion of Europe proved to further legitimate SOE's role.[20] Not everyone was in agreement about the use of sabotage and subversion, however. Dalton's perspective was often animated by his left-wing views, and he sought to incite rebellion thinking this alone would bring about German or Vichy collapse, dangerously overselling what most Britons thought irregular forces could do for the wider war effort. Each arrest or discovered operation in occupied Europe could then make Dalton and SOE look more and more foolish and futile. But Gubbins's belief that coordination with conventional forces was key to partisan activities nicely matched Allied needs. It was a historic moment in the history of twentieth-century partisan warfare. The SOE was now led by a man who believed that the best way to use a fifth column centered on its participating with the other "four columns" of conventional forces in a highly coordinated way.

Key though it was, this alliance posed huge challenges—of coordination, strategy, and perhaps especially morale and morality. Gubbin's leading planner for the Auxiliary Units encountered resistance that he believed was caused by defeatism. Following the fall of France, Peter Wilkinson traveled about England in the summer of 1940, organizing and preparing the Auxiliary Units to fight a German occupation from within Britain. He briefed senior Home Guard Army leaders, letting them in on the very secret preparations and soliciting their advice on how local efforts could best be coordinated for Britain's national defense. One of these briefings was what he later called an "awkward interview" with Sir Will Spens, regional commissioner for East Anglia. Before the war Spens, trained in the sciences, had been master of Corpus Christi College, Cambridge and later vice-chancellor of Cambridge—the equivalent of an American college provost—and Wilkinson knew and greatly admired him from his days there as a student. He briefed Spens in detail about the Auxiliary Units and their role in Spens's area of responsibility in the event of a German attack. "He listened attentively," Wilkinson wrote,

> while I described what Auxiliary Units hoped to achieve. After a moment's thought, he replied that he was not convinced that clandestine

resistance of this sort could serve any useful purpose. It was moreover, bound to provoke severe reprisals against innocent civilians whom it was his first duty to protect. He felt obliged, therefore, to warn me in no uncertain terms that if any member of Auxiliary Units was found acting illegally in his region, either before or after a German occupation, he would be arrested and severely punished. This remark was in stark contrast to Mr. Churchill's exhortations to fight on to the bitter end, but its logic was unanswerable and I walked sadly away for I had great respect for my Master's intellectual integrity. It was my first encounter with the *Pétainiste* argument against which SOE was to strive, so often in vain, while trying to fan the sparks of French *Résistance*.[21]

Wilkinson's inability to answer Spens's objection involves a question that remained unanswered during the entire Second World War, one involving the Western tradition of a country's armed forces being employed purely as a function of state power. Since the Romans had left England and local warlords had filled the resulting power vacuum, those men had controlled companies, regiments, and battalions that they would then provide to their king under certain circumstances. It is important to note that even after the shared consolidation of state power in the Parliament and the monarchy, the army units maintained their loyalties to the local lord first and the king second until the late nineteenth century. In this way, no king could become too powerful. On the continent of Europe, French, Prussian, Austrian, or Spanish forces were relatively, and more and more after 1648, creatures of the monarchy. Therefore, Spens's concern about managing the chaos and destruction of war is an age-old one that was largely solved with the consolidation of state authority around a central government and its prerogative to be the sole authority over the armed forces; by the late nineteenth century, this had occurred in Britain with the slow formation of power sharing between the king and Parliament. Such a tradition landed in the American colonies too, and persisted due to the inherent distrust many English and American political leaders had of a professional standing army belonging solely to a single person. American fears were fired by the memory, ironically not of a king, but of Oliver Cromwell, who defeated the king's forces due to his professional and well-supplied "Model Army." But in their own way, by the summer of 1940, the British had settled in on a way to command regular forces within the bounds of their own laws. Irregulars conducting combat operations and supporting conventional military forces inside Britain fell outside the tradition, and as such, Spens believed, they were also outside the law. Wilkinson's use of the pejorative *"Pétainiste,"* however telling, masked the issue. Who had the legitimate authority to use partisan forces and how would they be controlled? How would they be punished for excess and abuse when they went too far?

The answers would determine how the British government, according to its laws, could deal with the matter. Thankfully, as the Germans never invaded, the British avoided the issue, and other events changed the nature of the war considerably. But during the course of World War II, the British sought to use irregular warfare against the Germans in occupied countries, with irregular forces comprised of people from other nations, and the question of under whose authority they fell remained unanswered. As we will see, the issue remained a vital one for the French. The Soviet Union, which had signed a treaty of non-aggression with Germany in 1939, had been completely blindsided when Hitler launched Operation Barbarossa and invaded the Soviet Union in June of 1941. By the fall of 1942, Germany's efforts there were stalling; 1941 also brought the United States formally into the war. Upon hearing the news of the Japanese attack on the US naval base at Pearl Harbor, Hawaii, Churchill reportedly slept soundly for the first time in months and justifiably so, considering the enormous industrial might that was now going to be marshaled on the British side. Now the war took on a new hope for the British, and diplomacy and coalition politics became enormously important.

New allies drove shifting war aims and, as Churchill later remarked, "There is only one thing worse than fighting with allies, that is fighting without them!"[22] Having the Soviets and Americans join them in the war was not only crucial to Britain but it also meant grander objectives were possible. No longer was irregular warfare around the periphery of occupied Europe the only option. Large-scale offensive operations and indeed the invasion of the European continent itself were now within reach.

In the spring of 1942, President Roosevelt and his generals developed a series of plans to become involved in the war against Germany, a plan that never saw implementation and produced little but animosity between the three allied nations.[23] Stalin had been demanding it, but Churchill's resisting ultimately convinced President Roosevelt to delay invading France and instead aim for North Africa. However, in the run-up to planning that political decision, Wilkinson, now responsible for SOE's contribution to the overall plan for what became SLEDGEHAMMER, the earliest name for a trans-Channel invasion, put his mind to work. In the fall of 1942 he and a colleague worked under the assumption that the Allies would invade Europe the following summer and this "would trigger a wave of spontaneous insurgency in occupied Europe."[24] Partisan activities in France therefore became the focus of their attention. They knew, from their Special Operations Executive agents in France and from French émigrés who made it to England, of large number of young men who had joined the Maquis to avoid the Vichy and German draft labor programs, which were started nationwide in November 1942. Rather than be deported to Germany to work, many young men were living in the hills and woods of rural southern France or hiding with friends of family.[25] Wilkinson and many SOE planners were convinced the widely unpopular labor draft programs would provide the partisan army with its manpower. But how could they be trained and equipped to act according to Allied plans?

Over the fall and winter of 1943, they conceived the idea of small parties of British soldiers, three in a unit, who would parachute in to pre-identified Maquis bands and direct them in the accomplishment of tactical objectives. Thinking that they had only six months before the Allies would invade France, Wilkinson wrote, "The problem seemed to me to be two-fold. First, how to harness this considerable *Résistance* potential so as to support the regular invasion forces; and secondly, and no less important, how to prevent these volunteers getting in the way both of the regular operations and of SOE's clandestine actions."[26] He proposed that a small team—consisting of an officer, a demolitions expert, and a radio operator—be parachuted in uniform behind enemy lines at the time of the invasion. They would coordinate the actions of the Maquis with the nearest British or American corps commander who would have assigned to him within his operations staff a Special Force Detachment, a new term created to describe this team. Gubbins directed Wilkinson and others to start planning and develop the idea more fully.[27]

While Wilkinson and SOE Lieutenant Colonel Michael Rowlandson worked out the details, Gubbins started the approval process and began discussions with the American Office of Strategic Services. In July 1942, he or his representatives had won approval from the General Headquarters of the Home Forces to continue working and to come up with a set of plans. Over the course of August and September, Brigadier General Donovan, the director of the new American Office of Strategic Services, pitched the idea to the American Joint Chiefs planners for Psychological Warfare. He succeeded in convincing them of its validity and won approval by late August. Also, the United States agreed to contribute 50 percent of the men necessary to put these teams in the field. On July 22, the British and Americans agreed on a planning number of seventy teams. However, back in London, the British had to put a hold on the operation as the SOE's rival in intelligence work, the SIS, did not want the Americans involved in these matters at all. Bureaucratic turf battles do not give way to wartime demands, and when the director of SIS, Stewart Menzies, heard the idea, he quickly had it scrubbed. Things got put right again when the SOE promised that it would "share" its operations with the Americans and they would not run unilateral missions out of the United Kingdom into occupied Europe.[28] The SOE's Wilkinson and members of the American delegation, which included a very energetic and astute Captain Franklin Canfield, discussed the challenges of recruiting the right kind of men for the operation and what resistance fighters they might find in France.[29] Canfield fit the mold of the early OSS types; an attorney, with connections to Donovan before the war, he had joined the army and the OSS after the attack on Pearl Harbor and was one of the first OSS officers in London.

The earliest surviving planning document on the Jedburghs—as these teams were to be called—describes their mission as solving the dilemma of how to link the "Resistance Groups ('Secret Armies') with conventional forces on the day major combat operations commenced." As the document, written in April 1943, stated, they were to conduct operations that furthered military aims when neither the SOE agent nor the Résistance group was believed to be capable of conducting them. The authors, who are unnamed but most likely included Wilkinson, believed the Jedburghs, these teams of three men, should not be asked to undertake their task immediately upon arrival; they needed at least seventy-two hours to organize an operation. Moreover, the paper stresses that these teams not be deployed too near the front or their work will be given "short shrift," as SOE planners believed the Germans would have already policed up—rounded up—all local Résistance fighters near their front, leaving few Maquis to direct. Wilkinson emphasized that operations would concentrate on harassing or destroying aspects of the enemy's line of communications, enemy railways, enemy aircraft, enemy commands and staff, vehicles and ammunition, supplies, and other opportunities that might present themselves. Jedburghs would pass along intelligence on enemy movements, act as guides, or prevent the destruction of valuable resources the Allied command believed it might soon need.[30] The focus of the paper is highly tactical in that its tasks link the command of the Jedburghs to the closest corps or division and therefore Jedburgh objectives focused on aiding that commander's goals. The result of their initial exercise, called "Spartan," would influence Allied thinking on Jedburgh employment.

Approved by Home Forces to participate in Spartan, which was to be carried out in March 1943, Wilkinson and other SOE and OSS officers brought eleven Jedburgh teams to run a practice exercise against the Canadian army units in eastern England. SOE's teams of partisans and Jedburghs were integrated into the trial and immediately their benefits became obvious to the participating commanders. The results, however, "did not in all cases correspond with preconceived ideas on their employment."[31] Each team consisted of a British officer, a second in command, and a wireless radio operator. They linked up with resistance groups, code named "Boykins" after the American hunting dog, and focused their efforts on reconnaissance and scouting duties for the main forces. Wilkinson and his crew discovered that the army headquarters staff needed more people to work the link with the Résistance and suggested specific functions and roles. The teams also confirmed that the resistance tasks should not take place too close to the front due to the time lag it would take to organize a Maquis group to strike a target. The exercise planners suggested a time allotment of at least forty-eight hours, which meant that Jedburghs and resistance groups could best be used on strategic targets, benefiting regular army units, instead of tactical targets, such as blowing up railroads and ammunition depots. Wilkinson, Rowlandson, Canfield, and the rest of the exercise planners then believed that the teams would be best employed if linked at the army headquarters level and properly staffed.[32]

The last major lesson learned from Spartan was also one fraught with implications for the coalition. Rather than simply putting an officer on the team who spoke the language of the country in which they operated—French, Flemish, and Dutch, primarily—SOE now believed that it should have an indigenous officer as a team member. Requiring this necessitated the recruitment of natives. Furthermore, they were to operate in uniform, be given a set of tasks to accomplish prior to their deployment, and be received by SOE agents already operating in the area. That meant that the pace of SOE agent deployments, the number of them, and the nature of their mission became more and more focused on preparing the local Maquis for the invasion. These British agents then, inside France, began to argue with the Maquis leaders that all combat and sabotage action should wait while they husbanded their resources and made the best possible plans for D-Day. For these reasons as well as those noted in the exercise report, the teams were considered more as strategic than tactical operators. That is to say, the cumulative effect of many teams would be greater than sporadic action by individual teams. Moreover, SOE hoped that seeing a uniformed officer from their own nation on the team would have a positive effect on morale of the local members.[33]

The exercise had another important effect; it sold the Americans on the plan and assured their participation. Shortly after it was started on FDR's initiative in June 1942, the Office of Strategic Services staff officers and planners began appearing in London as a result of the first British/US cooperative efforts begun between the man FDR had appointed to be its director, William J. ("Wild Bill") Donovan, and the SOE officer William Stephenson. Donovan was the man Roosevelt turned to in 1941 to set up

American's first attempt at a central intelligence agency for the United States government. The Coordinator of Information, or COI, drew anxious and suspicious competition from the military services and the Federal Bureau of Investigation (FBI). They all wanted it killed, but after Pearl Harbor, Roosevelt seemed more intent on having it and instead of abolishing it, gave Donovan's outfit a new name, the Office of Strategic Services and financed his operations directly from emergency White House war appropriations. Stephenson was the intelligence operative the British had sent to New York in 1940 to run their operations in North America; he could not have been more pleased as he had campaigned for Donovan to run such an organization all along. His North American mission was twofold: first, to ingratiate British special operations and intelligence with their American counterparts, who were just now setting up their organization; and two, to develop Canadian resources for SOE missions, giving more manpower to the British effort. Donovan's role was to start America's first unified intelligence operation and build the capacity to conduct unconventional warfare, sabotage, intelligence, and counterintelligence for the United States. Donovan ran up against resistance to do this from the US Army generals, various theater commanders, and the formidable bureaucratic infighter, FBI director J. Edgar Hoover. Nevertheless, the OSS started and over the course of the Second World War would grow to nearly 13,000 personnel operating worldwide. Donovan also welcomed the coterie of people Stephenson had arranged to train Americans in intelligence and covert operations, among other initiatives. OSS became dependent on this British connection for expertise and sought to locate an office in London to begin work on the expected invasion of Europe.

However, the British, or more specifically, the British Special Intelligence Service, did not want the OSS, an organization that did both intelligence work and covert operations, in London to run unilateral operations in occupied Europe. An agreement was therefore reached that the OSS would not conduct unilateral operations. But the agreement did allow the OSS to get into the game, so to speak, by operating an office in what was going to be a major theater of operations. However, living under the promise made between Donovan and the British chief of the Secret Intelligence Service

Stewart Menzies in early 1942, grew more and more difficult, and by the beginning of 1944, OSS in London believed they were now capable of going it alone, independent of their British tutors.[34]

Donovan sent David K. E. Bruce to London to run the Office of Strategic Service's center that would provide its services for the Western European Theater. Bruce was the perfect man for the job. He had arrived in France just as the First World War ended in 1918, but instead of returning home, he had served as a diplomatic courier for the Versailles Peace Talks and traveled from European capital to European capital growing to love the diplomacy, intrigue, and social life. Returning to Baltimore in 1920, he took the Maryland bar exam, became a state legislator, and then married Ailsa Mellon, the daughter of Treasury Secretary Andrew Mellon. He and Ailsa were preparing for a career in the foreign service and set off to Rome. A career as a consular officer and diplomat was what Bruce had set his life to achieve after the First World War, but Ailsa's health grew poor and Bruce had to give up his dream. Nevertheless, by the late 1930s, Bruce had created a successful life, purchased his family's antebellum acreage near Staunton, Virginia, and been an accomplished attorney, publisher, Virginia state legislator, and trusted advisor to his very powerful father-in-law. Bruce had also become friends with several of New York's most powerful people, including Franklin Roosevelt. An internationalist, he volunteered to serve with the American Red Cross organizing war aid and was in London before the German bombing raids began in May 1940. It was there when in 1940, William Donovan arrived on a fact-finding mission for FDR. Bruce and Donovan struck up a friendship, despite being in opposite political parties. When the Japanese attacked Pearl Harbor in December of the following year, Donovan thought Bruce seemed the perfect choice to run OSS London. In early 1942, Colonel William Donovan asked Bruce to Washington, DC, and in May, Donovan offered him the job of his senior man at the OSS London field station, a job requiring solid connections and the ability to converse easily with British generals, politicians, and members of the aristocracy; Bruce provided the added bonus that the president would trust the information that came from London because he knew Bruce personally.[35]

But at their first meeting back in Washington, Bruce, who was now forty-four, told Donovan he did not know anything about running an intelligence organization. Not dissuaded, Donovan, who had long ago earned the nickname "Wild Bill," told him not to worry. "Nobody else does," he replied. "And I've already provided for that." He directed Bruce to see Stephenson in New York. After some schooling from the British in the United States and some time in Washington as OSS found its feet, Donovan sent Bruce to London. He kept his promise to run covert operations only in conjunction with the British, who soon determined that Bruce was a man they could work with.[36] However, the OSS needed to show results back in Washington, as Donovan was fighting bureaucratic battles daily against those who did not understand what OSS could do for the war effort.

Perhaps in this light the OSS's greatest strength was also its greatest weakness. While its birth can be attributed to FDR's friendship with and belief in Donovan, the OSS struggled for legitimacy and for the rest of his life Roosevelt was barely able to maintain the OSS against its detractors. And when Roosevelt died in April 1945, his successor closed it down. Lacking congressional approval, which would have given it a budget line and a measure of independence, the OSS was funded directly out of FDR's own wartime emergency funds.[37] Furthermore, he subordinated it to the Joint Chiefs of Staff. Therefore, the OSS was under pressure to show tangible results, results that benefited the army and navy, and not just the president. But the deal they made with the British, while getting them into the European theater, hobbled their ability to conduct operations for which they could claim sole credit. Therefore, when the OSS London observer, Captain Franklin Canfield, watched exercise Spartan in March of 1943, he realized the Jedburgh plan provided a golden opportunity.[38] The OSS could participate fully in operations that supported the invasion while doing it *with* the British. It seemed ideal. The OSS got access, and the SOE and the British received what they most needed from the United States: men and materiel.

2

Enter the Americans

When the Japanese attacked Pearl Harbor on December 7, 1941, the United States was profoundly unprepared for an industrial world war. While President Franklin Roosevelt and Congress had begun a national draft, and New Deal policies had largely put America in a mindset for industrial production on a grand scale, that capacity needed to refocus on war materiel. Shifting this focus would take months, and results would not become apparent for years. In the meantime, the United States would have to fight Japan and Germany with what it had. And what America had was not much. The chief of staff of the army, General George C. Marshall, reported in July 1939 that the regular US Army, which included the air force at the time, consisted of "174,000 soldiers scattered among 130 posts, camps, and stations."[1] Alarmed by war erupting in Europe in September, President Roosevelt convinced Congress to prepare the armed forces. Their series of legislative acts achieved a rather striking buildup for the time, and by the middle of 1941, the United States Army could now begin to ramp up to a desired strength of 1,418,097 soldiers organized in twenty-seven infantry divisions, four armored divisions, two cavalry divisions, and one cavalry brigade. But it had nowhere near the numbers to fill these lofty goals. Toward the end of 1941, it had just over 14,000 officers and 375,000 soldiers on active duty and 12,260 in the reserves. There was no Special Operations unit, per se, but merely training in extraordinary environments, such as arctic conditions, or beach landings, which Marshall referred to as Special Operations. Within the army, special operations was still an inchoate concept. The navy enjoyed the expansion as well but consisted of only 337,349 officers and sailors when the Japanese attacked Pearl Harbor on December 7, 1941. To fight the Second World War, it would ultimately grow to 3.4 million in July 1945. But of course, there is more to war than fighting, and so the other parts of the United States government involved in the conduct of its war strategy were profoundly changed, or had to be invented.

Among the capabilities they created was a centralized intelligence organization, and the person Roosevelt chose to realize it was William J. Donovan. There were few who understood irregular warfare despite the fact that it had been involved in nearly every war in American military history. But like the Sioux uprising of 1862 was eclipsed by the Civil War, a nebulous irregular war would quickly be overlooked when large actions with regular forces were occurring, as they are easier to understand. Only recently among some historians has this kind of warfare begun to be noticed as a part of America's history. So despite the country's experience fighting with and against Native American tribes from 1607 to 1890, in various guerrilla-style actions during the Civil War, in the long-running conflict that the United States conducted in the Philippines from 1899 to the 1930s, and in numerous engagements in Asia, Latin America, and North Africa by American soldiers or marines, guerrilla warfare has only recently been recognized as America's first way of war.[2]

Even though there was a brief fear of Japanese invasion, the United States, unlike the British government, never seriously contemplated the consequences of enemy occupation. When it came to establishing the national political war aims, such as defeating Germany before Japan or bringing both enemies to unconditional surrender, there was no constructive national discussion. Roosevelt simply broached the topic of unconditional surrender

with British Prime Minister Winston Churchill and then, with the somewhat surprised Churchill sitting next to him, made it a fait accompli by announcing it at a press conference at the Casablanca conference in January
1943.[3] The manner in which Roosevelt decided issues, even the grandest
issues of them all, such as unlimited war, often caught his political allies,
both foreign and domestic, by surprise. Fighting the war to such a conclusion could be achieved only by organizing the entire nation's economy, focusing all industrial energy for war, and making friends with a wide variety
of unseemly characters abroad who also sought the complete destruction of
Germany and Japan. Unconventional warfare is war waged only when the
goals are total and unconditional. A man who openly enjoyed this kind of
war, who would revel in this kind of complete, high-stakes fighting doing all
that was necessary to turn an advantage, and who could support unconditional surrender was William J. Donovan.

A First World War Medal of Honor winner and a New York attorney who
had known Roosevelt since they were at Columbia Law School, Donovan
re-initiated the old school acquaintance with Democrat and president
Franklin Roosevelt despite being a solid Republican. After serving in
President Coolidge's Justice Department in the 1920s he started a New
York City law firm specializing in anti-trust actions. He became fabulously
wealthy and entered elective politics, seeking to become New York's governor in 1932 as Roosevelt became president. After his defeat, he continued
running his New York City law firm and became an influential man in the
Depression-era world of corporate litigation.[4] When rumors circulated in
1940 that the president wanted to appoint a Republican to become his secretary of war, Donovan believed he would be the man chosen. But despite
initial positive indications from the president, and persistent lobbying by
his co-Republican and even closer friend Navy Secretary Frank Knox,
FDR nominated the venerable Henry L. Stimson for that post. Undeterred,
Knox continued to push Donovan's name to Roosevelt for other work as
Europe descended into war. Roosevelt's first priority was defeating Hitler's
Germany, and the president wanted to know if the British would fight.
Viewing the beginnings of the Second World War within the glow of the

First, he was bitterly disappointed in the French in the summer of 1940. As the Soviets had a treaty of non-aggression with Germany, Britain grew all the more vital as America would have no other partner in Europe with which to confront the Germans and Italians. Dispatched by Roosevelt on a globe-trotting intelligence and fact-finding mission in 1940, Donovan returned to provide the president an impressive assessment of issues in the Mediterranean and the Balkans, as well as British efforts to combat Hitler's war efforts.[5] Afterward, Donovan and journalist Edgar Mowrer, who had also been in London and had seen, as Knox put it, "the French debacle" firsthand, authored a series of articles entitled "Fifth Column Lessons for America." With these, they sought to enlighten Americans as to the methods used by Germany to weaken "the resistance of possible enemies and undermine the morale of countries they proposed to attack."[6] The articles may have served Roosevelt's overall purpose of domestic propaganda in warning Americans of the real and not so real rising threats, but it and other discussions with Donovan fostered Roosevelt's belief that he needed one centralized organization for intelligence.[7] Convinced, Roosevelt made William Donovan his director of the newly established Coordinator of Information (COI) in 1941, before the Japanese attacked. Donovan leaned heavily on the British and their man in North America, William Stephenson. Stephenson had made it his mission not only to school and train Donovan's future commandos but also to seek the active involvement of the Americans in the war. He knew he could influence Roosevelt through men like Donovan and Knox, and he often brought other British officers to Washington and New York City to do so. By May 1941, Admiral John Godfrey and his young aide, and future author of the James Bond novels, Commander Ian Fleming, visited Donovan's Georgetown home to reconcile efforts, advise him on organizational frameworks, and pass along intelligence.[8] With FDR's backing and British help, Donovan had succeeded in getting the intelligence organization created, but now he had to deliver.

When war declarations followed the attack on Pearl Harbor, Donovan convinced the president he needed more authority, and again Roosevelt agreed—this time making Donovan the director of the Office of Strategic

Services in June 1942. Roosevelt's support did not guarantee smooth sailing for the new organization, however. Donovan's appointment as a brigadier general with an independent budget from the president and a direct line to the Oval Office did not sit well with many generals and admirals in Washington or, and more important, with the various theater commanders. But by establishing a network of spies and contacts in North Africa, before the theater commander was ever named to the post, Donovan earned the respect of that theater's eventual commander, General Dwight D. Eisenhower. Eisenhower proved to be an exception among generals who jealously protected their command prerogatives. When Eisenhower arrived in London in January 1944 to take over the command of Overlord and the effort to invade France, he was willing to support what the OSS and SOE had spent months planning. Fresh from a frank and constructive conversation with General de Gaulle, Eisenhower must have been pleased by the agents in France, the British efforts to airlift arms to them, and the cooperation with the French Bureau Central Renseignements et d'Action for the invasion of France then scheduled for May 1944, just five months away. As he told de Gaulle, he needed the support of the French people, and the SOE and OSS operations were going to be the means to communicate and exploit whatever the Free French could accomplish.

William or "Wild Bill," as he was known, Donovan believed that one of America's greatest strengths was its rich ethnic diversity, and from the beginning he intended for his Office of Strategic Services to exploit it. He began to recruit representatives of all ethnic groups to aid in intelligence gathering and unconventional warfare around the world. The practicality of doing so was clear to Donovan as not only would first- and second-generation Americans speak the language, but on occasion, they understood the politics and perhaps had participated in and moved in political circles that the OSS needed now to understand. They could explain motivations, positions, and nuances involved in occupied Europe and Asia as the United States entered the war with little understanding of internal politics within occupied nations. For operations in Europe and North Africa, he sought Italians, Germans, Soviets, French, Greeks, Yugoslavs, Poles, Belgians, Danes, Norwegians, and Arabs. His first thoughts on using such operatives was to create Operational Groups, who could parachute behind the lines into their former homeland, conduct sabotage, and support nascent resistance movements.

Donovan intended these operations to be run by the Special Operations Division within OSS Headquarters in Washington, DC. If a volunteer did not wish to join such dangerous missions but still demonstrated an understanding of the occupied counties, Donovan knew he could still use him as someone would have to analyze all the intelligence he planned to collect. For this effort, he created the Research and Analysis branch, recruiting scholars who had specialized in these parts of the world to work alongside the people in this office. It would be these men and women inside Research and Analysis who conducted assessments on the war's impacts within the nations and provided advice to Donovan, the theater commanders such as Eisenhower, and President Roosevelt. Men such as Crane Brinton, a Harvard graduate and Rhodes Scholar who was an expert in French history, served in OSS Research and Analysis along with many others who after the war became recognized scholars in history, politics, anthropology, economics, and geography; they had cut their teeth on these Second World War issues. Donovan also created the Secret Intelligence Branch, a counterintelligence branch and a Morale Operations Branch in order to conduct psychological operations on the enemy. But Donovan miscalculated on a key issue. America fought the Second World War as a part of a coalition with Britain, the Free French, and later the Soviet Union. That meant that theater commanders such as Eisenhower would have operational control over much of what Donovan and the OSS ultimately provided. The mission of these divisions within the Washington office became focused almost solely on recruiting, training, and equipping Operational Groups for theater commanders. The British-conceived notion of Jedburgh teams was something no one in Washington would have anticipated.

Therefore, when Colonel David Bruce sent Captain Frank Canfield back to the United States to find approximately one hundred French-speaking American officers and non-commissioned officers, Donovan knew this was the way the OSS could become a player in Eisenhower's theater and in the invasion of France. But finding such men would not be easy. Candidates had to be in the US Army, Marines, or Navy; they had to be, or be willing to become, parachute qualified; they had to be willing to volunteer for duty behind the lines; and non-commissioned officers had to be highly proficient radio operators. Canfield and the OSS put out the call in army posts around the country sometimes drawing large crowds, only to see them dissipate quickly when all the requirements were listed. But the men Canfield and others managed to find started to appear at the OSS safe houses around Washington beginning that fall of 1943, some of them interviewing with Donovan personally in November and others interviewing with William Casey, a future director of the Central Intelligence Agency.[9] Those who made the cut then reported for training at what was referred to with the low-key name of Area B-1, the weekend retreat Roosevelt referred to as "Shangri-La"—what is now Camp David.[10] Donovan's relationship with William Stephenson and the British resulted in British instructors for the OSS commando and agent training, including the famous and colorful William Fairburn, the former Hong Kong policeman who had become a renowned commando instructor. They learned about lock-picking, plastic explosives, foreign weapons, how to use a knife in a fight, and other things that focused on the micro-level of guerrilla warfare.[11] When it came to guerrilla warfare training, the OSS seemed to be largely content with letting British take the lead.

It is not as if the United States military had no experience with such matters, but it had not included them systematically in its training. Perhaps the one exception could be found in the United States Marine Corps (USMC). The marines had experienced "Small Wars," as they called them, in the Philippines and China starting in 1898 and well into the first two decades of the twentieth century. They also had been the force the United States sent to in to Haiti, the Dominican Republic, and Nicaragua in the 1920s and 1930s. By the late 1930s, there was considerable understanding within the Marine Corps about the nature of guerrilla war, how such missions should be conducted. Marine officers debated their role, as well as whether they needed to think about formulating doctrine and principles of warfare. The debate became centered around the same debates taking place among the other services in the 1920s and 1930s. The difference was that the marines took this seriously enough to formally debate and then draft a handbook on how small wars could be waged. In the end, amphibious warfare became the defining function, though the USMC's Caribbean missions in the 1920s and 1930s prompted their drafting the *Small Wars Manual* in 1940 with the hope that they would no longer have to "re-invent the wheel" upon being ordered to their next small war.[12]

The manual is quite sophisticated, recognizing the relationship between political aims and combat, starting out by defining small wars as "operations undertaken under executive authority, wherein military force is combined with diplomatic pressure in the internal or external affairs of another state whose government is unstable, inadequate, or unsatisfactory for the preservation of life and of such interests as are determined by the foreign policy of our nation."[13] Furthermore, the Marine Corps manual anticipated operations in foreign countries, operations that fell outside legally declared war, stating that the United States "government has interposed or intervened in the affairs of other states with remarkable regularity," There was no reason to believe that this would cease in the future.[14] While the manual discusses all kinds of practical applications—regarding mules, setting up camps, and sanitation concerns—it also acknowledges that politics and the "decisions of statesmen" will require a smaller kind of combat than that engaged in the First World War. It also provided for what today military planners call a "Stability Phase" in which political power and authority would be handed back in phases to the locally constituted government. As the United States entered World War II, this manual was the only formal document any of the services had on how to conduct guerrilla warfare.

Such was the vacuum that Donovan and his men and women found themselves in when President Roosevelt created the OSS in 1942. Roosevelt's brief directive asked Donovan to "collect and analyze such strategic information as may be required" by the US Joint Chiefs of Staff (JCS) and to "plan and operate such special services as may be directed" by the Joint Chiefs. Such vague language allowed the creative and frenetic Donovan to then pursue nearly any effort he thought worth pursuing. But it also meant that the army and navy staff would have to bless and resource Donovan's ideas. In a meeting of the Joint Chiefs on August 19, 1942, the functions of the OSS regarding "Organized Sabotage and Guerrilla Warfare" were approved. The JCS approved sabotage actions and delineated four functions: organize and incite native groups in occupied territories; arrange for arms and equipment; provide training, direct or conduct sabotage activities; and set up reception committees "to meet and aid our armed forces" all in an effort to prepare the area for "offensive operations by our armed forces." Guerrilla warfare would be conducted by groups of foreign-born Americans loyal to the United States and currently in its military. They were to be given at least three months' training that would prepare them to operate behind the lines and engage in sabotage of key targets, perform reconnaissance, and support resistance groups of that country. The key was that they would coordinate with a theater commander's main invasion force. Where there was no theater commander for a particular area of operations, the Joint Chiefs of Staff would retain control of the OSS efforts. The army and navy were to provide the training personnel and facilities for these tasks. There had already been calls from the theaters for such people and support, and the OSS directive affirmed the Joint Chiefs' intent to answer them.[15] One can also sense Donovan's influence regarding the use of foreign-born Americans or resident aliens.

Nonetheless, when David K. E. Bruce arrived to lead OSS efforts in London to get its intelligence, counterintelligence, and special operations up and running, he also had to abide by agreements made with the British that proscribed unilateral American operations in northwest Europe. As the capability of their organization grew, Bruce and Donovan chafed under these restrictions. However, the Jedburgh plan, while not specifically designed with the OSS in mind, allowed American participation in what was, in spirit, something very much along their original directive. To make it happen, Bruce not only sent Canfield back to the United States on a recruiting drive to find French-speaking soldiers, sailors, or marines willing to volunteer for such duty, but he also had to staff his operation in London; and by January 1943, OSS Washington sent him personnel to conduct operations in support of what became Operation Overlord.

Arriving in London to help in the effort was Paul van der Stricht, a former New York lawyer recruited by Donovan, who along with several others began to work side by side with the British to run agents into France. They also began planning with the British-American military organization created to conduct detailed planning for the invasion. Formally called the Chief of Staff to the Supreme Allied Commander or COSSAC, it was the staff planning office created by Allied agreements during the July 1943 Quebec Conference. Its mission was *plan* for the invasion of Europe. COSSAC's relationship with both the SOE and OSS was a good one; it relied on them for ideas and information about the French Résistance, such as it could be understood, and on how to conduct guerrilla warfare against the Germans.

The issue was what to expect from French partisans. COSSAC's lead planner, American Major General Harold Bull, for one, always thought whatever the Free French could pull off would be a bonus, and therefore the Allies should not count on them for must-do missions.[16] This belief and skepticism set in early and provoked arguments within OSS London, the SOE Sections responsible for France, the Allied Staffs, and between the Allies and the Free French; as we will see, these mindsets would only resolve themselves at the time of the invasion. Nonetheless, that skepticism became a key factor, influencing the amount of resources the Allies were willing to devote to guerrilla warfare in France. And such efforts could require a great many resources. The Jedburgh plan would not come cheap. Not only would it require officers and NCOs to implement it, but getting them behind the lines and successfully linking them up with partisans required aircraft, airfields, thousands of rifles, pistols, hundreds of thousands of ammunition rounds and explosives, marshaling and packing facilities in Britain, hundreds of portable radios, and dedicated radio frequencies; also, there had to be people to monitor transmissions from France and encode and decode the messages and dispatch them to the correct place. In short, the OSS-SOE operation needed a grand effort that was beyond the capabilities of several staff officers in London, and there was less than a year to beg, borrow, or buy everything necessary.

Organizing that task fell mainly to two men: British Brigadier Eric E. Mockler-Ferryman and American Colonel Joseph F. Haskell. Mockler-Ferryman had experience with Allied intelligence and issues involving France. He was introduced to General Dwight D. Eisenhower, an American "no one had ever heard of," in August 1942 soon after Eisenhower's arrival in England. Eisenhower was then putting together the Allied staff in order to conduct what became Operation Torch and the invasion of North Africa. The British Army suggested Mockler-Ferryman as the one they wanted to set up an Allied intelligence staff. Eisenhower impressed Mockler-Ferryman with his affability and acumen—his not caring "which uniform an officer was wearing."[17] However, when German forces smashed the American units at Kasserine Pass in North Africa in February 1943, inflicting over 6,000 casualties and claiming over 4,000 prisoners, Mockler-Ferryman lost his job.[18] The negative domestic reaction to the first real combat between American and German soldiers was profound, and under pressure from Washington, Eisenhower fired him along with the American Corps Commander Major General Lloyd R. Fredendall. However, Mockler-Ferryman's reputation inside British Army circles remained undiminished, and Eisenhower himself decorated him for his service. It is very possible that his reassignment may have had little to do with his performance in North Africa. After the war, an unnamed but reliable source who knew about the incident informed him that the American government had insisted on a scapegoat from each country and Eisenhower decided to fire Mockler-Ferryman in order to share the blame among allies.[19]

In any case, Mockler-Ferryman harbored no ill will toward Eisenhower and was unhesitant about cooperating with the Americans on major operations, such as Overlord. General Gubbins quickly snapped him up and made him head of SOE's Western European Section. Three months later, Gubbins referred to him as an officer who "quickly grasped a most intricate method of warfare."[20] As the head of SOE operations in Western Europe, Mockler-Ferryman's duties were twofold. First he was to control the guerrilla warfare in Western Europe and second he "was to prepare with Overlord planning staff a scheme to dovetail the action of *Résistance* with the strategic bombing plan."[21] SOE's relations with COSSAC had by now become close, and its Western European Section formed what was informally called "the London Group" with their American counterparts from the OSS/Special Operations (OSS/SO) section in London—the office that came to be headed by Colonel Joseph Haskell.

The same month that Mockler-Ferryman became head of SOE operations in Western Europe, Colonel Joseph F. Haskell joined Colonel Bruce
in London. A West Point graduate, class of 1930, and the son of an army
general, Haskell had been serving as an intelligence officer on the COSSAC
staff since his arrival in London in March 1943. He arrived just as Wilkinson,
Canfield, and others began to press their Jedburgh plan to COSSAC as a
means to exploit partisan operations in Europe.[22] Haskell quickly became
a believer in the concept and recommended that COSSAC embrace it.
So when Bruce needed an officer to run his Special Operations section,
Canfield suggested Haskell, and his appointment gained quick approval all
the way up the OSS chain of command.[23] Connections helped. Haskell's
father, who was at that time running as the Democratic candidate for New
York's lieutenant governor, had been one of Donovan's commanders in
World War I. Furthermore, Haskell's older brother John was already in the
OSS and would later be OSS London's head of the Secret Intelligence
branch, or SI.[24] Donovan and Major General Harold R. Bull, another West
Point graduate and the chief of COSSAC Plans, and later Eisenhower's director of operations for Overlord, both liked the idea of having a military
officer they could trust in that key position.

Urbane and handsome, Haskell was a cavalry officer who had gone from
army post to army post prior to the war where he loved to compete on army
polo teams. He spoke French and was self-confident enough to lead in an
organization largely made up of non-career officers.[25] Requesting his assignment to OSS, Bruce wrote to COSSAC that "no other officer" could
undertake this work due to the short time before the invasion. He also believed that all the work Haskell had already done on the plan made him able
to come to the job without missing a beat. COSSAC approved Haskell's
transfer to OSS London on August 23, 1943, at the same time it approved
the Jedburgh plan and the London Group's efforts to control the partisan
movements inside Europe.[26]

By the late summer of 1943, with the Jedburgh plan approved and the
British and American leadership falling into place, it was now a matter of
finding the resources to enable the plan to come to fruition: staff assignments,

operational structure, training facilities and instruction, and of course supplies and equipment both for the Jedburghs and the partisans in Europe. Furthermore, it was one thing to have the agreement with COSSAC, but COSSAC would change personnel when the commander for Overlord was finally named—at this point George Marshall was still the leading American candidate—and he might look at partisan warfare and behind-the-lines operations in a different way. Marshall, who resisted the creation of the OSS and thought Donovan had too close a relationship to the president, nevertheless was not totally opposed to OSS operations and Donovan's schemes, as long as they were under proper authority. Whoever it might be, the London Group would have to come to an agreement with the new commander about the role the partisans should and would play.

By December 1943, the London Group established the role of the Jedburgh plan in support of the overall Overlord plan. The teams would be sent into the field based on the determination of the Supreme Allied Commander and how he would seek to control the partisans to conduct a guerrilla war supporting the Allied invading armies. Mockler-Ferryman and Haskell's London Group staff believed they had the broad operational outlines in place. The teams would be sent to a known resistance group and given at least seventy-two hours to organize the initial effort. They therefore needed to be briefed on their mission and the local resistance in the area, moved from their training base at Milton Hall to their briefing and isolation safe houses in London, and then on to one of the special duty airfields at RAF Tempsford or RAF Alconbury. At the airfield they would receive a meal and their equipment; the aircraft would be filled with their gear tailored for their tasks. Their radios would each be assigned unique encoding crystals. The British agreed to supply fifty officers, the Americans fifty, the French ninety-two, the Dutch nine, and the Belgians nine. The British would provide thirty-five wireless transmitter operators, the Americans fifty, and the French fifteen. Furthermore, to coordinate activities between the partisans and the conventional forces, the Special Force Detachments with each of the main Allied Armies had to be constituted, organized, and trained. These Special Force Detachments would be assigned to each numbered army, such as the US Third Army commanded by General Patton, and call in the alerted Jedburgh teams as they saw fit. At least that was the plan as 1943 ended.

Organizing all the support machinery for the Jedburghs did not mean starting from scratch. The British had been conducting operations in occupied Europe since 1940 and since 1941 had maintained networks of agents in France.[27] The British had also learned from their mistakes, and these experiences shaped their understanding of the Résistance and also of German efforts to thwart Allied networks; they had learned valuable lessons about how to run operations behind German lines. In fact, the German successes at catching the operators and rolling up networks was the SOE's biggest reason for wanting the Jedburgh program in the first place. Allied commanders believed they needed a strategic reserve of agents to operate in small teams after the invasion—when the Germans would round up the large resistance groups and their associated networks. They knew perfectly well that their agent networks were always on the knife's edge of survival and would not last long after the Allies invaded France. After the Germans and the French Vichy government had stepped up their anti-partisan efforts, the Jedburghs would replace all the SOE and OSS agents expected to be arrested, tortured, and killed.[28] The Jedburghs could still use the infrastructure to support their operations, but they would need a far greater support base. Moreover, it was clear by the end of 1943 that the French would have to be brought into the planning in a more robust way than they had been up to that point. The French efforts and how the SOE and OSS coordinated with them is discussed in the next chapter.

By early 1944 the challenges facing Jedburgh planning now included coordinating between the Allies, and specifically with the Free French. With agents regularly going in and out of France, aircraft dropping supplies, and operators ready with intelligence to send London, the most critical challenge was establishing reliable communications. The Allies found two different ways to overcome the challenge: the radio or wireless transmitter (W/T), and the British Broadcasting Company. The key person in any partisan circuit was the radio operator; his or her ability to communicate meant the difference between life and death. Relaying news of a circuit being discovered, a traitorous agent, or incoming equipment on a drop zone was key, and if the agents were incommunicado, things went terribly wrong. Because of their connection to Overlord, secure communications were even more critical for the Jedburgh teams, and by early 1944 the Germans had realized that they could triangulate the signal and locate a radio source. The German intelligence and police units used directional finding vans to locate illegal transmitters aided by a special military police (or Feldgendarmes) ready to arrest whoever sent the signal. In large cities, finding the exact room radio signals emanated from was more difficult. To help them home in, the Germans would switch the power off in the city section by section and when the signal stopped they knew where the radio was. Radio operators soon learned that broadcasting short messages meant better security and made it more difficult for the Germans to discover their location.[29]

However, even short messages sooner or later gave away their source and it often became impossible or impractical to send and receive on a dedicated radio set. To alleviate the number of messages to send or receive, Georges Begué, one of the SOE's first successful agents, came up with the idea of *messages personnels* over the BBC—probably because carrying around the enciphering books when there were so many Germans in the region caused him to despise the things. If caught, he'd be shot.[30] Over time, the Allies' broadcast of news and music would include pre-arranged phrases or poems, meaningful only to the person receiving the message. Thus, BBC announcers began the nightly broadcast with a stream of non sequiturs and nonsense, which, to resistance cells, contained orders or news of friends and comrades. To the circuit leaders it could be confirmation of an incoming flight of weapons or the orders to start an operation.[31]

To aid aircraft in getting to their drop zones, the Allies developed S-phones, which could transmit voice-radio signals in a secure way from the operator to an airplane. But with a range of only eight to ten miles, and special training required, the phones were a challenge to use. The Maquis rarely used the device, and when these phones were dropped in, the fighters focused their attention on the rifles, ammunition, and money, ignoring the strange radio contraption. Still, under the right conditions, the S-phones would have prevented many agents and material from being parachuted miles off target. As things stood in the winter and spring of 1944, the Résistance's methods of guiding aircraft to a drop zone could range from primitive to fairly sophisticated, depending on the skill and experience of the resistance group working the drop zone. In the most basic of receptions, four men used flashlights, formed a large "L" and signaled when they heard the sound of the aircraft. The reception party signaled a previously agreed upon Morse code letter, and the aircraft dropped the load over the "L" and flew on to another location to drop propaganda leaflets elsewhere, in an effort to make the Germans believe that that was the plane's only mission.[32]

Realizing that the Jedburghs needed a transmitter that could meet their task, both the SOE and OSS set out to develop a proper one. Their efforts resulted in a small suitcase-sized radio powered by a six-volt battery capable of sending out a signal that could reach London. All the team members were trained in Morse code, in case the radio operator was killed or captured. However, handling the radio required a high level of skill, particular when operating under combat conditions. Not only did the operator need to be an expert at Morse code but also deft with coding and decoding. To code Morse messages quickly, the Jedburghs used a process known as "one time pads." A "one time pad" had a set of letters five across and five down so the operator could overlay the normal alphabet on the pad, giving him a new order of letters. After using it once, the operator would then use the next code sheet. The person receiving the messages would have the same series of pages in order to unscramble the letters. A simple code for the Germans to break, but only if used twice.[33]

In addition to communications, the other key element of partisan warfare and coordination was air support. Almost all the aircraft that had been developed by 1944 were designed for strategic bombing rather than sneaking behind enemy lines and parachuting in men and supplies at low altitudes. Initial efforts to convert bombers for special operations immediately ran into many problems, not the least of which was the unwillingness of the Royal Air Force to provide aircraft. In August 1941, the SOE operated a total of sixteen aircraft from Newmarket Racecourse, a combination of Halifaxes, Whitleys, and single-engine Lysanders, the only aircraft truly designed for the SOE. A high-wing monoplane, stripped of arms and equipped with an auxiliary fuel tank, the Lysander could fly 450 miles and carry four passengers. It proved extremely valuable due to its ability to land in short and rough landing fields, providing flexibility. Lysanders could not be used for parachute operations but they could land to pick up and drop off passengers and equipment, and with the engine running, take on passengers and cargo.[34]

Whatever model was used, parachuting people and equipment clandestinely meant using an aircraft flying a low altitude mission at night. This required re-fitting aircraft and different training for aircrews. The first few months saw an initial mission success rate at a disappointing 45 percent, meaning that less than half the missions were successful. The problems stemmed from poor navigation, bad weather, and the often unprepared Maquis reception committee at the drop zone.[35] Air crews contended with Luftwaffe night fighters as well, attempting to fool German radar by flying with bombing formations until breaking off to their target area. And according to one SOE officer, the "moon was a goddess," as the moon's phases directed air operations. Aircraft could not land without some moonlight, and parachuting operations were best when the moon was at half or bigger. Dropping without moonlight was nearly impossible.[36] Despite the obstacles, the Royal Air Force units attached to SOE pressed ahead and developed their capabilities. By November 1942, SOE operated twenty-seven aircraft and had accomplished ninety-three sorties. Operations stepped up considerably during 1943, with 615 successful sorties. By the last week of September 1944, when most of the Jedburgh action described in this book was completed, the British had accomplished 742 air sorties with aircraft based in Great Britain to locations all over occupied Europe, delivering 854 tons of equipment for partisan movements. Nearly 75 percent of those missions were considered successful.[37]

By necessity, the Jedburgh plan had moved from a British project with continental partisan movements in tow to become a complicated coalition aspiration. The plan now required agreement and coordination between the British, who had the most experience with partisan warfare, the Americans, who were providing more and more of the resources and personnel, and the French, who were on the ground and whose country they were all trying to liberate. The OSS joined in the project to get into the Overlord campaign as the Jedburgh plan offered Donovan the opportunity to simultaneously support the invasion of Europe and to demonstrate to detractors back home that the OSS was worth having. After three years of warfare, finding highly trained and specialized British soldiers was becoming increasingly more difficult. Moreover, the Americans helped solve much of the aircraft-shortage problem, increasing the capability for night flying and aerial re-supply of the networks in France. Relations between Britain and the United States would prove somewhat challenging. However, at least from the British point of view, they must have looked much more inviting than relations with the Free French and de Gaulle. Understanding how the Free French began, how it drew its plans together with the partisan groups inside France, and what it sought from the British and Americans is a fascinating and compelling story. The details follow in the next chapter.

3

Recreating France and the Rise of the Résistance

Germany's diplomatic and military successes in 1939 and 1940 were stunning. The path the Germans traveled achieving them was remarkable. After their loss in the First World War and their bitter resentment over the humiliating Versailles Peace Treaty, the Germans endured despite the devastating Great Depression. In these circumstances they turned to Adolf Hitler's Nationalsozialistische Deutsche Arbeiterpartei, or Nazi Party, voting it into power in January of 1933.[1] Almost immediately, Hitler began reorganizing the German Army or Wehrmacht; over time the revitalized Wehrmacht became not only a source of his political power but an incredible military machine, developing rapid offensive maneuvering through the combined use of tanks, infantry, and aircraft all directed with coded radio communications.[2] France's doctrine of defense proved to be no match against the Wehrmacht's innovation and mobility, led by aggressive German officers. After the 1938 Munich agreement with Hitler, the French and British suffered months of successive and embarrassing setbacks, as Gubbins and Wilkinson experienced firsthand. From conceding to Germany's demand for Czechoslovakian territory, to the Soviet-German

Non-Aggression Pact, the loss of Poland, the Soviet-Finnish War, the sweeping German victories over Denmark, Norway, and Yugoslavia, and the inept leadership and poor preparedness accompanying Britain's loss of the Mediterranean island of Crete, the British and French governments seemed at a complete loss as to how to resist Hitler's relentless industrial might, lightning attacks, effective use of airpower, and sheer will.

And it got worse. Germany quickly followed its remarkable successes around Europe's periphery by invading Belgium on May 10, 1940. While the German tanks and aircraft were of similar quality to those of the French, the Germans used surprise, powerful offensive, and mobility; and led by officers encouraged to take the initiative, the Wehrmacht burst through the Belgian and French defenses. The French attempted a gamble to shore up the Belgian defenses, but they failed, largely due to their army's inability to maneuver effectively following years of preparation to fight a defensive war. From May 13 to May 17 the Germans succeeded in breaking through the French defenses at Sedan, Monthermé, and Houx on the River Meuse and wisely exploited their early successes by cutting off the British and French Armies in northern France from French forces to the south.[3] By racing to the English Channel, the Germans dislocated Allied efforts to defend France, leading the French Army Commander Weygand to admit to Churchill on June 12 that the French army could no longer conduct "coordinated war."[4]

Indeed, a complete lack of coordination and effective governance wracked France, its relations with the Belgians and the British, and its own army. Belgian King Leopold began armistice negotiations with the Germans on May 28. Fearing its army was going to be completely destroyed, the British began an evacuation at Dunkirk on the next day and by June 1, 350,000 troops including 60,000 French, had escaped across the English Channel. Moreover, Britain refused to employ Fighter Command's aircraft to defend French airspace.[5] German troops had advanced to the English Channel and other large formations were slicing southward getting between the French defenses on the German border—named after the engineer who designed the network of fortifications, the Maginot Line—and the French capital, cutting off French forces on the east side of the country. And to add to the consternation, Mussolini joined his German ally and declared war on France on June 10. "It's only fair, don't you see?" Churchill quipped upon hearing the news; "they were on our side the last time."[6] But France needed more than pithy remarks. When General Weygand spoke to the British delegation two days later, Churchill's cajoling and threatening of the French government to remain in the fight must have seemed obscenely incongruent with Britain's own actions, as no British forces remained in France.

Besieged with confusion, parts of the French army continued fighting in piecemeal and uncoordinated actions while the German Army captured some 2 million French soldiers and eventually shipped them to prisoner of war (POW) camps in Germany. The members of France's parliament scattered down the roads south to Bordeaux or other southern ports choked with fleeing refugees.[7] For many, such disorder and chaos were a greater threat than the Germans. On June 16, Pétain did as Churchill had feared and accepted the post as the head of the French government. The crafting of this eighty-four-year-old national hero into a leader in whom anyone could see what they wished to see was largely the work of Pierre Laval. Laval was a French politician who had been in and out of government during the preceding decade. Fervently anti-communist and contemptuous of the socialists, the freemasons, and the unions, he took the opportunity over his time as prime minister to make France into what he had long desired. In Pétain, he found a man he could use to renew France and who could symbolize justice and French national pride. Although Pétain did not trust him completely, he shared in the notion that an armistice with Germany should be sought.

But the cause for the rise of Pétain and Laval and their Vichy government cannot be placed entirely with these two men. As Robert Paxton wrote, "In truth, there was rather an instinctive shrinking from chaos that made war to the end against Germany simply unthinkable. The final weapon of a people whose conventional army has disintegrated is chaos."[8] Pétain was old enough to remember the last time the German army had conquered France in 1871. He could recall the subsequent chaos, the revolution, and the installation of the constitution he now viewed as weak and fundamentally flawed. He and many others had a reason to fear the very real threat of what continuing the war would mean: guerrilla warfare and roving criminals ostensibly led by communists and quickly answered with German reprisals, hangings, theft, and deportations.

But while the authority of the state is a long and deeply held tradition in France, there was another way to maintain the state while avoiding chaos. Charles de Gaulle took that path. The most junior general in the French army took a plane from Bordeaux to England the day after Pétain became president. The next day, Charles de Gaulle got permission from the British government to broadcast a message on the British Broadcasting Company's programming where he, perhaps nervously and beginning in a shaky voice, called for "French officers and soldiers on British territory…to join forces with me." He explicitly stated his intent to use a "superior mechanized force" to ultimately defeat Germany and insisted the war was not lost.[9] In a very real way, this call was not the beginning of de Gaulle as a political leader of any future French Résistance movement but rather the culmination of his army career in which he had persistently advocated using tanks and aircraft and the adoption of a doctrine to exploit mechanized warfare.[10] At that time and in the bleak days that followed, de Gaulle only sought to organize such a force for the time when a resurgent France called upon it. He hoped to use weapons salvaged from France and purchased from the United Kingdom and the United States to enter France again alongside Allied armies.

However, when no political party or leader emerged from the ruin of France's prewar political class, de Gaulle picked up the baton of political leadership. But de Gaulle was poorly prepared and had never shown any inclination for national-level political leadership. He would, over the next few months, compensate for his inexperience with an abundance of pride. Just days before the French government collapsed, Premier Paul Reynaud named de Gaulle to a junior Cabinet position as he was impressed with de Gaulle's ideas on how to organize an offensive-minded army. But a few days as under secretary of state for war was nothing compared to the experiences of others in national politics, others he believed would step forward to lead while he re-constituted something on the order of a brigade or division to operate alongside the British. But later in 1940 when other parts of the French Empire began to support him, he was forced to think about political aspects as well as military ones. When no political leader outside of France took up the mantle of leadership, de Gaulle seemed the sole person for people to rally behind. When Pétain met with Hitler, de Gaulle and his burgeoning Free French organization issued a manifesto in Brazzaville, Congo, where they claimed to speak for France, as Pétain's government was subject to the will of an invader and therefore illegal.[11] The government at Vichy returned the favor and issued charges against de Gaulle condemning him to death.[12]

De Gaulle's claiming sovereign authority over France had substantial consequences for other governments in choosing sides. Speaking to de Gaulle on the evening of June 27 before the Brazzaville declaration, Churchill decided to "recognize you alone" as he could not surmount the Foreign Office's reservations in recognizing de Gaulle as someone who spoke for France. The following day, the British government announced that they recognized de Gaulle to be the "leader of all the Free French, wherever they may be found, who rally to him in support of the Allied cause."[13] But later, when de Gaulle's group claimed the authority to speak for France, the Free France-British relationship began a long and stormy relationship as it careened from one point of contention to another over the next five years. That relationship found its first test with the incident at Mers-el-Kébir. When Pétain refused to order all French naval ships to sail to England or neutral ports, Churchill believed he had to order the Royal Navy to seize or destroy them. When they did so at Mers-el-Kébir, near Oran, Algeria, on July 3, killing nearly thirteen hundred French sailors, de Gaulle reacted with his furious temper at first. After some time to collect his thoughts, Churchill was struck with de Gaulle's understanding and his explanation to the French people regarding the matter. As de Gaulle stated bluntly, "No Frenchman worthy of the name can for a moment doubt that a British defeat would seal forever his country's bondage."[14] De Gaulle made clear that France's future was heavily invested in British fortunes. And when, as explained in the previous chapter, a few weeks later the British created the Special Operations Executive, that organization would prove to be the best vehicle for de Gaulle's links with the independently developing resistance movements inside France.

But interior movements had to have an animating idea that would motivate their inception and birth. As long as the shock of defeat continued and the Pétain government presented itself to the French as their savior from chaos, few movements had the reason to begin. Pétain's meeting with Hitler at Montoire, France, in late October of 1940 and his subsequent pursuit of a policy of collaboration provoked the origins of a French resistance opposing him. However, the vast majority of Frenchmen believed Pétain and his ministers, such as Laval and Admiral François Darlan, were doing their best to defend France, maintain order, and negotiate the release of French POWs. As historian Julian Jackson accurately wrote, "Before it could be joined, the *Résistance* had to be invented."[15] Therefore, animating ideas that appeared in the form of newspapers and posters extolling political goals were France's first forms of resistance. The first of the newspapers began to appear in the fall of 1940 while the more enduring and influential underground newspapers such as *Libération* and *Combat* saw their first editions roll off the clandestine presses in the summer of 1941.[16] The driving force for the early papers was complaints that Pétain's government was not the protector of France, as it claimed to be, but was instead a vehicle for Germany's abuse of France.

Pétain may have realized this himself when in December 1940 he arrested Laval and reshuffled his Cabinet and placed Admiral Darlan in charge of his government. While the drastic nature of Pétain's move has been ascribed various dramatic meanings, the result was not dramatic at all. Over the course of the next year, Darlan accumulated more and more government posts and by August of 1941 he was the vice-president of the Council while also holding the Foreign, Interior, Naval, Information, and the Defense Ministry posts. But despite all these responsibilities he was unable to repair the damage done to relations with Germany when Laval was arrested by the Vichy government. Furthermore, he supervised a deteriorating relationship with the British and a puzzling one with the Americans. To Darlan fell the dubious task of convincing the Germans to collaborate with France in its recasting of Europe under Nazism, but under a more subtle guise. He sought to go beyond the Armistice agreement of 1940 and formalize a relationship with Germany that would grant France a more respectable status. He persisted in this until replaced by Laval who had convinced Pétain he could do better. After Darlan failed to win any improvement in France's standing with Germany, Pétain submitted a list of replacement candidates to the German and the US ambassadors. Both disapproved of the list and Laval used the consternation to emerge from the political doldrums of house arrest to become prime minister for a second time.[17] Pétain had hoped Darlan would secure the agreements he sought, but such an agreement was not forthcoming from the German government, as was bluntly stated by the German state secretary at the Foreign Ministry who directed, "Squeeze the country dry," but give nothing to them in return.[18] Darlan lost the top position but retained his Defense and Navy posts and remained a power in the Vichy regime until the Allied invasion of North Africa in 1942.

One can quickly see Hitler's war aim for France by the map the Germans drew defining occupied and unoccupied territory. The occupied zone gave the Germans full control over the industrial north, Paris, and French ports on the North Sea, English Channel, and Atlantic Ocean. Hitler's modern industrial warfare now had more factories, workers, and mineral resources and the German Navy and Luftwaffe had the facilities they would need to conduct operations against Britain. Alsace and Lorraine were incorporated officially into the German Reich and the Italians got an occupation zone along their border with France. The line of demarcation between occupied and unoccupied France became a "virtual border" requiring identification cards, permission to cross, and restrictions on the amount of mail and goods allowed over the border. Running from central eastern France, south of Paris, and taking a southerly turn at Tours, the line of demarcation terminated at the Spanish border east of Hendaye. Those living along that line now underwent the curious change in life of becoming citizens near a border town where wartime want and rationing made smuggling an underground industry.[19] But as German aims shifted from defeating Britain toward operations in the east against the Soviet Union, its focus on France became more ambivalent, and clear direction for the German military occupation authorities governing France was often absent.

Germany needed France's resources, and Hitler still viewed France as a mortal enemy due to the France's victory in the First World War, but the German need for first-rate troops in the Soviet Union had an effect on how it could operate in France. Hitler, as in other areas, failed to govern or provide his commanders in France a coherent or unifying idea for occupation. He wanted racial cleansing, but the army commander for the occupation—the MilitärBefehlshaber im Frankreich (MBF), General Otto von Stülpnagel—did not enforce or follow up in such efforts. He was not a Nazi ideologue but instead a traditional Prussian officer who believed such activities were unprofessional and dangerous. Von Stülpnagel had within his command the FeldKommandanturn, an organization similar to military police that he stationed throughout France, even in the unoccupied zone where they were coyly called liaison officers. Von Stülpnagel also had an organized effort that focused on extracting economic and material wealth from France. Last, he possessed a staff element that produced intelligence and propaganda, and maintained a secret police. His attitude toward the treatment of the French people was one of severity for his own Germans who broke the law or murdered Frenchmen. Punishments against German soldiers acting illegally were harsh. However, von Stüpnagel's days were numbered in that position as he was finally ousted on February 16, 1942, by the political maneuvering of the other powerful people in the German occupation of France.[20]

In addition to von Stüpnagel, the German Foreign Office, Reichmarschall Hermann Göring, and the SS all believed they had an interest in how Germany governed France. The Foreign Office dispatched Otto Abetz to France to see to its concerns. In his two meetings with Hitler, Abetz was told to work toward collaboration with Pétain. But most evidence suggests Hitler was merely attempting to play Abetz, as it was not what he really sought from France. He did not trust Abetz since he was married to a French woman, but he believed Abetz could play a useful role if manipulated well. Abetz worked to encourage the anti-Jewish laws Vichy passed while urging his superiors in Berlin to collaborate with the Vichy regime. He also furthered Vichy's aims of their anti-Jewish laws and assisted with the process of deporting French Jews to Germany. While Göring had considerable sway with Hitler, commanded the Luftwaffe, and controlled a great deal of the economic effort to support the war, his major concerns in France came down to his personal interests in fine art and other French goods. His tirades about matters often left Stülpnagel confused and angry.

Another German entity and powerful player in French affairs was the SS led by Heinrich Himmler. He arrived in France without the knowledge or permission of the MBF authorities, and over time he developed a working relationship with Abetz—one he could use against his rival Göring. Himmler's SS sought French collaboration and along with Abetz supported the elements in the Vichy government that were pro-fascist and pro-German. Over time, the SS would become a powerful force in the radicalization of the war in France and would emerge as an influential player regarding security, police, intelligence, propaganda, and education. But the German Army's occupation authorities had been better prepared for occupying a nation while the Foreign Office, Göring, and the SS all sought to advance their own agendas, which were often counter to the aims of the MBF. This dysfunctional relationship within the German hierarchy contributed to Germany's confused efforts to occupy and govern France.[21]

In important ways, the MBF found itself somewhat lulled into complacency by the slow development of any widespread and well-organized resistance in France. This complacency, coupled with the competition among the army and other Nazi organizations involved in the German occupation, made governing France incoherent on many issues. But the Germans did not really have to go up against a Résistance resembling a military organization until the summer and fall of 1943. By that time Germany's strategic situation had shifted. Its invasion of the Soviet Union had stalled at Stalingrad in a long and protracted mauling by the resurgent Soviet Army. The Americans, British, and Free French had gained control of North Africa and Sicily and had launched operations on the Italian peninsula. Faced with these realities, Hitler issued strategic guidance on November 3, 1943, communicating his views regarding the west as "the crucial scene of the war due to the expected Allied invasion of France."[22] These two events changed the nature of the MBF's mission but found it lacking the forces that could defend France from the Allies and deal with a rapidly growing, reckless, and sometimes fierce, resistance.

Meanwhile, the Résistance needed to get its act together and to expand beyond distributing newspapers into an organized political movement. Growing and centralizing around a political goal proved to be a very slow process hampered by an incoherent animating aim and the development of effective and persistent German methods for arresting resistance leadership.

The reasons for its slow development can be attributed to the shock of the 1940 defeat, the popular belief that Pétain and his government were working toward what was best for the country, and a lack of an underground society or culture able to sustain the long struggle of the Résistance. Such a society would eventually be built, but developing it took time; whenever it got to a point that it could claim some kind of organization and sense of itself, a wave of arrests would deal it severe blows. Due to the nature of clandestine living involving pseudonyms, illegal identification cards, stolen money and weapons, passing of coded messages, and the fear of arrest and death, it is not hard to see why those who remained inside France took umbrage with those who attempted to direct resistance activities from abroad. There is a pride in living and surviving under such conditions that encourages the belief that because one is bravely suffering under occupation, one's actions are more legitimate than the actions of those who do not undergo such traumatizing experiences. Tapping into that legitimacy proved to be de Gaulle's greatest aim, for while he could get resources to fight the war through foreign backing, real political power would have to come from France.

The French occupied and unoccupied zones also provided another political dividing line. As prewar political parties had been ineffective and circumstances of occupation were quite different on the two sides of the line of demarcation, the Résistance became the purview of those untainted by political party records and developed in quite different ways in the north and the south. With German troops, barracks, parades, and aircraft flying overhead, the Résistance in the north had the more immediate aim of fighting the Germans, while in the south, resistance movements took a more political approach, resulting in arguments among them regarding aims and strategy as they vied with one another for members, influence, and resources. The difference became a source of conflict between southern and northern groups. After traveling around the unoccupied zone, a northern movement's member acidly remarked, "What they lack is a few Germans on the street."[23] Southern movements had far more political rhetoric in their newspapers while northern movements tended to focus on organizing for military action.[24]

The three main non-communist southern movements, Libération, Combat, and Franc-Tireur, reflected, in a very real way, each leader's enthusiasm, stubbornness, charisma, and ability to survive the clandestine life. Emmanuel d'Astier de la Vigerie began organizing the movement that eventually used the name Libération in the late summer of 1940, almost immediately after France's defeat.[25] French Army Captain Henri Frenay started his group in mid-1941 after realizing that Pétain and his mid-level intelligence and security officers were not interested in resisting occupation. He merged with another group whose focus was more on politics while he still retained his desire for armed action, and so he named the paper, and later their group Combat.[26] Jean-Pierre Lévy joined a group of philosophical and more politically experienced people than those in most movements. Urbane and charismatic, he became the head of Franc-Tireur after the arrest of its previous leader in March of 1942.[27] There were other movements, but these three became the largest and most influential in the southern unoccupied zone.

At the same time, in northern France the German presence governed the groups' development. Many of their newspapers failed to maintain any publication continuity and many of them pursued assassination or sabotage against German and Vichy targets from early in the occupation. These attacks, mostly in Paris, provoked severe German reprisals. Hitler and the German authorities viewed such acts as illegal violations of the armistice and international law. Under this kind of attitude, acts of resistance were viewed as simply terrorism and punishable by death.[28] But when Germans began to be assassinated in Paris, this was not enough for Hitler. He wanted the clear signal sent to the wider French population and sought 100 French Jews to be executed and 1,000 Jews and 500 communists to be deported in reprisals for the continued attacks on Germans in France.[29]

The communist participation is perhaps the most complicated aspect of the interior movements, but it serves to demonstrate how unified the Résistance became by the time the Allies invaded. The Particommuniste français (PCF) or French Communist Party was a presence, with waxing and waning parliamentary membership in French politics from the 1920s to the present day. However, the communists have traditionally maintained two key characteristics: their political independence and their views on action. The PCF eschews forming or participating in coalition governments as they regard the purity of their cause to be more important than the price they would inevitably pay by participating in a coalition government that would insist on bargaining away certain communist aims in the inevitable political horse trading. Therefore, before the Second World War, they had supported various left-wing governments but did not join them in a formal sense. They believed doing so would send the wrong signal to the French people and that the PCF needed to maintain an independence that it would not have if it joined a coalition government. Even during the Popular Front government of Leon Blum in the mid-1930s, the PCF supported the government but did not join it.[30]

The second aspect of the communists in the Résistance was how they had to navigate the PCF's reputation both before the war and in the early stage of the occupation. The party's leadership supported and participated in the international communist organization, the COMINTERN, and took direction from it. In the 1930s, that meant taking their cues from Soviet leader Joseph Stalin. When Stalin's foreign minister signed the non-aggression pact with Hitler, the French communists were obliged to propagandize, as Stalin directed them to do, that the Germans were not the enemy but rather capitalist nations such as Britain and the United States were the foe. When Germany invaded Poland, officially beginning the Second World War in September 1939, the French Communist Party forced French communists into attempting to hold to that party line, but the reality of it led many to believe that by doing so, they were indeed supporting German capitalists in a war on Poland. The logic became even harder to maintain when Germany invaded France *before* it invaded the Soviet Union, and this put the party in the position of having to advocate an alliance with Germany even though the German Army attacked and occupied France. Such advocacy laid bare the bankruptcy of the PCF's position as more communist than French, which was more than many French communists, much less non-communists, could take. Such a situation forced considerable defections from the party resulting in a split.[31] The Communist Party head, Maurice Thorez, went into exile in the Soviet Union for the duration of the war, while a new communist organization formed, taking the name the Front National (FN).

While communists directed the FN, it sought to maintain a non-political image and to fight German occupation and the Vichy collaborationist policies. Therefore, the FN dropped the international aspect of communist ideology from its cause while it held firmly to the central tenet of communist ideology calling for armed action to force revolutionary change. Its desire to fight attracted many adherents, whether they were communist or not, into its armed Résistance organization, called the Franc-Tireurs et Partisans Français (FTPF or often simply the FTP).[32] For the Front National, and later the PCF, resistance meant violence, not simply printing underground newspapers or spiriting downed Allied airmen back into Allied hands, but persistent attacks on Germans whenever a good opportunity arose. They wanted to kill Germans and Vichy officials despite the very real threat of reprisals. Action was more important than lives and in their view was worth the price.[33]

And, of course, when their actions achieved the death of a prominent German official, it played into the occupation authority's propaganda. The Germans and Vichy could then claim that the Résistance was a fringe movement of communists and Jews, using this as an excuse to arrest any they found and label resistance efforts as a part of the global communist/Jewish movement the Nazis had always portrayed as a great threat. When the Germans enacted counterterrorist policies in Paris focusing on communists and Jews, it ironically furthered the Front National's and later the PCF's own propaganda attempting to convince the French people of the communists' role as *the* leading way to resist occupation and collaboration. The belief, or myth, that the communists were more active, violent, and effective than all other resistance movements persists due to effective Nazi, Front National, and PCF propaganda during and immediately following the war.[34]

But things changed again when Germany invaded the Soviet Union on June 21, 1941. Obviously no longer on Hitler's side, Stalin quickly directed the French communists to resist Germany. Moreover, when Germany declared war on the United States on December 8, 1941, Stalin eventually directed Thorez and the remaining French Communist Party members back in France to support the Allies and fight against the German occupation. With Stalin's backing, communist participation in de Gaulle's Free French movement was just a matter of working out the details.[35] But the Front National's leadership had more to bargain with, and signing on under de Gaulle's banner was not a foregone conclusion. Nevertheless, their FTP units, mostly in southern France, proved to be an attractive alternative to staying at home when Vichy persisted in implementing a policy that directly affected men in their twenties and thirties. In February of 1943, Laval and the German labor minister agreed to institute a labor draft that sent men to work in German factories. The numbers of people involved in the Résistance increased as a result. Popular reaction to the Service du Travail Obligatoire (STO), the French name for the labor draft, was the single greatest cause for young men to join the Résistance. German Labor Minister Fritz Sauckel came to be known at the time as the "recruiter, *par excellence*, for the army of the *Maquis*."[36]

But how many people were in such movements? Or more important, how many would become Eisenhower's guerrillas by picking up arms to fight under the Allied Command? Membership numbers in all of these groups is very difficult to establish with certainty. Libération had told de Gaulle's BCRA chief Dewavrin in January of 1943 that they had 23,000 members to be armed while Franc-Tireur claimed 16,000.[37] It appears that Combat had 70,000–75,000 total active members in its organization by the end of 1942.[38] When a document from the Résistance to the OSS requesting arms, ammunition, and funds fell into the hands of the Vichy police during the winter of 1943, it estimated the national total, including the communists, to be at 241,350 men.[39] Such numbers may be high due to a group's exaggerations and or double counting, and certainly they are off considerably if an intelligence report from the Supreme Headquarters Allied Expeditionary Forces (SHAEF) is correct. Completed in November 1944, as the combat in France shifted from guerrilla action to static fronts in the east and west of the nation, SHAEF's intelligence analysts took numbers from the Jedburghs and the reconstituted French Army headquarters. It explained that the armed FFI numbered 91,500 during the summer months and that the numbers in the French Army by October, which had mustered in FFI units, swelled the regular forces to approximately 300,000 men.[40] But all that was yet to come.

UNIFYING THE INTERIOR GROUPS AND LINKING THEM
WITH THE FREE FRENCH

While the interior groups created themselves according to their conditions and the actions and reactions of the occupying Germans and the Vichy Regime, de Gaulle's understanding of them was slight. His intelligence chief André Dewavrin had, with the help of the British Special Operations Executive RF Section, sent agents into France but had gleaned no useful insight into how the movements worked or who led them. Furthermore, the Free French suffered from a complete lack of appreciation for the circumstances of the interior movements and the factors that created them. The position of the Free French relative to the Allies continued to be a tenuous one and, as discussed in the next chapter, de Gaulle had persistently poor relations with the British and Americans. De Gaulle's fortune changed, however, when Jean Moulin found his way to London and met with him on October 25, 1941.

Before the war, Jean Moulin had been a department prefect, roughly comparable to an American state governor, for the Department of l'Aveyron, and he was serving as prefect of the d'Eure-et-Loire Department when the war began. He had been educated in the French national bureaucratic manner but was not the typical government manager. During the Spanish Civil War he had served as an aide to the air minister, where he supported the Spanish Republicans by smuggling arms across the Pyrenees Mountains despite the French government's embargo. But in spite of this, his energy and skill impressed the government, which led to his appointment as the youngest prefect in France. When the government signed the armistice with Germany he attempted to work with the Germans for the good of his department, but when it seemed too much to bear, he attempted suicide. Denounced by Vichy for his reluctance to accuse the French Senegalese Army unit of war crimes, as the Germans were pressuring them to do, he went into the Résistance in November 1940.[41]

He then made good use of his time in the wilderness before boarding a British plane from Lisbon. Before leaving France, his activities are not precisely known, but he tried to meet and ingratiate himself into various resistance groups with modest success so that when he spoke to the BCRA and SOE debriefers upon his arrival in London, he impressed them with his understanding of matters inside France. Of course, when they knew next to nothing of the groups behind enemy lines, increasing their understanding would not be difficult. Moulin had met Henri Frenay, for instance, and knew something of the emerging Combat movement. But during his private meeting with de Gaulle, he made such an impression, as de Gaulle did with Moulin, that the two men decided they needed each other and that Moulin should return to France as de Gaulle's representative in an effort to unite the movements.[42] De Gaulle provided him with money and arranged with the British to parachute him back into France via an SOE-operated aircraft. Moulin's letter and directive from de Gaulle was written in a tone of equals and stated that military actions and political actions should be separated. It left open the option of political leadership and encouraged the movements to intensify their propaganda efforts. Moulin also brought some money to be split among the movements with a promise of more funds to follow. De Gaulle asked for regular reports on the groups' progress and setbacks. The only thing he demanded was that all military action should be coordinated through him in London. Moulin returned to France on New Year's Day, 1942.[43]

That year, 1942, was a turning point year for the Résistance. Certainly the entry of the United States into the war, it was hoped, would be a boon to a Free France and the defeat of Germany. But due to incidents over French colonial possessions, especially in the Caribbean and off the Canadian coast, President Roosevelt now forced issues with de Gaulle while at the same time losing faith that Vichy would ever resist German aims. Moreover, Vichy cost itself dearly in public support when it conducted trials against those who had been in the government of France in the 1930s, attempting to prove that they were the ones culpable for France's defeat due to mismanagement and bankrupt ideologies. The trials quickly demonstrated no such thing and Darlan had to abandon the effort. This embarrassing event, plus Darlan's failure to gain German agreement for collaboration, forced Pétain to fire Darlan and return Laval to his former job in the government in April. On June 10, General Koenig, a French commander of an armored division, scored a victory against the Germans at Bir Hakeim in North Africa. The morale boost this provided cannot be underestimated, as it became the rallying cry for Frenchmen everywhere and proof that the French Army could defeat the Germans on the battlefield. General Koenig became famous and the battle became a rallying cry for Résistance movements, including several Maquis group that called themselves Bir Hacheim. These events inside France in May and June both drove people away from Pétain and gave them an example of what the French could do to the Germans under resolute leadership, such as that of General Koenig.

On November 8, the Allies invaded French North Africa in a move that caught Vichy, de Gaulle, and most especially the Germans by surprise. General Dwight D. Eisenhower commanded the Allied forces landing in Morocco and Algeria with the goal of seizing ports along North Africa's coast, picking up French support, and getting into action against German and Italian troops in Tunisia and Libya. However, since it violated Vichy's neutrality, Eisenhower had been secretly working with the senior French general Henri Giraud in the hope that the landings would be unopposed. Giraud, the intrepid general who had been a prisoner of the Germans and then managed to escape, had an arrogance that the affable Kansan could not take in large doses. Meeting him on the island of Gibraltar, Eisenhower was surprised when Giraud asked Eisenhower when Giraud would assume command of all the Allied troops. Eisenhower quickly surmised that Giraud was only interested in himself, but he proceeded in the discussions as he was convinced Giraud was the only French general he could work with. But there was another twist: Admiral Darlan, who still retained control of the navy after Laval returned as prime minister, surprised the American negotiators when they were informed that he was in North Africa to see his polio-stricken son. The French generals advised the American State Department envoy, Robert Murphy, that Darlan was the senior Vichy official, higher in the government than General Giraud, and the one person he should deal with. Murphy and Eisenhower followed this advice, and the sporadic firefights that did take place ended when Darlan ordered a ceasefire.[44] Germany could not allow the French to join the Allies, as it threatened German forces in Libya attempting to press toward Cairo and control the Suez Canal. Hitler's reaction made it clear to all who was really in charge when he directed his forces to rush across the Demarcation Line and occupy all of France. Now Germany possessed the deep-water port of Marseilles as a point of control on the Mediterranean Sea. Apparently realizing Vichy's complete impotence in the matter when told that Hitler was going to occupy the entirety of France, Laval's only comment was, "Those Jews on the Riviera are in for a nasty surprise."[45]

The effect of this event was to create a precipitous drop in support for Pétain by the people inside France. As John Sweets points out, "the most dramatic and definitive loss of prestige for the Marshal accompanied the Anglo-American invasion of North Africa and the occupation of southern France in November of 1942."[46] Events such as this drove more people into the Maquis and the southern resistance movements, for now they had "Germans on the street," and combined with the forced labor draft, which came the following February, much of Vichy's legitimacy vanished. But while Allied intentions were seen to be finally producing meaningful action, the Free French could not have been more disgusted with the Darlan-Eisenhower agreement. De Gaulle and the movements greeted this news with a white-hot rage. Writing to American Admiral Stark, the American de facto representative to the Free French, de Gaulle remarked caustically, "I understand that the United States buys the treachery of traitors, if this appears profitable, but payment must not be made against the honor of France."[47] While Stark chose to ignore the letter, and de Gaulle apologized, Stark got the point again when the gist of the letter appeared in the London press. But the discomfiture and embarrassment of Churchill, Roosevelt, and Eisenhower was suddenly alleviated by blood when a twenty-year-old Royalist named Fernand Bonnier de la Chapelle walked up to Admiral Darlan in a hallway near his office and shot two bullets into his chest. The short, stout, former head of the Vichy government died instantly. As the next in line, General Giraud took charge and had Bonnier de la Chapelle executed the next morning. Who was behind the assassination or how large the conspiracy was remains unknown, but certainly Churchill, FDR, de Gaulle, and Giraud in their own way all benefited by it. Roosevelt wished now to advance Giraud and make him the head of the French in North Africa while maintaining Eisenhower as the overall governor of the French territory.[48] The French believed Roosevelt had no right to make such decisions. And as time progressed, the next expected Allied action—their invasion of France, or lack of it—forced the Free French and the resistance movements along two lines of thought that would animate their hopes: inevitable German defeat brought about largely by an Allied invasion and the punishment of the Vichy regime. As 1942 ended, with Allied successes in North Africa, numbers in resistance movements steadily growing, and Pétain looking weaker and more illegitimate, Germany's defeat seemed all the more possible.

But the greatest proof that the Germans would lose the war came when the Soviet Army successfully held out and then ultimately annihilated an entire German Army at Stalingrad at the end of 1942. The belief of German invincibility had collapsed. The communist underground newspapers extolled this victory while nearly all the underground newspapers in early 1943 showed their great anticipation about when the Allies might land in France and begin the final push to defeat Germany. As their expectation continued unrequited for the next year and a half, their sentiments toward Britain and the United States turned more and more harsh.[49] Living under occupation was long past tolerable for the committed resister.

In January 1943, Roosevelt and Churchill met for a conference near Casablanca, Morocco, and discussed Allied strategy for the coming year. The talks started on January 14 and continued for ten days, and the British prevailed in convincing the Americans that the conditions were not yet favorable for landings in France and that operations needed to continue in the Mediterranean theater.[50] Roosevelt also sought to merge the two senior representatives of France: Giraud, who was largely his man, and de Gaulle, whom he distrusted.

Roosevelt and de Gaulle had planned to meet in Washington in early January. In preparation for the visit, de Gaulle had spoken to Admiral Stark and stated that the governing class of France had found itself lacking in French history, but leadership talent was so diffuse within the population that a new class of leaders could always be found. De Gaulle impressed Stark with his description of how Joan of Arc and Clemenceau appeared in French history from different parts of the population to successfully save the country and thoughtfully expressed to Stark that "perhaps at this time

I am one of those thrust into leadership by circumstances, and by the failure of other leaders."[51] Stark believed de Gaulle could make a useful and positive impression on Roosevelt and encouraged the trip. But when Darlan's assassination occurred, events overcame the meeting and de Gaulle never left for the United States.

When de Gaulle and Roosevelt did finally meet during the Casablanca conference the tone had shifted a great deal. When it was apparent to de Gaulle that Roosevelt and Churchill believed they had the right to name the leadership of France, de Gaulle became very defensive and wary. He was also upset that Churchill had threatened to cut off his supporting funds if he did not attend the meeting at Casablanca. FDR's continued pressing of Churchill to produce the "unwilling bride" (de Gaulle) for the "bridegroom" (Giraud) only rankled Churchill on the matter. When they finally did meet, after the swelling of all these tensions, things got even worse. After some polite discussions between the two French generals, they shook hands for the cameras but both left completely unsatisfied. De Gaulle had attempted his historical illusions that had worked so well with Admiral Stark. But perhaps due to a muddle of translations, Roosevelt understood de Gaulle to be saying that de Gaulle was indeed Joan of Arc. The event became the signal event in the president's subsequent discussions about de Gaulle to others and he often embellished it to make de Gaulle seem outlandish and extremely arrogant.[52]

Seeing how FDR and Churchill tried to govern affairs for the French, "de Gaulle tried to coordinate, with even greater focus, all the efforts of metropolitan France."[53] Legitimacy had to be expressed and de Gaulle began pursuing that expression via two paths. The first involved getting the interior resistance movements to unite behind him, and the second path was to create a governing entity that the interior groups could join. These efforts would consume him and the Résistance for the next year and a half. Nevertheless, looking back at this time, de Gaulle wrote that he was full of hope, for "the die was cast; the scales began to tip the other way. The huge resources of the United States were transformed into means of battle; Russia had made a recovery, as we were to see at Stalingrad; the British managed to re-establish themselves in Egypt; Fighting France was growing....An operation of major scope was under way in the west."[54]

But de Gaulle was beginning to realize that the Allied landings he was referring to required successful linkage with the Résistance's actions. Such conditions required unity of action between the interior resistance movements and the exterior Free French. That meant constituting a provisional government that would be widely recognized in North Africa and the interior of France. How could it be constituted in such a way that all the movements and groups recognized it sufficiently to follow its orders? A normal course of action in a Republic would be for the political parties to participate, but their stock was gone and most of the more powerful resistance movements wanted nothing to do with prewar political parties that they believed had so disastrously let their nation down. Moulin, who had returned from France with news of the movements, and the intelligence chief Dewavrin had to impress upon the movements that only de Gaulle's political leadership could unify France and provide the necessary legitimacy. Both men would go into France and provide the necessary plans of what to do when asked by that legitimate and unifying political leader.

Dewavrin parachuted into France in February 1943 with Pierre Brossolette, having a mix of things to accomplish. Brossolette was a profoundly charismatic man, a journalist before the war; he had risen through the resistance ranks by assisting and planning the organization of various movements in northern France and knew them as well as anyone. Having spent most of 1942 in London growing influential in the Free French organization, Brossolette knew how to use a dramatic performance on the BBC and in large groups to gain more and more influence. Now parachuting into the country west of Rouen on February 25, 1943, with Dewavrin, the two had many details to share with their interior resistance brothers. Planning had been done in London on what they wanted their secret army to do, and to begin their preparations, they carried with them the microfilmed versions of Plan Vert, the effort to cut railway lines in certain key locations around France. They also brought more funds and attempted to pull the northern resistance movements together and under de Gaulle's banner.[55] Moulin, operating somewhat independently of Dewavrin and Brossolette, sought to get the southern movements in order and working together.

Their work, with great risk and effort, resulted in the formation of the Conseil National de la Résistance (CNR) on May 27, 1943, and its first major decision was to promise its loyalty to General de Gaulle. The Conseil was a mix of compromises and nearly did not happen due to Frenay's independent dealings with the American Office of Strategic Services. For months Frenay's delegate had corresponded and met with the OSS station chief in Bern, Switzerland, Allen Dulles. Dulles had been taking information and giving Frenay's Combat financial support. Realizing that this meant the Americans had independent power directly into one of the movements, Moulin became furious. It demonstrated further proof of de Gaulle's point of view that the United States meant to control the governing of France. But ultimately, Moulin's skill at manipulating rivalries smoothed over the differences within Frenay's Combat movement. The seats on the council were divided up among northern and southern movements and some of political parties, including the communists.[56] While the unification was tenuous, de Gaulle announced it, trumpeted really, as proof that he was more in tune with and more legitimate than Giraud.

With Moulin's mission enjoying success, de Gaulle left London for Algiers to work on the political unification of the exterior Résistance. Now firmly believing that he would have to be a political leader after some thoughtful communication from former French prime minister Léon Blum and other French politicians, de Gaulle arrived with an aim. The organization he sought to create was a committee that could govern French interests in the colonies. But now de Gaulle aimed for more and worked to develop it as a French provisional government that would be recognized as such by foreign powers. As historians John Sweets and Peter Novick have observed, de Gaulle was far shrewder than Giraud. Each of the two generals named members of the committee, and de Gaulle's members were more politically skilled while Giraud's were more technically oriented—and over time, they were turned or removed from the committee. As Novick stated, "When subsequent appointments were made, de Gaulle's nominees formed a solid bloc of able politicians, while Giraud's—mostly technicians—were not equally loyal to their sponsor and voted individually according to the issue under discussion."[57] De Gaulle and Giraud constituted the Comité Français de la Liberation Nationale

(CFLN) on June 3, 1943, and over the rest of the year, de Gaulle's political skill, compared to Giraud's complete lack thereof, began to emerge. By November 1943, they had also constituted a legislative assembly called the Assemblée Consultative Provisoire and a few days after its constitution, the CFLN members voted de Gaulle their sole leader. Giraud left the committee entirely. Remarkably, within a year of the Allied landing in North Africa finding the French political scene one of confusion, hatred, and assassination, de Gaulle had now risen from a small London office and had succeeded in organizing a political entity that could speak for the resistance, inside France and out. But it was not enough for Churchill and certainly not for FDR.

Churchill and Roosevelt quickly realized how Giraud was being maneuvered aside and feared their waning influence. In a memorandum to the Special Operations Executive chief Lord Selborne regarding funds to the Résistance in France, Churchill instructed him "to take care that the direction of the movement of *Résistance* does not fall under control of de Gaulle or his satellites in England; if not, he will use this enormous capacity at its own political ends in France and not in the interest of the allied effort of war."[58] Roosevelt also feared de Gaulle's efforts to decrease American control over affairs in France and became furious when French officials in North Africa had been removed and some were arrested. FDR had General Marshall send Eisenhower the terse note, "Please inform the French committee as follows: you are directed to take no action against them at this time." Continuing, Roosevelt told Eisenhower and Churchill, "It seems to me that this is the proper time effectively to eliminate the JEANNE D'ARC complex and to return to realism."[59] However, he gave no means or suggested no method to do so. Roosevelt did not because, short of assassination or some ham-handed attempt to arrest de Gaulle, it seemed apparent to all that de Gaulle was the person with whom the Allies would have to deal on matters regarding France.

But while de Gaulle struggled to force the American president to deal with reality, the Free French did not use their time idly. Dewavrin and his colleagues in London were busy planning how they could make Plan Vert better and came up with other plans to enhance the Allied invasion when it occurred. Their planning office, known as "Bloc Planning," began aggressively preparing for all kinds of scenarios. Roughly translated into English it means unit or group planning. Created in December 1943, the Bloc Planning group designed detailed plans to cripple the railroads (Plan Vert), sabotage the underground long distance telephone system (Plan Violet), and disrupt electrical installations (Plan Bleu). These plans had been roughed out from an early planning group, and due to reorganizations the continuation of these efforts fell to the BCRA office in London on Duke Street, about a fifteen-minute walk from the SOE's main office on Baker Street. General François d'Astier de la Vigerie led the effort in his position as the commander of the French Forces in the United Kingdom. In late 1943 and January of 1944 they conducted two staff studies to assess the best use of the Maquis in France and how they could assist in the Allied landings. When they shared the results of these plans with their British and American counterparts, the strategy was greeted with great interest. The studies showed that not only did the Free French have plans on what to do, but the French also had an organization in France with increasing capabilities and might be able to carry them out.[60]

The leadership of the interior Résistance had worked out many command and control arrangements with the Free French via their contacts and by working with Dewavrin during his visits to France. They agreed that France would be divided into regions, largely decided along former political tradition, and led by a political head. But this political leader would also have a Délégué Militaire Régional (DMR) or a regional military delegate who spoke for de Gaulle. In all practicality that meant he worked for the senior general in London or Algiers, depending on what part of France fell under those two Allied spheres of operation. Northern France would fall under General Eisenhower and SHAEF in London and southern France would fall under Allied Forces Headquarters (AFHQ) in the Mediterranean commanded by the British General Maitland Wilson. That meant that General d'Astier de la Vigerie would command the Résistance in the north while General Gabriel Cochet, whom the CFLN had appointed as their representative to General Wilson's headquarters, would command the southern Maquis. After deciding on this basic regional organization, the interior resistance and the London and Algiers Free French would have to agree on who would be the military delegates from the pool available for work in

France. While beginning the appointment and training of some of them in September of 1943, the effort of parachuting them into France began in January of 1944 and continued as necessary through the spring. The RF section of Bureau Centrale Renseignements d'Action (BCRA) and the Special Operations Executive (SOE) selected, trained, and deployed men to be de Gaulle's regional military delegates (DMRs) in France and supplied them with funds, radio sets, radio operators, weapons, and assistants to prepare for the Allied landings.[61] But much of their planning continued separately due to the frosty relations between de Gaulle and the Allies, causing problems in meshing the Jedburgh and other Allied plans. The issue had to be solved at a higher level and involved the political concerns of the United States, the United Kingdom, and the French CFLN in Algiers.

As the resistance movements inside France came together and organized with de Gaulle's France Libre organization, pressure continued to build on Pétain due to the lack of Germany's interest in collaboration and the loss of North Africa. The interior movements had been born, matured, coalesced, and with Moulin, Dewavrin, and Brossolette's effective negotiations and courage, merged with General de Gaulle's France Libre. De Gaulle managed to assert French rights on the international scene and never failed to maintain the notion of French sovereignty as an idea that still existed despite Vichy, the German occupation, and the lack of diplomatic recognition. The communist Front National's agreement to join in should have demonstrated to the world that all those who sought to defeat Germany and Vichy now followed de Gaulle. The United States, with the exception of the OSS, made no material support to the movements, even when they clearly announced their unified support of de Gaulle. In fact, Roosevelt hindered the resistance movements' wishes by supporting Giraud, a man the movements saw as far too close to Vichy. As 1942 wore on, it became evident that Giraud's sole source of power came almost exclusively from the White House. American support was not worthless as it meant materiel for rebuilding the French Army and re-entering the war with forces equipped to fight alongside the Allies. But it did not mean recognition from Roosevelt, nor did it gain the internal resistance movement's approval of Giraud. In fact, it weakened him when compared to de Gaulle who railed about the insistence of the United States on determining how the French would handle their affairs. Roosevelt kept recognition off the table, to be used as a bargaining chip when the time was right.

While recognition is something of a diplomatic exercise, it meant the Overlord commander could not relate operational details regarding the landings to the French. That forced the SFHQ and BCRA planning staffs, some of whom had become good colleagues and friends, to keep secrets from each other. With the row continuing between Roosevelt and Churchill on one side and de Gaulle on the other, it remained to be seen how soon the to-be-named commander of Operation Overlord would approach the effort.

4

North African Rehearsal

I n 1942, General Eisenhower was a student. He was learning how to be a coalition commander. Operation Torch, the British and American landings in Morocco and Algeria, had gone as well as the Allies might expect. Churchill and the British General Staff convinced President Roosevelt that 1942 was not the time to mount a cross-channel attack into France. The target was too hard, they argued, and despite the US General Staff's disagreement, Roosevelt concurred that the first major combat operation would be in the Mediterranean theater. Invading neutral French North Africa to get at the Germans and Italians offered a way to control vital sea lanes and put pressure on the German forces fighting to get to Cairo, and the effort could be supported by the Allied navies. The US and British troops would launch from Great Britain and the Virginia coast and land on the shores of North Africa with few enemy troops in their immediate landing zone, but there would be several regiments of French soldiers. France had declared its neutrality since the armistice with Germany in June 1940, and the French soldiers could be expected to fight back. Therefore, the challenge lay with the diplomats to work with the French in Algiers to stay their resistance. Robert Murphy, the senior American diplomat to French North Africa, had been working to do just that. Murphy had been in North Africa from the summer of 1940 negotiating trade and other agreements with French officials; before that he had served in the American embassy in Paris. His efforts had paid off in many ways and seemed prescient when FDR and Churchill agreed to invade North Africa, as the State Department and Donovan's OSS knowledge of the area did much to enable the landings. Murphy laid the groundwork for re-armament and mineral trade agreements, and had learned how to ingratiate himself to the senior French authorities in North Africa.[1]

His French bargaining partner was General Henri Giraud, described in the previous chapter, a man viewed as sufficiently non-collaborationist since the Germans had captured him in 1940 and he had subsequently escaped. As Giraud had been assigned by the neutral French regime to govern North Africa, Murphy had been quietly visiting with him in anticipation of Allied landings, seeking to get a sense of what the French would do. In Giraud he found a leader he could work with, but of course he could not be blunt enough to clearly explain that an invasion was approaching, nor could he get a firm alliance. However, he and General Mark Clark believed that when the landings occurred, Giraud would openly join the Allied efforts. Their work negotiating with Generals Henri Giraud, Alphonse Juin, and other senior French Army commanders had proved frustrating, and at moments embarrassing, especially when Giraud met Eisenhower and asked when command of the operation would pass from Eisenhower to him. The misunderstanding probably resulted from Murphy and Clark's cagey discussions with Giraud's supporters in Algiers as they were not able to reveal the plan's details. But their work proved not to be a total loss. With the decision to invade North Africa, Eisenhower needed French support to stall Axis efforts at the front and govern French territory in his rear areas, as well as not to engage in combat with American and British soldiers. But the effort was not without gaffes or outright mistakes intolerable at the political level.

As the invasion forces positioned themselves secretly off the coast, Eisenhower set up his command center on the island of Gibraltar. From there he hoped to maintain secure communications with the landing forces, London, and Washington, and to maintain contact with Murphy and Clark working with the French in Algiers. As the invasion began, Eisenhower, however, felt anything but informed of what was occurring. Nervous and unsure of himself in his first major operation, the new commander with not a minute of combat experience found himself in the dark about how the landings were proceeding and anxious to smooth out matters with the French.[2]

Murphy had made arrangements for Giraud to go to Gibraltar and meet with Eisenhower. When the two met, the senior French commander, festooned with decorations from three wars, was under the impression that he would be named the Allied commander of Torch, the code name for the allied invasion, once the landings began. When he met Eisenhower on Gibraltar, just as the invasion was beginning, he asked when the command would be transferred to him. Eisenhower had to disabuse him of this misunderstanding and gently stated that he had no knowledge of such an arrangement; if Giraud wished to pursue it, he would have to ask Roosevelt and Churchill for the command. But the discussion had to be done tactfully so that Eisenhower would not lose the support of the French commander, turning the whole effort into a disaster. The first conversation did not impress Eisenhower at all. He believed Giraud to be arrogant and more concerned about his own place in the scheme of things than for the welfare of his soldiers or his country. His initial negotiations with Admiral Darlan did not leave him with any better impression of the French commanders. In a November 9 message to General George G. Marshall in Washington, he declared his frustration with the observation about the French leadership that "All of these Frogs have a single thought—'ME.'" And later the same day in another message he sounded off again about "these stupid Frogs."[3]

When Eisenhower received a message from Robert Murphy, the senior American diplomat in Algiers, that the former French prime minister, Admiral Darlan, had arrived and had begun negotiations, Eisenhower seized on this surprising opportunity to deal at an even higher level skipping Giraud's ego in the process. If the French would negotiate a ceasefire that would stop the fighting and bring the French forces over to the Allied side, he would take it. But while Roosevelt and Churchill were aware of the negotiations with Giraud and some of the other French generals, they were shocked to discover a deal was in the works with the former Vichy official, Admiral Darlan, a dubious man, too closely linked with collaboration and Germany. While this made sense at the military level, his political masters found it a loathsome move, and when it became public, the British and American people and press were shocked.

President Franklin D. Roosevelt and British Prime Minister Winston Churchill had been eager to work with French General Henri Giraud, a leader they believed would provide unity to the French in North Africa while never having served in the Vichy government. His proclivity to disregard politics made him the perfect choice from Roosevelt's point of view as he could be asked to do what Roosevelt wanted. But when Darlan appeared on the scene they found the more senior Vichy official willing to discuss matters and more able to deliver for the Allies from his more senior position; also, he could bring the French Navy along in the deal. Over the next six weeks, Eisenhower and Darlan attempted to hammer out various civil and military details while Roosevelt and Churchill persistently thundered out their disapproval of the arrangement in messages to Eisenhower and expressed their reluctance about it to the press. Darlan could see that he would not prove to be a lasting part of any agreement with the Allies. Writing to Eisenhower he lamented, "I did what I did only because the American Government took the solemn engagement to restore French sovereignty in its integrity as it existed in 1939 and because the armistice between Axis Powers and France was broken by the occupation of the whole of French Metropolitan territory." He went on to complain about the Allies, implying that Roosevelt and Churchill were "spreading doubts" about his work to unite Frenchmen.[4] But he would not have long to fret about his reputation.

Enraged about the admiral's collaboration with Germany, a few young Frenchmen in Algiers plotted to kill him, drawing straws to determine who would be the assassin. Among them was future French Jedburgh Philippe Ragueneau who drew a long straw. While serving in a machine gun company in June of 1940, Ragueneau never surrendered and immediately started his own resistance movement. Later he merged it with the larger

National Liberation Movement led by Henri Frenay. Arrested for his activities by the Vichy government, he served six months in prison and then left for Algiers. While with the underground movement Combat, Ragueneau participated in efforts to ensure that the French Air Forces were not going to resist the Allied landings in November of 1942.[5] Disgusted with Vichy collaborators, he wanted them dead. The young man who drew the short straw was Fernand Bonnier de la Chapelle. Six weeks after the Allied invasion, Bonnier de la Chappelle simply walked up to the admiral as he entered his office from the street on Christmas Eve and shot him. Eisenhower was several hours away by car when he got the news and raced back to Algiers immediately.[6] Over the course of the next two days, Eisenhower listened to the French generals in North Africa regarding who they thought should be the civil and military leader, received telegrams from de Gaulle in London expressing his alarm about the assassination, and received messages from Roosevelt and Churchill. All the input pointed to Giraud as the replacement for Darlan, as such an arrangement would quiet fears of internal disorder within the French population in North Africa and make Churchill and Roosevelt happy; also, those loyal to de Gaulle seemed to approve.[7]

But Eisenhower asked for input from more than just high-ranking officials and his superiors. French Lieutenant Joseph de Francesco served in the Allied headquarters doing odd jobs and helping the American staff find its way in Algiers. From time to time he was a driver for senior officers. De Francesco, who had been captured in 1940, escaped, and made his way to North Africa, believed Darlan deserved what he got for collaborating with Germany. At some point shortly after Admiral Darlan's assassination, Eisenhower got into the staff car driven by de Francesco and asked the French lieutenant what he thought they should do with the assassin, evidently unaware that Giraud was deciding to have him executed. De Francesco bluntly replied, "They ought to give the guy a medal."[8] Eisenhower sat in the backseat checking his temper, but he was beginning to learn that French politics would be an ever-present concern.

Their short conversation in the staff car serves as a metaphor for Eisenhower's learning and negotiating his way through French politics. Several months after his short conversation with Eisenhower in the staff car, both de Francesco and Ragueneau had joined the Allied Special Force and parachuted into German-held territory as two French officers on the Jedburgh teams. But in December of 1942, while de Francesco served as a driver, he spoke to his future Allied commander and registered his visceral disgust with the French who had collaborated. More important, such beliefs were widely held among the French in North Africa, while inside metropolitan France, sentiments were shifting from Pètain's government and toward the Résistance as the French underground groups evolved and merged under the leadership of Charles de Gaulle. To Eisenhower, Darlan's assassination appeared to be symptomatic of French chaos, but to de Francesco, it was justice.

Immersed in military operations and the diplomacy required to support them, Eisenhower wanted nothing to do with French politics. For him, the military objective was paramount; nevertheless he could not escape political issues as they defined his military aims. But Eisenhower learned from Darlan's assassination and several other disagreements with the French over the course of the next year. He determined that the French Résistance would follow the Supreme Allied Commander if led by a man chosen by the Résistance itself, not by the governments in London or Washington.

Eisenhower's journal and other personal correspondence demonstrate his persistent frustration with those far from his situation, holding views, and persisting in policies he believed were unworkable. Perhaps he realized that those comprising the Résistance movements should determine its leadership. Those movements would confer upon a national leader the authority to deal with the Allies as well as organize a government able to take over from Vichy after the Allied invasion. When Roosevelt and Churchill agreed that Eisenhower should take command of the Allied Expeditionary Forces in December of 1943, they charged him with leading the Allied forces in entering northwest Europe and destroying the German military. Doing this task meant going through France, and this necessitated support from the French people. But if Eisenhower could get active Résistance cooperation to support Operation Overlord, it could create a severe challenge to the German army's rear areas by disrupting communications and transport, and ambushing German combat units. The Résistance could also provide vast quantities of tactical intelligence for more effective operational use of Allied forces. These units could also, if armed and organized for it, comprise a guerrilla force that might be useful under the right circumstances. But even more important, a provisional government, such as the Comité français de la Libération nationale or CFLN, would relieve the Allies of the troublesome and manifestly complex task of setting up an interim civil government.

Realizing what the CFLN meant to his efforts for Overlord, Eisenhower made a point to see de Gaulle before he left the Mediterranean theater for his new command in London. He had corresponded and met with de Gaulle on other occasions over the past year and a half. When Darlan was assassinated, Eisenhower attempted to get Giraud to meet with de Gaulle and passed messages between them over his cipher communications. With the goal of getting them to work together, he praised de Gaulle's CFLN achievements to Giraud. After being rebuffed by Giraud on December 29, 1942, about a meeting, de Gaulle persisted. In his second request, de Gaulle was clear in what he wanted the two to achieve. He wrote, "Only a provisional central French authority, based on a national association for the prosecution of the war is capable of guaranteeing direction of French effort, the maintenance of French sovereignty, and the just representation of France in foreign lands."[9] De Gaulle understood the difficulty and uncertainty in Algiers and offered to meet in Brazzaville, Beirut, or wherever the senior-ranking Giraud chose to meet. However, his second request failed to change Giraud's mind and the opportunity was lost. The two would not meet until Roosevelt and Churchill awkwardly forced them to shake hands at Casablanca nearly a year later.

Roosevelt made it clear to Eisenhower and to Churchill in various messages in early January of 1943 that North Africa was under Eisenhower's military occupation. However, having to deal with the reality of Giraud and governing the French demonstrated to Eisenhower that things were not that simple. He did not want to be in the position of telling Giraud to do something and then have the awkward silence that would follow if Giraud should refuse. Eisenhower and Giraud had worked out how to get French forces into the action against the Germans at the front, and if Giraud were to cause problems, those valuable troops would have to be pulled out of the line and the French forces covering Allied lines of communications could not be trusted with this key task.[10] The Allies needed a sovereign authority such as de Gaulle described above to cover those issues and support Allied military efforts.

And when it emerged in June 1943 in the form of the CFLN, Eisenhower cautiously recognized its utility to him and Allied military operations.

Nevertheless, Roosevelt and Churchill did not. In a message dated July 8, FDR directed Eisenhower and Robert Murphy to stop considering official recognition of the CFLN. "Under no condition are you to recognize the Committee without the full consultation and approval of The President."[11] As president, FDR certainly had the authority to direct his generals on matters, especially issues of a political and diplomatic nature, but he never worked to resolve affairs with de Gaulle at his level. Roosevelt pressed this position and restated it whenever he felt necessary over the course of the next year. De Gaulle, on the other hand, apparently got along well with General Eisenhower, and the two men's correspondence provides evidence of their mutual respect and cordiality. In a congratulatory note soon after Eisenhower's selection to command Overlord, de Gaulle graciously declared that the CFLN had "full confidence in you for employing French forces under your command for the next Allied operation."[12] So while de Gaulle and the CFLN granted Eisenhower the authority to command its forces, FDR and Churchill denied de Gaulle the authority to make such a grant. But if the French Résistance groups were now united behind de Gaulle, the people in those groups might consider Roosevelt and Churchill as much of a threat to French sovereignty as Germany.

For the president and the prime minister the issue revolved around their suspicion of de Gaulle and the fact that the French people had not had an opportunity to express their approval of the CFLN. Of course, while the Germans occupied France, a vote was impossible. Nevertheless, there was overwhelming evidence that de Gaulle and the CFLN were viewed as the sole leadership of the Résistance. Paradoxically, the only other source of authority in France was Pétain's collaborators. But how legitimate was the CFLN and de Gaulle's leadership of France? The American Office of Strategic Services, Research and Analysis Division, produced a detailed and revealing seventy-page report on the various Résistance movements and their political, trade union, and religious subgroups. In the first sentence it answered the president's unfounded belief with the blunt assessment: "The French underground enjoys the support of the vast majority of Frenchmen." The report continued, "Since 1942 the underground has recognized the leadership of de Gaulle."[13] Furthermore, as I described in Chapter 2, post–World War II scholarship has demonstrated this to be true. De Gaulle was the undisputed leader of the unified Résistance movements.[14]

So if the underground enjoyed the support of a majority of Frenchmen who recognized de Gaulle's leadership, why would the president of the United States insist otherwise? What could make him go against his commanders and his chief of intelligence? The reason may be in the influence of one particularly well-placed French émigré who had arrived in Washington, DC, just after France's defeat in 1940. Alexis Léger was an accomplished poet and an experienced diplomat who could command attention within the State Department and the White House due to his reputation and ingratiating style. Soon after his arrival he began a connection with the US State Department with descriptions and opinions of European events. President Roosevelt came to hold Léger in "high esteem." Léger had been fired from Paul Reynaud's government just before de Gaulle was brought into it. This may have been the source of his hatred and distrust of de Gaulle, a man he never had met, and his persistent words to Roosevelt and State Department officials regarding the impossibility of de Gaulle's worth as a leader.[15] It is certain that FDR sought Léger's advice often and always received words back that de Gaulle's efforts were illegal and that de Gaulle would prove to be dictatorial.[16] Hearing anti-de Gaulle beliefs repeatedly from such a qualified source bolstered advice he was getting from his former ambassador to France, William Bullitt. After de Gaulle visited Stalin and brought the communist resistance under his umbrella, Bullitt misinterpreted what was happening and told FDR that de Gaulle was in the pockets of the communists. Furthermore, Bullitt theorized that Stalin and de Gaulle had an agreement on postwar France. Bullitt feared that an alliance of the political right and the communists would team up and "crush democratic elements."[17] Such an event would defy imagination, however, as de Gaulle's conservative politics and devout Catholicism would never allow him to team up with left-wing atheists, unless, of course, France itself was at stake as it certainly was in 1942. After the war, sustaining such a political alliance seems exceedingly fanciful.

If de Gaulle did not want an Allied military government in charge of France, neither did Eisenhower. After leading successful combat operations against the Germans and Italians in Algeria, Tunisia, and Sicily, Eisenhower now prepared to do so in France on the Allies' way to Germany. However, he had more than good experience as an Allied combat commander. Before his departure from the Mediterranean theater, Eisenhower requested an appointment with de Gaulle. De Gaulle had sent him a note of congratulations and a Christmas note on December 23 declaring that he had "full confidence in" Eisenhower and furthermore would place French forces under his command "for the next inter-allied operation."[18] Eisenhower then visited de Gaulle, and as de Gaulle recounted later, their conversation was vital for both men to initiate the kind of relationship and support each needed from the other. Eisenhower reportedly told de Gaulle, "'You were originally described to me,' he said, 'in an unfavorable sense. Today, I realize that that judgment was in error.'" Eisenhower went on to say, according to de Gaulle, that a successful invasion required the participation and coordination of de Gaulle's forces and the "moral support of the French people." De Gaulle reportedly responded, "'Splendid!...You are a man! For you know how to say, 'I was wrong.'"[19]

Whether he had ever been wrong or not, Eisenhower seemed convinced at least by January of 1944, soon after arriving in London for his new position as the supreme commander, Allied Expeditionary Forces, or SHAEF, that "the French National Committee, whatever its faults might be, represented the beginnings of civil government in France." Furthermore, he believed the president, and the War and State Departments largely concurred.[20] At SHAEF he met with the senior French military representative General d'Astier de la Vigerie on January 22 when they discussed several issues. During the conversation that ranged from the desire for liaison officers in Eisenhower's staff to a role for medical supplies of recaptured French territory, they also discussed the role of the resistance movement and the Maquis. Ike told d'Astier that he spoken with "de Gaulle and Giraud [about] the role of the Resistance and the problems involved in combining their action with allied forces."[21]

Unfortunately, indications that Eisenhower was going to treat the CFLN as an entity possessing some authority caused the Darlan-like episode to play out again. In a note dated January 25, Churchill rebuked Eisenhower by stating he did not think Roosevelt would be "prepared to trust to the French Liberation Committee as the dominant authority." Furthermore, he intimated that the selection of those who represented the French Committee must be agreed upon by the Allies, and that Eisenhower should not simply accept anyone they sent.[22] Continuing with the attitude exhibited regarding earlier disagreements with the CFLN, Churchill and Roosevelt pressed their right to select who the French could have in key roles. When Churchill met with de Gaulle in London five days later, he highlighted the British and American long list of complaints and related to de Gaulle that he and Roosevelt had little confidence in the CFLN, "nor by implication, in its head." Churchill dryly commented to the American president that de Gaulle "seemed upset by this."

But Roosevelt's arrogance outmatched Churchill's. In early February 1944, the prime minister and the president conducted a debate via message concerning who should have which parts of Europe as their sphere of influence. Previous conferences had determined the general guidance, but now the War Department was cueing up Overlord planning and postwar occupation duties that required decisions from Roosevelt. In setting up the nature of the issue with the British, he baldly told Churchill, "France is your baby and will take a lot of nursing in order to bring it to the point of walking alone. It would be very difficult for me to keep in France my military force or management for any length of time."[23] So while he insisted on setting up, as the Allies had in Italy, an Allied Military Government of Occupied Territory (AMGOT), over Eisenhower's request not to do so, FDR knew he could not commit the forces required and was going to lean on the British to do it!

When the Combined Chiefs of Staff formalized Eisenhower's invasion mission in a directive on February 12, 1944, it not only told him what to do but made provisions about his task, logistics, forces, and other broad-brush issues. It also gave him the use of agencies that conducted sabotage, subversion, and propaganda. However, the last paragraph of the order concerning relations with liberated Allied territories conveyed to Eisenhower that "Further instructions will be issued to you on these subjects at a later date."[24] Such language covers up a non-decision. With the invasion scheduled for

May, just four months away, Eisenhower needed to make arrangements with France, but Roosevelt and Churchill refused to grant political recognition. De Gaulle later referred to this entire episode in his memoirs and observed that FDR's similar attempt in North Africa had come to naught, and yet he attempted it again in metropolitan France. The French leader wrote, "The President's intentions seemed to me on the same order as Alice's adventures in Wonderland."[25] The Free French had always wished to accomplish two major goals. The first was the defeat of Germany, the second was the purge of the Vichy government. But a new one developed around the fear of an AMGOT, and it was largely fueled by FDR's actions. De Gaulle and the CFLN were prepared to press this matter like a game of chicken, and it seemed that Roosevelt's obstinacy was prepared to crash Overlord's success over the issue. Exasperated, Eisenhower wrote in his private journal on March 22 that the president "has thrown back in my lap" the resistance issue, telling him to work with anyone "capable of assisting us." He desired to work with de Gaulle, but Roosevelt did not permit Eisenhower to work with de Gaulle alone, and de Gaulle would not work with SHAEF unless the Allies recognized him as the sole political authority.[26]

OVERLORD AND ALLIED PLANNING TO USE THE RESISTANCE

Shortly after the creation of the Anglo-American SOE/SO, or the London Group, the chief of staff to the Supreme Allied Commander, or COSSAC, published on December 20, 1943, the "Basic Directive" on Jedburghs' defined objectives, roles, team composition, tasks, and other details. The teams were to support the invasion of Europe and consist of "three men, of whom at least one will be a native of the country in which the team is to operate. Teams will consist of a leader, a second-in-command, both of whom will normally be officers, and one wireless operator." Functioning as a liaison with any Maquis in their area, Jedburghs were not to command the resistance, "but it is felt that the arrival of Allied soldiers, in uniform, behind the enemy lines, will have a marked effect on patriotic morale and that these teams, representing as they do the Allied High Command, *will act as a focus for local resistance*." Sent to areas with known resistance elements, the teams would communicate the Allied Command's orders to the local groups. The team would then train the *résistants* on sabotage, organize guerrilla operations, arrange for arms to be delivered via nighttime parachute drops, and coordinate the Maquis groups' operations with Overlord objectives. Surprisingly, the directive contained no guidance on how to coordinate Jedburgh operations with conventional units, despite the British long-held belief that the Jedburgh teams would be called into the field by the nearest Allied land force.[27]

COSSAC's work on the possible use of Résistance had been informed by SOE, OSS, and other intelligence agencies. Its director had the staff finalize a detailed planning document in July 1943. It was lengthy and attempted to cover every scenario. "Annex P" of the plan, "Support of Military Operations by Resistance Groups in France," defined Allied assumptions and potential missions for the Résistance groups. It assumed four things about the situation that the Allies would not be able to control. First, that the "general situation in France will be substantially the same as that of 1st June, 1943." Second, that the resistance groups would maintain themselves until the invasion date and the "labour draft will be successfully countered." Third, they would not be called upon, other than for various and directed sabotage activities, to take action prior to D-Day. Their last assumption was that the required material would be made available for them to carry out their plan of action.[28]

COSSAC got the second and third assumptions correct. However, adequate weapons and materials would not be made available to the Maquis, due to an argument over resources and objections of Allied senior leaders who believed that attempting to deliver them would be a waste of resources and valuable airlift missions with little or no gain. Furthermore, this lack of capability was exacerbated when the landings occurred due to the larger than predicted numbers of Maquis that rose to fight, all needing weapons and ammunition. Thinking conventionally, most army leaders did not support the idea of using scarce bomber sorties to arm thousands of civilians in the hope of coordinated military action.[29] Furthermore, pre-invasion estimates on what would be required to equip the resistance were woefully short.[30]

While the Résistance was united at the senior levels, the scattered local resistance groups presented another reality. The typical Maquis member was a runaway, hiding out from the German labor draft. Indeed, Vichy policies that attempted to extract concessions from Germany on various key issues, by offering up thousands of young men to work in German factories, only served to fuel popular French discontent with Vichy and drive the discontented workers into the Résistance. Groups of Maquis began to form in early 1942 and by 1943, especially in southern France, and they began to set up localities where they were the actual power. Vichy authorities and the German army and Gestapo continually worked to eradicate their growth, but completely stopping them was futile. By 1944 many of them were linked with the Algiers-based CFLN or groups outside France via networks of spies and underground newspapers. Their political strategy sought the twin goals of toppling Vichy and ejecting the Germans. Therefore, over time, groups emerged whose desire for liberation rose while their belief in Pétain and collaboration dropped considerably. These groups often took on the mold of French prewar political groups, but with one difference: whatever prewar goals their political party or group may have advanced, they now all had the twin goals of overthrowing Pétain and removing the invader.[31] Nevertheless, while those goals united, they often had no firm agreement among themselves as to local roles and responsibilities.

As the groups matured, no national leader could claim to exercise firm control with such fine precision as directing military targets at the local level until after D-Day. Local leaders were independent and conducted themselves in ways garnering the local assistance necessary for survival. Their activities were often centered on local political or military necessity and while they agreed on the national aims, they often felt detached from their national-level leaders in London or Algiers regarding their day-to-day duties. Nearby inhabitants required the resistance to demonstrate its usefulness by carrying out local aims, not necessarily those desired by de Gaulle or the British government. Toward this goal, Maquis attacked targets that could supply them with clothes, arms, or other equipment or vandalized property symbolizing Vichy or Germany, demonstrating how the resistance played on local resentment against Germany.[32]

British and American knowledge and understanding about the interior resistance groups and how they worked at the local and regional level could only be described as vague. Britain confronted the challenge of supporting them but without knowing how, or whether it should support de Gaulle, General Giraud, or any other French personality. Indeed, the British were not above working with even the most ideologically motivated communists, as their open alliance with the Soviets demonstrated. Furthermore, they supported Josip Broz Tito's partisans in Yugoslavia in order to fight the Nazis. Indeed, could putting British efforts behind one man who failed be too much of a setback to overcome? France was not the only country with an active resistance, and the British learned a lesson from supporting the wrong Yugoslav group when they backed the royalists and then found out about the Yugoslav king's people and their double dealing. When they were discovered collaborating with Germany, Britain shifted and backed the communists, siding with their ideological enemies to combat the Germans.[33] With the stakes so high, all had to decide who their allies would be, based on their actions, not their talk.

ALLIED SPECIAL FORCE PLANNING WITH THE FORCES FRANÇAISES DE L'INTÉRIEUR

When the Special Operations Executive first organized to conduct operations in France, the British leaders did not wish to throw all their weight behind de Gaulle, skeptical of his political ability and unwilling to risk trusting him to maintain Britain's secrets. Such distrust was not necessarily a distrust of him per se but a pragmatic concern of whether de Gaulle and the Free French could keep secrets, codes, and communications out of the hands of an extremely tenacious and effective German intelligence operation. Therefore, SOE established two offices to work in France. Unknown to the French, the SOE's "F Section" was for unilateral British activity while the "RF Section" coordinated activities with the Free French's Bureau Central Renseignements d'Action. However, the RF Section and the BCRA relations were complex, and in many ways it is inaccurate to conceive of them as two operations or separate entities who happened to talk to each other and share the results of their independent labor. Instead, their operations were largely co-conceived and planned while the French agents saw themselves as French who merely used British resources. Furthermore, F Section lost its secret status from the Free French when de Gaulle found out about its existence. General de Gaulle exhibited his displeasure in a temper tantrum when he berated the British officer responsible on November 6, 1941. But while he could exhibit his Gallic temper, there was nothing he could do about stopping unilateral British operations in France.[34] Curtailing such offensive British behavior would have to wait until he had more control of events.

The typical way in which the RF/BCRA agent became an operative occurred something along the following lines. A French man or woman would find his or her own way out of France to London and attempt to contact the Free French. But British authorities normally detained them before they could speak to Free French representatives. The British Secret Intelligence Service questioned them to ensure they were not enemy agents. If the SIS approved of them, they would be conveyed to BCRA headquarters and would undergo something of an acculturation process at the "Patriotic School" run by the BCRA in southern England. If they made it out of that with their loyalty affirmed and expressed an interest in going back to occupied France, the BCRA would devise a mission for them based on its needs and an assessment of the kind of mission that would fit the skills of the agent. Then the BCRA would arrange with the RF section for the agent's training and clandestine insertion back into France. Training consisted of parachute jumps; small arms skills and maintenance; use of explosives, codes, and radio equipment; and any special training an agent might need for special tasks pertaining to the mission at hand. Jean Moulin's path back into France mirrors this description.[35]

The system largely worked with modest success considering all the bureaucracies involved and their secretive and conspiratorial nature. The SOE, SIS, and BCRA had hammered out this process over the course of their early relations, and if one of the organizations broke the agreement, nasty letters from senior administrators quickly attempted to correct the matter. The letters, files, and records in British and French archives affirm a level of consternation at the time that would rise again over the course of the war when someone broke the procedural agreements. The bureaucracies operated along a seam of sovereignty creating a vagueness of loyalties for the bureaucracy, but the individual agent grasped his individual loyalty very clearly. Navigating through the archives makes that apparent, especially when one sees dozens of dedicated French patriots like Jean Moulin listed as "British agents." It is hard to believe that Jean Moulin would have thought of himself in those terms. Nevertheless, the F and RF Sections were distinctions with a difference due to the type of agent who might gravitate toward and be useful to one section or another.[36] Of course, de Gaulle and the BCRA could not stop the British from running their own operations in France in full ignorance of the BCRA. From an operational standpoint, this led to duplicative efforts while from a political and sovereign point of view, it empowered local groups to assert their own independence from a resistance uniting around de Gaulle when it could be resourced from Britain via F Section. As described in the following chapters, various Francs Tireur et Partisans Maquis groups asserted their power with money and weapons from F Section agents who did not care about the political leanings of the group they armed, nor did they always understand the local politics and how it would affect national political formations after the war. When everyone sought the defeat of Germany, this point may seem petty, but when de Gaulle and the French eventually needed to assert civil control and order in the confusion of 1944 France, their work was made far more difficult due to the British unilateral F Section operations.

RF and BCRA cooperation had become well rehearsed by the beginning of 1944, but nevertheless, the Jedburgh plan seemed to have to catch up to much of their efforts. As the head of the RF section, British Army Lieutenant Colonel James Hutchison wrote that "there was continuous consultation" with Dewavrin and others of the BCRA.[37] That may have been, but with the standing up of SHAEF and the arrival of its new commander General Eisenhower, the D-Day planning began to push their cooperation in different ways. Quickly after Special Force Headquarters briefed the French on the Jedburgh plan, they enthusiastically grasped the opportunity it provided them—but not without shifting it to meet their needs. The BCRA planning organization, known as Bloc Planning, believed in early January that "It was not a question of creating a new doctrine of employment for the Jedburgh, but of adapting their employment to the doctrine of the *l'Armée Intérieure* defined in our proceeding projects."[38] In other words, the Jedburgh plan could best be implemented in ways that furthered Free French current planning with the interior Résistance groups and the Armée Secrète. The document discouraged its leadership from attempting to get the Allies to change their current plans for the use of the Jedburghs but advocated the creation of a French military command to direct the Jedburghs and to look after the interests of the l'Armée Intérieure. Within this context, the Jedburghs would be an operational reserve. These words are eerily similar to the two-year-old SOE thinking that the Jedburghs would be a reserve of agents that would replace their pre-D-Day agents who would presumably be lost soon after Overlord began. Both the British and the French assumed they would lose their networks and agents currently operating in France and saw the Jedburghs as the means to overcome that loss. But more important, the BCRA planners realized that the Jedburghs provided another means for the assertion of authority. The French understood that if F Section commanded the Jedburghs, it would be another source of consternation and political illegitimacy introduced into France at the very moment of its liberation.

Therefore they quickly seized on the opportunity and began recruiting French officers and radio operators in order to participate and perhaps command the Jedburgh plan. The numbers levied on the French were high considering the paucity of qualified officers in the French Army for such work. Since every team would have a French officer, one hundred such officers would have to be produced. The Free French set up a Jedburgh planning section and appointed officers to flesh out the details from their point of view. Realizing that their desires exceeded the availability, one of the planners still believed that two hundred teams would be a minimum of what they would need and advocated recruiting in the UK among their airborne units and staff elements. Knowing that they only had eleven such candidates in the United Kingdom, General d'Astier de la Vigerie telegrammed Algiers on January 11 emphasizing that it was "absolutely necessary that you send to me 80 officers of the first rank."[39] Recruiting even the Allied Special Force's request of eighty-two officers and fifteen radio operators would be an amazing feat given their late start. It took the United States nearly a year to find, recruit, and train their promised one hundred Jedburghs officers and radio operators. When d'Astier met with Eisenhower on January 22, there is no record of their discussing the specifics of the Jedburgh plan, but it is clear that d'Astier and his Bloc Planning staff were attempting to use the Jedburghs as a link to the Maquis.

Colonel Dewavrin discussed the Jedburghs and their liaison work with the SHAEF and SOE liaison officer Lieutenant Colonel Robin Brooke during various meetings from January 14 to 20. Noting that it was useless to discuss changing the doctrine the British had so far devised for the Jedburghs, internally the French decided to press the issues of how to best use them given the current status of the Résistance. The BCRA was very concerned about the confused command arrangement that would ensue if the Jedburghs reported to the SOE while the resistance reported to General d'Astier. With no command relationship for the French forces established within Eisenhower's staff, such a situation was bound to create confusion in the field during the first fragile moments of the invasion.[40] The fact that some Maquis groups would follow British SOE agents, as they had been doing for months, drove Dewavrin's London staff to wonder if they and the Free French government-in-waiting could quickly assert its authority. Also, how would the military delegates they were sending into France resolve disputes with SOE-controlled Jedburgh teams even when it had a de Gaulle-approved officer among them? Who would decide the priorities for air re-supply? How could they maintain effective coordination with the nearest conventional force commander? Myriad issues could arise causing confusion if there was not a unified command arrangement integrated into the Allied organization for their Armée Secrète, the Free French regional military delegates, and the Jedburghs.

Striking out on his own, Dewavrin ran an operation independent of the British but right under their noses and with their support. Indeed, the evidence suggests that Bloc Planning's most secretive and daring officer Gilbert Renault, who used the code name Rémy, built a plan that sent Capitaine William Jean Savy, also known as Jean Millet, into France to reconnoiter drop zones and areas for Jedburgh operations.[41] Savy and his small team were directed to find one hundred safe houses for Jedburgh teams and to locate sufficient drop zones and reception committees for the Jedburgh teams' initial arrival.[42] Such an effort demonstrates the BCRA's suspicion of British-led Jedburgh planning as the documents demonstrate that SOE F Section would be calling the teams into the field and therefore deciding which resistance groups would get arms. BCRA planners feared a loss of control, duplicative efforts, and political intrigue if F Section ran the Jedburgh plan unilaterally. Afraid of losing the argument with them, BCRA apparently sought to deploy Millet to France to set up circuits independent of F Section circuits in existence in order to maintain some shared control over Jedburgh operations.

Millet's mission ran under the code name Eclaireur, which is French for "Scout" and departed for France on March 2 with two radio operators.[43] The mission is an oddity for many reasons. First, it is the only Jedburgh mission that deployed prior to D-Day. Second, the team commander did not train at Milton Hall but appeared to have been selected unilaterally by BCRA, and only then agreed upon by F Section and the OSS. Third, there is clearly some internal subterfuge occurring between BCRA and their British and American fellow spies. The American OSS liaison officer to the French, Paul van der Stricht, recalled that Millet "was a real *éminence grise* to General de Gaulle."[44] The British officer who ran F Section spoke highly of him and the services he had rendered to their mutual efforts prior to his being sent back to France on Eclaireur. But other than that, little is known about him. He was an accomplished and well-traveled attorney before the war but had not served in the French Army due to a prewar aircraft accident that left one of his arms incapacitated. Not letting that or the injury's disfigurement stop him, he had served in conjunction with the British network, Bricklayer, providing false papers and other supporting issues. The British brought him out of France in July 1943 and he had floated between the BCRA and RF Section since then.[45] Bloc Planning chose him to run this mission probably because neither the British nor the Americans knew much about him, nor had they trained him in any meaningful way. M. R. D. Foot's work *The SOE in France* lists Savy as the head of the Wizard Circuit that was active in France the same time as the Eclaireur Mission and with the same radio operator. He also reports that the Wizard circuit discovered the location of a thousand V-1 Rockets in a depot near Creil, France, and that Bomber Command attacked the site in July.[46] The details about the V-1 rockets were explained in Churchill's memoirs, but frustratingly there is no mention of them in the Eclaireur report. Furthermore, no report for a Wizard mission exists in SOE files. Was the French BCRA hiding the true nature of their mission from British F Section and then throwing them a bone of prized intelligence so F Section officers would not ask any questions about what Savy had been up to in France? It seems very possible, especially when such well-informed scholars as Foot not only mistake Wizard for Eclaireur but fail to ask what was really happening with this mission and focus on the story about the V-1 rockets.

Savy's real mission is more interesting than finding a large number of Nazi rockets. As the French were not privy to D-Day planning, Savy parachuted far from the invasion area, landing near Châteauroux in central France. Tellingly, he met with General Pierre Dejussieu, the commander of the Armée Secrète. He and Dejussieu traveled around France and gathered information on Maquis strength by region, their weapons requirements, and possible drop zones. Savy spoke to or gathered information on each of the regions. In total, it was a large and successful fact-finding mission that did far more than find safe houses and drop zones. It also may have given the BCRA a certain amount of confidence that the Jedburgh teams would not have to be dropped blind; instead, the teams could be cued up for certain groups and leaders who would expect them to arrive at a designated time.[47] Most important, it armed the French Jedburgh planners in the BCRA with up-to-date information they could trust from one of their own sources. However, the Gestapo, never far behind the resistance, arrested General Dejussieu in Paris on May 5, two months after Savy returned to the UK. Dejussieu spent the rest of the war in concentration camps as the Gestapo classified him a political prisoner who apparently was worth keeping alive. Two weeks before Paris began fighting for its liberation that August, the Germans shipped Dejussieu to the concentration camp at Buchenwald-Dora.[48] The former French resistance leader was liberated when Allied troops overran the camp in 1945. Later in July 1944, Savy's radio operator, Eileen Nearne, who had stayed on in France to serve with another circuit organizer, was also arrested and spent the rest of the war in German forced labor camps.[49] Furthermore, the Germans arrested the SOE F Section circuit organizer Maurice Southgate just a few days before they snatched Dejussieu. Southgate's circuit was then split between his second in command Rene Maingard and his radio operator Pearl Witherington. Southgate also survived the war but endured the nightmares of the Buchenwald concentration camp.[50] Did the Gestapo learn anything regarding the Jedburgh operations from Southgate and Nairne, who Savy may have kept in the dark? Or did they learn anything from Dejussieu, with whom Savy discussed the details of the Jedburgh plan? It is unknown. What is fairly clear is that the French now were asserting command over the Jedburgh planning and fooled the British into deploying the Eclaireur mission while not knowing its full purpose or its results.

Eclaireur's results, as useful as they were for planning, were toned down in the report currently in the British archives while the same details are expounded on in BCRA documents. But now that BCRA had run a "scout" mission into France, had determined a great deal about the lay of the land, and had accurate information on Maquis units throughout the country, it still could not prevail upon the British or Americans to allow them into the command organization which for the French rendered the entire affair's "execution impractical" and "unacceptable."[51] Of course, General Eisenhower knew it was unworkable as well and that issue still lay churning at the highest levels.

MILTON HALL AND THE JEDBURGH PREPARATIONS

Getting the most out of the French Maquis required well-trained Jedburghs. As previously described, Major Frank Canfield had gone to the United States to recruit the Americans. First, men had to be found who could operate behind enemy lines, speak French, parachute, and show the ability to operate independently. Every team needed a parachute-qualified radio operator with great skill at Morse code. A September 1, 1943, OSS London memo asked OSS Washington for forty-four staff officers, fifty officers fluent in French, and fifty enlisted W/T operators. Washington viewed recruiting Jedburghs more important than any other requirement and refrained from recruiting for other units until they filled all Jedburgh positions. The OSS believed that finding French-speaking junior officers was the most difficult mission, so they focused their search on New York, New Orleans, and the Fort Benning paratrooper school where they believed more qualified officers existed. Recruiting signs appeared at Fort Benning asking for French-speaking officers willing to operate behind enemy lines, and by the end of November 1943, OSS had filled the requirement.[52]

Getting qualified candidates released from their current duties often proved exceedingly difficult and bureaucratic. The candidate who became the senior Jedburgh, Horace "Hod" Fuller, had served in the French Army from May to July of 1940, joined the US Marines in 1941, and commanded a machine gun company in action on Guadalcanal in 1942. Initially requesting his transfer from instructor duty at Quantico, Virginia, to the OSS in May, Fuller finally got the word of his reassignment to OSS in September. The son of a Harvard archaeologist and a well-connected man, Fuller pulled out all the stops to get reassigned to OSS and to go to the European theater. After being injured in the Pacific, he had been posted to instructor duty at Quantico, Virginia. Fuller described instructor duty as "a fate worse than death."[53] President Roosevelt's son James, Fuller's Naval ROTC classmate at Harvard, wrote to General Donovan urging Donovan to write directly to the Marine Corps to "shake him loose."[54] Once he was in the OSS, Frank Canfield worked to get him assigned to the Jedburgh project where his French skills and combat experience afforded him a great deal of respect among most of the Jedburgh candidates who had little military and no combat experience. After the war, one of the Jedburghs wrote that Fuller "most typified the Jedburgh." His leadership was evident on the way to the ship in New York, when the train from Washington stopped at the public siding instead of a planned and more discreet location. Undeterred, Fuller led, the young commandos to "march through Penn station in pile jackets and caps, dangling fighting knives."[55] To them, his willingness to complete even this simple mission of making the next train on time, while violating regulations served as a great example to the younger officers.

Jedburgh candidates received orders to Washington, DC, with the guidance to leave the train station and find a cab once in the capital city. The recruits then told the driver to drop them at a certain corner where they would wait to be picked up by an OSS car. The OSS recruiter stressed the secrecy of their assignment and instructed them to tell no one the nature of their reporting instructions. Evidently the procedure was not subtle enough for one cab driver. When a few recruits asked the driver to drop them off at the right corner he said, "Oh, you're those OSS guys!"[56] Much to the Jedburgh recruits' delight, the training area was the Congressional Country Club in the Maryland hills near the present-day Camp David. There the Jedburghs were instructed in small arms and self-defense, took psychological tests, and trained in room-by-room combat with human-like targets. The golf course became their running track, the woods served as survival training areas, and they lived in the best quarters any had ever seen in the army. Later, the wireless/transmitter or W/T operators trained at another OSS camp in the nearby Pennsylvania woods before rejoining the officers overseas.[57]

Fifty-five American Jedburgh candidates left New York on the Queen Elizabeth I and arrived in Glasgow, Scotland, on December 23, 1943. From there they traveled to Arisaig, Scotland, for further training and evaluation. The instructors took trainees on cross-country hikes in the rugged Scottish hills; gave them further training in small arms and hand-to-hand combat; and sent them to Stodham Park in three one-week cycles for more psychological testing. After the mental tests determined how the subject handled stress and emotional strain, the instructors told him he failed. By observing how the man handled rejection and the other aspects of the test, examiners measured his strength of character and willpower.[58] One British candidate was asked when he had stopped wetting the bed? Without missing a beat the Welsh officer replied, "When my father took me to see a psychologist!" He passed the test.[59]

Those who made it past the evaluations proceeded to Milton Hall for final training and team selection. The large Milton Hall estate, four miles north of Peterborough, England, became the main Jedburgh training and holding area. A large country manor with many rooms for billets and offices, Her Majesty's government acquired the estate and scheduled it for use by January 1, 1944. The W/T operators joined the officers after three weeks of radio training at Henley-on-Thames, west of London. Almost all the Jedburghs were at Milton Hall by February 1 and started more training in demolition, map reading and field craft, German and Allied small arms, guerrilla tactics, German tactics, reception committee work, anti-tank mines, street fighting, motor cycle and car driving, German Army vehicle and equipment recognition, and more physical training. Jedburgh commanders and seconds-in-command received a general history of resistance movements in northwest Europe, ways to utilize the resistance, functions of Jedburghs, first-aid, practical wireless training, French geography, and observation and memory training. Special Force Headquarters directed that training be completed by April 1 so they could be deployed before Overlord began, at that time expected to start in early May.[60]

Unfortunately, Milton Hall was not ready for the officers so temporary training sites were found at Fairford, Gumley Hall, and Walsingham. All Jedburghs visited one final training school for parachuting at the jump school at Altrincham, Manchester. Even the men already parachute-qualified attended the training, as jumping out of the B-24 "Joe hole" varied enough from jumping out of regular aircraft to require familiarization. The school scheduled three jumps; the first two would be in daylight from a balloon at seven hundred feet and the third jump would be at night from five hundred feet. For the seventeen-year-old Prince Michel de Bourbon-Parme, parachute training proved trying. While waiting for the proper command before parachuting from the balloon, American W/T operator Sergeant Bill Thompson, French Michel de Bourbon-Parme, and the British instructor lost their balance when unexpected winds came up, causing the Prince to fall out. Descending toward the earth, the Prince yelled to his instructor, "I'm sorry!" and the British officer calmly replied, "That's all right chap, don't bother to come back."[61]

Milton Hall finally became available for Jedburgh use the first week in February 1944. The British modified the old mansion for classrooms, offices, and billets and set up temporary buildings for non-commissioned officer housing. Beginning in late January the French soldiers began arriving, but they were not all there until March. Recruiters made a concerted effort through North Africa, the Middle East, and the United States; one French Jedburgh even came from Guatemala. The seventy French Jeds began to mix with the rest, and curiously, politics was rarely discussed. The factions gripping French society and crippling French unified action failed to have any impact on these soldiers. One French Jedburgh remarked that "they were professional soldiers and didn't think much about politics." Apparently, de Gaulle knew about the French Jeds but never visited Milton Hall, nor did any of his generals.[62] In a brief interview with one of the Frenchmen, who as circumstances had it, served in the US Army, General de Gaulle said to him, "Oh, you are going off with those people? Fine."[63]

However, a Washington OSS civilian did visit Milton Hall late on a Friday afternoon forcing the training-weary Jeds to delay their weekend pass. The British commandant of Milton Hall, Lieutenant Colonel Frank Spooner, was an unpopular man and the Jedburghs felt no obligation not to embarrass him in front of the distinguished visitor. Prior to the visit the American Jeds had started a tradition they would often repeat when they believed superiors ordered them to do something stupid. It first began when a Jedburgh officer arrived late to a formation and the British NCO asked the officer to drop and do fifty pushups. The officer counted them off in front of the formation and getting to the punishment's end he grunted out, "48, 49, 50," got on his feet and exhaled an angry "some shit!" The group laughed and in short order it became a sign of Jedburgh indignation when one in a group would yell, "48!" another chimed in "49!" a third "50!" and all yelled, "Some Shit!" The innocent and surprised Washington visitor heard such a cheer and dropped his speech on the platform. Lieutenant Colonel Spooner let out a characteristic snort in shock and disappointment but could do nothing but be embarrassed. Spooner also had been under investigation for certain unpaid bills and perhaps Gubbins and Mockler-Ferryman were somewhat exasperated with him. They replaced him shortly afterward with an enormously well-respected Rhodesian Lieutenant Colonel G. Richard Musgrave.[64] The Jedburghs were an unconventional unit, not afraid to speak their minds and unfazed by normal military punishment when they did so, but they quickly took a liking to Musgrave and he commanded their respect as the invasion approached.

One more thing remained prior to deployment: the teams had to be put together. Special Force Headquarters allowed them to "get married"—in other words, they would choose their own teammates. Over the remaining time before D-Day, the Jedburgh officers paired up and then selected their radio operator. Training together, many of them had the opportunity to form friendships and learn whom they could trust.[65] Soon they would be in combat, and despite the rigorous training, none knew what to expect. Choosing their teammates then came down to personality traits each Jedburgh thought to be most crucial. Since there was a French officer on each team, they had a certain amount of say over whom they "married." French officer Paul Moniez had wanted to go back to France with an American, but impressed with the French-speaking abilities of British Captain James O'Brien Tear, he opted to pair up with him. "I thought it was a very important skill," Moniez said very sternly. Speaking sixty-three Septembers after his deployment to France, one could still see his great despair over the French defeat in 1940. He wanted to make sure they did well and so he wanted to go into combat with the best teammate he could find.[66]

British Brigadier Mockler-Ferryman and American Colonel Haskell, co-directors of Special Force Headquarters, also wanted the Jedburghs to do as well as possible. On February 24 they went up to Milton Hall and shared the classified details with the Jedburghs about what they would be doing in occupied Europe. Most of them were going to France while others would go to Belgium and the Netherlands. Their function was strategic, the brigadier told them, and they would work with the resistance on three main missions: liaison, organization, and leadership. Liaison meant representing General Eisenhower to the local Maquis, using their wireless transmitter for the necessary communications, acting as advisors on methods and tactics, and supplying weapons via clandestine air drops. Organization meant providing some order to groups not necessarily organized along military lines by task or function. And if the group had lost its leadership due to German efforts, they must be prepared to step into that role. Noting that each team's situation would vary greatly from the next, Mockler-Ferryman emphasized that whichever of the three missions they did, "liaison was the most important one of all."[67] When asked from the audience, "how many Germans were in France?" the brigadier replied, "not many over half a million." After a silence, one of cocky Jeds joked, "Oh, that's all?" and the room erupted in laughter.[68]

AIR SPECIAL OPERATIONS PICKS UP THE PACE

General de Gaulle took every opportunity, both publicly in press conferences and privately with Winston Churchill, to get the RAF and SOE to do
more to equip the interior resistance groups. De Gaulle met with Churchill
in Marrakech in January 1944 while the prime minister was traveling back
to London from Cairo. The conversation prompted Churchill to meet with
Minister Selborne, Commander of Bomber Command General Harris, and
Air Minister Sir Charles Portal immediately upon his return. He sought to
make southeast France similar to Yugoslavia in its effective partisan groups.
Churchill's prodding resulted in placing the priority of the Maquis' needs
second only to the strategic bombing effort and above even the SOE's own
circuits, attacks on German V Rocket installations, and sea mining. It also
resulted an increased monthly sortie rate of 120 from the Mediterranean
theater and 60 more sorties from the RAF transport group No. 38 in Great
Britain. And according to the SOE's official history, "for the first time, in the
course of the first three months of the year, the BCRA networks were better
supplied than the Allied circuits."[69] Furthermore, the British agreed to help
train the American aircrews just now organizing Special Operations air
missions. If the Allies maintained the new number of sorties, it would mean
16,000 more men could be armed each month.[70]

The Americans had been late participating but eventually they surpassed
British efforts. Getting involved in late 1943, Colonel C. S. Vanderblue,
commander of the European Theater, Office of Strategic Services, sent a
letter proposing the creation of two squadrons to supply European resistance groups. The senior American officer in Britain at the time, Lieutenant
General Jacob L. Devers, commander of the United States Army, European
Theater of Operations, approved the concept within a week, but it took
more than two months before 8th Air Force's commanding officer General
Ira C. Eaker designated two squadrons and created the Carpetbagger project. A memo dated December 30, 1943, gave OSS operational control of
the aircraft, but 8th Air Force retained a measure of administrative control.
That meant that missions would be determined by the OSS/SO London
requirements, but the aircraft and people retained their US Army Air Force

status for all other matters. As the British and American SOE and OSS merged their efforts into an Allied Special Force Headquarters, they set out missions each moon period, and 8th Bomber Command detailed a liaison officer to approve them.[71]

Lieutenant Colonel Clifford Heflin commanded the 801st Bomb Group or Carpetbaggers. When their squadron's mission of flying anti-submarine missions from the Azores was discontinued, Heflin and other officers were reassigned to fly their modified B-24 bombers into occupied territory in this new special operations mission. Heflin had joined the army immediately after graduating from Fresno State University in 1939 and received his commission the same year. With the onset of war he won quick promotions and at twenty-nine, he took command of two squadrons each maintaining sixteen aircraft.[72] For southern France, air support would have to come from 15th Air Force in North Africa. When General Eaker took command of the 15th Air Force in the Mediterranean theater he found the OSS air capability in a shambles and sought to do the same for his new command as he'd done in Britain. The unit that was airlifting supplies to the Maquis in France and the resistance groups in the Balkans was poorly equipped and trained. It took three months of asking and arguing with Army Air Force Chief of Staff General Henry Arnold in Washington, for the authority to reorganize his aircraft and personnel in order to do the task at hand. General Arnold also heard from American generals Eisenhower, Devers, and Donovan, and British RAF Air Marshal Charles Portal, who all agreed with Eaker. After several weeks of back and forth, General Marshall and the American Joint Chiefs decided to grant Eaker the authority to create a special operations squadron at Blida, near Algiers, with three B-17s and 15 B-24s and the required crews and support personnel. By May 1944, the new unit had flown eighty-eight missions. In what became the 885th Bombardment Squadron (Heavy)(Special), commanded by Colonel Monro MacCloskey, the Americans contributed to the special operations airlift to France from the Mediterranean theater, as well as from England.[73]

But organization was one thing; flying effective missions proved to be quite another. In Britain, the crews, unfamiliar with the correct flying procedures, had to spend a month flying with British crews. Moreover, the required facilities were not ready at RAF Alconbury so the Carpetbaggers moved to RAF Harrington in Northamptonshire.[74] Also, the B-24s required several changes to make them special operations mission ready. The two waist gun positions were eliminated to save weight and the aircraft was painted black to elude searchlights. Mechanics removed the bottom machine gun turret and converted the space to a "Joe hole" covered by a round plywood center hinged door for the Jeds to jump through. They placed reinforced static line points above the "Joe hole" with a static line long enough for eight parachutists. The bombardier and navigator required more room to work, so they removed all unnecessary equipment. Next, the Carpetbaggers installed green and red jump signal lights, and static lines in the bomb bay for dropping cargo. In order to find their way to the drop zones in the dark, the air crews trained in celestial dead-reckoning, pilotage, and radio navigation, and the bombardier position became a second navigator, a waist gunner became the "Joe" dispatcher who managed the jumpers, and the pilot, co-pilot, engineer, radio operator, and tail gunner filled out the rest, for a crew of eight. Crews trained to drop "joes" at an altitude of 600 feet traveling 125 to 135 miles per hour: any higher and the person would land off target, any lower and the chute would not have time to deploy.[75]

Rigging and packing all the weapons, fuel, ammunition, leaflets, radios, and personnel chutes required a special facility close to Harrington. Approximately 100 men worked at the facility; during the first quarter of 1944 they packed 2,348 containers and the second quarter they packed 13,071 containers and 8,323 personnel chutes. By D-Day, Maquis groups had received 7,404 containers filled with explosives, light machine guns, pistols, carbines, anti-tank weapons, and grenades.[76] The standard drop consisted of 12 containers with the following supplies: 6 Brens with 1,000 rounds, 36 rifles with 150 rounds, 27 Stens with 300 rounds per gun, 5 pistols with 50 rounds per weapon, 52 grenades with 18 pounds of plastic explosives, over 100 field dressings, over 6,000 9mm rounds, 3,000 .303 rounds, and 40 empty magazines. If more containers were dropped to the same drop zone, they contained more ammunition, not weapons.[77]

Not satisfied with merely a two-squadron effort, General Eisenhower's staff sought still more aircraft. In January 1944, the Allied Expeditionary Air

Forces received a strongly worded letter from SHAEF complaining about the lack of support.[78] Both Churchill and Roosevelt became concerned about the possible poor perception caused by lagging arms deliveries, and Eisenhower was attempting to mitigate the concern. Anxious, General Donovan believed if the French Résistance regarded the United States and Britain poorly, the viability of Allied missions to France—like the Jedburghs'—would suffer.[79] On February 11, 1944, Eisenhower signed a Donovan-drafted cable to Eaker saying, "Believe it extremely important from viewpoint our government that United States participate as fully as possible this program and that anything you can do to expedite delivery of modified planes necessary for this purpose will be of great assistance."[80] A follow-up phone call between Major General Bull, Eisenhower's director of operations at SHAEF, and General Spaatz, 8th Air Force commander, produced no results as General Spaatz refused to degrade the strategic bombing effort. Clearly, his views were different from those of General Eaker, his predecessor. Bull and Spaatz considered the possibility of having planes perform conventional bombing missions during the non-moon period and then make them available for special operations sorties. However, the time and effort required to convert the bombers to special operations and back to bombing made it impractical.[81] Spaatz held firm and despite Eisenhower and Donovan's wishes, the OSS received no more than their already assigned two squadrons.

But ironically, while the higher headquarters tried to solve a problem of too little support to the Résistance, the Carpetbaggers and their British counterparts apparently delivered more than current Allied and French underground networks could hide. The joint SOE and OSS March report to SHAEF related that if deliveries increased, the Allied French Résistance groups would be the ones to absorb most of the additional supplies. Up to March, the *parachutages* concentrated on areas under the control of Britain's unilaterally run "F Section" in France and the British supplied Résistance. However, by the May report, few difference existed as the F and British-Free French "RF Section" appeared to be receiving supplies based on the health of their circuit, not political alignment. The next month, the airdrop reports no longer distinguished tonnage by their SOE affiliation of F or RF Sections.[82] The fusing of the two categories may also have been an effect of the command

arrangements Eisenhower worked out with General Koenig by the beginning of June 1944. By the time the invasion neared, the British and Americans
had delivered 1,549 tons of weapons and supplies in nearly 3,500 sorties.
More than half of the total sorties flown were between April and June 1944.[83]
Aircraft losses amounted to forty-one British and American aircraft due to
enemy action and accidents.[84] Now up to the task, the air forces could modestly deploy and re-supply the Maquis with Jedburgh liaison elements, at
least along the assumptions General Eisenhower's staff officers held in early
June regarding Maquis numbers, their expected needs, and the pace of the
war. They would find out very quickly that their assumptions were wrong.

The Politics Running into D-Day

General Eisenhower knew that President Roosevelt's confrontational approach with de Gaulle was proving ineffective and perilous and Prime Minister Churchill began to come around to the same conclusion. In April and May, while Roosevelt enjoyed some vacation time at what is now Camp David, a draft policy letter on how to guide Eisenhower's relationship with the French painstakingly made its way through the War Department, the British Cabinet, and the Combined Chiefs of Staff. It indicated that Churchill wanted Roosevelt to hash out the issue with de Gaulle in Washington, but FDR would not invite him to the White House and wanted de Gaulle's representatives to request a visit. Only then would he agree to see him and by that time it would be the middle of May with only two or three weeks for Eisenhower to coordinate plans with the Forces Françaises de l'Intérieur (FFI). De Gaulle, still in the dark as to when Overlord would launch, had returned to Algiers to stew over the Allied Military Government of Occupied Territories (AMGOT) issue. When he found that Eisenhower would be the sole authority for the printing and dispersal of French currency as well as other civil matters he fumed all the more. But he was no longer the lone crusader of 1940, casting about for men and equipment. He now had them, and Churchill felt the need to remind the American president of it. "He commands considerable forces," he telegraphed Roosevelt, "including naval forces.... [H]e presides over a vast empire, all the strategic points of which are at our disposal."[1] Furthermore, General Donovan forwarded an intelligence report to the president on April 3 with more information confirming the allegiance of the interior Résistance to de Gaulle. Not only that, it ominously stated the Résistance's disillusionment with the United States and its increasing bewilderment at Roosevelt's delay in recognizing the Comité Français de la Liberation Nationale (CFLN). All of France knew, according to the OSS source, of the Soviet Army's Eastern Front successes and its murderously high casualty rate. They knew the British were dropping tons of weapons and ammunition to the Maquis in France. In comparison, the American presence in the war seemed suspiciously weak, and they drew their own conclusions that Roosevelt sought to undercut the CFLN and therefore, its effectiveness to fight the war.[2]

Such attitudes were punctuated by what the Germans did to a large Maquis encampment in southeast France near Glières in the rugged Vercors mountains. On the same day Donovan passed the report to the president in Washington, General d'Astier in London reported to Eisenhower's chief of staff, General Bedell Smith, that seven hundred Résistance fighters had been "annihilated by the troops of occupation, without receiving the aid they had asked of us." After Vichy forces failed at negotiating with the Maquis, then made a faint attempt at fighting them, a task force of elements of the Wehrmacht's 157th Reserve Infantry Division attacked the redoubt in the French Alps. The Germans made a concentrated and well-coordinated onslaught defeating the Maquis in a three-day effort.[3] In London, the FFI's repeated requests for RAF strikes only resulted in a staff meeting fifteen days after the dramatic deaths of the stranded Maquis. The British and American planning officers believed that such a location was too far and the danger too great to send in Royal Air Force planes. But the frustrated French believed otherwise and pointed out that there were "no known" anti-aircraft batteries in the region. General d'Astier pointedly wrote to

Eisenhower, "The Forces of the French Résistance have the honor of being amongst the first troops engaged in combat against the common enemy in the theater of operations under your command."[4] Churchill's desire to get more arms to that part of France was succeeding, but he had not thought through the implications and results of such actions. The next few weeks and into May, while the political problem festered, Eisenhower's staff pressed ahead with planning on what it wanted the Résistance to do once the Allies landed. What the Maquis would do before the invasion was seemingly in no one's control and this added to Eisenhower's, de Gaulle's, and Special Force Headquarters' fears that guerrilla action would only provoke German reprisals. They hoped that some control of the Maquis could be brought to bear after the invasion, furthering Allied aims.

To implement those aims, on March 23, 1944, the Supreme Headquarters Allied Expeditionary Forces (SHAEF) ordered its special operations planners, now mostly British and Americans in a subordinate Special Force Headquarters in London, to have seventy Jedburgh teams trained for D-Day. Eisenhower gave it total authority over Résistance groups, who were not yet under his control, and directed the Résistance to concentrate efforts against German air forces, lower the morale of German forces by sabotage, inflict damage on the German war effort in general, and *prepare for the return of Allied Forces to the continent*. It seems that Allied planners expected the Jedburghs to deploy well ahead of the conventional invasion force, despite Special Operations Executive (SOE) and Office of Strategic Services (OSS) strategy to use the Jedburghs as a reserve and a backup for clandestine networks that would be endangered when Overlord commenced. Although Jedburghs and Operational Groups (American commando teams deployed for the single purpose of destroying specified targets) were to be ready by April 1, SHAEF insisted that no invasion plan details, especially the date, should be conveyed to any resistance group.[5]

What targets did General Eisenhower want the Résistance to attack? The commander stated his priorities in a dispatch sent to his colleague, Supreme Allied Commander, Mediterranean, General Maitland Wilson. The 2nd SS "Das Reich" Panzer Division was in southwestern France refitting, and based on their location he directed that the railroad from

Montauban-Limoges-Vierzon on D + 1 through D + 3 be the first priority. Second were the railroads from Bordeaux-Poitiers-Tours that presumably could carry the 11th Panzer from the Bordeaux region northward. They were to be attacked four days after the invasion until seven days after the landings. The cable listed other railroads as well as roads, indicating all Germans moving north should be impeded as much as possible. Significantly, the Jedburghs were not to enter France sooner than ten days before D-Day. Eisenhower thought it too risky and a security hazard to have anyone in France with Overlord plans.[6] But there was another reason that SHAEF passed even more restrictive orders to Special Force Headquarters as D-Day neared. The Jedburghs could not deploy to France prior to the night of D-Day. General Bedell Smith warned of the need to do everything possible to safeguard Overlord and feared that dropping Jedburghs into enemy territory risked compromise with doubtful gain.[7] It is unclear, however, whether the security concern was a cover story being used by Eisenhower and Smith to conceal the political disagreements between FDR and de Gaulle from his Special Force planning officers. And while later SOE and OSS official histories wrote that the intent was to use the Jedburghs after D-Day, the contemporaneous SHAEF documents and indeed some of the Jedburgh memories reinforce what may have been the original plan: to go into France sometime between April 1 and D-Day.[8] If that was the case, it seems Roosevelt's argument with de Gaulle was the only thing holding the Jedburghs back. But while the operations were being curtailed, the Allied and Free French planning went ahead.

It is clear now that Eisenhower's railroad targets described above are based on the Bureau Centrale Renseignements d'Action (BCRA) plan Vert, which by now had become Special Force Headquarter's plan. Indeed, many of the plans that originated with the Free French in London now became Allied plans, via the working links among British, American, and French officers. Bloc Planning had been busy, working mostly in a vacuum since they were not allowed to know the invasion areas. Nevertheless, they produced a considerable amount of work, and in the spring of 1944 they shared it with their British and American colleagues. Plan Bibendum focused on German military road traffic and armored columns. But SFHQ planners were uncertain about its viability due to the arrest of its BCRA organizer in May of 1944; the last word from him was that he was far short of the armed teams required to put the plan into full effect. Plans Jaune, Noire, and Rouge were for small-scale guerrilla attacks against enemy munitions dumps; German military command posts and major headquarters; and fuel storage depots, respectively. Their effectiveness was also in doubt as planning had not passed its initial stages when Maquis units began to grow and new challenges arose as to how to organize more and more units into the guerrilla warfare plans. The French BCRA canceled those plans on March 2, but the British SOE put in their place a merged plan that was to be rolled out by region or area as required depending upon the progress of conventional forces through France. There were other plans, not sufficiently accepted by Special Force planners, and one that even the BCRA cast a doubtful eye on such as the Grenouille plan. It involved French railway workers of the Société Nationale des Chemins de Fer (SNCF) who, when ordered, were to misroute trains and discreetly but effectively sabotage key machinery and signals. But the most controversial plan was Vidal, the plan for widespread "national insurrection." Few outside of France advocated this kind of widespread action, and SOE's commander General Colin Gubbins, Brigadier Mockler-Ferryman, and American Colonel Haskell believed that it had little relation to the landings and would offer minimal support for the regular forces. In their estimation it would have little benefit while risking brutal reprisals on civilians. They had no disagreement on this point with senior French leadership, with the exception of some members of the interior Résistance, often the communists, who saw the Vidal effort as vital to liberation.[9]

General de Gaulle, who by now had clearly learned how to use his officers for their greatest effectiveness, appointed a new commander to replace General d'Astier. General Marie-Pierre Koenig arrived in London at the end of March and assumed his duties on April 1. The rank-and-file Maquis loved and respected Koenig, if the underground newspapers are any guide, due to his leadership at the battle of Bir Hakeim when the French defeated German forces for the first time in the Second World War. Other Allied generals found him to be professional, eager to get along, and effective.

Even the acerbic British general, Lord Alanbrooke, thought him to be "quite pleasant and ready to cooperate."[10] Eisenhower met with Koenig after his arrival and believed he could be trusted with the invasion month; however, he did not want the information leaked to the French commanders in Algeria.[11] Indeed, one of the results of Churchill and Roosevelt's distrust of the Free French was their insistence that no messages be sent from their liaison officers in London to Algiers for fear of leaks.

Overlord's greatest asset and most closely guarded secrets were the unknown location of the initial attack and the date. Keeping them under wraps forced the Germans to spread their forces thin and to position their reserves farther back from the coast so they could move them toward the front line when the location became clear. Eisenhower guarded the location beaches, time of attack, and kinds of forces with an elaborate and immense deception campaign. A leak from a collaborator to the Germans would be disastrous. However, just as in North Africa, he was caught between working with the French to achieve his military aim and waiting for clearance from Roosevelt on proceeding with the CFLN. Nevertheless, he was willing to share details of the plan with the right person and did so with General Koenig to a limited degree.

Assuming command of what had grown from the small number of émigrés and adrift soldiers in June of 1940, the France Libre organization now had more staff and was working toward placing a division of conventional forces under Eisenhower's command for Overlord. Koenig served as the commander of all French forces in the United Kingdom and as the senior military liaison to General Eisenhower and the British General Staff. However, Koenig's other title was commander of the l'Etat Major Forces Françaises de l'Interieur (EMFFI) or Headquarters of the Free French Forces of the Interior.[12] In other words, General Koenig would be "commanding" the Maquis, and in that capacity, he was the perfect person for Eisenhower to coordinate with. On April 19, Koenig met with General Walter Bedell Smith, Eisenhower's chief of staff, who told him that Eisenhower intended to bring him formally into the Supreme Headquarters' organization and that in effect he would become a subordinate commander of forces similar to the American, British, and Canadian commanders who led forces in combat. Furthermore, Eisenhower told Koenig he intended to include him in the planning "well in advance to their being committed to these operations."[13]

But while Eisenhower and Koenig may have made some progress on getting their respective efforts to mesh, de Gaulle kept doing things that upset Roosevelt. In Algiers on April 25, de Gaulle had a press conference in which he reiterated a list of his war aims and made it clear that France would "accept no administration that is not French." In a charitable moment he praised Allied efforts to arm the Maquis over the past three months and, probably recalling his own conversation with Churchill in January about the efforts to arm the Maquis, he added the words, "thanks to the British." On FDR's transcript of de Gaulle's press conference, this slight to the US effort, even though the United States had contributed two more squadrons and tons of materiel, elicited more disgust as the President marked the transcript with two exclamation points. Then reinforcing FDR's fear about French postwar colonialism, de Gaulle also expressed French concern about war against Japan, saying that "France did not yield rights to any Pacific possessions."[14] There it was, summed up for Roosevelt in one press conference transcript: all of FDR's most vital concerns and confirmation of French stereotypes, solidifying the president's suspicions regarding his valid assumptions about postwar French colonial aims and de Gaulle's arrogant lack of appreciation for the increased American efforts to arm the Maquis.

But while the ice remained cold and solid at the presidential level, thawing continued to occur between the Anglo-American staff and the French in London. The first meeting between relevant senior military officials and General Koenig and his staff occurred on April 28. It consisted largely of some polite comments, introductions of staff members, and a statement of each side's aims. Eisenhower's representative made clear to General Koenig that he had no problem with members of the French side being comprised of civilians, since many of their issues concerned civil affairs. Perhaps this venue could provide them some room to maneuver while still staying within the president's and prime minister's guidance to avoid any hint of recognizing the Free French provisional government. The SHAEF staff and BCRA officers closed the meeting by dividing up issues to be addressed and creating subcommittees to handle the various tasks. Present at the meeting was the BCRA's Colonel André Dewavrin, who of course knew the inner workings of the resistance as well as anyone in London and who had probably participated in recruiting the French members of the Jedburghs. There is no indication that the French realized their planning time was short and indeed, Koenig and his staff were still not aware of the invasion date.[15] But with the actual date so close, this level of effort was not going to suffice, and it had become alarming to Eisenhower and the implications more clear to Churchill.

On May 1 the British and American Special Force Headquarters pressed ahead with integrating the French, as far as possible, while they finalized their own D-Day plans. On May 8, SHAEF approved its planning annex to the overall Overlord plan regarding the use of the Résistance. Added to the main Overlord plan several days after the rest had been completed, the addition specified that Special Force Headquarters (SFHQ) was to direct the Maquis in

widespread, pre-arranged and to a certain extent controlled,— acts of sabotage [which] will be carried out against specific types of targets, principally railway and telecommunications. Action will also be taken to delay the road movements of ENEMY reserves, especially armored units. In addition, wide-spread guerilla activity by small bands of lightly armed FRENCHMEN operating in the ENEMY's back areas will undoubtedly take place. This activity will be organized and coordinated to the fullest extent possible by SOE/ SO Headquarters, LONDON through BRITISH, FRENCH and AMERICAN officers already in the field and by others who will be dispatched before and after the invasion.

The directive concluded its first paragraph with the low expectation that "guerrilla warfare may reach a scale approaching that of minor military diversions." The lessons of exercise Spartan, described in Chapter 1 resonated in the directive, for the staff not only finalized Jedburgh issues but added a capability to the field armies, just as Spartan had sought to do.

Furthermore, Eisenhower's planners made the provision for Special Force Detachments to be created in the 21st Army Group and its subordinate armies to enable coordination with the main forces. It also reiterated that the effect of the Résistance was thought to be strategic and not tactical; in other words, the impact would not just serve to blow up one or two bridges, but cumulatively would have a dramatic impact on the campaign. It also highlighted the two main kinds of resistance groups—"Allied French" meaning the groups that had been taking direction from the BCRA since the unification of the movements with de Gaulle's Free French, and the "SOE/SO directly controlled groups" that the British and to some extent the Americans had been running without French coordination.[16] If the "Allied French" failed to act, at least the others might. It seems that Mockler-Ferryman and Haskell believed they were to attempt to direct the Maquis groups by using the French BCRA plans, without informing the Free French or General Koenig.

On the same day, the director of SHAEF Operations, Major General Harold Bull, signed a directive telling Special Force Headquarters to arrange with the BBC to broadcast the warning messages on Y Day and Y + 1, and then the action messages at H Hour minus 7.5 hours. Y Day and Y + 1 meant June 1 and 2 while H Hour minus 7.5 meant seven and a half hours before the first landings commenced on the Normandy beaches code named Utah, Omaha, Juno, Gold, and Sword. Brigadier Mockler-Ferryman then had to coordinate with the British Broadcasting Company for more air time as the increased number of messages went far beyond their normally allotted minutes.[17] Furthermore, it meant bypassing General Koenig as no details could be related to the French, even when Eisenhower had made it plain to Koenig that he would give him the invasion information. Roosevelt's running argument with de Gaulle made it impossible for General Eisenhower to keep his promise. It also put into question whether the orders, if broadcast without Koenig's concurrence and participation, would be carried out. Eisenhower, Bedell Smith, Bull, Mockler-Ferryman, and Haskell would have to sort out the timing for telling Koenig, and have the tact to do it.

Also on May 8, the *Capetown Castle* arrived at the Algerian port of Mers el- Kébir and fourteen Jedburgh teams stepped off the ship. The forty-two

Jedburghs, including Major "Hod" Fuller, transferred their gear onto a train for Algiers and the shared SOE/OSS base code named Massingham.[18] These teams would be inserted into southern France from North Africa because the hours of darkness each night did not afford enough cover for aircraft to reach southern French locations, allow the men to parachute out, and return safely to Britain. Prior to their departure, the Jedburghs—whose friendships were now solidifying around all kinds of spirited competitions—decided to have a parting challenge. With the fourteen teams departing Milton Hall, American Bill Colby proposed a contest to see who could make it through one of their obstacle courses first. Then a little betting occurred with Colby's money on French Lieutenant Paul Aussaresses. But Aussaresses came in third and Dutch Captain Arie Berstebreurtje won the race, while Colby lost his money.[19] Additionally, now that Colonel Musgrave considered all the Jedburghs trained, those who were not setting out for North Africa had a chance to enjoy some leave in London. "It was a wonderful time," recalled Michel de Bourbon-Parme. "If you were in uniform you could not pay for anything in a restaurant or night club. It was absolutely fantastic. I'll never forget it.... All the nationalities were there...we were all there together, Poles, French,...everybody. All united...all wanting to go to Germany to kick the Germans...in...the...butt."[20]

Unfortunately for Eisenhower, SHAEF, Special Force Headquarters, and the Résistance, Roosevelt, Churchill, and de Gaulle were not so unified. Several issues remained in contention, particularly occupational civil affairs as D-Day neared. The political leaders' inability to work out details of occupation policies, including whether Allied currency or only French printed notes would be used, caused Eisenhower great embarrassment. On May 11, he cabled Washington asking US Army Chief of Staff General George C. Marshall for further guidance. "The limitations under which we are operating in dealing with the French are becoming very embarrassing and are producing a situation which is potentially dangerous."[21] Until Roosevelt sanctioned de Gaulle as the legitimate French leader there was no one to whom Eisenhower could communicate an active Résistance plan, squandering a valuable advantage against the Germans. Would de Gaulle countermand the BBC action messages? Would Eisenhower be forced to invade France without aid from the Free French? Eisenhower was stuck in Roosevelt's catch-22.

But some of the Special Force HQ planners feared a grand failure for two other reasons. The noticeably greater number of "message personnels" that Mockler-Ferryman asked the BBC to broadcast would certainly tip off the Germans. But even more fundamentally, they believed the increasingly centralized organization in France was certain to place too much information in the hands of a very vulnerable and precious few French leaders. Few arguments between the British SOE and certain French leaders had a longer history. The British sought a decentralized resistance organization for security purposes, but some of the French leaders wanted a centralized French resistance organization inside France in order to control their hoped-for "national insurrection." Ironically, the British gained the most help from the Gestapo on this issue with arrest after arrest of senior Résistance leaders making it impossible to create such a centralized structure for any length of time. There was even debate about General Koenig parachuting into France, but that never got serious consideration.[22] In any event, Special Force Headquarters did not intend to bring about Plan Vidal, the national insurrection, but because of the way the BBC action messages were broadcast on D-1, many Maquis units got that impression and they went full throttle into doing what they wished.

The debate within France's CFLN and its constituent elements on this point was a long and continuing one. What did it mean to espouse a "national insurrection" from a political point of view? And what would its utility be to the military effort? The British and later the Americans sought only Maquis activity that supported the Allied landings and subsequent operations. Many French leaders, including de Gaulle, Koenig, and the BCRA staff officers agreed with this, but various communications, broadcasts, and their official newspapers parachuted into France used language that could be read the other way and only served to stoke the smoldering hatred many French had for the occupiers and the collaborators. For instance, during the Glières battle, the French language accounts about the battle on the BBC contained vivid descriptions and were a source of inspiration to other like-minded Maquis. De Gaulle's own language often elevated the issue and he failed to clearly dissuade those *résistants* from pursuing such a course of action.[23] Churchill's supply of weapons and ammunition further reinforced the wrong message. Therefore, SHAEF's decision to broadcast all the action messages for Plans Vert, Tortue, the aggregated guerrilla war plans, and the telecommunication plans to all the French regions as well as the SOE circuit leaders could be construed as supporting Plan Vidal, the national insurrection. However, this was not Eisenhower's or General Koenig's intent.

Koenig's chief of staff Colonel Henry Zeigler, BCRA planners, and the Special Force Headquarters planners clearly achieved some progress, however. On May 20 at Finchampstead, west of London, American Colonel Joseph Haskell had scheduled a meeting for detailed discussions about the military effectiveness and estimates of various regions and sought the BCRA's advice. Even with the invasion area not divulged, the meeting nevertheless resulted in detailed planning and some guidance from Koenig on regions of France that should receive Special Force Headquarters' attention with aerial re-supply, Jedburgh team deployments, and British Special Air Service (SAS) missions. The purpose was to "provide agreed upon recommendations to the Supreme Allied Commander" for activities after D-Day. Furthermore, the ice was melting regarding a single command under Koenig. The British representatives noted that it was Eisenhower's wish to have a French command exercised from London. With all in agreement, the discussion turned to what assets would be deployed and where inside France. The group discussed the Vosges, central France, the Morvan, and Brittany. With the recent arrest of Brittany's military delegate, the BCRA had selected a replacement to deploy as soon as the British could arrange it. They noted that they had to notify their agents in eastern France that the summer moons prohibited flights there for at least two cycles, meaning no weapons would be delivered to them until late August at the earliest. In the Drôme and the Grenoble area, the OSS, SOE, and BCRA at Algiers was to prepare re-supply of ammunition and ensure that the Maquis there were not to attack the enemy installation in Grenoble until directed. When Koenig was later briefed on all these issues, he concurred but overruled one thing. He directed that the Morvan area southeast of Paris should be raised in priority and classified as a *réduit*, or protected place, from which raids could be staged against enemy lines of communication.[24] Colonel Haskell and Brigadier Mockler-Ferryman accepted this idea and later assigned a mission to that area led by the former RF section chief, Lieutenant Colonel James Hutchison, who had transferred to the Jedburgh teams.[25]

But while SHAEF and its Special Force Headquarters were making progress with the French, no word came from Roosevelt regarding an agreement or a way forward with de Gaulle. Realizing the gravity of the situation now, Churchill sent a cable to FDR on May 26 taking up the cause. He tried to make clear that de Gaulle was becoming more and more important, the situation was becoming more and more dire, and that the press, Parliament, and political considerations were forcing their hand. Churchill believed that if their disagreement caused unavoidable casualties, the cost could be a political one as well. In what can only be described as obvious, Churchill bluntly reminded the president that "after all it is very difficult to cut the French out of the liberation of France."[26] FDR made no reply.

Carrying on, Special Force Headquarters did achieve some progress at lower levels when it succeeded in merging their Algiers special operations staff with itself for operations in France. In April the Mediterranean theater's Allied Force Headquarters had agreed to take direction regarding their activities with the French Résistance and on May 23, the Special Projects Office Command (SPOC) stood up under British General Maitland Wilson's Allied Force Headquarters. General Wilson now had SOE and OSS personnel in his theater working together on French issues and SHAEF agreements with him regarding each headquarters' role in Overlord and a division of labor for France between them. The hoped-for invasion of southern France, Operation Dragoon, could now be conducted on a more equal footing in that both headquarters had an entity conducting Allied unconventional war in France.[27] With the command of the irregular warfare in France solidifying, the first Jedburgh team orders were finalized on May 27 and 28. Special Force Headquarters ordered Team Hugh to deploy near Châteauroux in central France with some elements of the 1st Special Air Service Battalion comprised of British commandos. Hugh's mission was to "act as a liaison between the SAS troops and such Résistance as may be available in the area." The SAS battalion was to assess the feasibility of establishing a base of operations from which it could conduct raids on the enemy's lines of communications. SFHQ gave the British only F Section responsibility for running the operation and would determine the SAS and Team Hugh's reception and drop zone. Remaining compartmentalized, however, it also directed that the BCRA "will not be consulted during preparation." Team Harry's mission was similar in that it was going in with elements of the 1st SAS Battalion under the auspices of F Section with no notice given to the Free French during the planning. Special Force Headquarters directed Team Harry to parachute into the Morvan area approximately 200 kilometers east of Team Hugh.[28] Team Harry partly fulfilled General Koenig's desire to emphasize the Morvan region. But Koenig's impact was much larger. He had now completely changed SOE's original plan to use the Jedburghs as reserves for captured agents. Now they were parachuting in as links to Koenig's own Free French while the long-running British F Section circuits in France would operate in parallel. The aspect the Free French had noted as a problem in January—namely, the British and Americans commanding the Maquis and asserting control of liberated France—and indeed the issue General Eisenhower had sought to avoid all along, was now occurring because Roosevelt and de Gaulle could not settle their arguments.

General Koenig had just begun rearranging things and would have precious little time to get FFI integrated into his Allied structure the way he and Eisenhower wanted. Five short days before Overlord's launch, Eisenhower's chief of staff, General Walter Bedell Smith, met with General Koenig to discuss command arrangements and integrating the French into SHAEF's organization. Bedell Smith reiterated Eisenhower's long-held desire to bring the French into SHAEF and told Koenig, "those dropped with the role of making contact with *Résistance* groups should be under your command." In all practical terms this would mean General Koenig and his London staff element would command Jedburgh teams, Special Air Service units, and all other missions sent to the Maquis.[29] Brigadier Mockler-Ferryman and Colonel Haskell's boss, the OSS London chief Colonel Keith Bruce, also met with General Koenig late on May 30 to tell him that the BBC warning messages were going to be sent out on June 1 and 2.[30] The meeting was a courtesy as SHAEF had already directed the messages to be sent not only to the Anglo-American circuits in France but also to the resistance regions controlled by the BCRA. How firmly the Allies controlled them is demonstrated by their bypassing the FFI's own commander to direct his forces to prepare to accomplish their part of Plans Vert and Tortue, conduct guerrilla war, and attack enemy telecommunications in accordance with the Free French plans, which by now had been subsumed into SHAEF's. After the conversation, Colonel Bruce took a train to meet none other than General Donovan who had just arrived from Washington to witness the coming invasion. Together they boarded the USS *Tuscaloosa* and were on board as it participated in the maritime operations supporting the landings on D-Day. Colonel Bruce, Colonel Haskell's boss, did not return to London until June 10.[31]

With the action messages cued up, the political pace of events and tension quickened. Churchill had heard nothing from President Roosevelt and so he decided to handle the matter himself. He wrote General Eisenhower that he believed "it essential that the French Committee should be told before the operation starts and the only safe place to tell them is here where we have them under our influence." Agreeing quickly, Eisenhower wrote back to Churchill that "it would be of the greatest possible value" to have de Gaulle make a broadcast along with the other nations' heads of governments in exile, such as Norway and Poland.[32] Churchill invited de Gaulle and a small staff from Algiers to London. Koenig now awaited de Gaulle's arrival knowing that the BBC messages had been broadcast on June 1, but he did not know that on the next day Special Force Headquarters drafted still another set of Jedburgh orders for Teams Frederick and George to go to Brittany with elements of a French SAS battalion. Philippe Ragueneau, the participant in the plot to shoot Admiral Darlan, was alerted with his Team George teammates and prepared to get their mission brief in London. Special Force Headquarters wanted the French SAS unit to establish a base from which they could raid enemy bases in south central Brittany while other French SAS forces would establish a base farther to the west. Both Teams George and Frederick were to "arrange such assistance from the *Résistance*" as the SAS needed. The Jedburgh teams were in effect working for the SAS and were to arrange local Résistance support for whatever the French SAS commander might desire. The London BCRA office was not to be informed of the use of French forces in combat until after they had departed.[33] But certainly Koenig knew the great event was near. The time between the broadcast of the warning messages and the broadcast of the action messages could not be more than a week, probably less.

Around 6 PM on June 3, de Gaulle landed on English soil and received a note from Churchill inviting him to lunch the following day. The prime minister asked to meet him near Portsmouth where he was inspecting the invasion preparations.[34] The result of the meeting was important, as Eisenhower wrote in his diary, "We have direct means of communication with the *Résistance* groups of France but all our information leads us to believe that the only authority these *Résistance* groups desire to recognize is that of de Gaulle and his committee. However, since de Gaulle is apparently willing to cooperate only on the basis of our dealing with him exclusively, the whole thing falls into a rather sorry mess."[35] But of course he had more to see to than only the French Maquis. The magnitude and level of effort regarding Overlord was staggering. It involved over 7,000 ships and more than 11,000 aircraft carrying and supporting 150,000 soldiers across the English Channel onto the Normandy beaches and northern France.[36]

Around 9:30 that same evening Eisenhower assembled his senior staff and commanders to hear the last invasion details. For the command machinery to effect the operations on the intended day of June 5, Eisenhower had to give the go order by the morning of June 4 allowing the amphibious landings, the airborne landings, the air support, the maritime activity, and the deception operations enough time to get to their final assembly points and run their preparation plans. Thousands of soldiers had to board ships and aircraft, which would take hours. At Eisenhower's briefing, the RAF meteorologist gave a pessimistic report, so he decided to see what the weather looked like in a few hours and requested the same group to reassemble at 4:30 the next morning. If the weather prohibited the landings on June 5, they would still have time to postpone.[37]

Before dawn on Sunday, June 4, Eisenhower's senior generals were back at SHAEF Advance Headquarters near Portsmouth only to learn that the weather was not improving for the following morning. They decided to postpone the operation for twenty-four hours. General Eisenhower, who had not been feeling well, returned to his bunk. Around 6 AM General Bull called to speak with him, and when his aide, American naval Captain Harry Butcher, told him Eisenhower was sleeping, Bull passed along the bad news that the SHAEF press office had mistakenly sent the teletype message that Allied forces had landed in Europe! The story was immediately canceled, but the Soviets, Germans, and some of the wire services in the United States had the story. All the last-minute details were weighing on the staff, and failing to keep the invasion details secret could mean a catastrophic Allied defeat. Captain Butcher's patience with all the issues facing them was wearing thin and when he heard the CFLN leadership was coming he exclaimed in his diary, "Cripes, even de Gaulle coming to this camp today, to see Ike of course."[38]

As news arrived of the Allied victory in Italy and the fall of Rome, staff cars brought Generals de Gaulle and Koenig and other French officials to meet Churchill along with his ministers Bevin, Eden, and his generals Ismay and Smuts of the Imperial General Staff. Both Ismay and Smuts, a South African, had a great deal of experience in unconventional warfare; Smuts had participated in the Boer War forty years earlier when Churchill was an enemy lieutenant on the British side. For Churchill, it seems, experience in guerrilla war was a cause for befriending someone no matter what side he had been on. De Gaulle and Churchill discussed the invasion and Churchill informed him that the time was imminent. De Gaulle responded that he thought so, since the sudden increase in BBC messages led many in Algiers to conclude it must be near. After lunch the subject turned to politics. The prime minister tried to convince de Gaulle to concur about the American and British occupation policies. With such an agreement that day, Churchill indicated that he could arrange for de Gaulle to go to the White House for a cordial and fruitful meeting with FDR. Now deeply suspicious, de Gaulle wondered how sincere the American and British governments were in this matter since he had attempted to meet with them and discuss these issues nine months earlier. De Gaulle verbally ticked off a long list of affronts that he had, until now, reined in, and he ended by raising the currency issue and registering his complaint about the Allies printing French money without his consent. The discussion degenerated into a shouting match culminating with Churchill exclaiming, "Between Europe and the deep blue sea, I should always choose the sea. Each time that you force me to choose between Roosevelt and you, I will always choose Roosevelt!" Labour Minister Ernest Bevin quietly commented that Churchill's views were not those of the entire Cabinet. With the air somewhat tense, Churchill proposed a toast and de Gaulle answered the toast with, "To England, to Victory, to Europe." Like de Gaulle's final decision on Mers el-Kébir nearly four years before, he knew France's future still depended on British victory.[39]

The meeting adjourned at 4:30 PM and they made their way to Eisenhower's headquarters where they were greeted with an honor guard. Eisenhower briefed de Gaulle and the other French leaders on the amphibious assault portion of Overlord and de Gaulle, very much impressed with all the preparations, graciously congratulated General Eisenhower on his preparations and planning efforts. Then Eisenhower discussed things alone with de Gaulle on the path outside where de Gaulle would have room to "to wave his arms and talk."[40] Their discussion centered on the task at hand, specifically the broadcast de Gaulle had agreed to make. Eisenhower handed de Gaulle a version he had written, saying it was a draft. De Gaulle agreed to review it but did not like the tone and the content regarding inferences that Eisenhower was the chief authority in France.[41] General Koenig, who had accompanied de Gaulle, promised to bring back a copy of a completed draft the next day for review. If done in time, Eisenhower's chief of psychological operations, Brigadier General Robert McClure, could complete the recording of de Gaulle for use during D-Day.[42] With that tenuous agreement for de Gaulle to make the broadcast, Eisenhower returned to his tent and after supper grunted when given a copy of the false Associated Press release.[43] Between that mistake, the high volume of BBC messages, and everything else that might tip off the Germans, it seemed a trifle at that point. The next day, with the weather still causing great concern, Bedell Smith informed Captain Butcher that de Gaulle refused to broadcast, and Butcher thought it was because of the words in Eisenhower's draft stating that civil control of France belonged to the Allied Command. When Butcher informed his boss of this, Eisenhower replied, "To hell with him.... If he doesn't come through we'll deal with someone else."[44] Of course, there was no one else. That evening, beginning at 9:15 PM, the BBC took a full fifteen minutes to broadcast 185 action messages to waiting F, RF, and BCRA networks of Maquis.[45]

Most of the messages were nonsense, such as "the duck's wings are still busy." But others were inspired. The SOE code writers, in this very fitting moment, also used a line from *Cyrano de Bergerac*: "at the end of the refrain, I thrust!"[46] But how sharp was this sword, so long prepared, but hotly contested and doubted? And how many swords would appear after so many dangerous night flying missions delivering them to secret drop zones? Special Force Headquarters gave the Supreme Allied Command a fairly sanguine estimate that it believed 577 targets would be attacked in the railway plan, 30 roads would be cut, and 32 telecommunications sites would be sabotaged. Additionally, and in a decision Eisenhower would later regret, they backed up those efforts with the all-out guerrilla plan as explained above and sent the message for guerrilla warfare to engage in maximum interference with road, rail, and telecommunications at the same time. More targets could have been attacked, but the Maquis still lacked arms, and the special operations planners indicated this.[47] A somewhat pessimistic account came from an SOE planner when his American counterpart asked what the opening days would bring. The SOE planner revealed that all the planning assumptions started with 100 men rising on D + 1 and culminated four days later with 100,000 Maquis having participated in operations at some point during that time. But he warned that the figures were only estimates and not to be used for planning any other operation that depended upon their support. After all, he reminded his American colleague, the Résistance was "an entirely unpredictable and nebulous force."[48]

6

The Struggle for Control

I ncluded in Prime Minister Churchill's daily read file shortly after the invasion was the following intercepted message from the Wehrmacht to its army units in France: "The tasks of the French *Résistance* organization are...1) In the landing area, direct guerrilla support, 2) in the hinterland demolitions and minor harassing operations, 3) In the interior mobilization zones—organization for major operations." Continuing on, this intercepted message warned that the Allies intended to parachute detachments of uniformed officers "along with a considerable increase in weapon dropping" and to accomplish these missions during the weeks of May 28 to June 9 when the moon provided the required illumination for night operations.[1] German assessments of Allied intentions for the Résistance proved to be largely accurate. Furthermore, their information on the intentions of the Forces Françaises de l'Intérieur (FFI) was substantial. Their persistent arrests provided a great deal of fidelity regarding the directives from London and Algiers to the interior. For example, on April 22, 1944, the MilitärBefehlshaber im Frankreich (MBF) distributed a translated copy of the directive from the Savoie's regional FFI leader to his department leaders. The Germans acquired the document in its entirety, translated it, and sent it throughout France.[2]

But knowing what the Allies sought to achieve and being able to do anything about it are very different things. The MBF, the Wehrmacht's senior element in France Oberbefehlshaber West (OB West), and the Vichy authority's Milice and Gendarmes were often at a loss to effectively stop Allied actions with the Résistance. Perhaps the greatest challenge for the Germans was caused simply by the wide variety of forces the Allies and the Comité Français de la Liberation Nationale (CFLN) inserted into occupied France over the next four months. The multiplicity of special units and intelligence agents parachuted into France before and after the invasion signal the wide variety of tasks as well as the necessity for redundancy that the Supreme Headquarters Allied Expeditionary Forces (SHAEF), Special Force Headquarters (SFHQ), and the Bureau Centrale Renseignements d'Action (BCRA) thought were necessary to harness the Maquis. Besides the Jedburgh teams, the Allies parachuted in British and French Special Air Service (SAS) teams and American Operational Groups (OGs) in order to attack specific targets or to defend key assets such as bridges or power plants. The Allies also inserted intelligence teams into France code named Sussex, Brissex, and Ossex teams to observe enemy troop movements and radio that information back to Britain. The Special Operations Executive (SOE), Office of Strategic Services (OSS), and BCRA all had networks of spies attempting to store explosives and ammunition for D-Day and subsequent operations. More recently, at Finchampstead on May 20, the three nations also conceived of Inter-Allied Teams comprised of military officers directed to represent Allied political aims to various *réduits*, or centers of guerrilla activity, where relatively large Maquis formations would probably rally and where Allied leadership would be needed.[3]

But probably the most important and long-term asset of all the various kinds of clandestine people deployed to occupied France were the previously discussed Délégués Militare Régionales, or military regional delegates (DMRs), charged with consolidating the CFLN's authority in that region. Many of the DMRs had been parachuted into France in late 1943 or early 1944 and the ones who had survived to the Allied invasion on June 6 began to consolidate the CFLN's authority as the various Franc-Tireurs et Partisans Français (FTP), Armée Secrète (AS), Organisation de Résistance de l'armée

(ORA), and other assorted Maquis units drew more and more men and boys into their ranks. The seventeen men in the twelve regions who attempted to perform this key duty were charged by de Gaulle to unify the military effort under the authority of the CFLN. Or as Clausewitz might say, they were responsible for bringing military action in line with the CFLN's political aims. Specifically, that meant France's liberation from Germany, the punishment of the collaborators, and the avoidance of an Allied military government of occupation. Waiting in the wings, the CFLN had regional liberation committees in Algiers or in France expecting to take the reins of civil power before the Allies could. Their mission then was to unify the Résistance at the regional level, mirroring what de Gaulle had achieved at the national level.[4] Toward that end, the support of the Jedburgh teams, working for General Koenig, as were the regional military delegates, meant an increased chance that their political unity would translate into effective military effort.

But to many, that day was far off, and to the Germans, the specter of defeat had not yet settled upon them. Leading German combat operations in France was Oberbefehlshaber West Field Marshal Gerd von Rundstedt headquartered in Paris. He took orders from Adolf Hitler in Berlin supported by his overall German Army staff headquarters, Ober Kommando der Wehrmacht (OKW). The Luftwaffe and Kriegsmarine headquarters in Berlin, in actual practice, commanded their air and naval forces in France, so not only did von Rundstedt lack authority over much of the MBF's occupation forces but he also did not command the air and naval forces in France. The OKW and von Rundstedt had organized his forces into two army groups, Heeresgruppe B commanded by Erwin Rommel and Heeresgruppe G commanded by Johannes Blaskowitz. Rommel then commanded two armies, the 15th Armee headquartered in Belgium that had the task of defending the Channel coastline from Belgium to the Seine River and the 7th Armee at Le Mans covering Normandy and Brittany and back to the Loire River. Blaskowitz's forces covered southern France with the 1st Armee in Bordeaux and the 19th Armee in Avignon. In addition to active forces covering France's perimeter, numerous reserve divisions were stationed around the interior, training and awaiting the arrival of more replacement soldiers and equipment in order to become fully mission capable.[5] The Wehrmacht unit already discussed at Glières, the 157th Reserve Infantry Division, was one of these units. Another was the 2nd SS Panzer "Das Reich" Division undergoing refit in the southern French town of Montauban. Eisenhower wanted the transportation routes cut so this very powerful division could not participate in Normandy combat.

In the opening days of the invasion, Eisenhower's objective for SFHQ and the Résistance was for them to assist in the first phase of Overlord, meaning the assault and establishment of the beachhead in Normandy, and in the second phase, which entailed assisting in the enlargement of Allied territory "west of the Seine and north of the Loire" rivers.[6] The sixteen Jedburgh teams deployed during this first phase of operation is described in this chapter. Their tasks were to ensure that certain railroads and roads were cut, making it difficult for the Wehrmacht to bring up reserves; that communication lines were sabotaged, making it hard for the enemy to coordinate a coherent defense; and to liaise with the local Maquis in order to train them for appropriate guerrilla activities when directed by SHAEF. In Koenig's first order to the FFI he declared their mission was to fight. But he was careful to remind his forces to fight in a prudent and effective manner. Those who were armed were to remain available as directed and those unarmed were to remain in contact with their commanders in order to receive weapons and training when arms arrived. In other words, they were directed to wait until they could fight.[7] Koenig and his British and American counterparts at SFHQ prepared Jedburgh teams to deploy to France along with SAS parties and drafted orders and briefing teams; over the course of the first and second phases of Overlord they would send in sixteen Jedburgh teams to liaise with the FFI and train their Maquis units. Chapter 7 describes the activities of some of those teams and their experiences in France as Eisenhower's direct means of communication to the Maquis.

TEAM HUGH

Just after 11 PM on June 5, an RAF Halifax bomber took off from Tempsford air base with Jedburgh Team Hugh. After getting through "quite a bit of FLAK" from German anti-aircraft guns along the route, the team parachuted into the French darkness, north of the small town of Saint-Gaultier in the department of l'Indre. Along with them were two of the officers of the British Special Air Service (SAS) mission, code named Bulbasket. French Captain Louis L'Helgouach, using the nom de guerre Louis Legrand, led the Jedburgh team.[8] The second officer was British Captain William Crawshay, and the radio operator was the French non-commissioned officer Rene Meyer, using the name Rene Mersiol. L'Helgouach had been recruited out of the Colonial Spahi Regiments in North Africa for Jedburgh duty.[9] Crawshay found his way into the Special Operations Executive (SOE) via a very circuitous route. When the war started, he was a student at the University of Poitiers in southwestern France. His step-grandfather was ambassador to France and he had spent a great deal of his childhood in Paris.[10] When available for service in the British Army, he was too young to serve in his home regiment of the Royal Welsh Fusiliers and so he volunteered for the 5th Battalion, Kings African Rifles, training Masai and Swahili soldiers in Somalia. While serving in that unit, he was mistakenly strafed and wounded by a South African Fokker-Wolfe fighter aircraft. That wound and a subsequent severe case of malaria sidelined him in Mombasa, Kenya, for more than a year. After being placed back on active service, he volunteered for the British Military Mission as a liaison officer to the Free French Brigade in Egypt where he met General Koenig just after his successful defense of Bir Hakeim. "I see that you have chosen a good regiment," said Koenig, meaning to insult the English while at the same time being kind to the young Welsh officer.[11] After watching, and missing, the battle of El Alamein from the heights above, Crawshay sought out more exciting work than he believed his current posting would provide. A friend arranged for him to meet with General Gubbins in Cairo and during that discussion Gubbins agreed to take Crawshay into the SOE and sent him off to the Jedburgh program, without revealing to Crawshay what the duties were. The Welshman returned to the United Kingdom in November 1943 with orders to report to Milton Hall for training. Comments in his records are not that hopeful, however, with one of his superior officers, American instructor Lieutenant Bill Dreux, remarking that Crawshay was "inept in many phases of military training."[12] Crawshay must have improved, however, as Colonel Musgrave allowed him to be on the first team into France.

Crawshay was familiar with this part of France, having studied in Poitiers, just southwest of his drop zone, and he knew the region to be made up of many small villages and farms. The 1936 census counted the population of l'Indre at 245,622 with a population density of 36 people per square kilometer, making it one of the least populated departments in France. Châteauroux was the largest town, with a population of no more than 6,000 people living in rural or small village settings. There were large swaths of wooded areas in the south side of the department and the terrain rose into what emerges as the Massif Central south of l'Indre. The department is defined by rivers, with the Creuse River on the southwest, the Indre River running through the department's center, and the Cher River running past the town of Issoudon on the east, all flowing into the Loire River to the north. The farmland, woods, and vacant buildings all were conducive to hiding weapons and small bands of men. Other than agriculture, a small aircraft engine factory, two small automobile factories in Châteauroux, and a bicycle factory in La Chatre contributed to the department's economy. On l'Indre's southern edge was one of France's principal hydroelectric plants along with the requisite high-tension power lines leading to Normandy and the Paris region. Further increasing the area's strategic value were the rail lines that transited the department. A national north-south rail line running from Paris to Toulouse bisected l'Indre, which was also cut by the east-west rail line serving Nantes and Lyon.[13] In the 1936 elections, the last real indication of political sentiments, the Popular Front had won 57.5 percent of the votes and 64 percent of the seats in the National Assembly with the Parti communiste français (PCF) winning just under 10 percent of the vote. Therefore the department could be described as center left.[14] But the railroads were SHAEF's primary concern, and with Plan Vert in operation, they were receiving a great deal of attention from the local Maquis.

The area's attributes were well known to the SOE as the first successful insertion of an SOE agent in France had occurred in the region in 1941.[15] Maurice Southgate's arrest mentioned in Chapter 4 had left the department in the hands of his two assistants, René Maingard and radio operator Pearl Witherington. They made the decision to divide up Southgate's network of contacts, and Maquis associated with Maingard planned to move off to the east into the Vienne Department while Witherington remained in northern l'Indre. These two ran the F Section circuits Hugh had been ordered to contact and whose Maquis Hugh was to train for guerrilla work.

Recognizing the incongruent tasks between their Special Air Service (SAS) colleagues and their own Jedburgh work, the members of Hugh and the Bulbasket mission all agreed to ignore their Special Force Headquarters (SFHQ) orders and separate. Maingard concurred with this and after receiving more weapons and gear in a parachute drop on June 6, inspecting the department's Maquis units on June 7, and receiving more of the SAS team members on June 9, team Hugh and the SAS parted company.[16] On June 7 and 8, Hugh's messages back to SFHQ signal their certainty at keeping the rail line from Toulouse cut, and noting that the population was enthusiastic, they declared that the "existing *Maquis* groups were doubling in 48 hours" and they asked for more equipment, radios, arms, and another Jedburgh team to help with more work than they could accomplish. SFHQ responded that their first priority was keeping the rail line cut, in order to keep units like the 2nd SS Panzer from coming north, but it also tempered Legrand's and Crawshay's enthusiasm somewhat by warning them to "keep out the undesirables" and limit the growth of the Maquis to those they could arm and train due to the fact larger groups are harder to keep moving and harder to supply. Radio operator Meyer signaled back, "Impossible to limit the numbers joining the *Résistance* owing to spontaneous uprising," and he confirmed their need of the second Jedburgh team.[17]

The spontaneous uprising of the Maquis occurred in more than just Hugh's area. SFHQ received similar reports from other places in central France, in Brittany, and in the southeast between the Rhône River and the Italian border. Such an influx was not what SFHQ wanted and neither did Koenig. Only four days after the invasion, the situation compelled Koenig to send an order to the DMRs, and the Bureau d'Opérations Aériennes (BOA), the Free French organization running the drop zones, to limit their actions. For many reasons, Koenig did not want widespread action and feared its chaotic results. Koenig's order came to the DMRs in clipped telegraph language, "CURRENTLY IMPOSSIBLE PREDICT NORMAL SUPPLY WEAPONS AND AMMUNITION YOU LIMIT TO A

SIMMER ALL GUERILLA ACTION STOP WHEN POSSIBLE BREAK CONTACT EVERYWHERE WHILE WAITING FOR PHASE OF REORGANISATION STOP…THIS IS A FORMAL ORDER STOP CONSTITUTE SMALL GROUPS RATHER THAN LARGE GATHERINGS STOP GOODBYE"[18] Having broadcast the order for general guerrilla warfare on June 5, SHAEF did not now like the surprise it had on its hands. The "unpredictable and nebulous force" that all had believed would fail to rise in significant numbers had exceeded SHAEF's expectations considerably. As one of the senior BCRA leaders in France at the time later wrote, the order, but more important, the slowing down of the aerial re-supply of arms, "effectively contributed to the avoidance of the useless sacrifice of the French population."[19] Koenig had a tenuous command structure in place that could not operate in the open; therefore, if SHAEF did not want the Maquis to do anything, it simply would not authorize aerial re-supply of weapons. The supply flights now became a blunt instrument for Eisenhower to use to control the Résistance.

Nevertheless, having an increasing number of Jedburgh teams in France would be a more effective way of controlling the Maquis, so their deployment kept pace. A "Carpetbagger" B-24 took off from RAF Harrington with Team Hamish and their twelve containers of equipment and weapons at 10:32 PM on June 12. The eight-man crew, commanded by Major Robert W. Fish, flew their aircraft to the drop zone with no enemy opposition and good weather. Hamish and its twelve containers of equipment departed the aircraft over the drop zone at 2:08 AM, and in keeping with the procedure to avoid detection, dropped the men and equipment from only 580 feet above the ground. After delivering the Jedburghs, the crew circled back around to drop off one container that had gotten hung up, and then flew a route distributing propaganda leaflets over three towns in France. Fish and his crew arrived safely back at their base a little after 5:00 AM.[20] Team Hamish, comprised of American Lieutenant Robert Anstett, French Lieutenant René Schmitt, using the nom de guerre Lucien Blacere, and American Sergeant Lee Watters had arrived, fulfilling Hugh's request for more help, and just in time. German combat units were organizing themselves, and activity in the region was beginning.[21] SOE agent Pearl Witherington was nearly caught on June 11 and her organization was momentarily scattered. Hugh and Hamish could now fulfill the long intended use of Jedburgh teams as a reserve force taking the place of arrested or disestablished F Section agents.[22]

Over the next two weeks, these two teams moved around the region splitting the work load and coordinating their activities not only with each other, to the degree possible given the German ability to intercept radio communications, but also with the F Section agents and the FFI leadership. So instead of replacing Jedburgh teams, the new ones often augmented them. They received at least three more night parachute re-supply drops and attempted to organize the Maquis in manageable groups defined by the team's ability to arm, train, and equip them. Team Hamish radioed SFHQ on June 24 reporting that "Railroad and telephone finished, roads difficult. Impossible stop Boche but can slow down by ambush. For this need mines and booby traps.... Been playing games with Boche patrols. Its fun."[23]

But what was not "fun" was the multiplicity of French units, many unaware of the others, beginning to impede coordinated action. The Maquis in the area, comprised of Franc-Tireurs et Partisans Français (FTP), Armée Secrète (AS), and Organisation de Résistance de l'armée (ORA) units, were unable to coordinate actions at this point forcing the Jedburgh teams to consider evacuating the area and heading south since the Germans were conducting such strong actions in Indre. Making the issue more complicated was the belief in the region, true or not, that the British had favored the FTP in their policy of arming the local groups, leaving the AS and the ORA not only bereft of weapons but suspicious of any link to the Free French and SHAEF in London. On June 20, Jedburghs Crawshay and Legrand met with Colonel Raymond Chomel who was the commander of the ORA in the department.[24] Chomel used the pseudonym Charles Martel, which recalled France's successful defense of Christendom from the Muslims near Poitiers in AD 732. An officer in the regular army, he commanded a unit of regular infantry and was "horrified" that he might have to take orders from Theogene Briant, pseudonym Alex, who was the FTP's leader in that part of Indre.[25] During two meetings they began to work through the ways the groups could cooperate, aided by the BCRA's operations officer for the region, Georges Heritier, pseudonym Croc, who had parachuted into the region in January.

Heritier had been captured in April but had escaped and now served as the assistant DMR.[26] But their meetings were halted on two occasions due to raiding parties of Germans. In one instance, they all had a narrow escape with the Jedburgh team's driver having to hide in pile of coal and Crawshay in a basement closet across from a wine cellar. The Gestapo officer, seeing the wine cellar and not wanting his men to get into it, ordered them all to leave the basement where the Jedburghs hid.[27]

Nevertheless, they again attempted negotiations and overcame the disagreements when Legrand and Crawshay agreed to pass orders to the ORA, the AS, and the FTP claiming that those orders were coming from Eisenhower through Koenig. Chomel agreed to take orders from "Surcouf," the commander of the AS in the region. Chomel would command "mobile" units, and the French and the Jedburghs and created sector chiefs for the area and agreed that the rest should be in reserve since they did not have arms for all.[28] On June 25 and 26, they managed a two-day discussion at Team Hugh's command post without being hunted by Germans. Present were Chomel, Heritier, and other FTP leaders; regional military delegate Eugene Dechelette arrived and led the discussions. Dechelette had been in France since February, a few days after marrying a British woman in London. The BCRA then arranged for Dechelette to parachute into France but his jump was not as fortunate as the Jedburghs' had been since he broke his ankle on landing.[29] By June his leg had healed and now he was attempting to assert the authority of the CFLN in the R5 Region, the Free French name for this part of France. Crawshay and Legrand wrote later that during his two-day discussion with all the leaders, Dechelette approved of their previous arrangements but wanted to take more action against the Germans. The Jeds disagreed. They believed, and London concurred, that few of the Maquis units were ready for major action against the enemy. But impressed with Dechelette, the Jedburghs later commented that he "was most clear headed" and "completely dominated the situation" during this key meeting that settled command of the Indre, the northernmost department in R5, with the FTP and AS Résistance firmly under the control of Koenig.[30]

But in all this, Team Hugh seemed not to recognize that Dechelette also reported to General Koenig, and that Dechelette's own radio messages were also informing SFHQ and Koenig of what was occurring. Koenig seemed to take more notice when contacted by Dechelette and often gave personal direction to regional military delegates that few Jedburgh teams received. In this case, the Allied Jedburghs, with more tactical liaison duties, seem to have been regarded as a reinforcing mechanism for DMR actions. In telegrams to Dechelette on June 24 and 25, while the meeting was being conducted at Team Hugh's headquarters, EMFFI told Dechelette, we "warmly thank you for this very precious information" and furthermore relayed to Dechelette that Koenig was glad that he had conferred with Bourgès-Maunoury who was serving as the southern zones military delegate and Dechelette's superior. In a message to Dechelette, Koenig also "confirm[ed] the command and organization decisions"[31] that he and Hugh had made. While the Jedburgh team's report comes off sounding like Hugh acted in the absence of coherent direction from SFHQ and Koenig, in the military hierarchy, there is little reason to see why Koenig would send a message to a junior team of Jedburghs when he had related his wishes and congratulations to Dechelette, the senior man on the scene. Even while they were growing more connected, the Allied and FFI teams certainly had redundant ways to liaise with localities all over France with F Section agents, RF Section agents, DMRs, Inter-Allied Teams, and Jedburgh teams. General Koenig, SHAEF's commander for the Résistance, was deferring to his senior person while retaining the ability and prerogative to communicate directly to any one of his assets in France when he wished. Therefore, controlling the FFI inside France might have looked confusing, but Koenig was working diligently to get the Résistance to come together.

ORGANIZING THE RÉSISTANCE IN THE MORVAN

In the Morvan, Koenig's late May direction to his staff to consider sending liaison capability to this region resulted in the deployment of nearly all types of teams to the area. Teams Isaac and Harry, the SAS Houndsorth mission, and the Inter-Allied or political mission code named Verveine all deployed there in early June. Lieutenant Colonel Hutchison, discussed in Chapter 5, who had been the director of the RF Section and later requested assignment to the Jedburgh teams, was chosen to lead both team Isaac and the political mission Verveine. A French officer, Ferdinand Viat, who used the pseudonym Commandant Dubac, would later deploy to take command, but in the meantime, Hutchison and his radio operator were to establish the initial base while attempting to ascertain the efficacy of Maquis activity in the region.[32]

Alerted by Musgrave to depart from Milton Hall to London, Hutchison and his wireless/transmitter operator (W/T), Sergeant John Sharpe, were briefed in a London flat the Special Operations Executive (SOE) used to instruct agents prior to their deployment. They looked at and studied maps of the area with the briefing officer to familiarize themselves with the departments of Nièvre, where they were to go, and the surrounding departments of Yonne, Côte d'Or, Cher, Allier, Loire, and Saône et Loire southeast of Paris and directly east of where Team Hugh was also being prepared to deploy. Hutchison realized, as General Koenig had two weeks before, that the confluence of roads, railroads, and rivers all winding through the forests made it "a part of France which the enemy was likely to use, as he hurried troops towards Normandy through the Vosges or as he made his way south to the Mediterranean."[33] Not only that, but later the Germans could be harassed going the other direction as well, for in their movement east, they would find the Maquis perhaps better ready to deal with them. In either case, Koenig's selection of this region and ranking it higher in priority seemed wise, but when Koenig had suggested on May 20 that the area become a *réduit*, making it high on SFHQ's list of regions to cultivate, there now seemed to be no recognition on Hutchison's part that he needed to tamp down Maquis activity instead of inciting it. Specifically, as stated in Team Harry's orders, the Jedburghs were warned against premature Maquis operations because the distance from Britain and the phases of the moon made flying to this part of France prohibitive after June 9. With no way to get weapons to the Maquis, Hutchison's duties were to be confined to relaying directions from London and finding out the nature of the local Maquis groups. But Hutchison never realized the implications of his orders nor how desperate he would be in the months of June and July and over time his frustration became too much to contain.

Hutchison's and Sharp's cohorts on Team Harry were supposed to depart with their elements of a British SAS mission on June 4, but weather delayed them until June 6. While boarding the plane, British Captain Duncan Guthrie, Harry's team leader received a copy of Team Isaac's orders telling him at the last moment that he would be under the combined mission of Isaac/Verveine once in the field. Harry was to liaise with any Maquis who might come to work with the SAS in order to conduct raids on enemy lines of communications, keep SFHQ informed regarding Résistance strength in the area, but be careful not to "encourage any mass rising by resistance unless ordered to by SFHQ."[34] The difficulty this presented to the Jedburghs proved to be substantial. They could relay orders and send information back, but being reduced to passing messages from SHAEF to Maquis incapable of much action went against the very nature of their training and what the Jedburghs believed their mission was to be. Furthermore, it de-legitimated their authority in the eyes of the Maquis when they arrived and promised weapons and then failed to keep those promises.

But the subtle shift in mission was only one aspect for which the Jeds had not been prepared. Hutchison later complained that this merging of his Jedburgh mission with the political mission of Verveine, compounded by the late arrival of his commander, only served to increase his confusion regarding his mission's intent and his role in the local resistance organizations. Hutchison also complained that Viat and other French personnel were not coming to the field until the following moon cycle "for reasons which were never explained to me." Perhaps it was because the French personnel could not be released without the knowledge of the BCRA, and General Koenig as SFHQ directed that the planning for this mission be done without informing the French. However, Hutchison and Viat had lunch at the Cavalry Club prior to Hutchison's departure and they discussed their mission and agreed on their methods and general philosophy about issues.[35] A curious point is that if Viat could not deploy until later, and if the French could not be informed, it seems that it would have been against orders to have met at all.

Once in place, Teams Isaac and Harry linked up with each other and began their work with the DMR for areas P1 and P2 southeast of Paris.

André Rondenay, who went under the code name Leminscate, and his assistant for drop zones, Alain Grout de Beaufort, who used the pseudonym Pair. Pair's duties of controlling drop zones meant that he determined who was given weapons and was therefore a major player with the regional or local Maquis. Having heard the BBC messages on June 1 and 5, the two met in Paris with their group and, with a few vehicles and arms, made their way out of the capital toward the Morvan where they were to implement their portion of plans Vert and Tortue, the attack on the railways and on the roads thought to be used by German armored units reinforcing the front. However, since their plan had been designed *believing that the invasion would occur north of them at the Pas de Calais* instead of further west at Normandy, the German traffic through the region was not as heavy as they expected.[36] Rondenay, who was a railway employee and engineer, had also studied the best tactics for stopping and delaying armored columns. Knowing how they operated, "it was essential to make the charges explode only to the immediate contact of the armored columns, after the passage of the motor cycles" that escorted the columns. Surprise was essential to get the desired logjam of traffic and avoid allowing the motorcyclists to divert the column or call for support.[37] Having managed to carry out many of their Plan Vert actions, Rondenay met up with Jedburghs of team Harry on June 10. On June 14, Team Isaac was directed to them in their small forest village of Lormes, 260 kilometers southeast of Paris.[38]

Together they began to select the Maquis units that all agreed were worthy of maintaining and began the process of training them and receiving weapons via air drops. But due to the distance from Britain, the shortened nighttime hours, and the moon phase, no supplies would be sent. Hutchison, who protested this situation on June 21, evidently was not informed of this key issue prior to his departure on the June 10 even though Team Harry was briefed about this prior to its departure. Also on June 21, a row began over the command of the region's Maquis. Arriving to see Hutchison was Colonel Dupin, who claimed to be their new commander. Buttressing his claim was a letter of appointment from Comité d'action militaire du CNR or COMAC. Here we see the influence of the COMAC, the committee created by the interior Résistance charged with overseeing military actions. One can also see the struggles then between the Résistance and the Allies over control of the Maquis' actions. The COMAC has often been referred to as the voice of the communists and it represented probably the most consolidated influence they had on the liberation. But their role was redundant with Koenig's role in London as both entities claimed command of the FFI. Both de Gaulle and Koenig agreed to their creation and existence largely due to the COMAC's limited geographical influence and the need for their participation. As historian Julian Jackson remarked quite accurately, "COMAC controlled less of France than the early Capetians."[39] So while the communists may have controlled COMAC, COMAC itself proved unable to control more than even Koenig did. Furthermore, de Gaulle and Koenig participated in choosing COMAC's members, increasing Koenig's influence and creating a sponsorship role for him over the committee. However, from Hutchison's as well as Rondenay's point of view, Dupin's arrival only sowed seeds of discord and confusion. In an unusually long message, Hutchison updated SFHQ on many things, requested arms and more Jedburgh teams for the region, and stated that COMAC's Colonel Dupin had arrived to command in the region but would recognize Koenig's and SHAEF's authority.[40] While Hutchison believed this kind of arrangement to be essential, since those in France were better able to command in France, the question then became what exactly was Rondenay's role as regional military delegate? On July 3, Hutchison received instructions from SFHQ that he was "to treat no further with Colonel Dupin," to which Hutchison protested only to be directed not to compete with Rondenay. Hutchison was now completely mystified. It was "a gratuitous piece of advice that showed that London was not conversant" with his original orders or mission and he chafed now under the reality of having to wait for weapons as well as Colonel Viat, who had yet to be deployed and assume command of Verveine.[41]

But while Hutchison and Dupin dealt with command issues, Harry and the SAS kept organizing hit-and-run ambushes with some of the Maquis units when arms permitted. Their ability to conduct railway cuts and run ambushes was modestly successful and infuriated the Germans who pressed the hunt to find the Maquis groups and the Allied units. As reprisal for an ambush done by the village Maquis units, the Wehrmacht "completely burnt" the village of Montsauche.[42] Fifteen villagers were killed the next day, and another severe reprisal was conducted on the village of Dun le Places, north of Montsauche. Instead of effectively discouraging further actions, this only inspired and infuriated the local French Maquis. The only restraint the Jedburghs could maintain on the Maquis was the ever-diminishing supply of weapons. As one of the first air supply missions to reach them was closing in on the drop zone, the RAF aircraft struck a USAAF B-24 in the mid-air darkness.[43] All the British and American airmen were killed and Captain Guthrie feared the Germans would discover the drop zone. He worked quickly with some of the local villagers and Maquis to bury the bodies and cart off pieces of one of the aircraft so the Germans would incorrectly assume that only one aircraft had crashed due to flak instead of finding two and deducing the crash site was an active drop zone. Guthrie's plan succeeded and "the Germans never realized anything more than one plane crashed."[44]

While Harry and Isaac in the Morvan and Hugh and Hamish in Indre worked to create unity of action in their regions, the same struggles were continuing at the national level between the United States and de Gaulle's CFLN. In the mind of President Roosevelt, D-Day seemed to change nothing regarding American recognition of de Gaulle's leadership and the CFLN. Two days before D-Day, the OSS sent maps with overlays and other briefing papers to the president. The materials demonstrated that the Maquis groups were in various states of organization and readiness, that the British and Americans had links with some groups but not others, and that the French had their own, much larger Maquis groups independent of the ones that the British had fostered beginning in 1941. The Résistance Regions were all precisely shown and included the DMRs' code names, their assistants, and their operations officers as of the latest information. The OSS also provided the estimate that the aggregate strength of the Résistance in France was 313,180. In raw numbers, this translates into the equivalent of nearly twenty-one American Army infantry divisions. Of course, as the OSS made clear to Roosevelt, only a mere 6,630 of the Allied French Maquis, meaning the Maquis unequipped or connected with the SOE or OSS, were considered "well armed" while 18,200 were considered armed who were in contact with SOE or OSS circuits.[45] Furthermore, these numbers were best guesses and in many ways irrelevant. The questions most animating Roosevelt had to do with de Gaulle's actions now that the invasion had begun.

On June 8, the American ambassador to the Court of St. James, John Winant, telegraphed Secretary of State Hull and related the frustration the British government had with de Gaulle's actions since his arrival. De Gaulle had made the D-Day broadcast, but not without consternation and only in his own words, not those drafted by Eisenhower for him, nor did he speak at the time requested, but later in the day so he would not appear to be last among all the exiled European governments who had spoken in quick succession of one another. But now that the broadcast was done, the currency and French liaison officer issues needed attention in order to aid division and brigade commanders dealing directly with the French population near the combat zone. De Gaulle had blocked both, but Winant now told Hull that the French had released some of the liaison officers for duties with American and British units. The currency was another matter and as of yet unresolved. De Gaulle believed that the currency issue was indicative that "France was being treated in this respect precisely like Italy" and was stirring up French fears of an Allied Military Government of Occupied Territory (AMGOT). The Allied proclamation explaining their use of the new French currency would be broadcast at midnight when it would not receive much attention, since the solution did not have de Gaulle's consent. Furthermore, Winant hinted that British popular sentiments, as Churchill had warned FDR in May, were beginning to coalesce around de Gaulle and the CFLN, and that the Parliament and the British press believed de Gaulle "was not being given proper consideration." Winant went on to suggest that as leader of the CFLN, de Gaulle could be invited to Washington to "agree to the plans which have been worked out for the civil administration of France"[46]—a tactful urging to Hull and the president that something must be done or relations with France would sour postwar relations with the United States. However, this urging was lost on the president. Admiral Leahy drafted a reply that FDR approved on 13 June stating that he looked forward to de Gaulle's visit when he would "direct his attention to our war effort toward the liberation of France."[47] In other words, FDR believed that de Gaulle should do what the United States wished simply because of American actions to free France from German occupation; de Gaulle, on the other hand, saw too much evidence that the Allies sought to govern France and separate it from its colonies.

Roosevelt's refusal to recognize de Gaulle had implications for all sorts of practical matters. The day after FDR replied to Winant's telegram, Secretary of War Stimson spoke with his deputy John J. McCloy about the issues with France. Stimson was very concerned that American soldiers would not be able to purchase needed supplies and materials from the French population if they refused to accept the Allied currency. Several weeks of progress and work regarding the matter before the invasion seemed to be vanishing. Furthermore, the disagreement about de Gaulle's refusal to allow French liaison officers go along with the landing forces found its way into the press, embarrassing Churchill and de Gaulle; Stimson believed that McCloy had probably leaked it to a reporter. While in England, General Marshall had "dressed down" two of de Gaulle's "chief lieutenants" during his recent visit to London, probably in frustration about what the French were demanding regarding recognition, the currency, and being frozen out of Overlord planning. Stimson could see that Eisenhower was in a very poor position regarding de Gaulle and grew frustrated with Secretary of State Hull who "hates de Gaulle with such fierce feeling that he rambles into incoherence whenever we talk about him."[48]

Stimson was arguably the most experienced person regarding foreign affairs in FDR's Cabinet. He had served as the secretary of war for President Taft, then as a colonel in the artillery in France during World War I. He had successfully mediated a civil dispute in Nicaragua for President Coolidge and later became his governor general of the Philippines. President Hoover appointed him secretary of state and in that capacity he had overseen the American negotiations of the London Naval Treaty, a major accomplishment in interwar disarmament. Now in his second stint as secretary of war, for a president of the other party, he was overseeing the largest-ever expansion of American military might and the arming, training, and equipping of over 8 million men and women. All that experience served him well and he could understand Eisenhower's embarrassment and desire for the United States and Great Britain to get together with de Gaulle on the issue. Roosevelt's draft policy remained in London unsigned because Anthony Eden and other members of the Cabinet were advising Churchill against signing it. Stimson distrusted de Gaulle, but he realized that while FDR's and Hull's policy sounded good in theory, it was not working in practice. France would not be treated like a minor nation that allowed the United States to show it how to run its own affairs. In an hour-long phone conversation with FDR, Stimson tried to talk to him about all this, but after speaking glowingly of how the Maquis were slowing down two divisions in France's interior, Roosevelt then said that General Donovan had told him there might be other options for French leadership.[49]

Suspicious of this claim, Stimson and McCloy talked to Donovan the next day. Donovan backed off such a positive representation of other leadership possibilities in France. In fact, he had written a memo to FDR based on his discussions with de Gaulle's representatives in London and Washington and his recent trip to the invasion zone, and evidently he was pressing FDR to fully recognize de Gaulle and the CFLN. But after speaking with Secretary Stimson, Donovan tore up his memo. Stimson and Donovan realized that the president was not going to change his mind, so they shifted their tack hoping to make some progress. Instead Donovan recommended to the president that Eisenhower recognize de Gaulle as a military leader and in that capacity, which was already being filled largely by Koenig in London and Cochet in Algiers, de Gaulle could be approached regarding French civil affairs concerning Allied operations.[50] Such a plan seemed completely unworkable from de Gaulle's point of view and perhaps after discussions with Stimson, who also wished to push the matter, and McCloy, who had been an advocate of de Gaulle's for over a year, it demonstrated that the three were no longer willing to continue to sing a tune the president refused to hear. As FDR's close advisor Harry Hopkins remarked, "One more crack from McCloy to the boss about de Gaulle and McCloy leaves town."[51] While they were Republicans, serving in a Democrat's administration, Stimson and Donovan may not have felt the same pressure regarding a political future that McCloy and others would as Democrats; nevertheless, even their advice became self-muted by FDR's and Hull's feelings and fear of de Gaulle's intentions. So despite all their efforts, the recognition issue continued to fester.

But while the president and his senior officials still pondered how to recognize de Gaulle, Eisenhower's efforts to bring in French military command of the Résistance was getting into gear. However, it would not come without severe reshuffling and dislocation of Special Force Headquarters at the very time they were now executing their long planned use of the Maquis. Koenig had been officially recognized as the commander of the FFI on June 6 but was not given the resources to execute his mission. Obviously those resources already existed in the form of the SFHQ staff comprised of the British and American officers as well as his own Bloc Planning staff in what was now the Bureau Rensiegnements et d'Action Londres or BRAL, as the BCRA had moved to Algiers with the rest of the French provisional government. On June 9, Koenig informed Ike's chief of staff General Bedell Smith that he had received de Gaulle's approval to form a tripartite command under SHAEF, that he was declaring the creation l'Etat Major Forces Françaises de l'Intérieur (EMFFI), and that he had named French Air Force officer Colonel Henri Zeigler who used the pseudonym Colonel Vernon to be his chief of staff. Koenig's final statement to Bedell Smith was that he awaited Eisenhower's directives regarding the activities he desired from the Résistance.[52]

General Eisenhower's directive established that the priorities were first to "foster active Résistance to the Bridgehead area and in Brittany" and to be ready at a later date for larger scale guerrilla activity in Brittany. The second priority was to delay the movement of German troops to the battle area by focusing on the railway lines linking Normandy to the rest of France. Third, Eisenhower directed Koenig to attack the telecommunication system so the Germans and Vichy regime would continue experiencing difficulties coordinating their own actions. But the directive also reminded the French general that since the primary means of supply came from aircraft, he should "bear in mind the limitations of airlift" such as weight, weather, moon periods, enemy anti-aircraft capability, and the numbers of aircraft available for such work. Eisenhower also coordinated these issues with

General Wilson, commander in chief of the Mediterranean so he could coordinate SPOC toward SHAEF priorities.[53]

How much did SHFQ and its nascent parent for operations in France EMFFI manage to deliver to the Maquis in June and what were the results? The Maquis received 60 short tons of explosives, 9,937 Sten light machine guns, 8,800 pistols, 5,677 rifles, 5,505 Carbines, 2,110 Marlins, 932 Bazookas, 70 anti-tank mines, 2,142 Light machine guns, and 64,618 grenades. Accompanying the weapons were over 8 million rounds of 9mm ammunition, over 6 million rounds of .303 caliber rifle ammunition, 13,048 rockets for the bazookas, nearly 2 million rounds of Carbine ammunition, and 288 shoulder-fired anti-tank PIATs.[54] These arms and the weapons supplied previously had enabled the Maquis to make, as SHAEF touted somewhat gleefully, 500 railroad cuts in France due to FFI's planning with the Société Nationale des Chemins de Fer Français (SNCF) and the efforts around Plan Vert. Postwar inquiries into this have demonstrated that the SNCF, the FFI, and Plan Vert were indeed effective, achieving, for instance, 171 sabotage attempts in the eastern region—between Paris and the Belgium border—that produced 136 successfully cut tracks.[55] "The results achieved by the FFI have far surpassed the results generally expected" believed SFHQ, but "in spite of warnings, Résistance groups have been taking premature overt action before they were fully armed." Ominously, now the FFI and the civilian population suffered from reprisals "at the hands of superior German troops." Nevertheless the Special Force staff believed those enemy forces conducting the reprisals were then delayed from coming to the invasion area, seemingly failing to understand the reprisals were often carried out by soldiers under the MBF or reserve forces that were never going to be ordered to the front. But SHAEF no longer believed the number of aircraft available to supply the Résistance was the limiting factor. Instead, the limiting factors were aspects such as weather, moon phases, and enemy action; two of these SHAEF and its forces could do nothing about. The factors limiting the Maquis were "the lack of arms, stores, funds, and trained leaders." Furthermore, the report advised SHAEF that "SFHQ's original estimate of future supply requirements will be entirely inadequate."[56] The numbers of Maquis flocking to join Allied efforts against the Germans and Vichy overwhelmed SHAEF's ability to supply them, but not due to lack of aircraft; instead, meteorology and moon phases were the limiting factors.

SHAEF's growing faith in the Résistance brought a greater awareness of the risks the French Maquis were taking. With that understanding, they felt a greater obligation to supply more weapons. SHAEF directed the US Army Air Force to make up to 300 aircraft available for a single daylight operation code named Zebra. On June 18, SFHQ received confirmation from SHAEF of the aircraft availability and of logistical support from the British War Office; it promulgated its own orders to have all the containers ready for a massive mission on June 24. SFHQ representatives met with the US 8th Air Force planners to sort out the vast details of this complicated operation attempting to supply weapons to the Maquis of four separate SOE circuits: Marksman, Director, Salesman, and Trainer. SFHQ made arrangements to distribute the containers from five different depots to nine different 8th Air Force bases and also devised BBC messages for broadcast on the day before the aircraft departed. Weather forced a delay of a day, but on the June 25, the same day Team Hugh met with Dechelette and the Maquis leaders in Indre, 197 B-17s entered French airspace and flew to four different drop zones. Containers were dropped on their assigned drop zones by 176 aircraft; two aircraft were lost due to enemy action. The aircraft that turned back did so due to the lack of a good confirming signal from the ground. The Maquis and SFHQ personnel on the ground were relieved to get the weapons.[57] One American agent on the ground working in the R5 and R6 regions signaled, "Maquis thanks to U S Air Force for damned good show. When is the next?" However, that same agent painted a much bleaker picture on his return. Lieutenant Jean Claude Guiet, of the US Army, preferred to receive weapons from the British because American air drops became infamous for an apparent lack of concern about the rigging's quality. When the Americans dropped weapons, "we had to run all over the country to find the containers" and during the daylight operations 359 of the 1,296 containers suffered nearly a complete loss when their chutes failed to open. "The impression we got," stated this American officer, "was that the Americans did not care where they dropped the stuff or how they dropped it."[58] But the American Carpetbaggers, who had by this time gained proficiency in their work, did not do Operation Zebra. Instead, it was a first-ever drop for bomber crews, and the aircrews had little time to learn the tradecraft of flying at low altitude and dropping equipment rigged with parachutes instead of their usual load of bombs from high altitude. The fact that 75 percent of the containers actually survived intact is fairly remarkable given the short planning time and the complexity of such an operation.

One of the other targets for the 8th Air Force and SFHQ's efforts with Zebra was the Vercors and the growing numbers of Maquis now gathering on this rugged terrain east of the Rhone River about 100 kilometers south-southeast of Lyon. At this drop zone, the 35 aircraft dropped 450 containers. SFHQ received the signal from the Vercors organizers that they were "able to arm another 1500 men."[59] The F Section agent here was Francis Cammaerts who used the pseudonym Roger. A pacifist who joined SOE after his brother had been killed in action, he established the Jockey circuit in March of 1943. He left France later that year but returned during a harrowing stormy night when the aircraft he was to parachute from caught fire 250 miles from his intended drop zone. He and the crew all parachuted from an altitude of 10,000 feet while watching their aircraft burn, descending through the cloudy darkness, fog, and rain.[60] Despite the harrowing experience, he reestablished and matured his circuit, and the Résistance in the region had come to rely on him for his resourcefulness, courage, and imagination. On June 6, the Allies designated him second-in-command to the regional leader and ORA Colonel Zeller, who used the pseudonym Faiseau or sometimes Colonel Joseph. In the rapidly shifting leadership roles of the interior Résistance, Zeller had been appointed to take command of the FFI for both R1 and R2 by the CFLN in Algiers. They had lost their DMR, Laurent Burdet, code named Circonference, to arrest soon after D-Day and he remained imprisoned until around June 25.[61]

The loss of the DMR was only the beginning of the confusion. Having received the orders from London over the BBC for guerrilla warfare, the Region's FFI headquarters chief of staff, Colonel Descour, interpreted it to mean all-out guerrilla warfare. The F Section leader Cammaerts had to plead complete ignorance of a regional redoubt in the Vercors and the guerrilla actions of Plan Rouge as well as argue against the commonly held belief among the Maquis that the Allies were going to conduct a major air-borne operation on the Vercors plateau. As June wore on it brought the deployment of Jedburgh teams Veganin, Chloroform, and the subsequent inter-allied teams and an American Operational Group to the Vercors area. All this activity served to reinforce the mistaken but nevertheless hardening belief that the Allies were going to mount a major operation and that they should hold out.[62]

The team members of Veganin came up to the Vercors separately and from that point on remained apart. British Major Neil Marten had gone up to meet Cammaerts and the other Maquis leaders prior to the Zebra parachuting of supplies. The day after Zebra, French Captain Gaston Vuchot, using the nom de guerre C. L. Noir, climbed up to the growing and now fairly well-armed Maquis camp. Veganin's orders were to "harass to the maximum German communications" in the Rhone Valley with small groups of Maquis. The team had departed Algiers on the evening of June 8 with radioman Sergeant D. Gardner. But during the jump, Sergeant Gardner's static line failed and he was killed. After burying him with honors, the team spent the next two weeks meeting and assessing the situation in the region near the town of Beaupaire, north of Vercors. Before they arrived, the BBC messages provoked the local Maquis to attack various German installations for which the Germans called in air support. The Luftwaffe responded with great effect and elements of other ground units hunted for the "Terrorists" in the villages. Failing to find any, they burned the villages and raped the women instead.[63] The reprisals gripped the local residents in fear and they wished the Résistance would stop any more attacks. The FTP units, who had not participated in any of these attacks, then used local sentiments against their AS rivals, and Veganin, now just parachuting into this cauldron of revenge and hatred, had to rally the demoralized AS Maquis while Vuchot tried to organize the local Maquis units, including the FTP, but found the latter lacking in more than weapons, equipment, and know-how. The FTP had little sense of appreciation for military authority, but more dangerously, their way of life prior to Veganin's arrival was largely thieving and bartering for food while showing no interest whatsoever in fighting. Vuchot commented that their reputation in the region was poor and their sense of honor completely absent.[64] But having nothing else to work with, he tried to convince them of their new mission given by the Allied command. Additionally, he believed the two leaders of the various units had great courage and showed potential. Referring to one of his leaders at the end of Veganin's mission, Vuchot wrote with a dark sense of irony, "Malboux was remarkable brave and audacious...[but] was without scruple....He died heroically at the very moment when I was planning to have him arrested."[65] The other local Maquis commander was called Bozambo and had a reputation in the region for running a good Maquis group, one that could attract men to join it, but he was out for his own interests and Vuchot rarely got him to understand his part in the war.[66] Vuchot, a French soldier imbued with a deep sense of honor, forced himself to cajole, persuade, and plead with these two while he attempted to achieve his mission.

Notified of Gardner's death, SPOC deployed a replacement Jedburgh Team Dodge to reinforce Veganin with a W/T operator; they also sent American Captain Cyrus Manierre. A West Point graduate and boxing coach, Manierre had served as an instructor prior to becoming a Jedburgh. Canadian L. Durocher served as Veganin's new radio operator. Dodge parachuted in and met up with Vuchot on June 24 and accompanied him up into the Vercors. Vuchot had been told of the plans to make Vercors a Maquis stronghold and not only disagreed with this course of action but wished to inform the Maquis leaders on the plateau that it was counter to Allied orders. Taking Manierre and Durocher with him, they hiked the fifty miles up into the region and were reunited with Veganin's commander Major Neil Marten as well as Cammaerts. But up on the Vercors plateau, with a fresh supply of weapons for more than 1,000 Maquis, the attitude was different regarding the possibilities of Maquis action when compared to the Maquis Vuchot had to the north. When they arrived to discuss things with Cammaerts and the local FFI commander for the region, Colonel François Huet, who went by Colonel Hervieux, Vuchot could not persuade them to disperse. Unlike Veganin's original orders, they were convinced their orders were valid, had a higher priority than Veganin's, and that they needed Veganin's Maquis to join them on the plateau. Huet sought to create a redoubt capable of staging raids along the Rhône valley on large enemy units. Cammaerts informed Vuchot that the Allied Command in Algiers had made Cammaerts the senior Allied officer and that all the Jedburgh teams reported to him. That was not so much an issue, but then he proceeded to confirm the plans about the redoubt orders, that it took a higher priority than team Veganin's orders, and that he was to send the Maquis groups he had been in contact with up to him. Vuchot could not see the wisdom of any of this and looked to his British teammate for confirmation that Algiers had indeed altered Veganin's orders.[67]

But more was occurring than Vuchot could understand. Marten mysteriously said nothing to support his teammate and Cammaerts was firm and persuasive. In the end they compromised and Vuchot was allowed to keep two Maquis units but lost the argument about the validity of congregating at the Vercors as well as his radio operator, Sergeant Durocher. "With rage in my heart, I descended to the valley."[68] Now with no full-time communications link to Algiers or London, Vuchot and Manierre attempted to manage their FTP Maquis groups toward persistent harassment of the enemy.

They focused on sabotage, which Manierre specialized in, having been directed to focus his attention on the electrical plant at Beaumont-Monteux in the Isère department. By taking the plant out of action, they could deny the Germans the electrical power they would need in the region. Within the Maquis was a former electrical plant employee. Using his inside knowledge, they devised a plan and with about twenty-five men, approached the plant at night, killing the guards as silently as possible and then entered it. Manierre placed 30 kilos of explosives on the control panel and set the timer for 45 seconds and ran out of the area with his Maquis fleeing with him. When the charges exploded, not only was the control room destroyed, but so was the roof. There were numerous secondary explosions; large electrical hums and pops reflected and arced around the standing lines, and the shock of it all shattered windows of nearby homes. "We felt we had succeeded," stated Manierre dryly.[69]

Manierre spent the month of July conducting more sabotage and insisted on being part of the actions or leading them, even when Vuchot wanted him to remain behind. But Manierre insisted and often succeeded in his work, sabotaging troop trains, electrical facilities, and ambushing the enemy. He established relations with some of the local Armée Secrète

Maquis and they proved to be very effective. But the banditry continued. Manierre and Vuchot's greatest trouble was with a small group of FTP who called themselves the *equipe speciale* or "special team." Their job was to procure supplies for the rest of the area's Maquis. To them, this meant a license to steal, bribe, and vandalize. Having had enough, and with the persistent complaints of the local people, Manierre gathered a group who found them hiding out in a home. They refused to come out and a "brisk fire fight ensued, reminiscent of prohibition days in Chicago." The rifle fire and grenades killed them all, including the two women inside the house.[70]

With the Maquis swelling in the region to "six to seven thousand men," Vuchot and Manierre, now rejoined by Durocher, requested more Jedburghs to help arm and train them. Manierre continued with his sabotage work and went everywhere in civilian clothes. EMFFI organized another major daylight drop of weapons to the Vercors as well as several other drop zones. Operation Cadillac, similar in scope to Zebra, occurred on July 14, further infuriating the Germans but elating the French, who celebrated their Bastille Day, or national holiday, for the first time since 1940 with the belief that they once again would be free. The Veganin team, however, was conducting its own operations and, fortunately, the men were not on the plateau during the long battle that occurred from July 21 until August 6. However, the day before the Wehrmacht succeeded in sweeping the Maquis off the Vercors plateau, Captain Manierre's luck ran out. Stopped at a roadblock in what he believed to be a different Maquis group, he got out of his truck only to be handcuffed. While Manierre still believed it was all a mistake, the group found his US Army dog tags and their leader came up to him and chillingly said, "You Yankees must understand that there is one boss in France and that is Marshal Pétain." Captain Manierre now realized that he "was in the hands of the Milice."[71] It was August 5, ten days before the Allies would begin their second invasion of France with Operation Dragoon.

TEAMS IAN AND ANDY

As F Section agent Rene Maingard left Team Hugh in Indre, he arrived in Vienne and asked for a Jedburgh team for that area. On June 14, SFHQ drew up the team's orders to deploy to Vienne and work with Maingard.

Together they were to make sure that "the general uprising must not take place" as well as make it clear there would be no supplies for such efforts. Instead, Ian was to shut down the Bordeaux-Poitiers-Tours and Bordeaux-Niort-Saumur railway lines in SHAEF's effort to block enemy reinforcements. The orders also stated that Ian should radio back to SFHQ about the possibility of controlling a large enough area to support daylight drops. With planning under way for Zebra, headquarters wanted to get an assessment of doing something similar for Ian when it could be arranged.[72] On June 18, 1944, the Carpetbaggers attempted to take Team Ian to France; however, the aircrew could not find the drop zone and refused to parachute Ian blind. They attempted it again, taking off at 10:39 PM on June 20. This time the crew experienced good weather all the way to the drop zone and clearly saw the bonfires and code letters from the ground; they dropped the team and their equipment in two passes.[73] But for one of the Jedburghs, the drop went poorly. W/T operator American First Sergeant Lucien Bourgoin's parachute opened late and at an altitude of 400 to 500 feet; every moment was critical. Fortunately, Bourgoin landed safely; however, he found his radios severely damaged. Team leader American Major John Gildee and second-in-command French Captain Alex Desfarges, using the nom de guerre Yves Delormes, arrived in fine shape. Maingard's reception team met Ian, collected its equipment, and drove the team to a farm serving as Maingard's headquarters. The team got off to a very slow start organizing the local Maquis as their damaged radios hindered the effort. Bourgoin did partially fix one of the W/T sets, but for nearly ten days the only communication was via Maingard's radio.[74]

Special Force Headquarters (SFHQ) dropped ninety containers of arms prior to Ian's arrival, while Maingard related information to SFHQ concerning the area's Maquis. SFHQ briefed Ian prior to departure of three groups numbering "150 highly disciplined men," another 1,500-man group in the former unoccupied zone, and a third 2,000-man group in the former occupied zone. Ian was to train and organize these men into an effective force while also keeping the Bordeaux-Poitiers-Tours and the Bordeaux-Niort-Saumur railroads cut. Ian deployed with a modified Jedburgh kit with fewer Brens and carbines and took more special rail charges to enable more sabotage, and enable guerrilla activity. Maingard hoped to send them toward Chatellerault in northern Vienne giving them an area adjacent to Hugh, but unfortunately, heavy German activity caused him to change his mind, and instead Maingard sent them to southern Vienne and northern Charente.[75]

On June 22, SFHQ sent a message to Ian warning them, "German Infantry Division moving north Toulouse-Normandy. Keep us posted movement. Attack wherever possible." Unfortunately, Ian's damaged radios failed to receive the message and the team spent the next week attempting to get a strong reception from their W/T. Nevertheless, Ian organized the sabotage of the Bordeaux-Paris railroad and kept it cut until June 26. The Jedburghs also arranged to sabotage charcoal factories vital for German vehicles and attacked locomotive supply pumps along the railroad to Paris. When the Germans quickly repaired the railway damage, Ian asked SFHQ to bomb it.[76]

While pursuing minor operations, Ian conducted regional reconnaissance and attempted to arm and train the swelling Maquis ranks. As they traveled from village to village they found groups and leaders willing to rally and recognize Ian's role as a command link to SHAEF and de Gaulle. Working an approximately one hundred square mile area south of Poitiers, Ian placed a nucleus of Maquis in villages encircling the area. Using seven villages on crossroads, Ian created what they hoped would be a safe perimeter where they could train more Maquis and run drop zones. Another group of Maquis specialized in demolition and sabotage; called Sape, they ran their own drop zone, keeping themselves supplied. Major Gildee possessed great organizational skills and set training schedules, controlled supplies, and managed the drop zones. French Captain Desfarges made a point to show the French people his presence and "spoke to the assembled populations to encourage them and request their aid for future actions."[77]

As Maquis units received arms and trained and the sabotage unit became ready, they struck out to attack. From July 20 on, they turned their perimeter into a "fortified bastion" with tree barricades, masonry, and mined bridges. Ian also put officers and NCOs from the French regular and reserve army into their four battalions, which swelled to 6,000 men, freeing the Ian team to oversee the entire effort. The team soon became a "regimental commander," directing operations while leaving supply, discipline, and administration up to the separate Maquis "battalions." Team Ian arranged communications with telephone lines, motorcycle couriers, and carrier pigeons. Short of money required to carry on operations, Ian arranged a no-interest 12 million franc loan through the Free French from the Bank of Algiers. Also, some of the local French gendarmeries worked with the Maquis to set up police in their communities. Moreover, Ian recruited four doctors, set up two hospitals, and arranged for SFHQ to send medical supplies. All these events increasingly eliminated Vichy authority as well as Germany's.[78]

On July 20, an estimated 800 Germans broke through the defenses and lodged themselves in Champagne-Mouton, a village the Maquis had retaken. The enemy set up barbed wire, dug ditches, and fortified their positions. Taking numerous hostages, the Germans threatened to shoot hostages and burn the town if attacked. From Champagne-Mouton, they sent out patrols for five days and attempted to reconnoiter Maquis positions. Enemy columns probed the perimeter at other locations, but when met with strong organized Résistance, the Germans disengaged. However, the Germans managed to cut Ian's telephone network, causing other sectors to lose communications and slowing reinforcements, making a Maquis counterattack impossible. On July 26, Germany launched a 400-soldier attack near Ambernac, but as local Maquis were not yet fully armed they withdrew several kilometers leaving the village to the enemy. The Germans pillaged the town and shot civilians, but soon Ian arrived with reinforcements and forced the enemy back to Confolens. Over the next few days, more forceful attacks continued and Ian considered a withdrawal to Dordogne as their entire position "was at stake." Nevertheless, the inspired and spirited young Maquis fought extremely hard and despite little training and having only small arms, managed to use the blown bridges over the Vienne, woods, and other natural defenses to bog down the enemy offensive.[79]

On 1 August, Ian reported "Four days fighting near Champagne routed Germans," and they claimed the action cost "30 Germans killed and 3 prisoners. 2 Maquis killed and 10 wounded." News of a larger battle followed the next day and Ian requested more weapons, ammunition, and "shoes and

Jedburgh teams with approximate operating locations, June–September, 1944.
(Erin Greb Cartography)

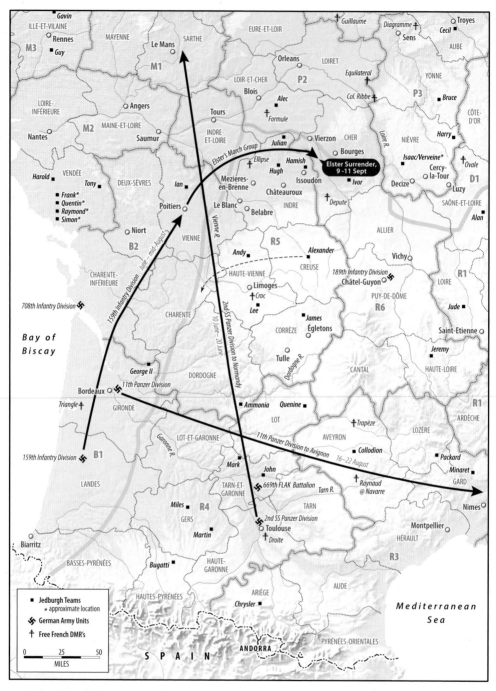

Jedburgh locations and actions described in Chapters 6 and 8. (Erin Greb Cartography)

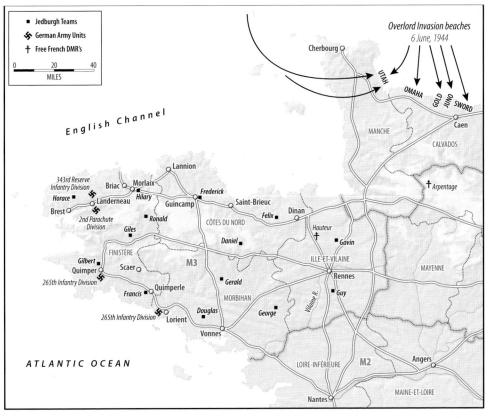

Legend:
- Jedburgh Teams
- German Army Units
- Free French DMR's

0   20   40
MILES

Overlord Invasion beaches
6 June, 1944

Cherbourg

UTAH
OMAHA
GOLD
JUNO
SWORD
Caen

MANCHE
CALVADOS

English Channel

Lannion

343rd Reserve
Infantry Division
Briac   Morlaix
Horace   Hilary
Landerneau
Brest
2nd Parachute
Division   Ronald
Giles

Frederick
Guincamp   Saint-Brieuc
Felix   Dinan
CÔTES DU NORD
Hauteur
Gavin

Daniel

FINISTÈRE

M3

ILLE-ET-VILAINE

Gilbert
Quimper
265th Infantry Division
Scaer
Gerald
MORBIHAN

Rennes
Guy

MAYENNE

Francis   Quimperle

265th Infantry Division   Lorient

Douglas
George

Vilaine R.

Vonnes

ATLANTIC OCEAN

LOIRE-INFÉRIEURE

M2

Angers

MAINE-ET-LOIRE

Nantes

Arpentage

Jedburgh locations and actions described in Chapter 7. (Erin Greb Cartography)

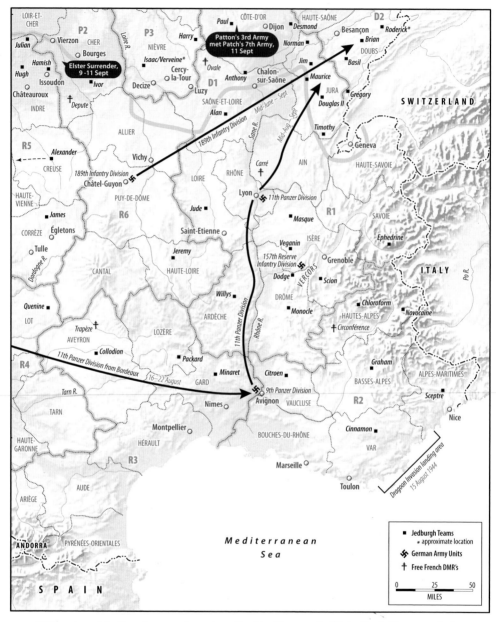

Events and Jedburgh operations described in Chapter 8. (Erin Greb Cartography)

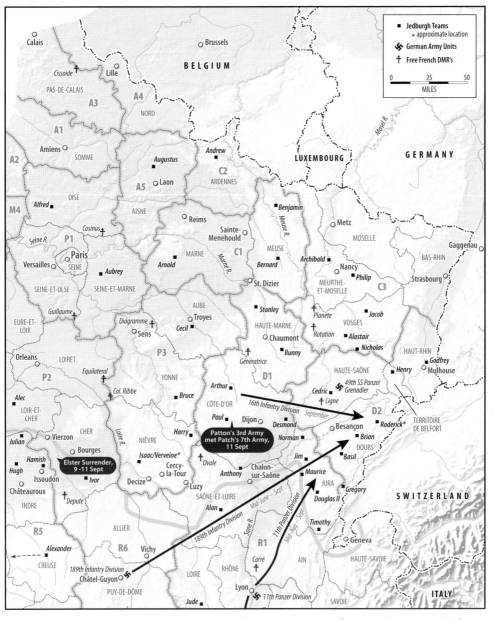

Events and Jedburgh operations described in Chapter 9. (Erin Greb Cartography)

General Charles de Gaulle and General Dwight David Eisenhower have a brief meeting in France just before Paris was recaptured from the Germans. Courtesy of the U.S. Army.

General Eisenhower and General Koenig pose for photos with other Allied generals celebrating the liberation of Paris. Courtesy of the U.S. Army.

Generals Eisenhower, Bradley, and Koenig chat while meeting in Paris after its liberation from Germany. Courtesy of the U.S. Army.

General Koenig, Whitney Shepardson of the OSS, and Colonel Joseph F. Haskell visited the American Army Air Force unit responsible for dropping supplies and agents into occupied France. General Koenig awarded medals to these American airmen that day. Courtesy of Julia Haskell Paine.

Maurice Bourgès-Maunoury served as a regional military delegate in southern France, then served as the leader for the entire southern zone of France during the summer of 1944. Like many Maquis and Resistance leaders, he went into politics after the war and became Prime Minister of France in 1957. Courtesy of the British National Archives.

Victor Gough started his war service in the Auxillary Units, whose mission was to conduct an insurgency against the Germans if they succeeded in invading and taking over Britain. He later joined the Jedburghs, parachuted into occupied France, and was captured and executed by the Gestapo. He was talented in drawing and art, and his design became the Jedburgh insignia. Courtesy of the British National Archives.

Major Arthur Clutton worked tirelessly to bring about the surrender of Major General Elster's forces south of the Loire River in September 1944. He also sought in vain for the French resistance to get the credit. Courtesy of the British National Archives.

Major Colin Ogden-Smith was one of the few Jedburghs to have considerable combat experience before becoming a Jedburgh. He was killed in action in southern Brittany on August 31, 1944. Courtesy of the British National Archives.

Eugene Deschelette, code named Ellipse, served as the Free French Military Delegate in central France. Overcoming challenge after challenge, his area conducted the best insurgency against the Germans of all the Free French military delegates. Unlike so many other French Resistance leaders, he led a quiet civilian life after the war and stayed out of politics. Courtesy of the British National Archives.

Jedburgh First Lieutenant John K. Singlaub, second from left, in a posed photo in a London safe house. Courtesy of the U.S. Army.

SOE file photo of Eric Mockler-Ferryman. Mockler-Ferryman ran all SOE operations that supported Eisenhower's SHAEF operations in France. He had also served under Eisenhower in North Africa, until relieved after Kasserine Pass, when President Roosevelt demanded that a British officer be fired as well. Despite that, he admired and appreciated Eisenhower's abilities and leadership. Courtesy of the British National Archives.

Jedburgh Team Ivor just before loading onto their B-24 flight into France for their mission. American First Sergeant Lewis Goddard, left, sporting a beard, would be dead by the next morning due to a faulty parachute. Courtesy of the U.S. Army.

Team Chloroform and local maquis in southeast France. Courtesy of Jean Louis Perquin.

Team Frederick: French Lieutenant Paul Bloch-Auroch, American Sergeant Robert Kehoe, and British Major Adrian Wise. Courtesy of the U.S. Army.

An undated photo from the drop zone of a resupply drop of weapons and other supplies into France. Courtesy of the U.S. Army.

General Eisenhower left, Winston Churchill (partially obscured), and General Charles de Gaulle meet for a conference at Eisenhower's headquarters just before the commencement of Operation Overlord. Churchill and de Gaulle had just had a very tense meeting, and now Eisenhower was going to have his turn. Courtesy of the U.S. Army.

President Roosevelt finally agreed to meet Charles de Gaulle. This was only their second meeting during the war, and it occurred far too late to solve Eisenhower's dilemma. Preparing him with an impromptu discussion just moments before their private discussion was Major General William Donovan and Colonel Joseph Haskell, with files full of photos of air dropped supplies and information on the role the French resistance was playing in France's liberation. Courtesy of the U.S. Army.

British Lieutenant Colonel Dudley G. L. Carleton-Smith (right) and British Jedburgh Training Commandant Lieutenant Colonel G. Richard Musgrave next to him in a formation at Milton Hall celebrating Bastille Day, July 14, 1944. Courtesy of Major General Sir Michael Carleton-Smith.

socks." The Germans finally retreated toward the south, but the attack killed an estimated 100 Maquis and an estimated 200 Germans. However, the determined Wehrmacht tried again on August 2 to penetrate the French perimeter. Team Ian hoped to spring a trap near the village of Champagne-Mouton but instead drove into an ambush.[80]

Captain Desfarges drove the team along with Louis Mondinaud and information agent André Very of the Maquis group Bir Hacheim. In their four-door Citroen they carried around 1,800,000 francs, their radios, and the BBC code phrases for their upcoming parachute drops. As they arrived in the village on this warm day, they heard a woman yell, "Malheureux, les Boches!" It was "too late!" as Desfarges later wrote, for as they rounded a curve and tried to stop, a German column opened fire with automatic weapons and small arms. Desfarges, wounded in the cheek, put the car in a maneuver protecting the passengers and everyone attempted to return fire. But the car was now immobilized and Mondinaud severely wounded. Everyone left the vehicle darting into available cover behind a house and in alleys. Desfarges, Gildee, and Very made an escape through a barn adjacent to the street. Captain Desfarges found a window at the other end of the barn and went through. Major Gildee, a bigger man, needed to be pulled from one side and pushed from the other to squeeze through. Sergeant Bourgoin realized the codes, money, radio, and radio crystals remained in the Citroen and returned to get them. But the Germans cut him down before he escaped a second time. The three survivors made it to a farm outside the village and found twenty Maquis, then made their way back to the truck to retrieve their equipment and find out where their comrades were; "10 meters from the car we were again spotted by the Germans" and they retreated into a wooded area, covering themselves with dirt and debris. Fortunately, the Germans had no dogs and the men came out of hiding after the Wehrmacht left twenty-three hours later.[81]

Bourgouin's body remained near the trees he attempted to enter for cover, while the Germans looked for the others. Unable to run, Mondinaud could not get away fast enough and a German soldier struck him in the head delivering a fatal blow. After the German troops left to look for the others, a Pleuville woman walked over to Bourgoin's body and covered his face with a handkerchief; local men came and moved the bodies into the church. The two were buried the next day in the church cemetery. Gildee and Desfarges, failing to retrieve their radio and other equipment, attempted to pull their operation back together but were bereft of their comrade and vital communication with London. Years later, Desfarges remarked, "I never saw Gildee show any emotion, but when the Sergeant was killed I thought he'd never stop crying." Unable to radio London for six days, the team finally found their wireless set at a farm of a former French Mercantile Marine radio officer and sent, "Our automobile attacked by column of 400 Germans at Poeuvill [*sic*]. Bourgoin and chauffeur killed." The message also explained the loss of all their gear, requested an air drop to replace the missing equipment, money, and gasoline and an additional arms for 1,000 men.[82]

SOUTHWESTERN FRANCE

One of SHAEF's major interests was in the 2nd SS Panzer "Das Reich" Division. The unit was in southern France reconstituting, training replacement soldiers, and resting after years of murderously difficult combat against the Red Army in the east. On June 6, this armored division of roughly 19,000 soldiers was located in Montauban, France 50 kilometers north of Toulouse and approximately 800 kilometers from Normandy.[83] Another of the armored units in southern France was the 11th Panzer Division located near Bordeaux. But both of these units were under their normal strength. In fact, the influx of new soldiers and the shortages of replacements in soldiers, non-commissioned officers, and officers make it questionable how good the quality of the unit was, given the lack of experience of a majority of their soldiers. The 11th Panzer Division had no more than 50 percent of its soldiers and approximately 45 percent of its officers and NCOs when it arrived in Bordeaux in April of 1944. The 2nd SS Panzer "Das Reich" Division suffered from similar issues and had to integrate a high number of Alsatian soldiers into their ranks. These two armored divisions, while feared by SHAEF planners and certainly capable of action, were not the units they had been. Nevertheless, the 2nd SS Panzer Division's Commander, Heinz Lammerding, received orders to move to Normandy on June 8 and directed his command to smash the "gangs" and assert the authority of Germany and the Vichy government.[84]

In an effort to delay and impede their movements, Special Projects Operations Center in Algiers deployed Jedburgh teams Quinine on June 8, Ammonia on June 10, and Bugatti on June 20. Team Quinine, comprised of British Major Sir Tommy MacPherson, Frenchman (but in the US Army) Michel de Bourbon de Parme, who used the nom de guerre Michel Bourdon, and British radio operator Oliver Brown arrived to great celebration at their drop zone. Since MacPherson parachuted into combat wearing his highlander kilt, one *résistant* called out to his comrades that there is a French officer here, and "he's brought his wife!"[85] But MacPherson, who had been in the war for three years by then and had experience behind the lines and as a POW, found that few in this Maquis group were really eager to fight against the Germans. Determined to do something, Quinine set about sabotaging whatever they believed would do some damage to the Germans while demonstrating to the locals that the Allies were present and were fighting. SPOC directed MacPherson to contact Droite, the DMR for the region whose real name was Bernard Schlumberger. However, no one MacPherson spoke to had ever heard of him.[86]

Instead the teams worked with F Section agents such as George Starr and Philippe Liewers, also known as Geoffrey Staunton, who were running circuits in the region, had built up groups of Maquis and operatives they could trust, and had organized to execute Plan Vert, Tortue, and the others when given the signal on June 5. Since the Jedburghs were not inserted until D-Day and after, and since it took time to establish a team's operations due to smashed radios, injured or dead Jedburghs, independent Maquis leaders and groups, and pursuit by Milice, Gendarmes, Wehrmacht, and Gestapo, it all became too much to overcome in such a short time. And since the Jedburghs were always designed as an operational reserve, asking them to literally jump into the situation, ignorant of that locality's ability to conduct operations, makes Ammonia's primary mission of the immediate "destruction of communication and harassing troop movements between Brive and Montauban" seem unrealistic. For instance, on June 13, Sergeant Jack Berlin of Ammonia radioed to SPOC that "2 SS is between Perigeux–Brive. Resistance GROUPS attacking. Need supplies and ammunition urgently."[87] Ambushing and delaying the 2nd SS "Das Reich" Division was accomplished, and Ammonia and Quinine participated in the effort, but more than likely it would have happened whether they had been there or not. The multiplicity of commands, both Allied and French, both exterior and interior, stymied unity of action until Jedburgh teams, DMRs, and FFI commanders on the scene could agree on who would be issuing orders and who would be taking them. But in the meantime the individual teams, often acting under the aegis of one of the BCRA plans, were what provoked the first few days of Maquis operations.

As Ammonia's commander American Captain Benton Austin had Berlin radio back to SPOC, "Local organization good but regional bad. Too many chiefs." Too many chiefs were indeed an issue and the regional DMR structure was for this part of France in complete disarray. Schlumbarger had been appointed DMR for R3 and R4 and was sending messages to EMFFI from the Lot department wishing to get help from Koenig to publicly assert his authority in the region. In other messages he described attacks on Germans during the first week of June and his hope of liberating the area before the Allies arrived. However, his area was large and he had to play catch-up with others who had been there longer. In many cases, the F Section agent, such as George Starr who had been there for over a year, or even Pearl Witherington, to the north, who had to recreate a circuit on the remains of her arrested boss's foundation, had a far easier time than EMFFI's own man who had just parachuted in days before the invasion with little regional knowledge.[88]

All three Jedburgh teams foundered to some degree attempting to harass these major German armored divisions, but they arrived too late to measurably impact or improve on what the Maquis would have done without them. While the 2nd SS "Das Reich" Division did take longer to arrive in Normandy than it would have had the Résistance not interfered, it is difficult, if not impossible to credit Jedburgh operations for slowing it down. Instead, as Max Hastings and Peter Lieb have shown, the decision by the

Germans themselves to deal with the Maquis along the way was essential and to some degree self-imposed. That decision was provoked due to the actions of Maquis, or as the Germans called them, "terrorists," prior to D-Day. The provocations that continued to occur after D-Day only heightened the SS Division's Nazi ideological sensitivities regarding the Maquis' communists and the FTP's sloganeering. Such activities drew in the SS who did not like such taunting. The ideologically minded Germans could not allow them to continue.[89]

Therefore, having not yet received orders to proceed to Normandy, Lammerding dispatched one of his battalions to strike "immediately and brutally against the terrorist bands." They sought to make the local population too afraid to support the Maquis. In the village of Oradour-sur-Glane on June 10, about 22 kilometers from Limoges, the SS arrived searching for the Maquis who had killed one of their comrades. Finding none, they shot all the men in the village and with the women and children in the village church, burned the structure to the ground. To make sure that all died, they threw grenades into the burning church and fired at whoever escaped the inferno. Within four hours, 642 villagers were massacred.[90]

DE FACTO RECOGNITION

In Washington, Donovan had shifted again from his previous position in his June 15 memo where he recommended that de Gaulle be treated as a senior military official only. On July 4, with de Gaulle's visit finally scheduled later in the week, Donovan sent President Roosevelt Ramon Guthrie's assessment on France and an account of the looming problems regarding recognition and the costs of continuing the current policy. Guthrie, a Harvard French literature professor before the war, argued that the situation called for a clear statement from the president on what the United States sought to achieve because the press reports, speculation, and rumors were persisting and doing real damage to Franco-US relations. Also, Guthrie noted that most of the French in Algiers "fail to see the validity of the American contention that the Committee does not represent French opinion." He pointed out that the committee may be the fairest embodiment of French public opinion and sentiments in its history.[91] Furthermore, the FFI's impact and American operations such as Zebra were having an effect beyond French drop zones. When Colonel Haskell's report of the event got to Donovan, the OSS director showed it to the Joint Chiefs and sent a copy to the president. It included all the detailed planning information, the locations of the drops, weapons provided to the French, and even dramatic photos that may have been taken by Haskell himself.[92] But Donovan, Marshall, and Roosevelt received a firsthand account as well due to the fact that Colonel Haskell came to Washington, evidently to bring his report personally. On Thursday, July 6, General Donovan and Haskell appeared on the president's appointment calendar, apparently as last-minute additions to the president's schedule. It is not recorded what they discussed, but with only fifteen minutes allotted to them, it could not have been a detailed conversation.[93] It was a fairly busy day for FDR with de Gaulle arriving for the first time later that afternoon. OSS Bern had also recently sent some of the first reports of the 2nd SS "Das Reich" Division's atrocities and Donovan also sent those on to FDR. However, none of it brought the president any further toward recognizing the CFLN or de Gaulle. The meeting would be about less concrete issues.

But while Roosevelt treated it as something less than a state visit, de Gaulle, with a great deal of public support and sympathy, maintained a schedule that had all the trappings of a visiting head of state. He paid a visit to General John J. Pershing in his Walter Reid hospital room and their discussion of Germany's future made the papers. He paid his respects to George Washington at Mount Vernon and the Tomb of the Unknown Soldier at Arlington Cemetery. He arrived at the White House at 4:30, three and a half hours after Donovan and Haskell met with Roosevelt. Photos were taken and the next day he arrived for a formal luncheon after a one-hour discussion and working session with the president.[94]

Their discussions that day and during the following day were not focused on civil administration in France and other matters of immediate concern as Stimson had hoped, but rather on the fruits of victory and the international system Roosevelt hoped to achieve. "It was by light touches that he sketched in his notions, and so skillfully that it was difficult to contradict this artist, this seducer, in any categorical way."[95] Indeed de Gaulle wrote how the still unwinding Allied victory, which he fully realized had been brought about by the United States and Great Britain, fueled FDR's and America's dangerous optimism. The continuing and assured successes created a rising sense of belief in America that the nation must be involved in the world instead of remaining isolated as it had been in the past. De Gaulle believed it meant that the United States would now pass "from one extreme to the other, it was a permanent system of intervention that [FDR] intended to institute by international law."[96]

After a trip to New York and a stop in Canada, de Gaulle headed back to Algiers where it was apparent to all that the CFLN was indeed the legitimate authority in France in territories controlled by Allied armies. At the local and regional levels, the provisional government's organization was planned and in most instances the personnel named. Since the summer of 1943, the CFLN had worked on a structure to seize power from Vichy at the moment of liberation. Each department in France would be governed by a committee comprised of local resistance leaders and notables overseen at the regional level by a kind of super-prefect. Most of the appointed leaders of the Committees Departmental de la Libération (CDL) and the commissaries de la République were from the Résistance.[97] Of course, this had all happened while FDR and the State Department insisted on participating in how and who within the Résistance would participate in the process, and when they could not do that, they hindered it at every opportunity. The resisters all agreed that this was an issue for the French—alone. As combat operations continued through June and July, and the first localities saw the implementation of the CDLs and the emergence of the regional commissaires, US and British Civil Affairs soldiers realized their work was going to be far lighter than originally planned. The Résistance, however, continued to be perplexed by America's policy toward it. The underground newspaper *Libération* had a short article on the bottom of the last page in its edition immediately after de Gaulle's visit. The article scoffed at FDR's announcement of the CFLN as the "de Facto authority" in liberated France. Such terms were confusing given the circumstances the article's author believed. Searching for the reason why, the writer attributed Roosevelt's persistent confusion on the matter to Alexis Léger, discussed in Chapter 4, for influencing him far too much. But more important, it stated in muted glee, "Adieu, therefore to the shadow of this AMGOT which did not have time to approach our shores."[98] The Résistance had long worked for its Revolution and recently coalesced on how to achieve it. At that moment in France it sought, via the Maquis to fight for it, and through the CDLs to begin the political path toward their France. The Allies, no matter how much they had done and were doing, were not to be a part of such an intimate matter.

CONCLUSION

The halting military progress the Jedburghs made toward Eisenhower's aim of harassing the movement of German reinforcements to Normandy was a manifestation of more than battlefield confusion and difficulty. Enemy action, Gestapo arrests, lack of resources and airlift, and the physical limitations such as the weather and the moon's phases all played a role. But the political ambiguity had its impact too. President Roosevelt's delay and "de facto recognition" at the Allied level reflected down at the military level in the still consolidating and not yet fully formed EMFFI, and at the local level with the Jedburghs striving for local unity of action among markedly different Maquis groups. Where there were competing local objectives or groups, Eugene Dechelette's successes in R5 began to mollify them. Teams Hugh, Hamish, and Ian were unfortunately parachuted into this chasm of political ambiguity but would assist in sewing the gaps together. What they found was greater enthusiasm embodied in more Maquis than they could train and equip, but now that they had arrived and were face to face with those wishing to fight, the teams immediately sought to do so, even when their orders were to discourage such widespread guerrilla operations. Ambiguity effected clarity of action and purpose at each plane of political expression and each node from the strategic to the tactical. While the American, British, and French Allied staff officers continued to plan and while their comrades in operational units worked to execute missions along these seams of sovereignty, their clarity of action was brought into stark focus by the presence and effects of the Wehrmacht, Gestapo, and Milice.

The unexpected and overwhelming numbers in the Maquis proved the Special Operations Executive (SOE) planner correct when he remarked that the Résistance was an unpredictable and nebulous force, but he believed it would be small, not the high and swelling numbers that materialized after June 6. Not wishing to have this occur and getting constant reports of reprisals, Eisenhower and l'Etat Major Forces Françaises de l'interieur (EMFFI) were forced to spend a great deal of their message traffic dampening enthusiasm, directing Jedburghs and others in France to refrain from anything other than sabotage and small-scale hit-and-run activities. Therefore, the liaison the Jedburghs thought they would be doing—specifically, exhorting the people to join the Allied cause—became instead trying to control the growing numbers, keep a check on their passions, and not dampen their morale so much they would not contribute when needed.

As July ended, Allied forces had painfully and slowly established themselves in Normandy, and now American General Omar Bradley was planning his next move. Becoming the commander of the 12th Army Group on August 1, he had to take the ports on the Brittany peninsula that were required to sustain the Allied armies. He also had the task of preparing to move east toward Germany. On the western wing of the Allied line, he sought to punch a hole through the portions of the German 2nd SS Division, the 352nd Infantry Division, and the 3rd Parachute Division directly on his front. This "Breakout" began around July 25. It would be reinforced by General George S. Patton's newly constituted 3rd US Army that shifted from its deception mission, fooling Hitler into fearing an attack on the northeastern coast of France at the Pas de Calais, into one of very real combat. Embedded in the 3rd Army was a Special Force Detachment led by Lieutenant Colonel Robert I. "RIP" Powell. His unit's role was to coordinate Patton's actions with the Résistance directly behind the enemy it faced. But the highest priority of Koenig, Powell, and all those within the EMFFI sphere was the liberation of Brittany and the advancement of Patton's forces to the Atlantic ports. That mission had been developing since D-Day and is the subject of the next chapter.

7

The Free French Battle for Brittany and Eisenhower Battles for the Free French

The same night that the Jedburgh team Hugh left for Indre and Team Harry deployed to Morvan, two Jedburgh teams were to depart for Brittany. Eisenhower made Brittany a high priority and Special Force Headquarters (SFHQ) and General Koenig focused a great deal of their attention on the peninsula over the months of June, July, and into August when it was finally liberated. Winning Brittany back from the Wehrmacht would protect the Allies' western flank and provide them the vital ports they needed to sustain their forces in France. Furthermore, taking those ports away from Germany meant denying the Kriegsmarine direct access to the Atlantic, further hobbling its ability to sink Allied shipping. For the same reason, Brittany was vital to Germany and Hitler had directed that the ports be made into fortresses, or *festungs*, so that they could hold out indefinitely. Therefore, pulling the Wehrmacht forces toward the two ends of Brittany to repel the invasion coming from the east and to hold the ports in the west often clogged the roads with moving troops. The relative closeness of Allied airfields in England to Brittany, compared to central or eastern France, allowed air power to have a greater operational influence with both daylight close air support and the night time re-supply air drops. Also, due to its proximity, the Supreme Headquarters Allied Expeditionary Forces (SHAEF) never had to be concerned with handing off portions of Brittany to Allied Forces Headquarters (AFHQ), and therefore SFHQ never contended with Special Projects Office Command (SPOC) for directing the Résistance there. But SFHQ was blinded by the Gestapo's ability to continually disrupt the networks of the Special Operations Executive (SOE) and Bureau Centrale Renseignements d'Action (BCRA) so that there was no operational contact in Brittany on D-Day. However, the SFHQ and BCRA planners did benefit, in a way, from Brittany's having only one major resistance organization and it was the Franc-Tireurs et Partisans Français (FTP). While other groups, such as Libération-Nord, had a presence and some leadership there, they had very few armed Maquis groups. Therefore, the Jedburghs in Brittany rarely had to contend with politics and polemics as they attempted to organize the Maquis into tactical operations. Last, the distinct culture and history of Brittany played a role as many of the villagers and farmers did not speak French but instead used their Breton language, so the French Jedburghs who came from the region proved critical, as did educated Breton schoolteachers and professionals who spoke French well. All these issues determined the nature of the war in Brittany and shaped it in different ways from the other parts of France.

Lieutenant General Wilhelm Fahrmbacher in Pontivy commanded the Wehrmacht's presence in Brittany, largely in the form of the XXV Armee Korps. He reported to the 7th Armee OberKommando commanded by General Oberst Friedrich Dollmann in Le Mans.[1] When the Allied invasion occurred in Normandy, General Dollman's forces shared the weight of the attack along with the 15th Armee OberKommando in Lille as the dividing line for the two forces fell nearly in the middle of the Normandy invasion beaches. Both these commanders reported to Armee Gruppe B commanded by General Feld Marshal Erwin Rommel, who reported to General Feld Marshal Gerhardt von Rundstedt, commander of OB West in Paris. Forced to pull combat forces from Brittany at the onset of the Allied invasion, Dollman left Fahrmbacher largely responsible for the defense of the peninsula along with the Kommandeur der Sicherheitspolizei und des SD at Rennes commanded by Obersturmbannführer Hartmut Pulmer.[2] Both Fahrmbacher and Pulmer had been involved in Germany's eastern campaigns, with Pulmer conducting Einsatzkommando actions in Poland.[3] These two had their views of how to deal with irregular forces and they believed the law and justice required the harshest of measures. But so did the Ober Kommando der Wehrmacht (OKW), and on March 4 it declared that partisans involved in sabotage or irregular warfare were not to be taken prisoner.[4] The implication of what to do with them was clear.

Fahrmbacher's combat forces remaining for Brittany were largely comprised of the 266th, 343rd, and 265th Infantrie Divisions with the 2nd Fallschirmjäger Division in reserve.[5] The 2nd Fallschirmjäger Division was reconstituting and not yet at full strength, and its commander, Lieutenant General Ramcke, had not yet arrived. Accordingly, it was placed at Landerviseau at the peninsula's extreme western edge. The readiness and combat capability of all these units was similar to others in France in that they lacked men and equipment that would, under different circumstances, make their consideration for combat use questionable. The 265th Division, for example, reported only 221 Officers, 1,651 NCOs, and 7,513 soldiers along with their allotment of 341 foreign soldiers, for a total of 9,726, and its commander rated his division suitable for defense only. Not only was Berlin unable to supply the necessary strength in men to their divisions, but pre-invasion combat had also taken a toll. During the month of May the 265th Division had suffered eight killed, two wounded, and one missing due to "energetic action against the terrorists." The 343rd Division commander did not make any comments limiting his capabilities as he was not in such a weakened state, but he did note eight killed, four wounded, and three missing due to enemy action while being short a total of 110 soldiers at the end of May.[6] But in addition to these somewhat weakened Wehrmacht divisions, for controlling the civilians, Fahrmbacher could call on Pulmer's Gestapo and the Feldgendarmerie units scattered around Brittany at St. Malo, Brest, Lorient, and St. Nazaire.

Special Force Headquarters' plan for Brittany had been thought out before D-Day and it consisted of dividing the peninsula into a northern and southern half. Each zone would have a detachment of the 4th French Parachute Brigade which was now a part of the Special Air Service (SAS). Commanded by French Lieutenant Colonel Bourgoin, this unit was to parachute into Brittany and establish operating bases for the Maquis to create a focal point for the region's Résistance. Bourgoin was about forty-five years old and a First World War veteran who had lost an arm in combat. With only one arm, special arrangements had to be made with four of his soldiers jumping with him in order to break his fall.[7] One Jedburgh team was to accompany each detachment and serve as a liaison with the area's Maquis; however, they would report to Bourgoin in the field while having their own radio and command link back to SFHQ for airlift allocations and orders. Since the SAS reported to SHAEF and later General Koenig when working with the Résistance, the problems inherent in a bifurcated arrangement like this may not have seemed too difficult to the SFHQ planners, but the teams tasked with this mission struggled with the problem straight away. Team George, consisting of American Captain Paul Cyr, French Captain Philippe Rageneau using the name Philippe Erard, and French radioman Pierre Gay, who used the nom de guerre Christien Lejeune, were directed to accompany the SAS and the regional military delegates (DMRs) for Regions M3 and M4, who were Alain Willk (Fonction) and Maurice Barthélemy (Hauteur), and establish a base named Dingson. In their orders they were told of the other Jedburgh team, instructed that they could call for an additional three teams, and given the locations of the boundaries between their southern zone and Brittany's northern zone. The orders make it clear that this was an F Section operation—for unilateral British activity only—and that the Bureau Rensiegnements et d'Action Londres (BRAL) was not to be notified.[8]

Captain Cyr could not understand who SAS reported to, for it appeared to him they were their own private army. Fortunately, Ragueneau had worked with the SAS commander previously and was able to smooth out their initial troubles, enabling them to come to a working arrangement. As described previously, Philippe Ragueneau had been involved in the plot to kill Admiral Darlan, and he was finally going to get into France, risking his life to liberate it. On June 8, Cyr's twenty-second birthday, the team boarded the aircraft around 11:30 PM with sixteen others; when they were over the drop zone their actual jump was quite different from their Milton Hall training. Cyr complained on returning to England, "We all stood up and ran down towards the tail of the plane, jumping out in a very unorthodox manner." Fifteen to twenty French met them and immediately "bounced" with joy at their arrival. They pulled them up, gathered the gear, and made such a noise that Cyr thought they would certainly attract too much attention. Confirming his fear, the Maquis told him the Germans were only 2 kilometers away. The Maquis brought Team George and the SAS soldiers to a farm, which then became the SAS base Dingson.[9]

The welcome given to George and the SAS party was a grand one. Cyr, Ragueneau, and Gay wrote when they returned England, "Women, children and men were laughing and crying with joy. At 3:00 in the morning girls came running out kissing us and giving us flowers and wine. The men between the ages of 12 to 75 were ready that night to march on the German garrison." In the morning, all went out to assemble and organize their gear. The Jedburghs discovered their wireless/transmitter (W/T) sets were not among the rest of the equipment. Later that afternoon, a farmer arrived with them in his cart. According to the farmer, the equipment parachuted into his field about 9 AM approximately 2 to 3 kilometers from the drop zone. But to make matters worse, the Germans immediately jammed the frequency, forcing Sergeant Gay to broadcast on their secondary frequency. Soon the Germans jammed the secondary frequency, forcing Team George to broadcast sparingly on their emergency channel and ask SFHQ for a new primary channel. Estimating the need to arm 4,000 men, George asked for arms and related which reception ground should be used. They also asked for 1 million francs adding, "Please we beg you send equipment immediately."[10]

Rather than building and maturing an SOE circuit as Hugh did, George worked with the SAS to destroy bridges, cut railroads, and arm the French. Camp Dingson became a base of operations for SAS nightly patrols out to a target and a rallying point for Maquisards. For the first few days, while the communications to SFHQ was intermittent, five to ten planes came each night dropping arms, fuel, and supplies. The SAS and Team George began organizing and arming the Maquis, re-established contacts between the

Résistance groups, and tried to keep London informed. Initially, a great deal of confusion clouded the situation concerning who was who in the Maquis. Thick with recriminations, some pointed to others as spies and double agents, forcing George to question almost every piece of information until verified by others they trusted or until they grew to respect the man or woman through their own experiences.[11]

Communications became worse as George continued pressing SFHQ for a new frequency and new W/T sets. SFHQ never granted their request because they grew dubious about George's security and suspected the Gestapo sent the messages. Using poor security practices, George repeatedly failed to authenticate its messages properly, causing SFHQ to grow more and more suspicious. Headquarters' fears were unknown to the Jedburgh team and they continued their mission but lamented in their final report, "Our radio communications were very, very poor and we sweat blood on them."[12]

As more and more arms and men came into the camp, Dingson attracted considerable attention from the Wehrmacht and it was only a matter of time before Fahrmbacher's XXV Korps attacked. Maquis, poorly controlled and amateurishly led, made several attacks on German garrisons and depots provoking the Germans to retaliate. Moreover, Frenchmen came from as far as 100 kilometers to receive weapons, then returned to their homes and farms spreading the word to others. With 5,000 men armed and another 5,000 men soon to be armed, George discussed their role with the SAS Commander Bourgoin who decided to detail them to the Loire Inferieure area, southeast of their present position. George considered the Maquis there to be "the worst department in Brittany" and also concluded along with the SAS commander that the region was too vital to ignore. Team George made preparations to leave and selected local men to guide them.[13]

Unfortunately, George stayed too long. Awakened by exploding grenades and machine gun fire on June18, the team began a desperate fight along with the remaining SAS and approximately 600 to 1,000 Maquis. Noticing the persistent supply drops and parachutes, the Germans organized a task force of some of the 2nd Fallschirmjägers, Infantry and Feldgendarmes. Bringing in forces from the west and north, the Germans were impressed with the size of the base and estimated it at 500 men. The phone calls back to headquarters noted that the partisans and SAS fought "skillfully behind hedges, walls, and trees."[14] The Jeds burned documents, hid their code books, and made arrangements on rendezvous points in case they became separated. When the German attack met more resistance than expected, it ceased for about an hour but restarted after more enemy troops came into the fray. The SAS radioed for air strikes and the RAF strafed the Wehrmacht around 4 PM. But the air support was ineffective, as the Germans found cover in nearby trees. After sunset, Cyr and Ragueneau took command of two Maquis companies and led counterattacks hoping to stifle German momentum and force the enemy farther away from the camp's headquarters. Meanwhile, the SAS unit sustained several casualties and the commander ordered all wounded loaded to be on trucks and the supplies they could not bring with them to be destroyed. A great deal of arms meant for the Résistance went up in flames.[15]

Ordered to break through the German lines and carry on guerrilla operations, the George teammates found each other and decided to take six British airmen with them. The airmen had parachuted out of crippled aircraft and found their way to the SAS camp days before. Forcing their way through the lines with a Maquis group, George soon found itself slowed down by the pilots unfamiliar with small unit tactics. After getting through the lines and dodging numerous patrols, the Jedburgh team and the airmen traveled approximately ten miles when nearly thrown to the ground by an explosion lighting up the night sky. The SAS and Maquis arms depot finally blew up in a tremendous explosion. Laden with their packs and radios the Jeds spent the rest of the night avoiding firefights. Getting a few hours' sleep in a wheat field, the team found its way to the rendezvous point meeting the SAS Commander, the remainder of his SAS team, and some of the Maquis leaders. French women and girls cared for the wounded, doing the best they could with inadequate supplies. George then teamed up with Willk and Barthelémy, and split off from SAS toward their area of Loire Inferieure.[16] SFHQ had prepared to send another Jedburgh Team to Dingson and prepared the orders on June 16, but when the attack forced Dingson to scatter, Team Gregory was scrubbed. Scheduled to deploy on the very day the

Germans attacked Dingson, French Jed Albert de Schonen and British Jeds K. D. Bennett and Ron Brierley were canceled and instead sent on July 8 as Team Daniel into Côtes du Nord.[17] Had they been sent as planned, SFHQ could have easily lost the three Jedburgh teams.

Starting from a point twenty-five miles from base Dingson, George made its way slowly, relying on local men and women as guides. Taking nearly a week to make their way carefully past enemy patrols, they traveled through several small villages on back roads and finally to the Maquis camp near the village of Saffre. Now nearly thirty-five miles north of Nantes, Gay radioed London, "Arrived safely 'Alarme' ground, Loire Inferieure. Begin tomorrow 28 dropping for 2,000 in slices of 500. Reception committee standing by every night from 28th." Hoping to impress the local Maquis with the team's ability to make arms appear from the sky, the team lost a great deal of respect night after night when no planes appeared. On June 30, SFHQ requested George to pass the word to Barthelémy and his aide to "Go to safe place and lie low for a few days. Keep in contact and await any instructions." Evidently, London wanted to see if it could salvage their agents from what it assumed was a Gestapo-penetrated Jedburgh team. They gave no instructions, causing Ragueneau, Cyr, and Gay great concern and undercutting their validity with the Maquis.[18]

To add to the terrible luck, a double agent betrayed the Maquis camp's defensive positions to the enemy. When George arrived, they found the defenses inadequate, fired the camp commander, and rearranged the defenses just in time. As Sergeant Gay decoded messages on the morning of June 28, the Germans attacked and the W/T set had to be packed up "while the Jerries could be heard only 100 to 200 yards away." Miraculously making their way past two machine gun positions, Team George hid with Barthelémy in a clump of bushes so thick that the Germans could not find them and grenades tossed into them exploded harmlessly. The Germans used dogs, but they proved useless as so many people tracked around the area that the dogs could not pinpoint any particular person. After the Germans had given up and departed the area, the group made their way to a wheat field and then decided to split, not telling others their destination. Team George lamented its sorry state and later described its condition bereft of nearly all equipment and possessing only "one radio, one battery, a few weapons and our clothes" as it made its way toward Ancenis.[19]

While George's operations in Brittany were sliding into disaster, Team Frederick was not faring much better. It deployed with an SAS element of the same unit as at Dingson and arrived near the Duault Forest southwest of Guincamp on June 10. This team was led by British Major Adrian Wise with French Captain Paul Bloch-Auroch using the nom de guerre Paul Aguriec, and American Sergeant Robert Kehoe. RF Section and SAS was to control this mission, but again BRAL was not to be informed until after D-Day.[20] The team arrived to similar fanfare that George had experienced but lost one of the SAS men during the jump. The dead man had wrapped primer cord around his legs for some reason and it had accidentally ignited killing him before he hit the ground. Also alarming to Kehoe was the noise made by the loud and excited people who had come up to meet them at their rendezvous point; the fires set to signal the aircraft, which were still burning, and his recollection of a German headquarters near their location. There seemed to be no security practices whatsoever and he feared the Germans would discover them immediately.[21]

The Jeds were transported to a farmer's home and provided with break-fast; they met up with the rest of the SAS team that had arrived with them but had been slightly scattered during the parachuting. French Captain Le Blanc of the 4th Parachute Battalion commanded the SAS base Samwest. He and some of the leading elements of the SAS party had arrived the day before and distributed weapons among the Maquis who had been with the reception committee. They also held some "spies" prisoner and the local Breton Maquis and French SAS had beaten them regularly and finally executed them. Wise seemed disgusted with his first impression of the Résistance and wrote, "In my opinion subsequent brutal treatment of SAS prisoners may have had something to do with this."[22] As the Jedburgh team was making its way to Samwest, a German officer stopped by a home in the nearby village of Carhaix to ask directions. The answer he received was Sten fire from one of those who had been at the drop zone the day before. The untrained and uncontrolled Maquis were already drawing too much of the wrong kind of attention with their passionate desire to kill Germans.

Wise, Bloch-Auroch, and Kehoe did not successfully transmit their message on the first day and discovered they got better reception at higher ground. On June 11, Kehoe managed to transmit their confirmation message to SFHQ saying, "Arrived safely with all containers and equipment. Have contacted local groups. Great possibilities Cotes du Nord area. Send Jed team and arms for them. Advise soonest possible dropping ground."[23] However, this would be his last message as the unprovoked attack on the 2nd Fallschirmjäger officer from the day before brought the division into the area hunting them. The German soldiers returned to the farm where the German officer had been killed the previous day and shot those they found and burned down the farmhouse and the outbuildings. After a brief fire fight between the Germans at the farm and the nearest SAS checkpoint, the SAS commander gave the order to move south to Dingson, which was still operating at this time. The Jeds moved east a few miles accompanied by an RAF pilot who had bailed out a few days previously. The move was so rapid that Wise lamented they "lost nearly all of our kit in the process."[24] The total Samwest group, now numbering over one hundred of the French SAS and the Jeds, moved out in small groups attempting to avoid a pitched battle in what had grown from an attack of approximately forty Germans into a "an estimated 400" methodically working through the area.[25]

Since D-Day, the 266th Infantrie Division commanded by Lieutenant General Karl Spang had received all kinds of warnings and indications of paratroopers landing in northwest Brittany. One report claimed that three hundred enemy parachutists had landed near the coast. The Allied use of dummies, as well as the nighttime bombardments and obvious fatigue and fear of the German soldiers is evident in their logbooks.[26] The Germans quickly constituted a task force from elements of Spang's division and elements of the 2nd Fallschirmjägers to conduct a repression column through the area.

Having hidden one radio and planning to take their other with them, the Jed team started moving out on June 12, but the nearby shooting seemed to heighten their fear of capture and they decided to hide the remaining radio as well. Also with them was an RAF officer who had come in with the SAS and who decided not to go with them on to Camp Dingson. Wise thought they should bring him along, but not being used to or fit for long nighttime journeys laden with gear, the tall man in his forties slowed the Jeds down. But Kehoe noted that "conventional military forces prefer to work in units and fear being isolated or surrounded." That gave the Jeds an advantage in speed and flexibility while the Wehrmacht worked methodically through the forest.[27]

Working to get as far from the forest as they could, they risked moving during daylight. Again, Brittany's proximity to British airfields and the RAF patrols paid off in alerting them to danger. As they were only seconds from coming on a German patrol, they heard a fighter plane overhead and its strafing attack on something immediately in front of them. When the aircraft had flown off, they looked up to see the frightened enemy motorcyclists fleeing in the other direction. Determined now to stay off the roads, the team hid for the night and next day in a ditch next to a farmhouse; they realized that if they asked for help from the locals it would mean death to those who aided them should the Germans ever discover it. But the next morning, wet, exhausted, and starving, Bloch-Aroch went to the farmhouse to ask for food. The Breton-speaking woman scared him as he did not understand what she was saying and feared she was German. He was relieved when her daughter, a schoolteacher who spoke French, agreed to help them.[28]

Their luck was beginning to change. Not only did the women provide them a wonderful breakfast, but the meeting led to more contact with the Côtes du Nord Résistance. Over the next few days, they moved again, established a command post, and began planning their operations. The women, Simone Le Göeffic and Louise Quennec, proved remarkably able to bicycle around the region passing messages to the nearby Front National and FFI leadership who ultimately made their way to the farmhouse. With the arrival of Yves Le Hegarat, using the nom de guerre Marceau, they met the leader of the Côtes du Nord's FFI. Le Hegarat who had come to the fore in the Maquis leadership of the FTP, had become the departmental leader of the FFI as he successfully convinced the members of the Libération-Nord movement to merge just prior to D-Day. He successfully convinced them they would all work to achieve military aims and so they made him the FFI leader and agreed to share the weapons that the Allies supplied.[29] Now the Jedburghs had someone with whom they could work, supply, and train. They decided to stay in the region and not make their way south to Camp Dingson. Another reason for them to remain was that the women had taken in some of the wounded SAS soldiers. Wise believed his group should remain and help them while the women arranged for a surgeon from Guincamp to come and see what he could do. In the end, the doctor saved the lives of the soldiers by performing an operation and providing enough care to allow them to survive.[30]

Now with trusted contacts and their decision made to remain in the region, the team needed their radio to operate. Kehoe would have to recover it from its hidden spot in the forest where had had buried it and was worried about how quickly he could make the trip bringing back the forty-pound radio. He was surprised, however, to be offered a car. Over the years of occupation, one of their new contacts had stored a vehicle, hidden the wheels, and stolen enough fuel over time to have several gallons for a vital moment such as now. With two of their new Maquis and one of the SAS sergeants, Kehoe took the car and traveled in the darkness to search for his team's means of communication with SFHQ. With no radio, they were just three uniformed men, but with it they were SFHQ's and Koenig's liaison. A great deal rode on Kehoe's nighttime search. They arrived back in the forest and found the area. Kehoe had buried the radio next to a very distinctive boulder, but now all the boulders looked alike. While the SAS sergeant went in search of his own equipment, and the two Maquis stood guard with the car, Kehoe went from boulder to boulder searching. Finally, just as dawn was breaking, Kehoe dug at the right spot and found it. Lugging it back to the car, his relieved comrades loaded it into the car and jubilantly drove back to their new hideout. Kehoe later wrote, "This was to be the rebirth of Team Frederick."[31]

It was just in time; the same day the 2nd Fallschirmjägers attacked the former Camp Samwest with an impressive and concentrated force. Unlike the SAS at Dingson, the men at Samwest had taken the opportunity to disperse so when the Germans came in expecting a difficult fight, instead they found only pockets of Maquis and a few of the uniformed SAS—but no Jedburghs or their valuable radio. But while the Jeds had found their radio, OB West was now gaining more and more information on Allied actions with the interior Résistance. The 2nd Fallschirmjägers claimed that during the two battles, they had killed an estimated fifty of the enemy. The intelligence report about the actions against the Maquis concentrations in Brittany resulted in the discovery of French uniformed parachutists and the understanding that they were SAS who had obvious links to the Allies in London.[32] But there is no guess as to their overall mission. Were these parachutists an advance force indicating larger airborne operations? The German commanders were left to wonder and to make preparations throughout the interior zone.

Team Frederick spent the next two weeks in one place, a luxury considering they were only 10 kilometers from the Foret de Duault. Now back in business with their radio they sent London, "SAS attacked Monday and dispersed. Jeds okay. Have contacted guerrilla leaders. Paris-Brest underground cable cut by us." Kehoe had used the correct security procedure in sending a coded message by omitting certain pre-determined letter groups, so London was quickly satisfied that Frederick was indeed back up and rapidly responded to the team's request for air-dropped supplies. After two weeks there, they moved to another location to arm another Maquis group. Newly located about 34 kilometers due south of Guincamp, they remained only a few days and had to move again when a German patrol noticed their radio antenna and investigated. Shots fired at their farmhouse provoked them to grab their codes and crystals and run into the woods. After hiding out during the day, they managed to escape, now for a third time, and make their way north. At this location, near St. Nicolas du Pelem, the team eventually coordinated the reception of two more Jedburgh teams.[33]

Team Frederick's ability to survive re-energized General Koenig and the SFHQ staff. The Giles mission was back on for Finistère, east of where Frederick was operating and as a part of a larger plan, so were six other teams. After being delayed by weather and on another night by lack of a confirmed drop zone signal, Team Giles arrived to much the same fanfare as the other teams. Choosing the location based on recommendations from Teams George and Frederick, SFHQ began pondering how to deploy a more sophisticated command and control mission.[34] Giles was to be the first team in among the broader plan. SFHQ believed that in Finistère alone there were 9,600 Wehrmacht along with the 5,000 Paratroopers of the 2nd Fallschirmjäger and 9,000 naval, marine, and anti-aircraft or FLAK troops for a total of 37,000. But Barthélemy's most recent cable led them to believe there were 30,000 men waiting to join the Maquis. Such information, along with the imperative from SHAEF to control Brittany, provoked l'Etat Major Forces Françaises de l'interieur (EMFFI) to now begin a more comprehensive plan that they then attempted to put in motion. It consisted of sending more Jedburgh Teams to Frederick, and ended with sending in an inter-allied command and control element led by Colonel Albert Eon, and seconded by none other than Colonel Dewavrin.[35] However, American Captain Bernard Knox and French Captain Paul Grall of the Team Giles seem to be oblivious to this part of the puzzle. Probably left out of the broader plan for security reasons, Giles' ignorance proved costly.

Specifically, their point of confusion seemed to center around SFHQ's directive to not take "offensive action" until directed to do so.[36] By the end of June, with thirteen teams in France, and reports of sabotage, spectacular numbers of people joining the Résistance, and the belief that armored divisions such as the 2nd SS "Das Reich" had been effectively delayed, the Allies began to believe in the Maquis effectiveness. Certainly getting 8th Air Force to provide more air to ground support sorties on June 25 indicates that even SHAEF had begun to believe in what was happening. But as the scale began to tip and as numbers in the Maquis grew throughout France, their enthusiasm and passion altered the role of the Jedburghs. Instead of inspiring, provoking, and leading the Maquis to action, now the teams' presence was to dampen and pass along the directive to wait. Instead of providing the fuel, they had to put on the brake. The Jedburghs who had been in France before the end of June had experience and had matured along with their Maquis and could temper their passions better than new teams, such as Giles now parachuting in; these late-coming teams did not have sufficient time to establish a rapport with the groups they met.

TEAM GILES DEPLOYS

American Captain Bernard M. Knox, French Captain Paul Grall using the nom de guerre Paul Lebel, and British Sergeant Gordon H. Tack comprised the seventh team dispatched from Britain to France. On June 16, SFHQ alerted and briefed Giles its mission to deploy to the Finistère region of eastern Brittany and organize and arm *Résistance* forces. SFHQ knew very little about the region's Maquis, and prior to the team's departure General Koenig himself briefed them, emphasizing the region's importance and how vital it was to learn more about the Maquis' potential for combat. Also, Koenig sternly warned Knox to act like a gentleman and behave himself as a good guest of France should. Evidently, he thought Americans chased women too much and would be parachuting into France with stockings and chocolates.[37] Immediately before the team left for France, Captain Grall went back to London to agree on the BBC signal for the Brittany large-scale attack. Grall suggested and SFHQ agreed the signal would be *"Le chapeau de Napoleon est-il toujours a Perros-Guirec?"* ("Is Napoleon's hat still at Perros-Guirec?"). After an unsuccessful attempt on July 4, Giles finally parachuted into the French night on July 8/9 from a Carpetbagger B-24.[38] Their mission flew in on a night that saw 15 sorties, from two airfields, to four drop zones now under the control of Maquis who were coordinating with Team Frederick.[39]

Captain Knox parachuted first out of the "Joe hole." Born in England and educated in languages at St. John's College, Cambridge, Knox had joined the International Brigade and fought in the Spanish Civil War. After he was wounded, he left Spain for Paris and fell in love with an American writer. They moved to Connecticut, and Knox became a naturalized citizen in 1943. After the bombing of Pearl Harbor, he joined the US Army where he was trained as an air defense officer. At the beginning of 1944 he was stationed in England, and when he heard about the OSS he volunteered, hoping to see some action. He served as an explosives and French instructor at Milton Hall, and after some parachute training, he was put in the mix to deploy on a team. Twenty-nine-year-old Knox acted as team commander for Team Giles. Captain Paul Grall joined the Jedburghs from the North

Africa recruiting drive. The Germans had captured Grall in 1940 and held him as a POW in Poland. He escaped and somehow got to Morocco. A member of the French Colonial Army, Grall was a well-built man with a large scar down his cheek from an automobile accident. Sergeant Tack served as W/T operator and Captain Knox considered him a first-class radioman. Tack followed Knox down the "Joe hole" with Grall exiting last.[40] The drop went well, with Knox and Tack landing close together; they found Captain Grall within two or three minutes. Excited young Frenchmen welcomed them almost immediately, greeting them with kisses. The reception party gathered up their gear and much to the Jedburghs' delight had vehicles to transport them to a safe area. Riding in cars and a truck carrying their equipment, the team members hoped to get to their base before dawn, but the distance was so far that the team did not make it there until daylight. At base the members found not quite fifty men whose leader was in Côtes-du-Nord, Team Frederick's area, attempting to acquire weapons. Captain Grall organized the defenses and distributed the weapons giving instruction as he went along. Later that afternoon, the team heard the BBC message informing them of another drop on the same ground as the previous night. Although they were leery about making the trip back to the drop zone, the Giles team decided to risk it in order to retrieve the weapons. They also sent word to London stating that the Résistance situation was different from the one they had been briefed on since Gestapo and Milice had recently arrested and shot many local leaders. The Giles message lamented, "situation at Finistère is not as informed," requested three more Jedburgh teams to work other parts of the region, and asked for an additional 1 million francs.[41]

Giles retrieved their supplies from the drop zone just in time. They discovered the next afternoon, that the 2nd Fallschirmjägers had an estimated three hundred troops going through farms searching for Résistance forces. The suspicious Germans heard the aircraft and arrived on the drop zone just five minutes after team Giles and their reception team left. After the near miss, Giles distributed the arms to another Maquis group and met the returning Maquis leader, Yues Legal, who led the most active Brittany group, the communist FTP. Team Giles and Legal quickly came to an agreement on dropping grounds and the strategy that Giles should remain in Brittany's center while letting the next Jedburgh teams work the coastal areas.[42]

On the night of July 9–10, two more Jedburgh teams parachuted onto one of Giles' drop zones without its knowledge, and the next day SFHQ radioed Giles of the arrival of Teams Francis and Gilbert. These two teams proceeded to the villages of Quimper and Quimperlé and by the time the ground received a drop of weapons for Giles' Maquis four days later, their cover was "blown." Hearing the noise four nights previously, the Germans suspected something was going on in the area and attacked the Maquis as they finished their work at the drop zone. However, the Maquis put up stiff resistance, surprising the Wehrmacht, and Captain Knox thought the Germans sustained so many casualties that attacking the drop zone was not worth their effort.[43]

The FTP sent their men from Finistère to Giles' camp to receive training, weapons, and instruction in organized Résistance activities for the region. Giles worked to coordinate every supply drop in an effort to control the Maquis and keep the materials out of German hands. Giles and the FTP selected seven drop zones and informed London of their location while training numerous Maquis on reception ground procedures. On July 12, the Free French (FFI) chief, Lieutenant Colonel Berthaud visited Giles' command post and discussed Résistance operations. Giles team members and Berthaud established a professional relationship at first and related their respective goals, agreeing to stay in contact with each other via Legal. Unfortunately, Berthaud, whose real name was Bourrières, and who had taken over from the recently arrested Libération-Nord leader in the area just before the Giles team arrived, lacked the quality and quantity of the organization enjoyed by the FTP. While meeting with him, one of the Maquis recognized a man in Bourrières's car as a spy, and Giles' report coldly stated, "we had to shoot one of the men in his car, who was a known Gestapo agent." Due to fears that Bourrières's organization had been compromised, Giles avoided working with him.[44]

Their fears proved true when the next day the mayor of the nearby village told Giles that "large German forces were in the area looking for us," using a map with "red marks against the name of the farm where we were taking our meals." Giles packed up camp and moved that night with its hundred-man company. Traveling by foot for the next two nights, they arrived at a high plateau near St. Thors where they set up operations and managed to stay for a week. While at St. Thors, they met with more Franc-Tireurs et Partisans Français (FTP) departmental chiefs anxious to begin offensive actions. Ordered by Koenig to avoid open warfare until directed, Giles worked to convince the Maquis that they fell under the command of SHAEF and their orders were to wait until the correct time. After a long discussion, the FTP chiefs agreed they would follow the Allied orders.

Unfortunately, Colonel Bourrières became jealous and complained to London concerning the FTP's influence with Giles. Radioing London in response, Giles stated the assertions were "true enough because in our region *Résistance* is mostly *Maquis* FTP." The message went on to remind London that the "arrangement was made at an interview between us and Berthaud." Giles was tired of Bourrières's complaining, and London concurred with Giles and its arrangements with the region's FTP.[45]

Meanwhile, Giles received the Jedburgh Horace and Hilary teams and three other French parachutists at one of its drop zones. Giles arranged for them to take up positions on the north Brittany coast and sent them off to their areas. To add to the confusion, one of the prisoners suspected of belonging to the Milice escaped, forcing Giles to relocate again. The Jedburgh team crossed the Aulne canal and set up camp in a valley 3 kilometers from the village of Lennon. Here Giles increased their number by one with Canadian Flight Lieutenant Brown. Shot down over Brest, Brown wandered into the team's area and remained with them as the normal escape routes closed when the Allies invaded Normandy. Brown spent nearly three weeks with the team helping Sergeant Tack handle the radio traffic. At this point, five teams worked in Finistère but the Fallschirmjägers still controlled major roads and aggressively sought to ferret out the Maquis.[46]

Team Giles also met with Major Colin Ogden-Smith and Captain Guy Leborgne of Team Francis and clarified each team's operating area. They discussed policy regarding the Résistance and Brittany's political groups. Unfortunately, the details of the discussion are not noted, but they presumably delineated each team's operating area and drop zones and exchanged information on the FTP and Bourrières.

Agreeing on every point, they parted and Knox lamented, "This was the last time I ever saw Colin."[47] Team Francis had parachuted near Quimperlé on July 10. Leborgne, who used the nom de guerre Guy Le Zachmeur, and radioman British Sergeant A. J. Dallow landed on their drop zone at approximately 2:30 in the morning. The team leader, Ogden-Smith was nowhere to be found. Leborgne met up with the Maquis leader in the region and Colonel Bourrières and reported no problems with his organization but seemed to work well with their FTP, who were again the most numerous in the area. Having dropped right near a town that was "the center of counterterrorist" activity for the Wehrmacht, they feared for their missing colleague and sent out some of the Maquis to search for him while they established links with the region's groups, arranged more weapons drops, and organized arms among them. Fortunately, on July 14 they found Ogden-Smith who had been hiding out the last four days. Their pre-arranged rendezvous point proved to be the town with the region's Wehrmacht garrison, making life difficult then for members of the team to find each other. Together now, they met with Giles on July 16 and again on July 19, while both were evading the enemy. But having had modest success in finding and equipping Maquis, by July 24 they claimed to have armed 500 men near Carhaix, another 500 near Scear and 300 near Guisgriff. Establishing a company near the coast presented a problem as there were fewer men there to recruit and the density of the enemy was greater; nevertheless, they claimed to have armed approximately 200. They had also been joined by one of the stray SAS soldiers, Sergeant Maurice Myodon. As to the overall plan for Brittany, Team Francis seems to have understood the overall nature of the Allied aims in the region for they wrote that they were storing up arms for later operations and worked to coordinate their operating areas and share communications not only with Giles but with Team Gilbert.[48]

Ogden-Smith was an experienced commando, having participated in the British Small Scale Raiding Force and had served in North Africa. Returning to the United Kingdom, he was reassigned within the SOE to the Jedburgh program and did very well in training. He befriended Knox while at Milton

Hall and they had spent time discussing their mutual interests and their separate experiences, each curious about the other's combat time. Ogden-Smith told Knox that he was jealous of Knox's having gone to college and expressed an interest in getting back to university after the war.[49] He had been recently married and his wife lived in London. His prewar occupation was working in the family business manufacturing and selling fishing tackle and fly rods.[50]

Having survived the separation from his team immediately on arrival and one close call on July 19, Ogden-Smith now led the augmented team of Leborgne, Dallow, Myoden, and two Maquis that helped keep watch and operate the radio. They made their headquarters at a farm in the village of Querrien, 12 kilometers north of the small port of Quimperlé. On July 29, they found themselves surrounded by "approximately 100 Feldgendarmes," led directly to their location by a neighbor. A burst of machine gun fire and a grenade was their first warning that Germans were nearby. Unfortunately, Ogden-Smith and Myodon were wounded immediately while Leborgne fired back and by chance killed the officer leading the operation. In the confusion that followed, Leborgne was able to escape. Sergeant Dallow, who had been about a hundred yards away, grabbed his carbine and some of the radio equipment and ran toward the house where his teammates were exchanging fire. As he was climbing up out of the ditch, he fell into some bushes and could not get out of them. Lying there unable to move, but unseen by the enemy he watched helplessly as the firefight ensued. Ogden-Smith lay wounded but managed to give himself morphine and fire his weapon at the enemy putting down some of the Germans. Myodon, wounded from the grenade, defended himself exhausting four clips of rounds before calling out, "you need not be afraid, I have got no more ammunition." Lying there in the open, firing at the Germans, he had enabled Leborgne and the two Maquis to escape. The Germans carefully approached and then shot Ogden-Smith dead. Another Feldgendarme walked up to Myodon warily, but killed him with a burst of machine gun fire and finally a bullet to the temple. Dallow remained in the bush the entire time with nothing but his pistol, unable to help. After two hours, with the Germans gone, he managed to climb out and departed the area.[51]

Informed of Major Ogden-Smith's death by radio message from Giles, SFHQ related the news to Major General Gubbins, on or about August 3. Gubbins had taken special interest in the Jedburghs and had interviewed Ogden-Smith personally for SOE. Now he wished to know more of the details about his death, and the first reports were not enough. His son Michael Gubbins had been killed at Anzio in February. Having been informed of his own son's death by finding the War Office message in his morning inbox, Gubbins sought something more so that he could write a meaningful letter to Ogden-Smith's family.[52] But that was not the only thing he was searching for. The French were now fully involved in the operations in France, and the influence of Special Operations Executive (SOE) in France was beginning to wane.

GENERAL KOENIG TAKES OVER GUERRILLA WARFARE IN FRANCE

On June 23, Eisenhower announced to his superiors and subordinates that General Koenig was now equivalent to any Allied commander serving under him in the Allied Expeditionary Forces.[53] In Washington, General Marshall greeted this news with the directive that it should be publicly announced at once.[54] But saying it was so and actually making it so proved to be two different issues. Bureaucratic loyalties, diminished egos, ignorance of the implications, firm opinions on the matter, and a lack of resources in war-weary London hampered the quick creation of the headquarters staff of the Forces Françaises l'Intérieur (FFI). Koenig wished to create his office and headquarters machinery in order to control the quickly expanding FFI inside France. Doing this required offices, vehicles, phones, and accreditations for his planning staff so they could get to work managing the SAS, the American Operational Groups (OGs), the Inter-Allied Missions, the DMRs, as well as the Jedburghs. Much of the structure already existed in the French Desk of the Anglo-American SFHQ. Still, Koenig had his own ideas, outranked the SFHQ co-directors Brigadier Mockler-Ferryman and Colonel Haskell, and indeed outranked the head of the SOE and the OSS. Furthermore, he had Eisenhower's backing on the matter and used that

trump card with the SHAEF staff or anyone else involved at every opportunity. In the end, he won every argument, but opponents appeared fre-
quently and came from many corners.

While it seems he could simply become the commander of the SFHQ
with the addition of some French officers, it was more complicated than
that. The portfolio of Special Force Headquarters (SFHQ) was grander
than just France as it ran guerrilla warfare in every country in SHAEF's theater, and placing a French general in charge of every nation's resistance
would not be wise. The compromise finally crafted was that the staff section
from SFHQ running French operations would be chopped, so to speak, to
EMFFI and General Koenig while the rest of SFHQ continued with their
work in the other nations. Therefore, Mockler-Ferryman and Haskell would
now have three jobs. Each was his nation's senior irregular warfare officer
for the theater. Each man was also a co-director of SFHQ. While these
positions may sound like the same job, they can be quite different. For instance, Haskell was responsible to Colonel Bruce and General Donovan in
Washington for requesting and justifying his personnel needs, equipment,
and the funds that kept his operation going. He also, with his British colleague, approved of operations and assessed how well their activities were
being conducted and what might need to be done next.[55] Together these
two tasks can be a burden, but when Eisenhower added the third task of
being the US or UK deputy to the French commander of the FFI, it created
too much complication for Mockler-Ferryman.

While Mockler-Ferryman got along well with Haskell, his relations were
not so cordial with Koenig. The specific issues of dispute cannot be determined from their written communication that survives in the various archives, but the tone of the letters and their habit of having to clarify what
was said during meetings with follow-up memoranda indicates that their
relationship was professional but strained. With the British brigadier and
the American colonel on the verge of taking on another deputy job title for
l'Etat Major Forces Françaises de l'Interieur (EMFFI) while maintaining
their Anglo-American co-director positions for Special Force Headquarters
(SFHQ) and their national responsibilities as well, they found themselves
having to develop methods for solving Résistance issues for France by

doing it the way Koenig wanted it while continuing with their agreed-upon procedures for their Anglo-American SFHQ for Belgium, Holland, Norway, Denmark, and Germany. Therefore, there were to be two methods for doing things: one for France and another for the rest of the theater.

Eisenhower seems to have anticipated this as indicated in his meeting with de Gaulle in December of 1943. However, Roosevelt's and Churchill's delay in coming to an understanding with de Gaulle meant that organizational agreements would not be agreed on until events forced them to be. That time had now come. On June 2, while Mockler-Ferryman was working with Koenig on the BBC messages, it appears that he and perhaps Haskell were working under the assumption that they would soon be "bringing them [the French] into our headquarters."[56] But instead, Koenig believed he would be bringing applicable portions of Special Force Headquarters into his. Since he was the senior officer, with the directive from Eisenhower, Koenig's belief is understandable. By June 12, the disagreement must have continued because now Gubbins and senior staff at SHAEF were involved in the matter. British Major General J. F. M. Whiteley who was deputy chief of staff to Bedell Smith, wrote Gubbins that Mockler-Ferryman and Haskell would contribute to SHAEF's operational planning and requirements but would not have access to them for France. Instead, their role in EMFFI would be to secure logistical capability such as airlift and weapons stores for France as the French were not conversant in that machinery nor was it acceptable to anyone in SHAEF for officers of one nation to have so much control over foreign assets. The reason boiled down to this, as Whiteley wrote: "As the smooth running of the whole affair must depend on mutual trust and confidence, there must be no occasion for a suspicion to arise in General Koenig's mind that Mockler-Ferryman and Haskell can approach SHAEF behind his back."[57]

Furthermore, Koenig's view on what the Jedburghs were to do was very clear. They were a liaison element. Koenig had regional military delegates (DMRs) and regional and departmental FFI commanders for *commanding* the Résistance; the Jedburghs' role was to communicate and equip, not to lead. As described in Chapter 4, Mockler-Ferryman would apparently concur, since during his speech at Milton Hall he had emphasized that for the Jedburghs, whatever else they might do, their mission would always be one of liaison. However, since so much planning from the beginning of the Jedburgh program had anticipated that the Jeds would replace arrested F Section cadres, Mockler-Ferryman and perhaps all the SOE and OSS planners were operating under the assumption that the SHAEF's means of controlling the Résistance would be via the Jedburgh teams and messages sent to them from SHAEF. SHAEF had long wanted a French general who would report to Eisenhower, but since he had also been accredited by the provisional government, to command the resistance, Koenig could direct the Maquis through his own staff. This meant that many of the planners working on operations in France within the SFHQ became superfluous and set up new tension between the Allies and the Free French. The Jedburghs were viewed by Koenig and his planners in Bureau Rensiegnements et d'Action Londres (BRAL) as merely a means to reach more Maquis units, assess their needs, and communicate them back to EMFFI, who would then decide whether to fulfill these requests depending on their priorities as they understood their directives from Eisenhower. Koenig's differentiation of the Jedburgh mission still served Eisenhower, while it left Special Force Headquarters (SFHQ) with a somewhat diminished operational role—and often perplexed the Jedburghs in the field. Lieutenant Colonel Hutchison's and Major MacPherson's frustrations, detailed in the previous chapter, are an example of this.

Mockler-Ferryman saw his influence diminish as operations progressed, and he grew more and more frustrated. Memos went back and forth between him and Koenig about how EMFFI should be structured, and finally Koenig had enough. Reviewing the paperwork on the matter, General Bedell Smith wrote in the margins of one that he did "not like the tone" of Mockler-Ferryman's letter. "Let's not have a childish squabble."[58] With SHAEF bearing down on the matter in order to resolve the issue without any further delay, Bedell Smith called a meeting to make it clear. On July 10, two days after Roosevelt announced his recognition that de Gaulle and the CFLN would be the "de facto authority" for France, Bedell Smith again emphasized Eisenhower's views on the matter and backed up Koenig.[59] Keeping up his efforts to get his headquarters going, Koenig asked for

Haskell to stay on but wished to have Major General Robert Laycock as his British deputy instead of Mockler-Ferryman. Laycock was one of the most experienced and well-respected among the British commando officers and perhaps more important, was *not* part of the Special Operations Executive (SOE). The British did not release him from being their chief of Combined Operations, a tame name for their headquarters of their commando forces. But the Americans agreed for Haskell to join coalescing EMFFI as long as he could remain in his other two roles. Haskell's ingratiating style backed up by his ability to pull off air operations like Zebra and Cadillac impressed Koenig. Mockler-Ferryman, however, saw the writing on the wall and tendered his resignation to Gubbins on July 27. Stating that he understood Eisenhower's reasoning on the matter, but that every French officer viewed Mockler-Ferryman with suspicion, something Whiteley had warned he did not want to see happen, Mockler-Ferryman believed resigning was his only option. Gubbins saw no other way out and accepted the resignation on the same day that Ogden-Smith was killed near Querrien.[60] But this did not mean that Mockler-Ferryman was leaving SOE, or even SFHQ. He simply left EMFFI and therefore SFHQ's French operations. Retaining his other positions clouded the whole incident and has evidently led M. R. D. Foot and William Mackenzie to miss the whole affair.[61] In his place, the British sent Major General Harold H. Redman, a man with little experience running special operations. He was not an SOE officer but was a French speaker serving on the Allied Combined Chiefs of Staff in Washington, DC.[62]

The American OSS did not put up such resistance, but General Donovan did fear the incapacitation of his London station's ability to continue its effort in Europe, just as OSS planning was beginning against Germany. Knowing that he would need agents and teams in central Europe and expecting that OSS London would run them, he feared that much of his machinery was being turned over to the French. In a response to Haskell's description of how the reorganization was progressing and what SFHQ assets would come under Koenig's command, Donovan fired off a message to Eisenhower claiming that "by tearing out certain vital tissues of our organization in your theater, compels me to ask for a reconsideration as to these matters."[63] Donovan went on to hint that he might be forced to take what was left of the Allied SFHQ and present OSS capabilities to SHAEF without the British.

But it was too late. Eisenhower had worked since January to bring the French Maquis under his command through a French general and he wasn't going to be persuaded otherwise now. He admired and appreciated Donovan and the OSS, but he was not going to slow the progress that was finally taking place. Furthermore, he was not going to let an Allied organization charged with working with the resistance in the other countries of his theater be broken up. He liked SFHQ and since the other exiled governments in occupied Europe were being comparatively pliant, he was going to run them as he saw fit. On August 9, Eisenhower told Donovan and Marshall that he disapproved of anything that dissolved SFHQ "for any countries except France." If Donovan needed OSS assets for issues in Central Europe, that was not Eisenhower's concern and he reminded Donovan that it was not SFHQ's either since it was a SHAEF organization. Bruce and Haskell followed the theater commander's telegram with a message that quite accurately reminded Donovan that Eisenhower had no responsibility for Central Europe and it was expecting a lot for Eisenhower to give up personnel for missions outside his theater. By sending the message to Marshall, Eisenhower was making sure that his superior understood his point of view.[64] Assuming Donovan was not willing to go to the president on the matter, Ike called his bluff.

General Koenig and his chief of staff, Colonel Vernon, had not waited for final resolution on the matter, but had been, since mid-June or so, taking over operations in France that related to the Résistance. Koenig focused his resources largely on Brittany, and since the BCRA and SOE contacts had been arrested, they now relied on the Jedburgh teams to make use of the growing Maquis. Their one functioning DMR for Brittany had been sending messages since his arrival with Team George and the SAS at Dingson. On June 18, Maurice Barthélemy, who used the code name Hauteur, radioed that he was meeting with the region's principal Maquis group leaders to agree to the overall plan for their organization.[65] But that was the same day as the attack on Dingson, and these plans were significantly altered by the enemy's actions. The scattering of Dingson and Samwest had forced SFHQ and EMFFI to reassess their timing of their next steps. Fulfilling their orders meant more than deploying several Jedburgh teams, and EMFFI began putting together a French led Inter-Allied mission that would serve as the overall command element for Brittany. SHAEF allotted thirty-five air sorties a night for Koenig's SAS and EMFFI forces, less than what was possible due to the concern of indicating too much to the enemy about how important Brittany was to the Allies. Eisenhower's orders to Koenig were clear: "The whole object of FFI planning and operations in BRITTANY is to give as much help as possible to enable the AMERICANS to capture BREST in the shortest possible time."[66] The US forces approaching Brittany now required FFI support, and Koenig believed he needed to send a command element to Brittany to coordinate the effort.

The mission was commanded by French Army Colonel Albert Eon, and his second in command would be Dewavrin. EMFFI gave it the codename of Aloes and put them on standby to be ready to go when the time was judged right to open guerrilla warfare. In the meantime, military command remained with the SAS commander Commandant Bourgoin, and the Jedburgh teams were reminded of that in messages.[67] Aloes planning included working with the 21st Army operations staff as it progressed west, increasing the parachuting of arms to the region; and Eon traveled to Milton Hall to brief the teams alerted for work in Brittany. Aloes planning began in early July, just as Giles departed for France, and their planning continued to the very day of their deployment on the night of August 4.[68] Team Giles missed all of this as their departure put them into combat prior to being informed of the tactical planning considerations.

Knox, Grall, and Tack of Team Giles were suffering from the lack of consistent direction as well as the Gestapo's control of Brittany. Under the threat of being found, the team moved again. Striking out north across the Pleyben-Chateauneuf road, the Giles team marched until 4 AM. The team hoped to settle north of that road, but by the next day it learned that Germans had captured one of Sergeant Tack's former radio assistants. Knowing they must keep moving, they decided to go back across the canal toward Kernoux that night. While on the move, they saw German signal flares and sent part of their company ahead to investigate. The scouts failed to return and Giles decided to strike out on their own, but the remaining men and boys were now without their own cadre and simply could not sustain a long forced march. Compelled to take to roads rather than going across country because the men were so weary, Giles reconnoitered a small village and could not believe its luck when they found an unguarded canal bridge. Just as they were all across, machine gun fire erupted from the bridge area they had just passed through and inspired the Giles men to keep going as long as possible, but by 7:30 the next morning only eight men remained with the team.[69]

However, during their movements they happened upon a great opportunity. Giles discovered the German main position in the region and hoped to capitalize on the information. The Germans had commandeered a chateau situated on the area's predominant hill. With such a position they could view a great deal of the surrounding area, but Giles informed London of the position and asked for the RAF to strike. On July 30, three dive-bombers rolled in on the target filled with hungover German soldiers still groggy from a party the previous evening. Giles radioed SFHQ and gleefully exclaimed the air strike "Couldn't have been better."[70]

By late July, the Franc-Tireurs et Partisans Français (FTP) Maquis and especially the FTP leadership sought to take the fight to the Germans, but instructions to do so still had not arrived. Giles informed London of the difficulty of keeping some groups in check and complained, "FTP getting very hard to control and we may not be able to do it much longer....FTP are reaching boiling point and explosion may occur if Boche continues to hunt them." But apparently Giles, and perhaps other Jedburgh teams, misunderstood a key aspect of their orders. SFHQ wanted the Maquis to refrain from general open activity but to engage in systematic and persistent guerrilla activity. In other words, small-scale harassment and well-planned guerrilla attacks were fine. But Giles, believing all such activity was off limits, worked hard to convince the Maquis to refrain from any type of engagement while London wished only to stop open warfare. In their exchange of messages, Giles and the l'Etat Major Forces Françaises de l'Interieur (EMFFI) seemed to be talking past one another to the extent that Grall and Knox responded to it all in their longest messages yet saying,

You (EMFFI) did not answer our question at all. We are not thinking of our own skins but of success of operation. We repeat in words of one syllable, if Boche attacks *Maquis* in this area, no power on earth can stop a general explosion. They can only attack if they have precise information. They can only get precise information through Feldgendarmerie. It may be already too late. Information this morning Boche about to install 25 companies between Callac and Chateauneuf. At least 500 at Chateauneuf. Our liaison is being completely cut by action of Feldgendarmerie. Messengers are arrested, tortured and shot every day. In these circumstances our work is becoming almost impossible. Central Finistère a powder magazine which needs only a spark and the Boche is going to provide the spark. As for moving when we are in danger, we have moved five times since our arrival. But 15 armed companies in the center. Cannot keep moving all the time. We have managed to keep *Maquis* quiet until now but if they are attacked, nothing can stop open fighting in Finistère.[71]

London radioed Giles on July 30: "We quite agree about action by small groups against field gendarmerie. Only mistake in interpretation made you interrupt all operations. Must keep enemy in danger everywhere cease-lessly by guerilla [*sic*] action, that is to say, generalized mobile offensive action by surprise and refusing large scale battle." Aggressively continuing the weapon supply drops, Giles kept warning London they needed the message about Napoleon's hat, otherwise they would not be able to control the FTP. Now, London gave them a way to relieve the pressure caused by the misunderstanding but they still seemed not to understand the nuances of their mission.[72]

Moving for the last time on July 31, GILES found its last headquarters back in its first headquarters, the village of Plessis. They carried out recon-naissance on the chateau recently attacked by the RAF. Piles of rubble and the odor of decaying bodies greeted them and they reported killing seven-teen more Germans. The Germans evacuated the ruins the next day and Giles intensified the drop zone activity hoping the wait would not be long until they were given the order for all-out action. On August 2, Team Francis radioed Giles with the news of Ogden-Smith's death and Giles radioed London that all Francis' drop zones were blown as Ogden-Smith had the locations on him when he died.[73]

But on the evening of August 2, the BBC transmitted the desired message: "Le Chapeau de Napoleon est-il toujours a Perros-Guirec," and team Giles quickly set up an attack on columns of Germans moving east. As the 2nd Fallschirmjägers moved toward the Allied forces now around Dinan in eastern Brittany, Giles brought the guerrillas to bear while sending London the message, "Lack arms and ammo. Going over to offensive tonight." Giles and the Maquis could press the fighting, but they continued to require more arms. The next day London obliged and the Maquis received four loads on one drop zone and one load on another. Giles succeeded at getting the orders and arms to the northern part of their sector and also succeeded at penning in the Germans by blowing up a bridge on the main east-bound road while running ambushes on the roads to the east where the Germans were attempting to head toward the front. The Germans, now forced to travel cross country rather than by road, slowed down considerably and took out their frustration on the French villages and farms by burning, looting, and other vicious actions. Team Frederick radioed that it had 2,000 men ready for work along the road to be used by the Americans as they came toward Brest.[74] Their work made the progress of the American tanks along the road from Dinan to Brest much quicker as the team worked to preserve bridges while staging hit-and-run attacks on the Germans as they fled the advance of American conventional troops, led by Major General Troy Middleton's VIII Armored Corps. In all the chaos, Giles and the Maquis captured enemy prisoners and Captain Knox questioned them, reporting that "all of them were Hitlerites to a man. They admitted to the atrocities they had committed, refused to believe that the Americans had taken Rennes, refused to discuss the Hitler regime and refused to explain why they had French jewelry, money, and identity cards on them." Knox added that the prisoners amounted to a "considerable number" and "were all subsequently shot by the FFI."[75] The Jedburghs could not stop the Maquis from killing the prisoners even had they tried, due to the tremendous pent-up hostility over the four-year occupation punctuated by the recent wave of repression and reprisals.

Jedburgh Teams Felix, Guy, and Gavin in eastern Brittany received orders to preserve bridges the 1st US Army needed to advance and to relay information on the Maquis who could perform reconnaissance for leading elements of the conventional forces. Felix radioed the SF Detachment assigned to the 1st US Army that it believed it had 4,000 to 6,000 men partially armed and organized just ahead of their front and provided their location to the American operations planners. By August 4 the SF Detachment in General Patton's 3rd Army radioed EMFFI that they had also contacted Felix and that the Jedburghs had organized the protection of the bridges and roads they intended to use from Dinan all the way to Guincamp and Morlaix in western Brittany. They also confirmed contact with the Inter-Allied mission led by Colonel Eon and Dewavrin on August 7.[76] Team Felix had parachuted into Brittany east of Team Frederick and consisted of French Major Jean Souquat who used the nom de guerre Jean Kernevel, British Captain John Marchant, and British W/T operator P. Calvin. Having had less than a month to establish themselves, they were probably at their most effective in explaining the FFI to the conventional forces who were abysmally ignorant of key issues. "In fact," Marchant wrote in his final report, "we met one Civil Affairs Captain at Dinan who did not know the name of General Koenig or what the initials FFI stood for. However we found him very cooperative."[77]

On the same night the action messages went out, EMFFI deployed the Aloes mission from England to act as the leading element of General Koenig's command. Colonel Eon's men numbered about thirty as they deployed into Brittany to set up their headquarters. With them was a Jedburgh liaison officer who hoped to build a healthy liaison between Aloes and the area's Jedburgh teams. On August 6, SFHQ notified Giles about the imminent arrival of Aloes and directed Giles to contact them, placing Giles under the command of Aloes as it was doing with all the other Jedburgh teams. Because Giles was in a central position, Aloes appointed them to be their main liaison to the Maquis throughout Finistère. Captain Grall concentrated on this new mission that put him in a key position regarding

Brittany's Résistance. Captain Knox also made reconnaissance trips with the Aloes commander and organized mopping up operations as the German army clung to scattered positions. Knox also met with American commanders entering the area, advised them on local conditions, and assigned French scouts to their headquarters.[78]

With the arrival of Middleton's VIII Armored Corps, the teams' role shifted to liaison work assisting the conventional forces. Crozon, a town on the end of the Brittany peninsula, served as the last German holdout in Giles' area. OB West had directed Ramcke's 2nd Fallschirmjägers to hold on to the port of Brest, and Ramcke and General Fahrmbacher's XXV Armee Korps had been preparing for such a mission for weeks. Giles aided the 17th and 15th Cavalry Squadrons' attack on the approaches to Crozon by coordinating actions with the FFI, and in the words of the Team Giles report, the Americans and French "cooperated magnificently."[79] EMFFI brought Giles back to England by sea prior to the final reduction of Crozon.[80]

TEAM GEORGE EVADES AND ATTEMPTS TO REORGANIZE THE LOIRE-INFERIEURE

Team George had reconstituted their mission after nearly three weeks of evading German patrols. Still working with the regional military delegate Barthélemy, they finally gained sound footing with a Maquis network to the northeast of Nantes. Once there and meeting in the home of a friendly local leader, they discussed how to get something going in their new area. Barthélemy, acting in his capacity as the DMR, prevailed upon the French Jedburgh Captain Rageneau to become the DMR for the Department of Loire-Inferieure. Rageneau protested since he believed this was beyond the scope of his mission. But since Barthélemy had no one else to do it, he agreed. So Team George became the de facto delegate for the department on July 4. As they attempted to create a guerrilla force capable of operating against the Germans, they discovered that this department had a wider variety of Résistance groups than most of Brittany. Those differences complicated their efforts. "The political situation was a nightmare," Cyr and Rageneau later wrote. In their view, the groups fell into four kinds: "political

groups interested in resistance, resistance groups interested in politics, political groups pretending to be interested in the *Résistance* but only really
interested in politics, and resistance groups not interested in politics (these
being the angels.)" Noting there could be more than one group for each
category, they tried to plow through the confusion attempting to ascertain
who could do what mission and whom they could trust. The Jeds believed
that the Front National leaders were in the first group and the Organisation
de Résistance de l'armée or ORA fell in the angelic last group. However, the
ORA was not without fault as numbers reported in their battalions were
often barely enough to fill a company. Realizing that the lack of weapons
depressed Maquis numbers, George attempted to get more arms but never
succeeded as the EMFFI suspected their transmissions to be a Gestapo deception and therefore sent them nothing.[81] Team George spent the month
of July and into August working to consolidate groups they believed would
actually conduct sabotage and raids. Having prevailed on the local groups
to unite behind them to fight the Germans, they succeeded in establishing
some sense of unity. They even met and were on excellent terms with Yves
Lemoan who was the regional delegate for the Comité de Libération. But
they also had to guard against German infiltration of their growing organization, and in many ways they became more like underground agents than
soldiers behind the lines. They were in civilian clothes and had blended
into the local scenery so cleverly that they often had lunch in their local
bistro while the same Gestapo officer occupied the table next to them.[82]

But as the US 3rd Army approached and their operations became more
important to Eisenhower's operations, Team George found little success.
EMFFI's disbelief in George's radio transmissions for weapons deliveries
resulted in nothing and their reputation with the local Résistance groups
dropped considerably after they had spent weeks establishing it. "We were
desolated and felt that our credit and authority could not stand much
longer on mere good words and promises," the team wrote after their return.
Upon hearing the BBC message declaring open guerrilla warfare, "we cried
like kids considering our useless set, our useless work and all the dangers
the patriots of the Loire Inferieure had gone through to get that point,
remembering how many guys in prison or under the earth had paid for

the trouble they had looking for useless grounds and organizing useless reception committees for planes which never came."[83] Their department's Maquis, which they estimated at around 4,000 men, lacked the weapons that would make them a part of the Allied effort. EMFFI did not believe George was actually who they said they were until August 10 when Cyr and Rageneau infiltrated Allied lines and presented themselves and some captured documents regarding the St. Nazaire port fortifications to the 3rd Army's intelligence director. Next they ran into Lieutenant Colonel Powell. He recognized them by their OSS jackets and finally now Team George could get weapons for their Maquis. They went back across the lines and in the end equipped their Maquis for the action against the German Festung at St. Nazaire and to help protect the 3rd Army's southern flank.[84]

BRITTANY CONCLUSION

M. R. D. Foot, writing the official history of SOE activities in France considered the Aloes mission to be a "striking success."[85] However, Knox believed differently and thought their presence irrelevant. Given his French teammate's opinion, perhaps it would be fair to say that Aloes was too late to effect the guerrilla warfare of July and early August, but that its presence served to support Major General Middleton very well when the Germans retreated into their defenses around Brest.[86] Relations with Aloes was certainly strained as Knox's language describing Eon's mission is heavy with sarcasm due to his disagreement regarding how Giles should be employed. Dewavrin reacted unkindly toward the American Captain Knox and told him that "the sight of my uniform made him feel ill."[87] By arriving so late, the Aloes mission became superfluous. According to Knox, he left Colonel Eon "and his useless staff alone."[88] But the command of Brittany's Maquis was largely performed by the SAS commander Bourgoin operating in concert with the regional military delegate (DMRs). Certainly, their ability to coordinate suffered because they had to stay on the move and avoid arrest, but as a command element behind the lines, Bourgoin, Willk, and Barthélemy and their Jedburgh teams pulled off some successes. The high density of German troops, the importance attached to the region by both the Allies and the Germans, and the relative political unity of the Maquis all created unique conditions in the region. The Jedburgh team deployments to Brittany exemplified the original operational concept the early SOE planners envisaged. In all, EMFFI deployed twelve Jedburgh teams to Brittany, several SAS missions with over 300 soldiers, and coordinated 206 tons of weapons drops during the month of July, resulting in Willk's belief that they had armed 18,489 Breton Maquisards by the time the order came to commence hostilities on August 3.[89] Recalling the early planning discussed in Chapter 1, the EMFFI deployed the Jedburghs to Brittany anticipating the widespread loss of their agents and wanting the Jedburghs to act as their replacements. However, the creation of a French-led organization, the EMFFI, that would run the whole operation was not foreseen by SOE nor did the SOE foresee the Gaullists eclipsing them as SHAEF's primary means to command the Résistance. Mockler-Ferryman was gone and there was, due to enemy successes and French assumption of control of the operations for France, no meaningful F Section presence in Brittany. General Koenig had succeeded in gaining complete command of all the SOE and OSS assets as well as the Breton Maquis. Some scholars estimate that the FFI in Brittany numbered around 35,000 armed men. Luc Capdevila notes the problem with such an assessment given the nature of the "spontaneous mobilization."[90] However, the number the Allies believed they armed at the time largely agrees with postwar historians' estimations of what was within the realm of the possible. So, if they did indeed have nearly 20,000 FFI under their command at the beginning of August, how well did they utilize them?

Due to a single Résistance group in Brittany, the Jedburgh teams rarely had to mediate between political factions or contemplate ramifications of supporting one group over the other. Team George is the exception to this and its members did have to negotiate their way through the local politics; but once established, they would have enjoyed some success had their communications not been suspect. Either politics, poor communications, or lack of arms proved to be the source of Jedburgh failures in France. Bernard Knox believed the communist philosophy had very little hold on such a rural and religious area and with the FTP filled with non-idealistic young men who simply wanted to fight the Germans, Knox considered politics to be "unimportant."[91] Since that was the case, and since EMFFI arranged for many of the drops that the Jedburghs, DMRs, and SAS requested, the Brittany FFI was largely successful during the first week of August in harassing the German forces as the American conventional units made their way into the region. However, there was a great deal of murder and mayhem, in addition to the legitimate military action Eisenhower and his commanders sought. German General Fahrmbacher's policy of ruthless actions against anyone suspected of supporting the Résistance turned on the Wehrmacht with the Maquis shooting prisoners and spies as Knox, Grall, and Tack's report makes clear. But it seems a stretch to blame the mere presence of the Jedburghs or the SAS for provoking the shooting of prisoners. Indeed, the presence of the Jedburghs and their work with the Maquis often mitigated such actions and kept the FFI leashed to Eisenhower's intent. Indeed, Bob Kehoe of Team Frederick wrote after the war that while the headquarters staff might often "talk of 'command and control' our role was better described as 'convince and induce'" when it came to the Maquis.[92] Such is the nature of partisan warfare and attempting to rein in the passion of the people, to use Clausewitz's words.

8

Setting the Trap

While Eisenhower and Koenig consolidated and reorganized French control over the Forces Françaises l'Intérieur (FFI), Allied operations in France continued with increasing speed. American Lieutenant General Omar Bradley's 1st Army and British Lieutenant General Miles Dempsey's 2nd Army had spent the days since D-Day attempting to capture the Cherbourg port and the city of Caen, respectively. Possessing Cherbourg would give the Allies one of the ports required to supplement their growing numbers while Caen sat astride key roads Eisenhower needed to drive to the east and south out of Normandy. On June 26 the Germans surrendered Cherbourg and Caen finally fell on July 8, the same day Bernard Knox, Paul Grall, and Gordon Tack of Jedburgh Team Giles landed in Brittany. The Wehrmacht countered the Allies with most of their armored forces facing General Dempsey's British and Canadians while the Wehrmacht forces that faced General Bradley's US forces were largely comprised of Infantry and Airborne units. The 2nd SS "Das Reich" Division that had been ordered to stop its "clearing operations" in southern France as they were committing their deadly work in Oradour-sur-Glane, struggled mightily to pass through the Maquis and Allied fighter bomber harassment. They finally arrived, regrouped, and began participating in the Normandy combat on June 20.[1] Teams Quinine and Ammonia had assisted in that delay, but the infamous 2nd SS Division's delayed arrival can also be attributed to F Section agents and their networks, as well as the BCRA-controlled networks such as those run by Eugene Dechelette, regional military delegate in R5, implementing their part of Plan Vert. Additionally, as Max Hastings has pointed out, OB West did not issue the order for the Division to move north until June 10. Therefore, part of the credit for the delay should be given to Gerd von Rundstedt and perhaps Adolf Hitler, who took that long to approve.[2]

The Wehrmacht succeeded in slowing down Allied efforts in Normandy while they mistakenly waited for what they believed would be Lieutenant General George Patton's First US Army Group (FUSAG) to hit the beaches in the Pas de Calais in northeastern France. But Hitler's suspicions were entrenched into firm belief by a sophisticated Allied deception campaign. In reality, Patton's force, the 3rd US Army, began to arrive in France in the middle of July and became officially active on August 1.[3] With that group was Special Force Detachment 11 commanded by Lieutenant Colonel Robert I. "Rip" Powell. His role was to be a part of the operations staff, or G-3, in Patton's headquarters and enable cooperation with the FFI as the 3rd Army pressed the attack into France. Each of the numbered Allied Armies had their own Special Force detachment but not all used it as Patton did, nor did they have the need for FFI support.[4] As Patton's superior General Bradley shifted his emphasis south and east along the north side of the Loire River, Patton wanted to race as fast as his tanks, fuel, and soldiers could go. This necessitated aid from two different methods of warfare than the 3rd Army could summon with their own soldiers and vehicles. To do it, Patton relied on the US Army Air Forces to provide close air support, but he also relied upon the irregular forces of the FFI to his south. Patton's fellow army commanders to his north were not in a position that exposed their flanks, nor were they encouraged to race as far as they could, so for them FFI support was not as crucial.

The Allied invasion of southern France was finally approved on July 2. Not knowing whether he would get the landing craft necessary for placing his forces ashore, Lieutenant General Alexander M. Patch began final planning and rehearsals for the southern invasion of France, code named Anvil and given the go ahead to land between Toulon and Nice on August 15. But Churchill, who had never favored an invasion of southern France and sought to use those forces for further landings in Italy or in the Balkans, continued to argue against it. He failed to convince Eisenhower to call off the southern invasion, and Eisenhower told him that if it was a political issue, he would have to appeal to directly to Roosevelt.[5] Churchill did so in a message to the president's close aide Harry Hopkins only a week before the invasion was to begin. Opening up with compliments regarding American forces and their quick movement into Brittany as well as east into central France, the prime minister complained, "I'm grieved to find that not even splendid victories and widening opportunities do not bring us together on strategy." He went on for another five pages on the reasons for canceling or diverting what had now been renamed Dragoon.[6] Hopkins would have none of it and answering for the president, who was at his Hyde Park home at the time, he replied to Churchill that it was far too late to shift things now, and that the way north "will be much more rapid than you anticipate. They have nothing to stop us." He went on to add, "The French will rise and abyssiniate [*sic*] large numbers of Germans, including, I trust, Monsieur Laval."[7] While the word "abyssiniate" is not in the dictionary, Hopkins apparently meant to imply that the Wehrmacht would suffer the same fate as Italian Dictator Mussolini's stalwart troops had in the Horn of Africa the year before. While Hopkins's hopes may have been more rhetorical than Eisenhower would have himself stated, the Allies did want Patch's 7th Army to drive up the Rhone River valley and eventually link with Eisenhower's forces coming across France from the west. Patch and Patton were to shut the door on fleeing German forces as quickly as possible. If successful, the Allies could potentially trap thousands of German soldiers in France. So while Patton wanted the FFI to protect his southern flank, Patch sought FFI intelligence for his forward movement and wanted Cochet's and Koenig's Maquis to harass the Germans along their routes to and from the battle area, cut their lines of communication, and sabotage enemy supplies and facilities.

Attempting to control this would be Special Force Unit No. 4 commanded by Lieutenant Colonel William Bartlett. Like his counterparts in SHAEF, Bartlett served within Patch's operations division and had a liaison to his intelligence staff as well as his subordinate units.[8]

Of course, Hopkins was exaggerating quite a bit when he told the prime minister that the Germans had nothing to stop Allied troops. The 11th Panzer Division and the portions of the 9th Panzer Division were still in the south, as well as several Reserve Infantry and Mountain Light Infantry Divisions. Additionally, there were anti-aircraft or flak units, naval and marine forces in the port areas, the Feldgendarmes scattered around the main cities, and thousands of civilian administrators working for the occupation authority, Militärbefehlshaber in Frankreich (MBF). But for the Allies, the focus of attention was the armored units, as they afforded the enemy an offensive combat force. The location and combat status of the 9th and 11th Panzer Divisions and smaller mobile units were of great interest to the Allied commanders. Therefore as the Allies maneuvered through France, they sought to use the Maquis to stifle the enemy's mobility and focused on these two divisions where possible.

As Patton's 3rd Army began coming ashore in Normandy behind Lieutenant General Bradley's forces in the middle of July, the Allies, including Churchill and Roosevelt, began to see the utility of Maquis action and sought to bring more of it to bear. De Gaulle's views were more circumspect, however, and he appreciated the situation with greater sobriety. He sought to emphasize what the French were doing for their nation's liberation but did not think things had gone smoothly. Writing to General Wilson at Algiers, de Gaulle stated that the Résistance in Brittany, the French Alps, and the Massif Central were having the desired effect, but believed that especially in the Vercors, "There is no doubt the opening of guerrilla activity was begun too soon" and that the supplies were insufficient and too late.[9] Eisenhower's staff, however, seemed to be amazed at what was occurring and viewed the German attacks on the Vercors, described in Chapter 6, as a strategic benefit. SFHQ's monthly report summed up the action as having diverted portions of the 11th Panzer Division, as well as infantry, artillery, and airborne troops estimated at 10,000 soldiers. "The forces of the FFI thus were able to divert a considerable ENEMY force which might have been used elsewhere."[10] Eisenhower's aide, Captain Harry Butcher, remarked that the "Résistance groups in France have stopped considerable rail traffic, out [sic] three main canals and have blown up 10,000 tons of ammunition and a depot." He also noted "severe fighting" in central and southern France and remarked that "We are still dropping into France SAS troops, Jedburgh teams, jeeps, armor and ammunition not only from England, but from North Africa."[11] Special Force Headquarters and its parent for France, General Koenig's EMFFI staff, sought to utilize the Maquis, but the swelling numbers necessitated careful selection of where to send those arms Butcher spoke of, and how quickly to deploy the Jeds.

With nearly one hundred Jedburgh teams in reserve for France as of July 17, only nineteen had been deployed, demonstrating a hesitance based on several factors. So far, SFHQ had deployed the Jeds focusing on central France with Teams Hugh, Hamish, Andy, and Isaac; southern France with Teams Bugatti, Ammonia, and Quinine; the Rhone River valley with Teams Willys, Veganin, Dodge, and Chloroform; and Brittany with Teams Frederick, George, Giles, Hilary, Francis, Gilbert, Gavin, and Guy. When the Maquis swelled to uncontrollable numbers, the Allies went through a major reassessment of how to use the Jedburgh teams along with a careful evaluation of their ability to supply the FFI. They also ascertained the available airlift with an appreciation for enemy interference, moon phases, and the certain delays from weather. Their planning was based on new assumptions now learned from experience but in many cases implemented by the new French staff officers as Koenig took over. His control can clearly be seen as F Section requests for sending teams to France went through either Koenig or his Chief of Staff Colonel Henri Ziegler as a note of July 28 suggests. F Section requested Jedburgh teams to be sent to various locations in France and the operations section of EMFFI considered them and approved of most, but they did so with an appreciation of their DMRs' views and Inter-Allied missions that were already in the area, and disapproved others based on the belief that uniformed teams were not yet appropriate to the region around Paris. One thing the British, French, and American officers who now comprised EMFFI wished to do was to send Jedburghs to eastern France and the departments of Doubs, Haute Saône, Aisne, Cote d'Or, and Vosges. The F Section officer, British Lieutenant Colonel Buckmaster, apparently did not object to any of Zeigler's points as his notes in the margins agree with all of the comments.[12] Written the day after Mockler-Ferryman's resignation, but a day before Gubbins approved it, Buckmaster, who was now EMFFI's British deputy for operations along with American Lieutenant Colonel Paul van der Stricht, evidently understood Koenig's growing role in France.

While the Allies did not all agree or understand the effect the Maquis might actually be having on the enemy, the Germans suffered considerable consternation themselves. Not only were they overwhelmed with enemy action, fuel shortages, sabotaged communications, and hit-and-run attacks throughout France, but the normal fog of war became increasingly thick when on July 20 elements inside the army nearly succeeded with their assassination of Hitler and an army coup against the Nazis Party. In Paris on July 20, the commander of the MBF, Carl Heinrich von Stülpnagel, received the first and incorrect report that Hitler was dead, and he began to arrest the Paris-based SS officers and troops. But when von Kluge, who had taken over from Rundstedt at OB West, refused to join the coup and everyone heard the truth of Hitler's survival, the estimated 1,200 SS who had been arrested were politely released the next day. Stülpnagel's days were numbered and he was recalled to Germany on July 21. His suicide attempt en route to Berlin only landed him in a hospital, and after a summary trial he was executed on August 30.[13]

However, throughout it all the Wehrmacht was able to develop a fairly clear understanding of what the Allies were attempting to get the Maquis to do. By the end of July the Germans turned their understanding of Allied special operations intent into propaganda. The *Pariser Zeitung* of July 29/30 ran a long article claiming that the Allies were conducting an illegal war in France due to the use of "so-called regular armed forces of General Koenig which consist of the French Résistance organization formed under English leadership. Englishmen, Americans, and de Gaullists form the framework and are parachuted in to try in vain to produce a rising of the people."[14] Clearly the Gestapo had succeeded in untangling the difference between the SAS or OG commando missions and what the Jedburghs were sent to do. How did they know this? By the end of July, the Jedburgh reports of Frederick, Giles, as well as other teams discussed their discovery of security leaks and traitors in their Maquis. The intelligence gained by these moles must have informed the Gestapo of the three-man Allied missions. Moreover, as discussed in Chapter 4, William Savy had told the internal commander of the FFI of the Jedburgh plan and it may have come up during General Dejussieu's interrogation after his arrest in May (see Chapter 4). So while no Jeds had yet been killed or taken prisoner, the Gestapo's penetration of various Résistance groups aided German and Vichy efforts to understand how the Allies were actively working with these groups against the Wehrmacht. Furthermore, their propaganda, by basing its argument on what was legal to do within the framework of the Armistice Germany and France signed in 1940, was a point that also concerned the Allies and General Koenig. De Gaulle's position had always been that because an armed enemy had invaded France, the Armistice of 1940 was null. His legal view of the matter flowed from this belief while the Germans of course thought otherwise and believed instead that what the Allies were doing was inciting an illegal rebellion against the legal government of France. While the Germans may have thought this way, they of course did not act like it since their occupation of the entirety of France demonstrated who Hitler believed was the real authority in France. As for the Jedburghs inciting the Maquis violence, it is clear the German propagandist also misunderstood the source of the inciting. It was German actions over the course of the long occupation that provoked the "Terroristen" as the Wehrmacht called them. Ironically, the Jeds, in most circumstances, were often found themselves trying to halt the spasm of violence the Maquis sought and, in theory at least, would be de Gaulle's voice, through Eisenhower and Koenig, regarding what violence was legitimate and useful.

Now too far along in the effort to reconsider or significantly alter course regarding the legality of the FFI, the Allies themselves groped for a way to present the FFI as a legally constituted force. Before the invasion, on May 20, General Koenig was given copies of the First World War's Armistice agreement of November 1918, the Geneva Convention of July 1929, and a copy of the German and Italian Armistice agreements with Pétain from June of 1940.[15] He may have requested these documents to see how far he could use irregular forces and the nature of their rights in a treaty that

Germany had signed. Before D-Day, SHAEF was also concerned about irregular warfare and decided to support the issue of armbands to identify
them as soldiers under the French flag, the FFI, giving them some international legitimacy granted to soldiers in uniform, and parachute them in
with the weapons and other supplies. On June 9, the Provisional Government of France officially adopted the FFI as an armed force under its authority.[16] SFHQ arranged for 14,000 armbands to be dropped on June 25
during the daylight Operation Buick.[17] The Germans soon noticed the armbands on FFI and reports of them quickly began filtering in to OB West
noting the presence of Maquis with the armbands by late June.[18] Furthermore, EMFFI messages to the DMRs emphasized wearing the armbands
and that the "Brassards" as the French called them, would be included in
the equipment drops. However, Colonel Zeigler radioed Dechelette, the
regional military delegate in Region 5, that it was unclear to what extent the
Germans would recognize this makeshift uniform.[19] General Eisenhower's
staff did not know either and did not think the French Provisional Government's proclamations nor the armbands would be sufficient for the typical
German soldier. General Whiteley of Eisenhower's staff requested General
Koenig to work out how he could begin the process of enrolling the Maquis
into the French Army and provide them with a service book "which while
not bulky" due to airlift constraints, could be viewed by the Germans as
a bona fide military document similar to what the Germans had done for
their own "Organisation Todt" members who were now being used as combatants.[20] All of this was being done in a large-scale game of catch-up due to
the lack of ability to plan out such key elements prior to starting Overlord.
The argument between FDR and de Gaulle had deep ramifications.

SETTING THE TRAP: CONVENTIONAL FORCES
AND COORDINATING WITH THE MAQUIS

On the same day that Operation Cadillac occurred—July 14—the Allies
wished to initiate a third such operation and EMFFI began organizing another daylight airdrop of weapons and supplies to the Maquis. SHAEF and
EMFFI gave the highest priority to the Vosges region of eastern France, but

after more than a week, they scrubbed that part of the operation due to "enemy action there being too great to allow a daylight reception."[21] For the nearly two hundred B-17s to reach their targets using low altitude daylight runs, enemy anti-aircraft concentration had to be light, and the Vosges did not qualify. After some re-assessment, Operation Buick was conducted on August 1 delivering 2,286 containers from 192 aircraft to 4 drop zones in southern and eastern France. Buick provided weapons to groups in southern France between Lyon and Dijon and to groups east of Lyon near the towns of Albertville and Annecy in three different Departments.[22] But this did nothing for the high-priority Vosges Maquis. Koenig's staff began planning another daylight mission but in the meantime, more of the normal Special Operations nighttime missions would have to make up the difference.

The day before Buick, EMFFI made arrangements to make up for the fact that the Vosges would not be supplied during the next day's operation and began planning a Jedburgh and SAS mission for the region with the hope of sending Team Jacob "to arm up to a maximum of about 7000 men...and keep them supplied" for this key region.[23] Indeed throughout the month of July, as EMFFI was organizing, SHAEF had instructed Koenig to arm "approximately 77,000" men by the first of August and to sustain them. Doing so meant canceling a French proposed Airborne Operation code named "Caiman" that was intended to develop one of the Maquis concentrations into a more potent sore point behind the German lines. But there were simply not enough planes to mount it, forcing Eisenhower to cancel it.[24] Allied planners knew there was a shortage of parachutes as well as airlift sorties but believed that 77,000 men was a realistic number. With Operation Anvil finally given a firm go, the intent was for those airlift missions to support the Maquis who in turn would conduct widespread guerrilla actions aiding General Patch's invasion in the south as well as Eisenhower's progress across France.

The southern theater's rough equivalent of SFHQ, the Special Projects Operations Centre (SPOC), communicated their priorities to General Koenig that explained how they sought to use the Maquis. The same day that Operation Buick dropped weapons north and east of Lyon, SPOC drew up its plan for how to use its fifteen Jedburgh teams. SPOC wanted teams to deploy to the Aveyron, Savoie, Hautes Alpes, and the Basses Alpes departments and cut the roads and railroads while the last three teams would also foment guerrilla warfare. Furthermore, two more teams would be sent to the Gard and a team to cover the Ariège and Pyrenées Orientales in order to cut roads and railroads out of Tarbes and Avignon while using the Maquis to block the Spanish border so Wehrmacht troops could not flee south into neutral Spain. SPOC's seven teams already in France were also to step up pressure on certain lines of communication, and in one instance, Team Chloroform would be shifted from its present location in the Haute Alps near Italy to come back to the Rhone valley in order to harass German troops behind the main invasion area. Team Packard, comprised of American Captain Aaron Bank, French Captain Henri Denis, and Canadian radio operator F. Montfort, departed Algiers the night before and were to cut the road between Bozouls and Mende Pont d'Espret and the St. Flour to Campagnac railway. One Jedburgh team was held in reserve and Operational Groups and Inter-Allied Missions were also factored into SPOC's planning for how it would get the Maquis to support General Patch's invading forces for his D-Day on August 15.[25] The effect of it all was to have the Maquis harass German forces as they came to the invasion area down from the center of France through the Rhone River valley or from Toulouse and farther west in France. Primarily the planners were concerned about the 11th Panzer Division north of Toulouse at Montauban, as the largest threat to Patch's invasion force; and if the Maquis could successfully sabotage railroads and conduct hit-and-run raids, they could buy the invasion forces valuable time.

The planning and cooperation between the two Allied theaters now began in earnest. On August 1, Eisenhower directed Koenig to equip 120,000 men into the FFI by the end of the year and use 400 sorties per month to do so.[26] On August 2, the day Sergeant Bourgoin was killed in Pleuville, EMFFI told their colleagues in Algiers at SPOC that they were sending two Jedburgh officers, British Major Osborne Grenfells and American Lieutenant Lucien Conien, to Algiers. They would be leaving for Algiers on August 6 and take the communications equipment and supporting plans for six teams that would be controlled by London. The teams had to deploy from Algiers due to aircraft range limitations. General Koenig approved the deployment of Teams Jeremy, Joseph, John, Mark, Miles, and Martin to various F Section agents in southwestern France. The message added that General Cochet could use the remaining four of the ten teams that had previously arrived in North Africa for "whatever you think fit."[27] The same day SHAEF received the Mediterranean Theater's Commander airlift priorities. General Wilson directed that fifty-five missions supply the Maquis in the Vercors, hoping to sustain them now as they were under a concentrated attack by elements of the 157th Infantry Division. The Drôme, Haute Savoie, Savoie, and Isère outside of Vercors were to get thirty sorties of weapons and supplies. The Department of Ardeche was to get fifty sorties, while Aveyron was to get thirty, Lozere twenty-five, and Lot et Garonne and Tarn et Garonne fifteen; Pyrenees et Gers was to get fifteen and then after the invasion it was to get seventy airlift sorties.[28] It appears that Allied planners were betting that the 11th Panzer Division would not leave their camps north of Toulouse until Anvil began, and the planners believed that inserting the Jedburgh teams just before the southern invasion's first day would be sufficient time to impact the 11th Panzer Division's attempt to reinforce German defenses.

While the plans for the Allied invasion of southern France were beginning to crystallize, EMFFI's plan on how to use the Maquis to support operations outside of Brittany seemed to get scant attention in early August. General Patton's 3rd Army officially came into being on August 1 with the schizophrenic mission of moving west to take Brest while moving south and east toward Rennes, Angers, and Le Mans. When German forces facing the northern Allied invasion withdrew to a line around Mortain in order to establish stronger defenses, it created a vacuum and Patton intended to fill it. Here one can see how events began to unfold due to circumstances rather than any specific Allied intent. In other words planning what one sought to achieve was easier than actually accomplishing this aim due to the constantly changing nature of events.

Operational plans had to be devised for how to use the new Jedburgh teams while the Jedburgh teams in the field had to be maintained and directed. Team Hamish in Indre worked the region between Châteauroux and Bourges.

They had been there since June 13 and needed help organizing the Maquis just east of their area in the Cher south of Bourges. They realized the need in Cher and related it to London on July 28 saying, "500 men located southeast of Bourges without arms. Evidently could use Jed team." Team Hamish offered to receive a team on one of their drop zones and help them move to the region to begin arming and training those five hundred men. Here, as well as in most of France, getting men into the Maquis was also no problem as Hitler had released a "mobilization order sending our recruiting way up."[29] The problem was how to equip, train, and employ them all.

EMFFI was probably aware of this issue, but offered no realistic solution for dealing with it. Illuminating the increasing problem, Captain Anstett of Hamish told SFHQ that organizing the Cher had just become easier as "We have found a French colonel who will take command....He has 12,000 men and all request arms." EMFFI staff decided to fulfill Hamish's request for another team and on August 3 completed orders for Team Ivor comprised of British Captain John Cox, French Lieutenant Robert Colin using the nom de guerre Yves Dantec, and American Sergeant Robert Goddard. The team was to deploy south of the village of St. Armand in the Cher, establish a relationship with the local FFI commander, identify more drop zones, and organize the resistance fighters into units of no more than one hundred men.[30] On August 6, SFHQ told Hamish, "sending Jed team IVOR and 1 million in containers marked with white cross on ground Paris tonight." Looking forward to seeing his friends, American Sergeant Watters of Hamish replied enthusiastically, "All set. Tell the boys to bring some American cigarettes for us."[31]

However, the tone changed dramatically in the very next message following team Ivor's arrival. "Goddard killed. Do not know how but he died instantly upon hitting ground. Chute opened but not completely....Burial tomorrow. More later."[32] The American radio operator's chute never opened properly and he and the radio equipment, did not survive. Cox, Colin, and the Jeds of Hamish along with some of their Maquis buried Goddard near Beddes, about 40 kilometers southwest of St. Armand-Montrond. The Cher's Maquis and Colonel Bertrand who was attempting to get organized and armed were now set back further until a replacement could be found for Goddard. SFHQ knew that Team Andy's officers suffered severe injuries on their parachute jump, making it a non-operational team. However, the radioman, British Sergeant Glen Loosmore, was able to perform his duties so they made arrangements for Loosmore to travel to the Cher to replace Goddard and become Ivor's radio operator. On August 13, Loosmore arrived in Cher and then had to resolve the technical difficulties attempting to use his Team Andy encoded radio while serving in Team Ivor.[33] For several days, EMFFI could not understand why "Andy" was broadcasting when the team had been deactivated, and Loosmore had to convince them he was now with Ivor in the Cher.[34]

Not only did the situation on the ground alter their intentions forcing administrative and policy shifts, but the takeover of operations by EMFFI led to a great deal of confusion in France. Primarily, the efficient routing of communications traffic became a source of failure within the staff. Coordinating communications within EMFFI and their counterparts at SOE who managed the stations became so poor that by the end of August two teams had actually deployed to France without the knowledge of the communications section.[35] That meant that when Team Alec, which deployed on August 10 and Team Bunny that was in France on August 18 broadcast on their appointed frequency at the appointed time, no one was listening. Alec's officers, never realizing what had occurred, later complained that "shortly after our arrival [in France] it became evident that we were not going to receive much assistance from London."[36] Instead, they coordinated as well as they could with the local FFI and later the conventional forces that operated near their area. Team Alexander's radio operator, Dick Franklin, realized his messages would be answered and understood if sent in French, but not English. In fact, it was clear to him that EMFFI had completely ignored all his messages as EMFFI sent him his first message in French, after the team had been in France for some time. Franklin realized that London still believed him to be in Creuse when the team had been in Charente for the last ten days.[37]

Airlift also became something too great to manage among the EMFFI staff largely comprised of French officers unaccustomed to marshalling Allied capacity. Airlift estimates that the Special Force planners had done in mid and late June demonstrate their understanding of airlift's capability and how many FFI could be initially supplied and then maintained for continuous operations. The Anglo-American planners had calculated that one planeload of 15 containers could arm 60 Maquis, and that another planeload of 15 containers packed with replacement arms and additional ammunition would re-supply 100 Maquis; from these estimations, the planners figured that their current force of 15,000 men would require 200 to 250 successful sorties to re-supply, and that the 78,000 unarmed volunteers would require *1,300 successful airlift sorties each month* just to give them their initial weapons and ammunition.[38] Therefore, for SHAEF to arm this number, it would need more than 1,500 successful missions each month. However, just before Overlord, SFHQ staff planners indicated that no more than 575 successful airlift sorties per month could be expected from the 115 British and American clandestine aircraft available in the UK and North Africa due to enemy activity, maintenance issues, moon phases, weather, and reception parties. Adding B-17s for the large-scale daylight missions contributed only an average of 200 more sorties each month.[39] Therefore, when Eisenhower directed EMFFI on August 1 to arm and maintain 120,000 FFI by the end of 1944 but only granted them 400 sorties per month, he seemed to be setting them up for failure. Re-supplying 120,000 FFI would require 1,800 successful sorties per month while 400 sorties re-supplied only an estimated 26,667 Maquis. The situation became even more problematic when one considers the sortie success rate was expected to be around 50 percent. For the Maquis, this meant that weapons would have to come from other sources and the FFI would never get enough from air drops.

Such shortages mandated that priorities be set and rigidly adhered to. Noting that more than four hundred sorties were unlikely—and the shortage of parachute silk made things even more difficult—Eisenhower defined his priorities on August 15 as Operation Dragoon's forces worked their way ashore near St. Tropez, France. Using the Free French regional designations of areas in France, Regions P1, P2, and P3 that are around Paris; C2 and C3 covering the Meuse and Moselle valleys and the Vosges; and A4 and A5 alongside the Belgium border were first priority. AFHQ's missions in R1 were second priority and the rest of France was third.[40] R5 and R6, the zones needed to protect the Eisenhower's southern flank were last in priority as were Regions D1 and D2 which comprised the Jura, Doubs, Côtes d'Or, and the Haute Marne Departments. Furthermore, the same directive complained to General Koenig that Brittany had received far more of its allotment while his current airlift pace supporting General Wilson's request in southern France could not continue for August.[41] So not only was the capability lower than the requirement, but the sorties that special air squadrons did generate in the first half of August were not getting to the priority regions. Mockler-Ferryman commented in his resignation letter on July 27 that he knew deliveries were "going to the wrong places" but was unable to direct corrections due to French suspicions of him.[42] Clearly the swelling ranks of Maquis could not count on the Allies to re-supply them; they could not even look to them for initial arms and equipment.

Despite the paucity of weapons for the overwhelming numbers of Maquis, EMFFI began the process to deploy more teams into southern France, an area that was the lowest priority. In addition to Team Ivor, EMFFI confirmed plans to send Team Alec to the northern section of Cher along with an SAS element. The team was to report to the F Section Circuit leader Philippe de Vomécourt and maintain a liaison between him and any Maquis groups they could establish contact with. The Jedburghs were to organize them into groups of no more than one hundred "and that as soon as equipment is available they should start guerrilla activity but not repeat not open warfare."[43] The same day, Colonel Zeigler ordered three more teams and three small groups of French SAS to deploy to central France. Jedburgh Team James was to go to the Correze, Alexander to the Creuse, and Lee to Vienne as Zeigler directed them to "prevent enemy movements on the railway lines Perigeux-Limoges-Chateauroux and Toulouse-Limoges-Chateauroux." The presence of the 11th Panzer Division must have been what provoked the interest in those railway lines as the 11th Division now was placed just north of Toulouse. The SAS and presumably the Jeds were not to "encourage formation of large units by resistance and will confine themselves to guerrilla actions, avoiding pitched battles and open warfare."[44] Teams Alec and Lee deployed to France on August 10, Team James deployed on August 11, and Team Alexander got off late not arriving until August 13. The 11th Panzer Division received orders to move east to Avignon on August 9 and began leaving on August 14.[45] Eisenhower did not need to worry about these tanks coming north because the 11th Panzer headed east to prepare to counter the expected Allied invasion somewhere on the southern coast. The day after the tank division began moving, that invasion became a reality.

When Anvil, now renamed Dragoon, occurred on August 15, Hitler and his commanders in France realized the nature of their situation had significantly changed and they began making different moves in order to save the German forces from being trapped. Partisan operations, which had gained a certain regularity for teams like Ian, Hugh, Hamish, and Harry in July and early August, now began to be more chaotic as the Germans decided to evacuate southwestern France. On August 16 Hitler directed the Wehrmacht, Feldgendarmes, Kriegsmarine, Luftwaffe, and all other German administrators to evacuate and they began making a concerted effort to leave resistance Regions B2, B1, R5, and R6 in southwestern France. The Wehrmacht's 16th Infantry Division was to be the northern covering force using the Loire River as a screen to protect their comrades from Eisenhower's forces to their north.[46] The 16th Infantry Division was a new designation for the former 158th Reserve Division.[47] Its commander, Generalleutnant Ernst Häckel, a veteran of the eastern front in 1941 and 1942, was to organize the defense of the German forces and personnel while they attempted to flee France via Dijon, then on through the Belfort Gap in Alsace, and from there into Germany.[48] Currently headquartered in a village southeast of Nantes and just south of where Team George was beginning to finally succeed in organizing local resistance, the Division began to move east to defend bridges at key locations on the Loire River.[49] Unknown to the Germans, their planned escape route lay in areas Eisenhower had made the lowest priority for arming. The Free French's DMRs Eugene Dechelette (Ellipse) in R5, Alexandre de Courson de la Villeneuve (Pyramide) in R6, Bernard Schlumberger (Droite) in R4, Jacques Davout d'Auerstaet (Ovale) in D1, and Pierre Hanneton (Ligne) in

D2 along with their Maquis and Jedburgh teams would have to perform their tasks with the weapons they currently possessed, fortified only by any leftover sorties that might drop them supplies when other areas could not be serviced. Evidently, Eisenhower was more concerned with what lay directly in front of his forces than what lay on his flanks.

The Résistance in R5 and R4 was a mix of nearly every southern group that had existed since the Armistice. The Provisional Government's Délégué Militaire Zone (DMZ) was Maurice Bourgès-Maunoury who went by the code name of Polygone. A politically astute man who turned thirty on August 19, he had originally come to France as the DMR for R1, the Lyon and upper Rhone River valley area. Due to persistent arrests, he was promoted to DMZ for the southern zone in February of 1944 and for a time was acting national delegate who "reorganized regions C and D after mass arrests there in March of 1944 with extraordinary speed and efficiency." When Chaban-Delmas was named the permanent National Military Delegate, (DMN) Bourgès-Maunoury then served as his assistant, while maintaining his DMZ position for the southern zone.[50] On his shoulders fell the task of creating a unity of action on behalf of de Gaulle and the provisional government in Algiers for southern France. He had even known of the Jedburgh plan as early as April when William Savy came to France on the Eclaireur mission and recieved intelligence about the nature of the Maquis, their numbers, and possible drop zones for the Jedburgh mission planners to use.[51] Bourgès-Maunoury had worked tirelessly and clandestinely for the Résistance and maintained communication with Koenig in London, the BCRA and Cochet in Algiers, his subordinate DMRs in the south like Dechelette, and the various FFI commanders in the Organisation de Résistance de l'armée (ORA), Armée Secrète (AS), and Franc-Tireurs et Partisans Français (FTP). Few understood the organization and nature of the southern Résistance as well as Bourgès-Maunoury. By late July and August of 1944, the months of the Libération, he was continually working with myriad local leaders, striking deals, demanding unity, and succeeding in his efforts. For instance, in August he visited R5 at least twice working with Dechelette and almost always succeeded at gaining the agreement among the parties that military action was what was necessary and that political issues needed to wait.[52] By their success, Bourgès-Maunoury, Chaban-Delmas, the DMRs, and the Commissaires de la République, who took regional political control on behalf of the Provisional Government during the Libération, proved to be the ones laying the foundation for postwar French political institutions. Their work was crucial.

Teams Bugatti and Quinine were now enjoying fits and starts of success in southern France and their work helped create the conditions that could slow down the 11th Panzer Division and capture as many other Germans as possible who were directed to evacuate on the August 16. Still lacking arms, Major "Hod" Fuller and de la Roche of Team Bugatti continually complained that "we were greatly handicapped by our lack of arms and explosives in spite of our daily message to Algiers for the same."[53] Nevertheless, when they received orders to begin "full scale guerrilla warfare" on August 14, they succeeded in organizing ambushes along the road between Tarbes and Toulouse, and on August 18 they captured the commander of Hauptverbindungsstab or HVSt 626, Generalmajor Leo Mayr, commander of the occupation forces for the Tarbes region. With the Germans now attempting to flee, the Jeds focused their efforts on protecting the Spanish frontier hoping to prevent "the Boches" from escaping into neutral Spain. Both Jed officers were pilots and the team managed to get ten small aircraft; de la Roche used an aircraft to scout out the best way to march their estimated 1,000 FFI up to Angoulême for operations against the Germans north of their area. On September 6 they also met with General Cochet on his visit to the area and worked to get their Maquis back from Angoulême and muster them into the French regular army now standing up in the region. Joining in on the liberation of Tarbes, Fuller was the Allied representative in the city's ceremony. But while, as one of the F Section assistants noted, Team Bugatti "was a terrific morale lifter on their arrival…the supplies they were promised and that they asked for were never sent and bit by bit disappointment followed enthusiasm."[54] While they achieved some successes in the southwest of France, in the end Bugatti was too far west to harass the 11th Panzer Division and too poorly supplied to fully exploit the area's Maquis.

But despite receiving nearly no weapons and poor communication, the Jedburghs in the region shifted their mission from what they were ordered to do and adapted it to fit their changing circumstances. MacPherson's team Quinine immediately began blowing bridges and tunnels when they heard of the invasion in the south and the Germans started to move, as Anvil started. Tommy MacPherson believed the number of dropped bridges and tunnels to be around a dozen in the Lot Department in the Massif Central, all attempting to prevent Germans from moving east, and the road from Aurillac to Saint Fleur received special attention. In one instance they contrived an elaborate ambush to trap Germans and Vichy police in a tunnel and succeeded in killing and wounding several hundred enemy soldiers.[55] Their success in cutting this road is greater when realizing what the teams north of them were also able to do.

Teams John, Collodion, Packard, and Minaret were in perfect position to harass the 11th Panzer's march from Montauban to Avignon. However, all of them ran into difficulties too great to surmount given the short time they had to work against the already moving 11th Panzer. Team John got to Montauban on August 22, just in time to radio back that the Panzer Division's former base was "liberated and department probably free of Boche" because they had simply left.[56] Team Collodian parachuted into the Lot, was met by MacPherson, and went into Aveyron as ordered to ambush Germans traveling through that department. But the FTP and the other Maquis in the region were shifting from being concerned about the Germans to being concerned about power after the war and acted with intent to use their weapons on each other after the Germans had left. The team did manage to get an arms drop and coordinate some ambushes, between the towns of Montauban, Rode, and Millar, but their mission in Aveyron was largely ineffective and when there were no longer enemy units in the area they sought to take some Maquis east to harass the departing Germans.[57] Team Packard had parachuted into the Lozere, on August 1 and thus had some time to devise plans and implement sabotage on roads and bridges in the Department. By August 22 the team and the local FFI leader had achieved some measure of unity and set ambushes and booby traps on the road from Ales to Uzez, to the west of

Avignon.[58] But by that time, the 11th Panzer Division had already passed through the area and was east of them in the Avignon area, preparing to cover the Wehrmacht's retreat to the north.[59] Team Minaret, that had been on alert for "nearly three weeks," finally deployed on August 14 to support Packard and concentrated on the road from Ganges to Alzon. However, this also was to the west of where most of the 11th Panzer was and thus these four teams were ineffective if SPOC's intent was slowing down the 11th Panzer Division. While the teams succeeded with many ambushes, killing, wounding, and delaying hundreds of the enemy from Montauban to Nimes, the Maquis only provided, as French historian Noguères noted in 1981, "a solid experience against guerrillas"[60] for the Germans but not a firm block to their escape.

SPOC sent Team Chrysler to the Ariège to work with the Fédération anarchiste ibérique (FAI), or the Federation of the Iberian Anarchists, a group that had been on the losing side in the Spanish Civil War from 1938 and had taken up residence in France. Many of the former Spanish Republicans were in Maquis groups in the region, and the French Provisional Government dealt with them warily. Team Chrysler, comprised of British Captain Cyril Sell, French Lieutenant Paul Aussaresses, and British Sergeant Ronal Chatten, arrived in the Pyrenees on August 16 with the mission of working with the FAI to prevent German formations from escaping across the border into Spain. Originally their mission was to have begun on the August 13, but when the pilot could not confirm the drop zone, he headed back to the airfield near Algiers. This delay forced a shift in focus. The team would not have a good opportunity now to work against the 11th Panzer Division so they focused on interrupting enemy lines of communication between Toulouse and Narbonne. They spent the last half of August sabotaging the road between these two cities, working to block Germans attempting to escape into Spain, and coordinating with SOE's George Starr and fellow Jedburghs Fuller, MacPherson, and Sharpe from three other teams. By the end of the month they began to be more concerned about stopping reprisals, and after meeting General Cochet on September 1, the team began to work their Maquis into service further east and to do communication duties for General Cochet as required. They originally had tried to find the DMR Schlumberger, but even on September 2 noted that he was "unknown in the region."[61]

THE LIBÉRATION IN R5

When Team James, comprised of American First Lieutenant John K. Singlaub, French Lieutenant Jacques de la Penguilly using the name Jacques le Bel, and American Sergeant A. J. Denneau, parachuted into the Correze with an SAS element, it began to cut the road connecting Tulle-Ussel-Clermont-Ferrand. Mission Tilluel—an Inter-Allied mission commanded by Major Jacques Robert, one of the former BCRA Bloc Planning officers—was also in the area. Their mission had received air-dropped weapons during July and they had given them to the FTP unit as one of the other Armée Secrète (AS) Maquis groups had received weapons and another AS unit had not. R5's Operations officer had partially armed some of the AS units; of the total 12,000 FTP and AS Maquis, 8,000 were armed. When James arrived, the various units each surrounded a German garrison along Route National 89. The Germans "did not come out, either because they were ordered to stay and hold or because they were afraid."[62] The team's weapons and capability status would not improve during the course of its mission as James "received absolutely nothing" while the SAS, OGs, and mission Tilluel received their drops. After Team James arrived in the area, they met the FTP and AS leadership and agreed to attack the German garrison in the village of Egletons, which lay along that Route 89. Inexplicably, the FTP began the attack hours before the agreed-upon time and the AS leader and Team James were forced to join the attack. Later that day, the BBC message came that every effort was to be made to attack German garrisons between the Loire and Garonne Rivers.[63] "During the battle of Egletons, Jacques [de la Penguilly] and I made an effort to be seen in the combat area where the shooting was going on and do training right there." Singlaub later recalled that his leadership example validated his teaching and combat credentials to the Maquis. "It showed them what one guy could do, who had some knowledge of the weapons."[64]

During the attack, a rumor began to circulate that Wehrmacht columns were coming from the southwest, which proved untrue, and the northeast, which was true. The Maquis partially lifted the sieges of these villages and took some men to conduct ambushes. But Singlaub and de la Penguilly believed they should completely abandon the sieges in order to have manpower to harass and ambush the traveling columns along Route 89. Unable to convince the FTP commander to contribute forces for this new operation, James and AS Maquis did what they could to ambush the enemy between Tulle and Egletons. After the Wehrmacht column retreated back toward Clermont-Ferrand and the region quieted down, the Jeds spent the next few days instructing the FTP on operating their weapons. When they believed that was complete, they decided to contact Dechelette in Limoges and arrange for a new mission. By this time, August 28, the Germans in the Gironde, Charente, and Dordogne were attempting to exit France via the route running through Limoges, Angoulême, Châteauroux, and Troyes and attempt to make Dijon where the major combat elements, led by the 11th Panzer Division, were already drawing a protective line. They had to go this way due to the FFI's success at harassing and ambushing forces on the routes, such as Route 89, that would have been a more direct route for fleeing to Germany.

When the James team found Dechelette, he had a mission for them and the AS unit from the Correze. Dechelette dispatched the AS unit to the Creuse and radioed London that he was sending Singlaub and de Penguilly back to Britain to get heavy weapons needed to handle the major German column now marching up from Bordeaux. He wanted heavier weapons, sixty machine guns, fifty mortars with plenty of ammunition, and gasoline within the next five days.[65] Time was critical, and the two Jeds along with Major Robert of the Tilleul mission departed via a C-47 on September 10 while Sergeant Danneau remained in Limoges.[66] On the same day, Dechelette informed London that Team Lee's work was done in Vienne but that he had another mission for them and requested them to remain in France.[67] Lee, along with a British officer of an Inter-Allied mission named Bergamotte, had worked with the FTP leader Georges Guingouin. Dechelette had named Guingouin the head of the FFI for the Department of Haute Vienne, and Captain Brown of Team Lee estimated that he had around 5,500 men. They knew that they needed to create obstacles for the retreating German forces and set about doing it. On September 14 they teamed up with some of the Operational Group members and blew a bridge on the only remaining railway line that exited the city to the east. The next day EMFFI radioed them a message: "German 159th Division reported on move northwards to battle zone. Make maximum effort prevent or hold them up."[68]

Dechelette's Maquis didn't need to be told to do this. The destruction of roads, bridges, railroads, and communication lines occurred non-stop all over the region.[69] Additionally, the Jedburghs requested air strikes when large groups of Germans could be expected to be moving on the roads. Teams Lee, Alexander, James, Hugh, Hamish, Julian, and Ian along with the SAS and Operational Group in the region all contributed to the chaos by leading or planning some of the sabotage; when the enemy troop concentrations invited it, they wired messages back to EMFFI giving locations of where to conduct air strikes. In the Vienne, the FFI commander Colonel Guingouin succeeded at getting the Vichy force to desert the Vichy side and join the Résistance. With the city surrounded, Generalmajor Walter Gleiniger, Kommandant des Verbindungsstabs 586, decided to surrender what was left of his three-hundred-man occupation force in Limoges. But Gleiniger was arrested by the "German police" when he informed them of the surrender and hustled out of the city, escaping all the Maquis ambushes.[70] He committed suicide on August 21, not ever knowing that most of his command had succeeded in their escape back to Germany.[71] As the destruction of roads, bridges, and railroads continued it was clear the 159th Division was attempting to flee. Divided into marching groups, more than 20,000 Germans from the coastal area now began to work their way through the region under the command of Generalmajor Botho Elster.

Believing that Elster's force of sailors, Luftwaffe, customs police, soldiers, and civilian administrators was the "159th Reserve Division" provoked a response from 3rd Army's SF Detachment led by Colonel Powell. Since August 2, the 3rd Army and the FFI had been coordinating their operations via Powell's Special Force Detachment. On August 18, Colonel Haskell, Lieutenant Colonel Paul van der Strict of the EMFFI staff, and Lieutenant Colonel Powell met with General Patton in France to discuss the role the FFI would play as the 3rd Army moved east. Recalling that meeting, van der Stricht later noted the absence of British participation in the planning. "No mention whatsoever was made of British participation or personnel in connection with the resistance matters discussed. This would of course have been entirely unthinkable only eighteen months earlier." Van der Stricht also remarked that when Paris was liberated, "there was no sign of any British SOE officer. Circumstances, and not any policy decision, had made the paramilitary operations of French Resistance a Franco-American affair."[72]

The Franco-American relationship continued when Generals Patton and Koenig met on August 24 and agreed in principle that the FFI could prove useful to Patton's drive east.[73] Their agreement then followed regular coordination between 3rd Army operations planners and Powell's small group of officers and local FFI commanders.[74] As the 3rd Army aggressively pressed east, covering the 435 kilometers from Rennes to Troyes in the next seven days, they continued to work issues with the FFI in formal meetings and informal communications that occurred along the way. On August 31 Powell met with F Section agent Philippe de Vomécourt and FFI commanders at Sens, 120 kilometers southeast of Paris. Taking information from the FFI commanders, Powell plotted out what they told him onto a map to get a sense of who was where and how strong each unit claimed to be. The 3rd Army's next objective was Troyes, 72 kilometers to the east, but its southern flank's lines now ran from Nantes to Sens, a distance of 500 exposed kilometers. With the reports from the FFI talking of tens of thousands of enemy troops on the move all corroborated by dozens of messages from Jedburgh Teams south of the Loire, Powell and Patton may have had a cause to be concerned. However, seeing the disposition of the FFI all along the river, and having coordinated with them over the past two weeks, Powell recognized their capability and sought to make it useful. After the conference, where he was informed of the paucity of weapons the FFI possessed, he knew he had get them arms to make them a viable force. Lieutenant Colonel Powell sent a frantic message to EMFFI that evening requesting more Jedburgh teams and weapons for the Maquis in the three departments soon to be on his southern flank. At around 1 AM on September 1, SFHQ received Powell's plea for arms for the area around the city of Dijon and Bourges, bluntly stating that "if Germans organize that area present drive may halt because of threat to flanks." Powell went on to request that Jedburgh teams Alec, Bruce, Cedric, and Harry needed to be given "top priority" for air-dropped weapons, and ended with the following ominous warning: "If these Departments do not receive arms Third Army now few miles from Germany may stop."[75] No one in 3rd Army wanted to tell General Patton he had to slow down, much less stop.

But Powell's reaction may have been excessive considering the type of enemy column coming in his direction. Generalmajor Botho Elster's Marchgruppe Süd, as it called itself, numbered just under 20,000 soldiers, marines, sailors, and assorted other kinds of personnel and was not looking for a fight; it was simply trying to get safely beyond Dijon and then on to Germany. Until the middle of August, Elster was the Feldkommandatur at Mont-de-Marsan south of Bordeaux. When Overlord started, he had attempted to quell the "terrorists" in his area with the "most ruthless and harshest means."[76] But now the tables were turned and he was fearful of similar methods being turned on him by the very people he had targeted. So were the German soldiers under his command. Forced to move north as the Maquis and Jeds had cut off routes through the Correze, Lot, and Cantal, which would have been a more direct route, his motley collection of troops now found themselves attempting to move north and then east through the Vienne, Indre, and the Cher and being harassed all the way by the FFI of R5. Under these conditions, everyone was getting desperate and the brutality was only increasing. On August 29, British Captain John Cox, of Team Ivor sent a three-line message bluntly stating, "The Germans are killing our wounded with kicks and rifle butts stop we are executing an equal number of prisoners [unintelligible] reprisals stop." He went on to request simply, "could you have this broadcast [unintelligible] to prevent further occurrences"?[77] But since his radioman was Sergeant Loosmore, and EMFFI was decoding the messages thinking the request was from Team Andy, the reader questioned the message's identity, not yet realizing it was Andy's radioman, working for Team Ivor. Furthermore, they probably did not want to broadcast that they were killing prisoners. Amidst all this confusion and brutality, someone had to rein in the madness.

Fortunately, R5 Eugene Dechelette was the Free French delegate and one of the most successful DMRs in France. He had by the beginning of August succeeded in achieving a great deal of political unity, but could not yet claim solid discipline. For instance, his negotiations brought in the FTP of Colonel Georges Guingouin in the Vienne and Theogene Briant's in l'Indre. Additionally, l'Indre had a substantial Organisation de la Résistance l'Armee unit led by Colonel Raymond Chomel with around 2,400 men. Chomel's ORA were not civilians who simply wanted to fight, but regular soldiers who had stayed in their homes as a result of the 1940 Armistice. They were light infantry, artillery, and paratroopers accustomed to organized military operations. There was also a substantial force of Armée Secrète and various other smaller Maquis groups. Furthermore, one of Tommy MacPherson's Maquis groups now organized as the "Schneider column" or "colonne Schneider" was across the Allier River firing artillery rounds at portions of Elster's Marchgruppe Süd by September 10, just as Chomel's forces had achieved his surrender.[78] The region Lieutenant Colonel Powell urgently requested arms for would never see these particular Germans, as Dechelette's combined groups of FFI, Allied Special Forces, SOE agents, the threat of the US division to the north, and the ever-present Allied bombing forced Elster to capitulate before they could get that far.

The surrender of Generalmajor Elster's Marchgruppe Süd proved to be a certainty but required many steps in which many different people participated at different times, allowing the Germans to achieve a remarkably good deal. Elster was the only person who participated in every step of the negotiations and used that as an advantage to gain as much as he could from the rolling negotiations that occurred from late August until September 16. During the process, three different Jedburgh teams participated in those negotiations along with Colonel Chomel and officers from his FFI unit, intelligence officers from the 329th Infantry Battalion (US), and the commander of the American 83rd Infantry Division, Major General Robert C. Macon. Indirectly participating in the negotiations were F Section Agents Pearl Witherington and Philippe de Vomécourt, and the Allied Air Forces that persistently bombed the German forces on their march through l'Indre. Team Hugh was by now in full operational swing having been in the department since June 6 and they kept up constant pressure on Elster, harassing and obstructing his movements and attempting to cut up his columns while radioing air strike locations. However, Hugh was completely unaware of Elster's willingness to surrender and took no part in the negotiations. But despite Elster's overall weakness against such odds, his negotiating situation became progressively better as the negotiations progressed through different Allied or FFI representatives.

Feelers between the FFI and Elster began on August 29 when Jedburgh team Julian sent a message to SFHQ that Elster's surrender had been demanded and they awaited his reply. The demand was made by the FFI in the region and Julian was merely informing EMFFI.[79] On August 30, Chomel sent out a notice to the FFI in Indre that the manner of warfare remained guerrilla warfare and that since large groups of Germans were expected to continue through the department, his brigade and all the other formations were to coordinate their activities in order to harass the enemy.[80] Next, Julian received notice from Colonel Chomel that the US forces north of the Loire River were going to send liaison agents to him and he wanted the Jedburghs to facilitate the meeting near the Loire River. There was a great deal of confusion about when this would occur with a window of September 1 to 14. Martel wanted to meet the 83rd Division and arranged to get mines and mortars in order to impress upon Elster the futility of his position. SFHQ, perhaps encouraged by Powell's message, also stepped up aerial delivery of weapons and dropped supplies on September 1, 4, 8, and 9. Additionally, Colonel Chomel's efforts to contact the 83rd Division directly paid off when Julian facilitated a meeting with the 83rd Division that arranged the transportation of 100 anti-tank landmines to Chomel's brigade.[81]

On September 8, representatives of Martel's command met with Elster, and the German general told them, "When I meet with a real obstacle provided by the Americans then I will see what I have to do but not before. I will not deliver my troops to the Maquis."[82] The discussions were short, but the negotiators agreed to meet the next day while Martel's men coordinated with Julian to get representatives of the 83rd Division to participate with them. On September 9, Allied efforts began to coalesce. Notified of a time and place to meet, General Elster met with Colonel Chislain, an officer in Chomel's Brigade and perhaps Lieutenant Magill of the 83rd Division.[83] Elster agreed in principle on the terms of his surrender, but expressed his desire to surrender to the American regulars. He had good cause to be afraid of the FFI since members of his command had committed reprisals and shot civilians in Vienne at the end of August.[84] Chomel considered his options and requested team Julian to represent the Allies at the next meeting set for 3 PM the following day. On the same day, Julian noted a planeload of supplies, but needing more told SFHQ, "If FFI this area still to operate against enemy troops further supplies essential."[85] On September 9, the French and the US delegation met with Elster again where they agreed to call in a demonstration air strike so Elster's soldiers could see what the nearly 300-kilometer walk to Dijon would be like if they chose to continue. Elster seemed to need the exhibition to convince his soldiers to agree to surrender. They agreed to meet again the next day at Issoudun where Elster had his headquarters. After the discussion with Elster was finished on September 9, Team Julian took Colonel Martel up to the Loire River bridge and introduced him to Major General Macon. Macon agreed to participate in the discussions and on September 10 he represented the United States while English Major Arthur H. Clutton of Team Julian participated in the negotiations on behalf of the British. Macon also brought along two colonels of his staff for the discussions at the sous prefecture office. Since Macon did not speak French and Elster did not *wish* to speak French, they spoke in English, forcing Chomel to continually ask what was being discussed. Furthermore, "Elster showed himself to be a very skilled negotiator and he succeeded in converting the exceedingly unfavorable situation in which he found himself to one of relatively great advantage."[86] General Macon began the discussions agreeing with Clutton that the FFI and SAS could be useful in maintaining control of the Germans, but after hearing Elster's tale of woe regarding how the FFI had been acting, Macon agreed to let Elster's soldiers retain their weapons until they crossed the Loire and could come *under the protection* of his Division. By the end of the conversation, Macon was convinced and agreed in order to save the Germans from the "bloodthirsty" Maquis. But

Macon also agreed that when the Germans handed their small arms over to the Americans, they would be given to the FFI.[87]

Marching armed Germans through French countryside and expecting no violence to occur required a precise agreement on all sides, with each soldier knowing there was to be no shooting. On September 11, Jeds John Cox from Team Ivor and Tommy MacPherson from Quinine took part in yet another discussion with Elster along with an American colonel from the 83rd Division. They worked out a procedure to place liaison officers along with the marching Germans, not to go through villages where possible, and not to purchase anything from the French population. Elster was difficult but finally agreed. Despite some violent incidents and one German killing a French civilian, Elster's forces made it to American lines across the Loire at Orléans on September 15.[88]

Macon's promise to return looted French property and hand over German weapons to the FFI was not kept, and Major Clutton found himself arguing with SFHQ and senior American officers in late September still attempting to enforce the deal. Due to Macon's unkept promise, the Americans kept the booty and allowed Elster to surrender with full military honors on September 16 after marching through Cher while the French fumed in humiliation. Their people had been killed and their property taken, their farms and villages looted and burned, but the US 83rd Division was completely ignorant of this and forced Clutton to go to de Gaulle directly to get his approval for the return of the French property. Not one to be put off, Clutton went to Paris, got de Gaulle's signature, and returned to Le Mans to pursue the matter further. But it was taking too long and EMFFI ordered the team, Clutton, and his teammates back to London.[89] The British Jeds and SOE agents involved in the matter could not stifle their frustration with the 83rd Division, General Macon, nor the Americans in general. The stalwart F Section Agent Pearl Witherington who had been in France since September of 1943 wrote, "The Americans went so far as to ask the Maquis to lend lorries for the transportation of those 'gentlemen,' which was promptly refused. When the Germans arrived on the Loire they were received by the American Red Cross with cigarettes, chocolates and oranges (things unknown to French civilians for the past five years), and were soon to walk arm in arm in French towns. This capitulation was a heavy blow to FFI pride, and totally undeserved, when it is considered that no Americans were anywhere near our circuit or further south."[90]

The surrender of General Elster is one of the fables of the Résistance but it has also been claimed by the 83rd Division and in one account made to look as if Lieutenant Magill stood down Elster all by himself. Press accounts in American newspapers at the time all pumped this strange story and credited Magill and Macon with the entire affair, barely mentioning the FFI. Since Clutton, Cox, MacPherson, and Witherington were clandestine and their work classified, they avoided questions from the press. Therefore, the link they provided between the FFI and American regular forces remained unknown in English language publications until Colin Beavan revealed more about the surrender in his book in 2006.[91] Even the US Army Air Force general attached to the 3rd Army, Brigadier General Otto P. Weyland, believed he was the one responsible for Elster's surrender and at least one author agrees, writing that "For the first time in history airplanes, unaided by ground troops, had forced the surrender of a large enemy force."[92] Such hyperbole is completely out of touch with the causes of Elster's surrender and reinforces dangerous beliefs many are all too willing to accept. The truth of the matter is that the FFI, in this case largely comprised of French Regular officers and soldiers armed with weapons supplied through clandestine Allied air drops, surrounded a large German formation of mostly non-combat troops being pounded by Allied bombing and weary from their long march. Unfortunately, French Colonel Chomel's only fault was believing in General Macon, who seemed to prefer to take the word of the enemy major general as if he were a peer, instead of the word of Colonel Chomel and Major Clutton, who were telling him otherwise. The insult is particularly harsh when l'Indre's Maquis suffered casualties of 368 killed and 547 wounded between 1943 to 1945.[93] Chomel's unit alone, referred to as the "Charles Martel Brigade," suffered 73 killed and 66 wounded.[94]

Chaos still reigned within the command and control structures in various regions, however, and to the east northeast, Lieutenant Colonel Hutchison of Team Isaac still had to contend with various notables coming to him and his French colleague attempting to assert authority. The commander of the FFI for Region P, Claude Monod, wished to stage an attack on Dijon, while the 3rd Army, most likely in the form of Powell's SF

Detachment, had requested the Maquis to guard Patton's right flank. With not enough weapons to do both, Hutchison disagreed with Monod. But Hutchison had to get written approval from General Koenig to enforce this mission instead of the dangerous head-on attack on the Germans.

By September 11, Hutchison had also made contact with General Jean de Lattre de Tassigny's forces moving up from the south and he agreed to get the FFI to cover their left or western flank. "This task fitted in perfectly with the protection of the 3rd US Army's right flank and all FFI companies and Battalions were ordered to thicken the number of ambushes and harry the enemy wherever they could find him."[95] The FFI successfully formed a blocking line through Decize–Cercy-la-Tour–Luzy–Autun to prevent the Germans from reaching Dijon, enabling Patton's and Patch's armies to link up on September 11, 30 kilometers west of Dijon. But Hutchison was not exceedingly cheery about their accomplishments and blamed London. His repeated "forlorn request for PIATs [Personnel, Individual Anti-Tank weapons] and Bazookas so urgently needed…while we were able to report something on the order of fifty small [engagements] were taking place, it was a swan song which produced no result." Not only could his team not get the weapons they requested, but orders from London often were not in accordance with local reality. In one case, the 3rd Army wanted the Loire Bridges blown, but EMFFI ordered everything to be preserved. By the time EMFFI changed its mind, the Germans had destroyed the bridges, provoking Hutchison to remark acerbically, "thereby presumably satisfying everyone."[96] But now the Overlord forces and the Anvil forces had linked up with the FFI's poorly supplied forces, killing or capturing approximately 79,000 Germans.[97] While this is probably more than Eisenhower would have thought possible on June 6, it was less than what could have been done. Elster's Marchgruppe Süd was 25 percent of the prize. But the ineffective use of the Maquis against the 11th Panzer Division, both on its march to reinforce the invasion area and then while it led the German 19th Army to the Dijon area, is disappointing when considering what the FFI might have done if organized more coherently and armed more effectively. The completely unexpected numbers swelling the Maquis caught the Allies in London and Algiers by surprise. Had they been ready for them, their trap could have had a quicker bite.

Why did some regions or areas succeed while others faltered? Understanding what worked and what did not is important, but one should understand the complicated series of events and actors as well to see how it all came together. Regarding Elster, not one of the people involved can honestly lay claim to Elster's surrender alone. However, it is no coincidence that this event occurred in Dechelette's region. Since his recovery from his broken bone after parachuting into France in January, he had hammered out agreements to create one of the most unified FFI-FTP units in nearly every department. For instance, in l'Indre, the ORA's Colonel Raymond Chomel was the commander of the FFI while in Vienne, Colonel Georges Guingouin of the FTP was the commander of the FFI. While all was not completely harmonious, there was a strong sense of political unity that brought about more effective military action. Furthermore, R5 was last in the airlift priority list, making the accomplishment all that much more surprising. The same could not be said of Regions 3 and 4. They suffered from less effective DMRs, a higher density of enemy troops, a significant Maquis population of Spaniards all tenuously woven together by the British SOE agents, the most notable of whom was George Starr. Complicating matters even more for R4 and R3 was their command structure: FFI military operations were externally commanded and administered by SFHQ, and then EMFFI; but other times during the summer they were led by SPOC that changed locations and later became Special Force Unit 4.[98] The timing of those changes depended on military and political necessities that had nothing to do with FFI regional issues. Sorting out who was in charge during the months of June, July, and August depended completely on when, where, and who you asked. In R4 and R3, many seams were being formed to define how French sovereignty was knit together. But in R5, all the evidence points to the wide acknowledgment that Eugene Dechelette was the man in charge, and he reported to General Koenig. And by August 25, Koenig was no longer in London, but in Paris where he became military governor of the city. Sovereignty was beginning to come home.

The Fog of War in Eastern France

Once the Allied armies from the two invasion areas linked up near Dijon, the nature of the war in France changed again. The first three phases—Overlord's initial landing; the breakout of the Allies toward the end of July; and the southern landings on August 15 and subsequent decision by Hitler to retreat—all created slightly different conditions for the Maquis and the way General Koenig's Free French could use them. When the Germans retreated to a defensive line running from the Swiss border east of Besançon to the Belgian town of Bruges on about September 15, the nature of the war changed again and the Free French may have tried to lay the groundwork for the last phase of irregular combat in France after early August. That is to say, their actions of inserting teams into eastern France could have paid great dividends, but other circumstances slowed these preparations and largely diminished their ability to coordinate the Maquis as a coherent force for Eisenhower. Prior to the link-up of Generals Patton and Patch near Dijon in the middle of September, Koenig's staff directed nineteen more Jedburgh teams into eastern France. These teams experienced a far different mission from that of teams such as Bugatti, Hugh, or Frederick, who had gone to areas early, contended with relatively few enemy, and had time to get to know the Maquis in their area. Such a luxury was not afforded to teams such as Augustus, Jacob, or Benjamin. As Keonig's headquarters and Special Force HQ attempted to support Eisenhower with Maquis in this region, a region Eisenhower made his greatest priority as described in Chapter 8 they did not grasp the shift in the nature of the fighting, and since it differed so greatly from their planning and recent operational experience, the staff failed to conduct a coherent operation.

The speed with which the Allied advance had developed from August 1 to the middle of September had many senior officers and staff planners mired in complacency and convinced that the Germans were about ready to collapse. The coup attempt against Hitler, the quick retreats, the continuous shuffle and re-creation of German units, little to no air cover from the Luftwaffe, and the paucity of fuel for enemy Panzers all seemed to be signs that the Germans were about ready to fold. Reading the German army message traffic provided by the codebreakers gave the Allies a skewed window into the German commanders' sense of frustration and their long list of difficulties. But the Allies' intelligence failed to convey the sense of fighting determination exhibited by the German soldiers largely unaware of their own nation's desperate state. Jedburghs who interrogated prisoners captured in France were often shocked the POWs did not know that the Allies had captured various French cities, or that their entire army was suffering as much as it was.[1] The typical German soldier's belief in an eventual victory enabled Hitler to continue the war despite the dwindling resources of every necessity, such as fuel, air cover, and experienced leadership. The exception to this stalwart belief that the Nazi war effort would succeed came from the soldiers captured around Dijon in the middle of September.[2]

But between the middle of August and the middle of September, two contending mindsets seemed to govern Koenig's staff planning actions and the dispatch of Jedburgh teams. First was the desire to get the teams into France while they could still have an effect on operations. Jedburgh teams were gaining a reputation for making a significant impact since the Résistance was doing much more than expected. Perhaps there was some chauvinism at work among the French since most at Supreme Headquarters Allied Expeditionary Forces (SHAEF) believed before D-Day that the Maquis would not have any meaningful effect. After the D-Day results began to come in, the doubters quickly became believers and credited the Jedburgh plan, the Special Air Service, and the Operational Groups with bringing it about. Donovan's continued use of Maquis exploits in his reports to the president is an example that indicates what the Résistance was doing when tied to the SOE and OSS efforts. The assumption one could easily make from the materials Donovan forwarded to the president was that all the combat activity was happening only with groups "stimulated" by SOE and OSS operations. Instead of soberly evaluating the conditions of any given success, a great desire developed within SHAEF and the Free French to override the initial plan to put Jedburgh teams in when requested by those in the field, and instead to insert them as soon as possible. Such a desire now competed against the original notion of the British Special Operations Executive that the Jedburghs were to be a reserve, replacing arrested agents to lead Maquis groups conducting open guerrilla warfare when the time called for it. But perhaps out of fear that the pace of operations would leave several unused teams in England, Maquis successes, which might or might not have been due to the Jedburghs, began to take on a life of their own and overrode the original plan of using Jedburghs as uniformed backups when they were needed.

The second factor that had originally served as a brake on Jedburgh deployments was a sense of reluctance the first planners like Peter Wilkinson had expressed in the original planning. First was the fear that deploying too many teams too quickly would leave no reserve if needed later. Staff officers also feared sending uniformed Jedburgh teams to areas thick with enemy troops. But in the desire to have the teams play an active role, the original SOE planning that the Jedburghs were to be a reserve for arrested SOE agents and operate in uniform was hastily revised in the first and second week of August. Koenig's persistent use of the teams to go into areas along with British Special Air Service (SAS) parties or Operational Groups developed into the norm, a deployment that was also completely new to the original planning. But since this pattern had been followed since D-Day with various success, it continued even though no modifications were instituted in the training of the Jedburghs still in reserve at Milton Hall.[3] By the end of July, it became standard practice within Koenig's staff that Jedburgh teams were sent in with commandos to be their liaison with any Maquis who might be in the area. In other words, it appears that even Koenig did not want to rely on a Maquis unit to carry out a specific task when French, British, or American regular and well-trained troops were available to do it. The Jeds could be a firm liaison with various groups not only to London but also to other Allied commando units operating nearby. Jedburgh teams were then used explicitly as liaison between the SAS and Operational Groups, and their communication links facilitated working with the local Maquis, where their language skills could augment the British and American commandos performing special tasks.

General Koenig's chief of staff, Colonel Henri Ziegler, now began cueing up Jedburgh teams to support Eisenhower's forces as they marched east toward Paris; at the same time, he began deploying teams to central France that could harass German forces that might come north toward Ike's forces or go east and south toward the southern invasion beaches. Beginning in the middle of July, the staff had anticipated the deployment of Jedburgh teams for the August moon period and wished to send two teams to the Vosges and one team each to the Ardennes, Oise, Seine et Marne, Marne, Meuse, Meurthe et Moselle, and Haute Marne Departments. Colonel Ziegler deleted the Oise, Seine et Marne, and Marne Departments from the approved regions because they "do not appear to be ready" for uniformed Jedburgh teams and reminded the British and American planners that those in the field requesting the teams should be asked to give an evaluation of their region's readiness for uniformed teams. Zeigler did approve the deployment of two teams each to the Doubs, Haute Saône, Aisne, and Côte d'Or, apparently anticipating the priorities he would be receiving from Eisenhower's staff on August 15.[4]

But the Vosges region in eastern France drew interest from General Montgomery's 21st Army Group. It requested a Special Air Service mission for the area. The idea of conducting an operation in the Vosges had begun in June but only now coalesced into Operation Loyton in early

August. The 21st Army Group tasked SAS to send ten men as an initial re-connaissance party to attempt to harass German lines of communication from Paris east toward Saarbrucken and Strasbourg. A Jedburgh team was to accompany the mission. During the same time that Koenig was working to get the Aloes mission organized for the command and control of the Brittany Résistance, his staff drafted the plans for Jedburgh team Jacob to accompany 2 SAS on its mission to the Vosges. The SAS was to run the mission, but since part of it involved working with the local Maquis, who were, to quote the SAS order, "not fully organized," Koenig's headquarters was interested in providing leadership to them. Team Jacob consisted of British Captain Victor Gough, French Lieutenant Maurice Boissarie, and British Sergeant Kenneth Seymour. Gough was one of the British Jeds who had started the war as an intelligence officer in the Auxiliaries that were to have fought behind the lines in England, had the Germans suc-ceeded in invading back in 1940. In November 1943 he was transferred from the Auxiliary Units to the Jedburghs as an instructor, and in the spring he joined the regular list of men to be deployed on a mission. Divorced the January before his deployment, Gough listed the woman running the boardinghouse where he lived as his next of kin. He and his French team-mate Boissaire both left their belongings at that boardinghouse while they were at Milton Hall and deployed to France. Gough was educated as an engineer, and his drawing skills were so good that he won the competition among the Jeds to design their Special Force patch.[5]

But Gough was not sent along with the SAS element to win drawing contests. They were to meet up with the regional French resistance leader and train and equip his Maquis. The Résistance in the area was led by Gilbert Grandval a man of great local prestige. He is also unique among regional leaders as he had not been sent into France by the Bureau Centrale Renseignements d'Action (BCRA), but instead had been appointed to the position after taking over the region's military affairs for the Résistance group Ceux de la Résistance. Nevertheless, he believed in the efforts of the centralized authority of de Gaulle, regarded General Koenig's authority for military matters to be synonymous with de Gaulle's, and viewed the politics around Algiers' military action committee to be harmful to France.

When Maurice Bourgès-Maunoury nominated him, the BCRA in London replied "that he would work out perfectly."[6] When members of the Algiers committee maintained that effective action could only be directed from inside France, Grandval did not believe it. "They knew perfectly," he wrote after the war, "... the scandalous and stupid intention of the Americans entrusting the government to the AMGOT; what counted before all this was the unity of France and only de Gaulle could assume it."[7] Grandval was just the kind of man the BCRA was looking for; he was loyal to de Gaulle, had knowledge of the local area, and possessed great leadership skills. Gough, Boussarie, Seymour, and the SAS team members of the Loyton mission parachuted from their aircraft to one of Grandval's drop zones lit up and looking "like bonfires on Guy Fawkes night," one of the SAS men reflected after the war.[8] The landing went well but Seymour broke his toe and it began to swell so badly he could not go as fast as the rest of them. On landing, the team quickly regrouped with the SAS and were met by one of Grandval's assistants. The Vosges is rugged country with thick forests and steep hills rising up from the river Saône that runs to the southwest and the Moselle which runs to the north into Germany. The valleys and forest naturally channel the region's roads and railroads into narrow valleys closed in with thick trees. The country is great for guerrilla tactics.

The Maquis made their command post on top of one of the mountains about six miles from their drop zone and they guided the newcomers back to it before the sun rose. Over the next two days, they made their initial plans.[9] Gough requested one of the SAS radio operators to send Jacob's first message to London saying that Sergeant Seymour had been injured on the jump but would be recovered within a week, and they believed they would be contacting Grandval soon. Team Jacob also sent a message on August 15 and 16 with the briefest of details on the local Maquis, which numbered eight hundred men, of whom fifty were armed. They had still not contacted Grandval but expected to on that day. For security reasons, they had to travel five miles from their command post to use the radio.[10] Germans were thick in the area, and by this time, the enemy was evacuating France and the roads were crowded with moving vehicles going into

Germany. But the regional Gestapo was also aware of their presence and was organizing an effort to catch them.

On August 17, two days after the landings in the south, one day after Hitler gave the order for many of the occupation forces in southern France to evacuate, and at a time when Patton's 3rd Army was still approximately 500 kilometers to their west, Gough and his comrades heard that the Germans were coming up the mountain toward them and took stock of their situation. With the Jeds were approximately one hundred men, inadequately armed with some weapons that had been dropped when they parachuted in, some weapons provided by previous drops, but mostly older rifles the Maquis had managed to hide after the armistice. They decided to leave a small rearguard at their position while most would attempt to make their way down to escape the trap. They set off around 4 PM with the SAS, Gough, and Boissarie up front and Sergeant Seymour in the middle of the column still hobbled by his injured toe. Unfortunately, there were enemy troops on their side of the mountain, and when the enemy initiated the firefight Sergeant Seymour "could not discover what was going on" after the group scattered into the trees and boulders to escape what was now a rapidly closing trap. The Maquis, according to Seymour dropped their weapons and moved off leaving him alone and unaware of what was happening to his fellow Jeds. He took cover behind a large jutting boulder and fired at the enemy with his large Bren gun, then when that ammunition was gone, fired at them with his carbine, and last shot at them with his pistol, expending every round. When a grenade landed near him but did not go off, he breathed a sigh of relief, but while the Germans drew nearer, he burned his radio codes and cipher pads. Realizing that he was alone and out of ammunition, a German soldier shouted something at him which Seymour assumed meant to come out and give himself up. Left with little choice and not knowing what happened to the rest of his group, he surrendered. He was marched over to "the nearest tree and stood against it. Two of the enemy were detailed as a firing party and were just preparing to take aim when a senior officer came rushing up to them." He wanted to interrogate Seymour instead of shoot him; and after he was walked down the mountain and taken to an office at a nearby German camp, Seymour was asked what he was doing and what his mission was. Seymour replied vaguely that he was in a "recce party," sent in to scout out the area and that his S. F. badge meant that he was a paratrooper. The interrogator seemed to be content with that and Seymour was moved to a prison at Schirmeck, France. He did not know what had become of his teammates, nor did he know what would become of him. But when later presented with some of the SAS team's radio equipment and codebooks, he insisted to his captors that did not know whose they were or anything about them.[11] Special Force Headquarters in London also had no knowledge of Seymour's teammates as London had no more messages from Jacob for several days.

But word did reach them regarding the fate of Captain Cyrus Manierre of Team Dodge who had been captured on August 3 near Grenoble. A telegram from Special Projects Office Center in Algiers to Colonel Haskell in London read that Manierre "has been taken to Vichy" and that the same information had been passed to the regional Free French delegate in the hope that he could effect some kind of escape.[12] Hearing nothing more for two days, Haskell directed Major Paul Van der Stricht to let him know the status of his Algerian-based counterpart's attempt to get Manierre out of prison, as the telegram from Algiers threw "some doubt on the question of whether everything possible" was being done to get Manierre out of Gestapo custody. Shortly thereafter, three men from Operational Group Alice received orders to proceed to Vichy with the intent of snatching Manierre out of prison.[13] Their effort to free him from the Gestapo was buoyed by the escape of the SOE agent Francis Cammaerts in the same area due to the quick thinking and cunning of one of his agents. Christine Granville convinced Cammaerts's captors to release him due to the eminent arrival of the Allied forces and they did so just three hours before he was to be executed. Cammaerts "has been released through quick wits" of Granville, the Special Projects Office Command (SPOC) wrote to Haskell on August 18 but went on to indicate that the Drôme's Free French commander believed the "Americans were not interested" in what happened to Manierre.[14] Nothing could have been further from the truth, with SPOC sending a team to retrieve him and Jedburgh team Monocle reporting on 20 August that they believed Manierre was "in prison but alright."[15]

Unfortunately, the three members of Operational Group Alice were unable to pull off their rescue attempt before "the Allied invasion of Southern France and subsequent northward advance of the Allied armies persuaded the Germans to send Manierre back to Germany."[16] They had indeed. After several days of thorough beatings and interrogations, the former West Point boxer divulged nothing of OSS. One morning a new German Army officer stiffly greeted Manierre and wondered how an American had come into the Gestapo prison. Manierre convinced him that he was a downed flyer and had been caught with some Maquis. This German "swallowed the story, hook, line, and sinker." Fortunately for Manierre, the southern invasion was progressing quickly and the Germans were evacuating the area. In the subsequent confusion, his new German guards sent him to Stalag Luft 1, near Barth, Germany. He arrived there and was questioned by a Luftwaffe officer who had records that he had graduated from West Point, was commissioned in the cavalry, and had been known to have taken pilot training. All this was true and very unnerving for Manierre, but the Luftwaffe did not know that he had failed in flight school and had joined the OSS.[17] Omitted from their records was all the information the Gestapo interrogators had gleaned as well as information from the Milice; as SPOC later became aware, the Milice who had arrested Manierre knew what his mission was as they had an informant inside Manierre's Maquis group. But while the Gestapo hoped to beat out more details after their evacuation from Lyon, those records and the interrogators who created them were killed in air strikes while being transported on trains out of Lyon.[18]

CAPTURING PARIS AND SUPPORTING THE 12TH ARMY GROUP

Anticipating Eisenhower's priority areas of eastern France, General Koenig finished plans for, at least he thought, the last of the Jedburgh missions for France. On August 8, the staff drew up the orders for deployment of twenty-five teams who were to leave "as quickly as possible." These teams were, in the main, the final results of the July requests described above. Their mission was to assist in the organization of the Forces Françaises l'Intérieur

(FFI); to provide additional means of delivering arms; and provide additional communications between London and the FFI groups. The teams would be sent to the Free French Délégués Militaire Regional Grandval, Hanneton, and Davout d'Auerstaet; the Citronelle mission on the Belgian border; and pre-invasion networks, or "circuits" of the British F Section code named Spiritualist, Pedlar, Historian, and Digger, among others. Clearly now little favoritism remained as Koenig's staff determined to send missions to all possible operatives in France. The teams would be commanded by Koenig unless the situation mandated them to be directed by those on the ground to whom they were being sent. Their planned dates of deployment were to begin on August 11 and continue until August 18, going long beyond the August moon period.[19]

But the rapid pace of Patton's Third Army forced a change. On the same day that the French cities of Le Mans and Angers were retaken, placing Allied forces less than 200 kilometers from Paris, Colonel Joseph Haskell requested that the staff consider deploying three teams to work a line from Paris-Orleans-Blois on August 8, but he wanted to ensure that sending them made sense as they would be operating in uniform. Two days later, this idea altered radically and developed into an operations order from Koenig that *eight* teams should be deployed to support the Allied advance, working the area south and east of Paris. The order itself is revealing as it shows how well, at least in theory, Koenig's planners sought to manage the Jedburgh missions in coordination with their regional military delegates. In a complete shift, these eight teams were to be inserted in *civilian clothes* in order to work clandestinely with the regional delegate, FFI commander, or circuit organizer and then send Maquis volunteers toward the Allied lines with the goal of making it through to American or British intelligence officers.[20] Such a mission was direct intelligence work for which others would be far more suited. While there were agents in the Paris region such as the Spiritualist circuit, EMFFI's action now shows their willingness to severely alter the Jedburgh operational methods to move these teams to the Paris region in front of the swiftly moving Allied armies. Much of this meant a major change in how the teams were originally planning to operate. In addition to being deployed in civilian clothes, the teams submitted handwriting samples so that any messages the Maquis brought from the Jedburgh team commander to the army intelligence staff could be validated as legitimate. The Jedburghs who were still awaiting deployment had to agree to enter France in civilian clothes. Not wanting to place undue pressure on them individually, Colonel Haskell directed that the Jeds be assembled by Milton Hall commander Lieutenant Colonel Musgrave and asked if they would agree to becoming clandestine. Haskell was clear on the matter and wrote, "On no account should the various teams be approached individually with a request that they operate in civilian clothes." Everyone knew what Hitler directed the Wehrmacht to do with civilian operatives. But the Jeds, itching to get to France, supported the change and a staff officer replied back to Haskell on August 14 that their response was "almost unanimous" and that Musgrave had more than enough men for the efforts east of Paris.[21]

Paris lay in front of the Allies' main force efforts. Eisenhower's initial desire to bypass the city proved impossible in the face of de Gaulle's clear desire to liberate it and in the way that events were playing out there. The 12th Army Group's rapid advance east, that spurred Haskell and SFHQ to suddenly consider sending Jedburghs there in civilian clothes, proved to be so quick that those missions to the area west and south of Paris never deployed. Teams Henry, Godfrey, Frank, Jim, Raymond, Quentin, Roderick, and Stanley, which had put on alert for the Paris area, were placed back in reserve status to await further requirements.[22] Also at work could have been some dissonance between the internal Résistance power structure and the external leadership of the Free French in London. The regional military delegate, Jacques Delmas, pseudonym Arc or Chaban, returned to France on August 14 at the same time that Koenig canceled Jedburgh teams for the region. Arriving at the newly liberated Le Mans airfield via an American aircraft, Delmas then traveled through the lines and arrived in Paris on August 16.[23] Chaban-Delmas, as he later came to be called, and the Comité d'action militaire or COMAC had sought to direct the Maquis from inside France instead of from London.[24] But after some time in London meeting with Koenig and others in EMFFI, Delmas now realized the utility of cooperating under Koenig's orders in order to line up with Eisenhower's efforts.

He agreed that the unity that could only be provided by London was the best way to proceed. Two days after Chaban's arrival in Paris, the city's Résistance began labor strikes as well as shooting at German soldiers and taking over key parts of the city. The German commander in Paris, General Dietrich von Choltitz, who had only taken that post on August 9 following the failed coup of Carl-Heinrich von Stülpnagel, now attempted to hold the city. Hitler's orders demanded that Paris be held or given to the Allies as "a pile of rubble."[25]

While the rapid pace of the Allied advance scuttled a comprehensive Jedburgh plan for the Paris region, one team did deploy east of Paris. Sent to the Seine-et-Marne Department on August 12, as a part of a planned deployment of twenty-five teams, Team Aubrey had agreed to go into France in civilian clothes and was the first team to do so. After parachuting to a drop zone south of the Seine, the Jeds were met by the leader of Spiritualist, Frenchman René Dumont-Guillemet. The team's two officers bicycled into Paris with members of the Spiritualist Circuit the next day. Over the next week British Captain Godfrey Marchant gave lessons in sabotage in an auto mechanic's garage, while French Jed Jean-Françoise Chaigneau traveled around Paris ascertaining who within the circuit might be able to do various tasks. Sergeant Hooker remained in the village of Forfey ill with the measles but still able to send and receive messages. By August 21, with more and more violence erupting in Paris provoking the Germans to respond with reprisals, Marchant and Dumont-Guillemet left the city and headed back to join British Sergeant Ivor Hooker at their safe house near the village of Forfry. Chaigneau arrived the next day with several other circuit members. But the fleeing Germans had hidden in the villages and woods all around them, and the team, along with the Spiritualist circuit, became involved in at least two battles with the Wehrmacht. On August 27, the Jedburghs and the men and women of the circuit became involved in a shoot-out with tanks whose fire "was like God's thunder."[26] The tanks had driven into the part of the forest in which the Jedburghs were hiding, and Dumont-Guillemet, Hooker, Marchant, and Chaigneau were forced to remain where they were as running would reveal their location. While they and other members of Dumont-Guillemet's group were able to fight back, doing so threatened their comrades hiding in trees around the German positions. Many of their weapons remained on trucks packed up with the manufacturing grease still coating them. Confusion reigned as some were hiding within the Wehrmacht's position and the others were ineffectively using weapons they were not trained to use. Very little went well, and Chaigneau was killed by a round from an enemy tank while attempting to escape along a stream.[27] As the SOE history of the Jedburghs stated, "As had been foreseen, the first overt action of this *Résistance* group resulted in its complete dispersal, and the death of the French Officer of the Team." Who actually had foreseen this was perhaps the British staff or the SOE planners who took the opportunity to make clear their disapproval of deploying Team Aubrey, which the French leadership had sent anyway. The British SOE staff member who wrote the line above made clear their reluctance to send in a team in civilian clothes to operate like spies in an area teeming with enemy troops.

But Team Aubrey was not the only one to deploy in this way. Team Augustus, another of the Jedburghs included in the August 8 order, deployed on August 15 to the northwest of the village of Colomfay in the Aisne Department. After confirmation from the A5 Region's operations officer, the team was given the green light to depart.[28] American Major John Bonsall led the team. He was a Princeton graduate who had received his commission through ROTC and planned to practice law like his father. But he was called to active duty in August 1941 and had subsequently joined the OSS. The twenty-five-year-old had just been promoted to major in April. The French member of the team was Jean Delviche who knew the region well, having grown up ten kilometers north of Laon. Few Jedburghs had greater knowledge of the area they worked than Delviche. The radio operator was American Technical Sergeant Roger Cote.[29] The team's mission was to link up with the region's operations officer, Pierre Marie Deshayes, who used the code name Gramme, and support his efforts in the area to arm his Maquis. Deshayes had parachuted into France in December 1942, the day before his twenty-fourth birthday, and successfully rose through the ranks of the BCRA network sent to liaise with the movement La Voix du Nord. The region's military delegate was Guy Chaumet who

operated under the code name Cissoide and had taken part in the same resistance movement as Deshayes. Together they had helped establish the
Bureau d'Opérations Aériennes (BOA) in this part of France.[30]

The team radioed to London on August 17 that all was well and "reception perfect." The arrival of the team brought spirits high as they all "managed a grand life in their house with good food (French) good wine etc."
Their next message on August 19 told London that they had met with
Chaumet and expected to meet with other leaders soon. They did so the
next day and radioed back local Maquis strengths, general locations, and
weapons requirements: 1,100 men were trained and had arms while 4,900
were not armed.[31] By August 21 the team's messages began discussing
German movements through the department and providing locations for
air strikes. They also acquired the German plans for the destruction of
the port at Le Havre. Their work cutting the railroad lines soon became impossible due to the number of enemy troops in the area. "Essential RR line
be cut by bombing," the team radioed on August 22. Two days later the
bombing, the Maquis actions, and the high traffic on the roads all were getting to be too much for the enemy as Cote radioed that the Germans were
"completely disorganized. Incapable of self defense against force." But the
team and the region's Forces Françaises de l'Intérieur (FFI) were having
their own problems which they related to headquarters on August 25. First,
the area was too thick with enemy troops; second, the region did not have
areas where they could shelter or hide; last, they lacked arms. Apparently
they did arrange at least one weapons drop as they continued on to say that
when the arms arrived, they divided them up and split up into small bands,
using guerrilla tactics when the opportunity arose. On August 26 the team
radioed that they saw the Germans preparing defensive positions but
not placing mines on the bridges. Koenig's headquarters radioed back on
August 30 that the Allied Army commander had ordered the "FFI to take
all possible steps to preserve" the region's bridges from destruction and
then specifically listed them.[32]

But there is no way of knowing whether the team received that message.
By the end of the month, some of the conventional British forces had pen-
etrated the area and the team had successfully made their way to Allied

lines traveling with one of the Maquis companies. At one point they were in several vehicles but had become spread out as each one had to travel through German checkpoints individually. While waiting for Augustus to catch up, one of the FFI complained the Jeds slowed them down. The FFI commander reflected and answered, "Perhaps they are good shots" and therefore worth a bit of a wait. They arrived without incident within the Allied lines, secured some equipment and gear for themselves, and passed on what they knew about the enemy in the area. They decided to return back across the lines. Captain Delviche, secured a car from a friend in the area and they drove back toward the lines at night in a torrential rain. At a checkpoint near the town of Barenton-sur-Serre, Germans stopped the Jedburghs and some of their Maquis. The Jedburghs may not have seen the German soldiers initially due to the weather, but as some enemy soldiers came out of the darkness, the Jedburghs may have attempted to bolt from their vehicle with their Maquis. Despite their civilian clothes and fake identity cards, the Jeds may have known the game was up because of all the radio equipment with them in the car. Two shots rang out killing Delviche and Bonsall; Cote must have attempted a run for it, but as he did, five more shots were heard in the rainy night. Later that night the two officers were found in the car and Sergeant Cote was found face down in the mud about a dozen meters from the car, all had severe head wounds. The German soldiers left the area without bothering to take anything.[33] The next day, the FFI arranged for their burial and later told the US Army investigator that they made sure to have an honor guard and a military burial despite the continued presence of Germans traveling through the area.[34] Completely ignorant of what had happened to their team, Free French headquarters radioed Augustus on September 16 to say that their mission was ended and instructing them to return to London via Paris.[35]

THE FINAL PUSH—THE JEDBURGHS RUSH IN

The lack of understanding in the Jedburghs' London headquarters of what occurred with Team Augustus is only one example of Free French Headquarters' difficulty in learning what was happening in France. Their order to deploy the twenty-five teams they had planned had been implemented slowly due to an inability to generate airlift sorties and for the Maquis to identify secure drop zones. These two factors provoked delay after delay for the alerted teams. Originally, the twenty-five teams were to all have been deployed by August 18, a rate of deployment that Colonel Zeigler seemed to doubt would be possible.[36] But while Team Aubrey deployed as scheduled, no other team did, and the order went through four amendments attempting to keep up with the changes forced by the delays.[37] But for the Jedburghs still cooling their heels at Milton Hall, it must have been difficult to see the war progressing and wondering if they would ever be involved. The day after Paris was liberated, Koenig's British deputy, Major General Redman, must have known their dissatisfaction with their situation and wrote a long letter to be read by all the Jeds awaiting deployment to France. Vaguely, he wrote that the reasons for the delay "have been many," but that "It has been necessary to keep a reserve to meet future eventualities." Continuing on, he stated that "the battle has moved much more quickly than had been anticipated. Dispatch by air to the areas required has not always been possible." But still emphatic that the Jedburghs had a mission to do, he said, "Should the enemy take up defensive positions on the frontier, it would be necessary to organize intensive guerrilla activity behind any such line taken up in order to reduce in so far as it may be possible his power to resist effectively the advance of the main armies." He noted that for the teams to be effective they would need to be inserted as early as possible, but "the rapid turn of events, unfortunately, has reduced considerably the time available, but we must make the best of the situation as it exists, and have confidence that most valuable work can be done by all now being sent in." Then seemingly contradicting himself as he had listed all the considerations regarding the methodical use of the teams, General Redman finished by announcing, "Orders have now been given for all Jedburgh teams trained and available and now remaining in this country to be employed as soon as the necessary aircraft deliveries can be arranged."[38] With this sentence, the deputy commander of the Free French notified the Jeds of General Koenig's August 24 orders that all available teams were to deploy as soon as possible.

But getting these teams into France proved incredibly difficult. Not only was the rapid pace of conventional operations too quick for Special Force staff to adjust to, but as they proceeded through their operations in August, Free French headquarters built more complexity into their war. For example, the Free French operations bureau wanted to conduct another mission similar to Aloes that had operated in Brittany in order to deploy a command staff to the regions in eastern France. L'Etat Major Forces Françaises de l'Intérieur (EMFFI) began a planning effort to learn the lessons from Aloes and send as many as four similar missions to eastern France. But realizing that Aloes' mission suffered from a great many faults, they sought to eliminate the errors they had made in late July and early August when it deployed too late via a very muddled process. These new missions would take Jedburgh teams as communication links and liaison units to the various Maquis units and operate alongside the Free French regional delegate and his FFI commanders. Furthermore, each team would be able to talk to other teams directly, something that generally was not being done for security and technical reasons. If correctly conducted and supported with airlift and weapons, this effort could have been very beneficial to the land forces as they made their way east.

From the middle of August until the first day of September, EMFFI's focus was on the area around Lyon and then north to Chalons-sur-Saône and Dijon and then blossoming out to an area from St. Dizier to Belfort and north to Verdun. Their aim was to harass the escaping Germans as they attempted to establish a defensive line on the west of the Rhine River. On August 15 Team Anthony deployed north of Chalons-sur-Saône and Team Jude deployed south of Lyon with an SAS team. When Jude arrived, it discovered more of a reception committee than they required. The way the Maquis had interpreted the BBC message they thought there would be 40 aircraft arriving, instead of 40 people, and so they had 2,000 people there with 100 vehicles to handle what would certainly have been a lot of weapons.[39] On August 16, Team Andrew deployed to join an Inter-Allied party near the Belgian border and Team Augustus left on its fateful mission to the Aisne. On August 18, Teams Bruce, Bunny, and Tony departed the UK for Yonne, Haute Marne, and the Vendee, respectively. Team Tony went to assist the effort now concentrating against the German garrison holding out at La Rochelle. On August 19, Teams Arthur and Paul left for Côte d'Or to the northeast and east of Dijon. On August 21, Teams Benjamin and Bernard deployed to the Meuse, with Benjamin going north of Verdun and Bernard to the south of the city. No more teams were sent until August 25, when Team Alfred deployed north of Paris and Team Arnold to the east of Paris in the Marne. On August 26, Team Cecil landed south of Troyes, Archibald went north of Nancy, and Basil managed to become the first team into the Belfort Gap, east of Besançon. On August 28, a record four teams departed, with Teams Alastair deployed to the Vosges, Cedric to the Haute Saône, and Norman to the Doubs south of Team Basil; Maurice was supposed to deploy and work with Norman, but their crew, distrusting the signal lights, aborted the mission and returned to England. Maurice finally made it to France on September 1 and successfully landed in Jura east of Chalons-sur-Saône.[40]

Summing up the frustration felt by many of the teams, Maurice's officer in charge, American Captain Charles Carmen, began his report with this rebuke—perhaps inspired by how he was spending his time while waiting to get into the war. "By the time we arrived in France," he wrote, "our state of mind was somewhat that of a woman whose lover has left without saying goodbye." He continued bitterly, "We had been led to expect that we would be sent in well before D-Day. Consequently, for three months we expected daily to be alerted. And for two weeks after we were alerted, the operation was daily postponed. Finally, on 28 August 1944, we arrive at Harrington Aerodrome for the third time, donned our parachutes for the second time, and climbed into the plane for the first time."[41] His report went on to vividly describe the inept and inexperienced B-24 crewmen who took part in a four-aircraft formation to insert two teams and the required arms for the area's Maquis. But when the reception party's signal lights were incorrectly thought to be anti-aircraft search lights, the crew decided to abort and return to England. Carmen and his French teammate Hubert Dumesnil went up to the cockpit and argued with the pilot, but to no avail. Team Maurice waited for two more days and then left on August 31 in a British aircraft from Tempsford. At last in France, they had the chance to celebrate their arrival with French wine, even though they were only "four kilometers away" from the Germans who were actively engaged with an FFI force. While Dumesnil developed their initial plans with the local FTP leader Lucien Chazeaux, Carmen and the radioman Technical Sergeant Francis Cole sent off their first message.[42] Carmen, in keeping with his playful writing, admitted that the two Jeds had to send the message "twice because of the Champagne."[43] Maurice finally had arrived and linked up with the local FTP leaders who just sixteen days earlier had merged under the FFI's leadership and therefore the DMR. The Jura's Résistance had gained a measure of unity without any Allied pressure.[44]

Also on September 1, Team Philip arrived east of Nancy, Roderick deployed south of Belfort, and Gregory parachuted on the eastern edge of Jura near the Swiss border. Gregory was the last of those that had originally been planned to deploy on August 8, and their on again, off again, alert posture was a function of their being a part of the command and control mission Orgeat, discussed below. Team Nicholas parachuted into the eastern Vosges on September 9 and Team Henry arrived on September 10 to a very friendly reception. In fact, it was nowhere near the German lines. By the time they had arrived, the Americans controlled the region north of Belfort. "You know don't you," Team Henry radioed to FFI headquarters, "that this area was overrun before we arrived," meaning that they had parachuted into friendly territory. Disappointed that their mission was entirely futile they continued, "We have done nothing at all…funny war."[45] But Henry was not the last of the Jeds into France. Team Godfrey arrived in Haut-Rhin on September 12, and four days later Teams Douglas II, Timothy, and Jim arrived in Jura as well. The French officer on Jim was none other than Lieutenant Joe de Francesco, Eisenhower's driver in Algiers who in December of 1942 wanted Darlan's assassin to receive a medal.[46] Joe had finally gotten to France twenty-one long months after that discussion with General Eisenhower. Discussing how he felt about that many years later, Joe stated, "There were a lot of angry guys at Milton Hall."[47] As Carmen stated above, they had been led to believe that they were going to be used before D-Day and according to de Francesco, the disappointment was especially sharp among the French officers.

But while their deployment seemed to be done in a scattershot manner, it was not planned that way. Instead, the process was a victim of circumstances brought about by the positive events of the advancing front lines and the negative aspect of the fog, rain, and cloudy weather everyone contended with in late August and September of 1944. The messages from the Free French regional delegates, as well as the Jeds, continually screamed for weapons, but when the aircraft could not deliver them due to the weather, there was not much that could be done. Free French headquarters did consider another daylight drop and planned a large mission similar to the previous ones. The planning for Operation Bentley began in the middle of August, and the first of the written directives on it appeared on August 20, long before the two invasion forces from the north and south linked up. Originally planning to drop supplies to eight drop zones in the six eastern Departments of Ain, Doubs, Jura, Haute Savoie, Haute Marne, and Saône et Loire, the mission planners believed there were 27,000 Free French willing to join in the combat, but who lacked the needed weapons. They estimated that approximately 13,000 were armed and believed to be in action. But the effort of inserting teams was beleaguered by the strict requirement that there could be no enemy anti-aircraft capability within 20 kilometers of the drop zones. That requirement alone, no matter the weather, would be hard for any Jedburgh team or intelligence agent to ensure given the constant traffic of German units moving through the region. Furthermore, the order directed that "In each case an assurance will be obtained from the Field that the ground situation provides adequate security, i.e. there must not be active enemy forces which might include light or heavy flak in the vicinity of the selected dropping point."[48] Given the thick population of Germans now crowding the region, such assurances were hard to attain. But this did not deter Koenig's plan with Operation Bentley on August 20.

Then the changes began. The very next day, the drop zone area shifted to the south, striking the Jura and Doubs from the list and adding Ardeche and oddly enough the Vercors whose Maquis had earlier been forced to flee the region and give up the ground to the concerted German offensive that had concluded on August 6.[49] With Operation Dragoon proceeding north with good success, it did make sense to re-supply those now engaged in fighting. But on August 24, a shortage of Bren guns and carbine rifles forced a shift in the weapons that could be sent, and therefore the effort had to be reconfigured, meaning further delays. On August 25 the progress of General Patch's forces forced a new change, and the Vercors and Ardeche were taken off as drop sites and the old list put back in the operation. On August 27 the operation was completely reorganized from an American daylight operation to a British nighttime mission and officially given the code name Bentley. On August 28 more Allied advances removed the Haute Savoie from the drop zone list. The order also noted that SHAEF had yet to approve of the operation and without that, the RAF 38 Group, cued up for the effort, remained waiting.[50]

Also waiting were the Maquis leaders. Apparently trying to get his weapons-starved region on the list of drop zones for the operation, Gilbert Grandval, the Free French delegate for C Region radioed on September 3 that there was no flak in the proximity of the five proposed terrains."[51] But for all the effort, Operation Bentley never happened, as permission from SHAEF was slow to come. On September 6, Eisenhower sent a message to Major General Redman describing his reluctance to supply the Maquis too "lavishly." Ike highlighted his reservations regarding the possibility that there might be "too many armed Frenchmen when hostilities cease who are not subject to military discipline" and that the soldiers now enrolling in the French regular army would go without weapons while the Résistance was still receiving arms. Adding that it was Koenig's decision, Eisenhower told Redman to discuss the matter with Koenig and "issue a categorical directive." Furthermore, Eisenhower wanted Koenig to notify the groups who were not going to receive arms of that fact.[52] Redman responded to the Supreme Allied Commander on September 11 that Koenig had directed Haskell and Zeigler, who were visiting Paris, to focus on the areas both Eisenhower and Koenig agreed were still worthwhile but told Eisenhower that some latitude might be necessary. The areas around La Rochelle on the western coast were still firmly held by the enemy and it is unclear whether Koenig knew German General Elster's formations had surrendered in l'Indre.[53] But by now the Royal Air Forces's 38 Group was no longer available for

Operation Bentley. On September 1 the unit was given to the British 1st Airborne Army for Operation Market Garden.[54] This operation was the largest Allied airborne operation of the war and began on September 14. Every aircraft suitable for paratroopers was required for it.

Eisenhower's fears of "lavishly" arming the Maquis seem completely incongruous with the views of Region D's DMR Pierre Hanneton. In a message to FFI headquarters on August 26 he decried as "deplorable" his ability to conduct operations "due to the total absence of any aerial operations for the last three months." but despite this his FFI had "perfect confidence in the French organization."[55] Hanneton is overstating the situation, but not by much as the SFHQ reports to SHEAF bear out. Only three tons of arms had been parachuted to Region D since D-Day.[56]

Attempting to operate in Eisenhower's highest priority area, the Vosges, at the end of August Jedburgh Team Alastair found their mission impossible and asked the obvious question in a message to Koenig's headquarters on September 5. "If you did not intend to give us any support why did you send us," and the team, led by British Major Oliver Brown with French Captain Rene Karriere went on to demand that Koenig's staff act and "For Gods sake do something."[57] London answered meekly stating that "Due to circumstances and reasons beyond our control it is impossible to send you operations at present." Colonel Zeigler, replying on behalf of Koenig, said that Grandval had been notified of this and that things were in the works but the timing of them was unknown. Zeigler's message back to Alastair ended with, "SORRY." Shortly afterward, another message arrived from Free French headquarters telling the Jeds that the daylight weapons delivery was canceled because Grandval "had not complied with some of the conditions under which the operations would be undertaken."[58]

Grandval, however, had been going back and forth with his London-based masters over their idea of mounting a large daylight drop over several drop zones on the same day in Alsace and Vosges. He protested, saying that the enemy would make it impossible to perform and that he simply wanted all the weapons they were prepared to send in one drop zone in the Vosges for the moment; later they could see about flying weapons into Alsace when conditions might be more favorable. Grandval pressed his case in messages to London as well as sending people to Paris to meet Koenig personally.[59] But the grand scheme was never worked out as it was impossible to expect the Wehrmacht to remain still thus allowing the information regarding the drop zones to remain valid for as long as it took the staff and aircrews to generate the plans and then execute their missions.

Therefore, instead of the RAF conducting Operation Bentley and delivering some of the weapons to the Vosges region, American B-17s conducted Operation Grassy to the Doubs only. In keeping with American practice, the operation switched back to being a daylight drop. On September 9, sixty-eight aircraft succeeded in dropping supplies, but to only one drop zone southwest of Besançon. Tasked by SHAEF to deliver arms to the Vosges, Special Force Headquarters coordinated the US Army Air Force effort that involved the drop zone being changed "four times before the operation was finally flown."[60] Furthermore, as the Jedburghs in the area could attest, the area south and west of Besançon was not really behind the lines at the time of the drop, but perhaps it was more accurate to say the area was in a state of flux. The Germans were quickly evacuating the area, so on any given day between August 16 and September 15, to predict which drop zones would be secure and which would not was very uncertain. This condition persisted in Jura and Doubs until the Wehrmacht succeeded at establishing a fairly firm defensive line roughly halfway between Besançon and Belfort on about September 15.[61] Nevertheless, Albert de Schonen, of Jedburgh Team Gregory had Sergeant Ron Brierley radio back to London that Grassy was a "huge success" for them. Furthermore, he radioed that Colonel Ziegler should "Consider this area armed." However, they asked that Zeigler tell them where other drops took place, as if they expected there had been other drops and other Maquis were now armed and equipped. There were no others, and Grassy was the last large-scale air operation in France.

Communications with the Free French regional delegates was a constant source of confusion. While it was not the single greatest issue faced by the London FFI and their delegates, it seemed to be one they believed could be solved and looked to the Jedburgh teams to do it. Learning from their deployed headquarters experience for Brittany and its Aloes mission, FFI's leadership in London thought they would "form, equip and despatch [*sic*] to Eastern France seven small mobile staffs to assist the local commanders of the F. F. I., particularly by the provision of communications both between groups in the field and between these groups and LONDON." Grandval would get three of these detachments, Hanneton was to receive three, and one detachment would be sent to Ardennes. The effort, which was easily the most complicated single mission yet designed, was to leave for France beginning on September 4, "subject to the procurement of the necessary equipment."[62] It is clear from that statement as well as the flurry of paperwork, amendments, notes, and memos regarding the mission that London did not have the radios, codes, drop zones, air sorties, or Jedburgh teams selected, nor did they even have the specific non-Jedburgh mission members identified. Over the next three weeks, ten amendments were made and portions of the effort were canceled resulting in only Teams Gregory, Jim, Douglas, and Timothy deploying instead of the originally planned seven teams. Reasons were largely lack of communications capacity, something that ironically was caused by a lack of communication between Koenig's own communications and operations staffs. The two parts of the staff rarely worked well together, as some of the examples discussed in previous chapters attest, and their relationship did not improve with the advancing complications and ambitions of the operations efforts.

By the end of August all of the Jedburgh missions in eastern France were transitioning to becoming reconnaissance assets for the advancing Allied armies. Usually, within a few days after their arrival, if not immediately, the Jedburgh teams met up with the conventional forces and decided to go back behind the lines and coordinate the actions of the Maquis, but with the specific guidance of the conventional forces in the area. In many cases, they found the Special Force Detachment and coordinated their activities with its planners. Team Benjamin, comprised of British Major James O'Brien-Tear, French Lieutenant Paul Moniez, and French radio operator Sous Lieutenant H. Kaminski, arrived west of Verdun at a very hastily arranged drop zone. The reception committee had only been notified "a few day [*sic*] previously to find a DZ at all costs and had never received any detailed instructions" on how to run such an operation. O'Brien-Tear and

Moniez later wrote that "the net result was that 2 days and 3 nights were spent rounding up and collecting the stores and parachutes, most of which were elegantly draping the topmost branches of the highest trees." Furthermore the Germans had recently moved some soldiers to within 350 yards of the drop zone.[63] Further complicating their pre-arrival plans was their smashed radio and injuries to Kaminski and the nearby team Bernard's French Captain Etienne Nasica. Therefore, the two teams decided to work together on the western side of the Meuse River instead of following the original plan for Benjamin to work the eastern Meuse while Bernard worked the west of the department. But Grandval's local Maquis were in a great state of confusion as he was attempting to bring about the large drop for the Vosges described earlier and was not in the area. Furthermore, the Gestapo and the local Vichy Milice had arrested many of the local Maquis group shortly after the Jeds arrived.[64] Those arrests gave the Germans the locations of all the drop zones the Jedburghs intended to use and "in effect," the team wrote, "all our immediate contacts with the local FFI were severed in one swoop."[65] Left with few choices or means to arm the Maquis, the two teams moved west at London's direction to link up with and perform reconnaissance for the 3rd Army. Lieutenant Moniez took some of the Maquis and conducted a patrol into the village of Sainte-Menehould killing four Germans, but they had to depart when the Wehrmacht reinforcing the village shelled them with artillery and mortars. The teams continued similar activities for the next two days, and in one action Bernard's Captain Nasica was wounded in the hip.[66]

Meanwhile, the lead elements of the US 3rd Army were rapidly overtaking their region. Finding the Special Force Detachment and Lieutenant Colonel Powell on September 3, the teams were directed to remain there for a new mission and given a new radio to replace the one destroyed during their parachute jump nearly two weeks earlier. Powell wanted to arrange for the teams to go south to the area between St. Dizier and Chaumont and assist the FFI's effort to protect the 3rd Army's southern flank. The team arrived on September 15 when they received their first and only aerial resupply. By the latter half of the month they were coordinating tasks the 3rd Army wanted the Maquis to handle, such as guarding captured enemy equipment and doing some tactical reconnaissance. The team wrapped up that mission and EMFFI directed them to return to London, which they did on October 2. Pondering their mission's effectiveness, O'Brien-Tear and Moniez believed the harm done to them by the arrests could have been mended, but "mending takes time in conditions where it takes 3 days for a message to be sent 10 miles and 3 more days for an answer to be received. And time is what we lacked."[67] Adding to the critique more than six decades later, Paul Moniez thought that his training did not emphasize adaptation or creative thinking. Little in what they did was what they had expected to do. His role in using the Maquis for rear area duties or organizing *Maquisards* to penetrate Allied lines to provide intelligence was not something he had been prepared to do. Furthermore, his lack of local knowledge, the very thing the he as a Frenchman was supposed to add to the operation, was also debilitating. His complete unfamiliarity with the Meuse was such that "parachuting me into the Meuse was just as if they had parachuted me into Arizona."[68]

GERMAN COUNTERINSURGENCY AND THE TRAGEDY OF TEAM JACOB

Team Jacob's relatively early arrival in the area east of where Team Benjamin parachuted did not make things easier for its Jedburghs. In fact, Gough, Boissarie, and Seymour were effectively destroyed as a team on August 17 while descending down into the Wehrmacht's sweep of the area under a small task force hastily organized called Kommando Schoner. That force succeeded in capturing Seymour, forced the Maquis to disperse, and sent the SAS and Jedburgh team scattering into the Vosges woods. The German task force commander Major Schoner, who had lived in New York before the war, stopped Seymour's summary execution immediately after his capture, brought him to their command post, and questioned him.[69] "He spoke excellent English with an American accent," Seymour noted.[70] Seymour was questioned and according to testimony after the war gave the enemy enough information to spare his life and garner decent treatment.[71] The next day the Germans moved Seymour to Schirmeck camp, "an ordinary slave jail," as Seymour called it and part of the Natzweiler prison system where he remained for ten days.[72]

But what happened to Captains Gough and Boissarie? Koenig's staff in London had heard nothing of Team Jacob since August 16, the day before Seymour's capture. The German counterinsurgency operations not only proved to be completely able to foil any coherent Résistance in Region C but were also able to capture and kill many of the Maquis, the British SAS, and the Allied Jedburghs sent to work with them. But while Gough and Boissarie had escaped the trap on August 17; they had no means to communicate to the Free French headquarters themselves, and regional delegate Grandval's message to London on September 3 reported only that he knew of the team but did not give any details of what they were doing or indicate anything involving their present condition.[73] Attempting to coordinate other things, it is clear that Grandval was merely repeating rumors back to London. But on August 26 Captain Gough succeeded with the aid of one of the BCRA radio operators in the area to send word that he needed new equipment and a new team. In a second message from a second operator he asked for "arms, ammunition, grenades urgently needed for 600 men," and that he needed a parachute drop of no more than seventy containers, and a radio. It ended with, "area getting hotter daily."[74] However, those messages probably were not recognized as being from Jacob as they were sent from another radio operator's equipment. A status report of Jedburgh teams done on August 27 laments that no communication from Team Jacob had been received since August 16.[75] But on September 5, Gough managed to get off two more messages. The first asked that his equipment be sent via the SAS air drop to take place in a few days and reported that he could not receive arms before due to being attacked. He needed money and remarked that getting food was difficult. Also on September 15 he telegraphed that Seymour had been captured and he feared that the Germans had executed him. He also stated that Boissarie was killed. "I am now sole member of team Jacob. 100 *Maquis* killed 100 captured in same battle. Rest dispersed." The next day his spirits seem to have risen somewhat. Gough apologized for such little communication; he stated that his Maquis leader was under surveillance and therefore could not operate but that Gough had rallied two hundred

Maquis and armed them with SAS-provided weapons. He signed off with the plucky remark, "Chins up." On September 19 Zeigler's staff finally replied saying it was sending money, and on September 23 telegraphed Gough again requesting details as to the fate of Seymour and Boissarie. They received nothing back from Captain Gough.[76]

Gough was Koenig's only man in the area Eisenhower had made a top priority and Koenig now sought to utilize him. On September 27, with Allied armies now approaching the Vosges and crossing the Meurthe River, Gough's operations could prove very valuable.[77] But it is unclear what messages Gough was receiving from London. Reports of the SAS note that Gough was operating independently of them and working with a group known as Maquis de Reciproque in October. But by early November the Germans had captured him.

The Gestapo had organized two operations in the area to defeat the insurgency after the Wehrmacht's initial efforts in the middle of August failed to do so. Operations Waldfest 1 and 2 began in September and were organized by the SS commander in Strasbourg, Dr. Eric Isselhorst, and his deputy Wilhelm Schneider. Isselhorst had been a member of the Nazi Party since 1932 and had worked his way up the party's ladder in Gestapo offices in Berlin, Erfurt, and Munich; after participating in and organizing Einsatzkommando detachments in Poland he became the head of the Strasbourg Gestapo in 1943.[78] His effective actions had largely succeeded in rounding up all of the SAS of another mission code named Pistol and nearly all of the SAS with Team Loyton. With Boissarie killed on or about September 4 and Gough captured at the end of October, Isselhorst had succeeded in destroying Team Jacob. Gough and Seymour were still alive, but while Gough was held at Schirmeck and later moved to a prison in Strasbourg, Seymour had been moved on into Germany.[79] The prison camp was organized to place special prisoners such as these parachutists in their own cells. So along with Gough were five SAS, four US airmen who had parachuted out of disabled aircraft, three priests, and another Frenchman. All were held there because they were taken while working with or being with the Résistance.[80] Also with them was Werner Helfen, a German NCO who had thrown his sawed-off shotgun in the river and ordered his soldiers to do the same. Helfen had been in the Schutz Polizei when his unit, then equipped with illegal shotguns, was ordered to turn over their legal weapons to frontline soldiers. He told his men to throw the weapons into the river because if they were captured, he was afraid the Allies would try them for having a weapon that was against the international conventions. However, he had been arrested by his own army for destroying Reich property and brought to Schirmeck as a prisoner. While there, he was given light duties bringing him in contact with the other inmates. He often did favors for the foreigners such as getting them medical attention, passing messages among them, and simply speaking kindly to them.[81]

As the Allies advanced, the camp commander Karl Buck received orders from Isselhorst to shoot any special prisoners that he might select, release the women, and burn down the camp. Buck did not carry out these orders because he "did not consider it wise to leave fresh mass graves behind, and secondly I considered the camp might have been useful to the Wehrmacht who were retreating." Instead, he arranged to transport the prisoners across the Rhine River to Germany and a prison at Gaggenau, on November 21. Captain Gough, having been told they were leaving, gave his silk escape map to Werner Helfen as sign of appreciation for the German's friendship. The next day, while they were all on trucks, Helfen, the only one of them who had been told of his death sentence, jumped from the truck and escaped. The others arrived at the camp at Gaggenau, Germany, on November 23. Witnesses after the war attested that they were all still at the camp at midday on November 25 but later that day the SAS, the three priests, the four airmen, the French civilian, and Gough were put back into a truck with soldiers and shovels.[82]

The truck drove through the town of Gaggenau and then into the Erlich Forest and pulled alongside a bomb crater. The execution unit took three prisoners out of the truck at a time, marched them into the bomb crater, and shot each of them in the back of the head. One of the priests attempted to flee but was shot down by the three men of the execution squad as he stumbled and fell in the trees. After killing them, they stripped them of their clothing, set fire to the bodies, and pilfered the best of the belongings from the pile of clothes, boots, and other meager possessions the prisoners had.[83]

After the war, despite the quagmire of Allied and judicial procedure and bureaucracies, Major Eric Barkworth of 2 SAS spent months attempting to uncover what had happened to the members of mission Loyton and Team Jacob. His relentless efforts resulted in the prosecution and conviction of the three executioners, Isselhorst, and his deputy, Wilhelm Schneider, who had conducted the Waldfest operations. Captain Gough's executioners received prison terms of no more than ten years. Schneider, even though Sergeant Seymour testified in his defense, was executed in January 1947. Isselhorst, who was tried for several other crimes, was finally shot by a French firing squad in February 1948. The Camp Schirmeck commander Karl Buck survived being punished for Gaggenau murders as the sentence was not legally confirmed under British law. But he too had plenty to answer for and was finally sentenced to death in the 1950s.[84]

That still leaves one Jedburgh unaccounted for, American Captain Cyrus Manierre. Sergeant Seymour who returned to the United Kingdom after being liberated from Stalag 9C near Frankfurt in April 1945, reported that he had seen Manierre while in a holding station awaiting further transportation. He caught just a glimpse but was sure it was him.[85] Manierre had successfully convinced his new interrogators in Lyon that he was an aircrew member and they turned him over to the Luftwaffe who took him into their system. While at the transit camp where Seymour saw him, Manierre realized his brother was just a few feet away among the crowd of POWs. William Manierre had been shot down with his bomber crew after flying his thirty-first mission one week after Cyrus had been captured. When the brothers made a bit of a commotion and the Germans realized two brothers were in the same camp, they made an event of it and due to their publicity the Red Cross was able to notify their mother of the two brothers' fate. Also making it somewhat easier Manierre recognized many of his West Point friends in the camp with him, which buoyed his morale a great deal. Having been promoted to major, he served the rest of the war as the adjutant to the group commander, Lieutenant Colonel Francis S. Gabreski, the famous World War II ace. On May 2, 1945, the Soviet Army liberated the camp and freed the last unaccounted for Jedburgh.[86]

CONCLUSION

General Koenig's headquarters could not overcome the myriad conditions that inhibited their ability to adequately support the Maquis in eastern France. Some were beyond their control: the constant turnover of the staff, the rapidly shifting front lines, the intermittent information and the staff's muddled awareness of what was occurring inside France; but the bifurcated command arrangements with the southern forces and the ambitious over-confidence that let them send teams without the ability to back them up with arms were self-inflicted problems. Koenig's lead Jedburgh planner, Lieutenant Colonel Dudley Guy Lancelot Carleton-Smith, must have been completely disgusted with the squabbling among the operations and communications planners and the lack of facilities in London needed to brief the teams when they were doing so many deployments in such a short amount of time. Furthermore, he and the other American and British officers on the staff often had to chase down what went wrong when a Jed in the field chewed them out for doing so poorly. One can only wonder how many of these issues could have been avoided had General Koenig been allowed to be fully integrated into SHAEF Headquarters when Eisenhower wanted him to be in early 1944. The fear of letting the French in on the secret was a valid concern, but despite waiting to bring the FFI in on the planning and conduct of operations, it is clear the Germans knew nearly everything about what Eisenhower's staff wanted the Résistance to do and how it was going to do it. But only in northeast France did the Wehrmacht succeed in disabling the FFI. The fate of Team Augustus, the only team to be completely eliminated; the casualties and prisoners of Teams Aubrey and Jacob; and the ineffectiveness of teams such as Maurice, Benjamin, and Henry attest to the fruitlessness of the Jedburgh effort despite the number of teams deployed to the area.

To arm the Résistance, Free French headquarters needed to have secure drop zones and favorable weather. But more than that, it needed to have secure drop zones that would *remain secure for nearly two days*. That was the time required to make all the arrangements and fly the missions bringing supplies. While such conditions may have existed in eastern France before

D-Day, or even before the middle of August when Hitler ordered the forces in the south and southwest to evacuate, those conditions did not exist when Eisenhower and Koenig needed to have them. The Wehrmacht's persistent traffic and movement through the region meant that Grandval, Hanneton, the Jeds, the SAS and the Maquis could not guarantee the continuing security of the area they identified when the Germans moved about as they wished. Moreover, the Gestapo's merciless actions against anyone found working with, as they called them, the Terroristen, proved to be extremely effective at rolling up FFI networks. Despite thousands of potential Maquis, operating in excellent terrain for guerrilla warfare and enjoying growing political support for the Libération, the effort to make them into a viable force never gained traction due to the thirty-six-hour planning cycle needed to line up aircraft, choose the proper containers of weapons, transfer the loads from the marshalling area to the proper aerodrome, properly rig the aircraft, and then fly the Jedburgh teams through the foggy moonless nights to the reception committee among the bonfires in the rainy forests of France. However, it was not for the lack of persistence and the "chins up" attitude displayed by many. The Jeds did need more time to establish themselves with Grandval's and Hanneton's organizations. But more than mere time on the ground, the teams would have had to have the Maquis armed and trained so that when the Wehrmacht's combat units transited the area, they could successfully harass them with hit-and-run raids coupled with persistent sabotage of key roads and railways. Of course, these operations, had they been able to occur, would have also required maintenance of secure drop zones amid the retreating and reorganizing Wehrmacht and SS units—a difficult prospect, no matter when the teams had arrived in the area.

Eisenhower's Guerrillas in History and Memory

During the course of France's liberation, the Allies deployed ninety-three Jedburgh teams to France. Those teams were a part of the Allied and Free French effort to control the arms delivered to France before and after they arrived. But the overall scale of the Allied effort to supply the French was massive. From 1941 until 1944, the Allies delivered 594,010 kilograms of explosives, 197,480 Sten light machine guns, 20,518 Bren heavy machine guns, 127,330 rifles, 57,849 pistols, 722,271 grenades, 2,440 Bazookas, 285 mortars, 9,373 Carbines, and 1,893 Marlin machine guns.[1] The number of armed Forces Françaises l'Intérieur (FFI) is elusive, but Supreme Headquarters Allied Expeditionary Forces (SHAEF) estimated it to be 114,000 by late October of 1944, nearly achieving Eisenhower's goal of having 120,000 armed men by the end of the year.[2] Within this atmosphere, we can examine Jedburgh operations during the summer and early fall of 1944 to see why some teams failed while others succeeded in attempting to understand the wisdom of using guerrilla warfare as a method of war. Furthermore, it allows us to examine the use of irregular warfare by nation-states, and in the case of the Free French, the re-emerging nation-state making use of its own irregular Maquis and how it dealt with the problems that arose.

Along with the Jedburghs, Allied headquarters in both the United Kingdom and North Africa deployed over eighteen Special Air Service missions, twenty Operational Groups, and twenty-six Inter-Allied missions to France. But of these Special Operations efforts, the Jedburgh plan was the first and most rigorously thought out and exercised effort the Allies put together. Not only were the Jedburghs specifically developed to liaise with another nation's irregular forces, but also the Jedburghs were *Allied* units working for an Allied headquarters that reported to the Supreme Allied Commander. Such an attribute is a rare thing to see in military units and so it is important to recognize how that came about and under what conditions it occurred. Coalition warfare is an incredibly complex affair to manage. This explains why alliances tend to maintain their coalition character at the highest level, such as at a headquarters, while leaving tactical units free from coalition politics as well as from the complexities of understanding myriad operational practices, language issues, and different capabilities. Doing so allows the operational level commanders and tactical units to operate more freely from political issues and maintain their own unique cultural cohesion, making room for clarity of intent and action. Placing alliance politics down to the tactical level forces very young captains, lieutenants, and sergeants to understand their teammates' culture while assuming they are cognizant of international politics. That is asking much of them. The Jedburgh experience of expressing the coalition all the way down to the tactical level is a rare occurrence. Perhaps it should remain so.

The Jedburghs sought to avoid politics in conducting their military mission. But many were forced to deal with politics when there were competing groups in their local area of operations. When the enemy attacked, unity often appeared within the groups who earnestly sought to fight back. But even in areas that had come together, Libération politics became more pronounced as the various political parties and groups vied for control in September or October as the Germans were defeated. As the first team into

France wrote at the end of their mission, "Fighting was over, politics began, [Team] Hugh left."[3] Major William Crawshay, Captain Louis L'Helgouach, and radio operator Rene Meyer operated in France from June 6 to the end of September 1944 performing various military tasks, but their mission was largely enabled due to the presence of sufficient local political unity. When that political unity was honed under L'Helgouach's auspices locally with their team, regionally with the regional military delegate, Eugene Dechelette, and nationally with General Koenig, then unified military action could occur and had a chance at being effective. Furthermore, operating inside the political sovereignty of de Gaulle and the Comité Francais de la Libération Nationale (CFLN), the teams exercised the committee's provisional sovereignty along with the Allied military authority. Therefore, what the Jedburghs did was give the CFLN's military commanders ninety-three more ways to reach their irregular forces scattered around France, assert some measure of control from Free French headquarters via their own regional military delegate or other representatives, in an effort to, as Clausewitz might say, control the people's passions.

A nation, whose will is embodied in its own sense of sovereign authority and the expression of its power, contends with other nations whether they are at war or not. As we have seen, those contentions are not only with enemies but also with allies. Free France's desire to reassert what it believed was the proper authority made it an aim, first and foremost, to allow no seams in its sovereignty. Philippe Pétain had no choice, he believed, but to bargain with Nazi Germany for as much sovereignty as he could get, but in the end he found only political illegitimacy. His fear of a communist-led internal revolution so clouded his views on the matter that he saw a collaboration with fascist Germany as preferable to losing the France he sought. De Gaulle, on the other hand, declared an outlaw in 1940, risked everything to liberate France from foreign powers, including the United States and Britain. He was so driven to do so, in fact, that when he found British Special Operations Executive (SOE) agents in France in September 1944, he demanded that they leave immediately. "We don't need you here." He scolded one British SOE officer who had been working clandestinely in France for months; "it only remains for you to leave. I have already told one Aristide, who was indulging in politics, to get out. Another that I have dispatched is Hilaire in Toulouse. You too must go home. Return, return quickly,... Au revoir."[4]

De Gaulle would have no more seams in French sovereignty. The Germans were to be driven out with combat while the British, in September of 1944, would be chased out with his scorn. General Koenig's easing the Special Operations Executive out of the command and control of the French Forces of the Interior via Mockler-Ferryman's resignation at the end of July is a portent of all this. While on the one hand, it seems obscenely ungracious and petty to lash out like de Gaulle did at the three British agents, since they had risked their lives for months. Nevertheless, ever since de Gaulle discovered that SOE's F Section was operating in France conducting British policy there as Britain saw fit, and not as a part of an alliance, it seems only natural that he would want them to depart France, as they were uninvited foreign intelligence and sabotage agents. Interestingly, there is no record of his seeking the hasty departure of Jedburgh teams who had the imprimatur of General Koenig in addition to having French officers on each team. In this regard, Eisenhower succeeded in gaining French participation the moment Overlord began by seeking to place a French general in charge of France's partisan warfare. Clearly General Eisenhower learned from his North African invasion experiences and improved markedly on the political chaos that had occurred there.

Given the strong evidence that suggests partisan warfare in France was at its most effective when German units were under strength, spread out, and forced to move through an environment where the population's hatred of them brought out more guerrillas than the Allies could arm or control, it seems incongruent to see why this method would be so popular as the twentieth century progressed. Indeed, it is difficult to see how it could be replicated later under other conditions. But then there never was a thorough vetting of how well and under what conditions the Jedburghs or the French Résistance proved to be successful. If all Jedburgh teams had met the same fate as Team Jacob or Augustus, then perhaps the institutionalized memory within the British, French, and American intelligence services and Special Forces would have sought a useful and sober assessment of why they failed.

Instead, the Vercors, Elster's surrender, and the operations on the Brittany peninsula were touted as examples of what is possible, and many of the commanders at the time accepted it while never seeking to understand why it was a success. But as shown above, these events were not what Special Force Headquarters believed them to be. The Free French viewed Vercors as a disaster while the British and American Special Operations planners believed the Wehrmacht units used there meant they could not threaten the conventional forces' progress through France. However, now we know those German troops would not have threatened Generals Patton or Patch—ever. The fact that the units employed by the Wehrmacht to conduct their anti-partisan actions in the south of France were units that never would have been moved to threaten main Allied forces in the first place never seems to have been appreciated by the British, Americans, or Free French. Vercors did nothing to divert those forces from being employed against Patton and the rest of Eisenhower's forces because they were units that never would have moved against them. The German 157th Infantrie Division, the main combat force at the Vercors, did fight against the Allied invasion force commanded by Patch, but only because Patch came to where they were. Elster's surrender was a grand success, due to reliable re-supply, Jedburgh teams with good communications and the ability to pick their battles, close air support, reliable intelligence, all operating in an environment of French political unity. The operations in Brittany utilized the same characteristics, with even more Jedburgh teams and greater air support for supplies and air strikes. These striking events, as well as the day-to-day sabotage and mayhem done to cut German lines of communications from D-Day through to the end of the Libération reinforced the efficacy of partisan warfare in their minds, even when the anatomy of the operations was not truly appreciated.

So how did Eisenhower's Guerrilla's support the war and did they help the Allies get to Germany? Lieutenant Colonel Robert Powell's August 31 message requesting arms for the FFI on his southern flank make it clear that he believed they could play a serious role. But it is also clear that the Wehrmacht to his south were only interested in securing their own northern flank along the Loire River to give them an escape route through the

Bourges-Dijon-Besançon-Belfort Gap corridor. Colonel Hutchison's comment that the German destruction of the Loire River bridges "satisfied everyone" is absolutely correct. Neither side wished to attack the other at the Loire River crossings; they *merely sought to outrace each other to Germany.* Not even Hitler's starry-eyed confidence in the ability of his armies could believe the newly re-designated 16th Infantrie Division was up to the task of outflanking the US 3rd Army. Instead, salvaging his forces from southwestern France was more important and the German 16th Infantrie Division's mission was to shield its comrades from any Allied forces that might seek to come in their direction. But Patton, quite correctly, was far too interested in racing eastward and happy to leave the other chore to the Maquis. Therefore, the success of the FFI had more to do with Wehrmacht choices than it did with their own. Given what the Germans faced and what their goals were after Operation Dragoon began August 15, 1944, they succeeded in establishing a defensive line, and successfully managed the escape of a significant portion of their forces. Koenig, Redman, Mockler-Ferryman, Haskell, and their staffs would have served Eisenhower better had they argued to make central and southern France the first priority instead of the last. Had General Koenig's headquarters succeeded in pouring arms into those regions by the day Operation Dragoon began, perhaps the Wehrmacht's 19th Armee would have been cut off and destroyed. Instead, the Herculean but ill-fated effort to mount a coherent operation in eastern France in order to use the Maquis as a force blocking the battle-hardened, combat-capable, and well-led German units retreating from Normandy merely resulted in some successful advanced reconnaissance while costing Special Air Service, Jedburgh, Maquis, and civilian lives. The only Jedburgh teams completely decimated, Augustus and Jacob, are a testament to the futility of General Koenig's efforts in eastern France. Since the Germans moving though eastern France were operating with the benefit of interior lines, far from Allied aerial re-supply and air support, Allied efforts to use guerrilla warfare there was ill considered.

My intention is not to criticize Koenig, Redman, Mockler-Ferryman, and Haskell, but rather to soberly assess their actions and to see why some of their efforts worked and while others did not. Operations in Brittany did meet with success and were the best of the four operational phases described above. Taking their mission from Eisenhower to assist the advance of Allied forces in capturing the Brittany ports, Special Force HQ and the Headquarters of the French Forces of the Interior developed a coherent plan and put it into action, albeit with some self-inflicted organizational tribulations caused by the poor relationship between Roosevelt and de Gaulle. Despite the lack of a solid, long-term regional military delegate for the Brittany, the replacements did manage to make an impact, and Colonel Bourgouin's role in commanding the area until the French Aloes mission arrived provided sufficient leadership and control for the region. The coherent nature of the region's Maquis, largely communist Franc-Tireurs et Partisans Français (FTP) meant that the group experienced little infighting, and coupled with sufficient French leadership, Brittany's Free French operations enjoyed much unity of action. But the greatest impact was the ability of the aerial re-supply to continue without any substantial German interruption. Drop zones were certainly lost, but when the effort succeeded in arming over 18,000 men by August 1, it indicates that the region was the best and most reliably equipped of any in France. This was especially true considering that Brittany received no major daylight re-supply operations such as Operation Cadillac. Furthermore, all the Wehrmacht units in Brittany were under strength and not equipped for rapid maneuver, a necessity to chase down partisans and defend against air attack. Even the 2nd Fallschirmjäger Division, the fiercest and arguably best led of any division in the region, was harried and unable to stop the Maquis from conducting much of what it sought to do. However, Eisenhower's whole aim was to capture the port at Brest in a usable state. But by the time German General Herman-Bernhard Ramcke surrendered in mid-September, the port's facilities were so badly damaged that Eisenhower could never use them.

It is no coincidence that German General Elster's surrender occurred in the region run by arguably the most effective Free French military delegate. Eugene Dechelette did all the things the Jedburghs wished they could have done. He arrived in his region in early March, established a relationship with the various Maquis groups, learned the region's geography and enemy makeup, secured the BBC code words for the alert and action messages, and had managed several drop zones. By the time D-Day occurred, he had things well in hand and had formed a small but capable organization that could operate independently should communications with him be cut. After the Normandy landings occurred, changing the nature of what the Germans were doing and what the Maquis could do, he successfully executed his plans, worked with Jedburgh teams sent to him, requested more, and assigned them areas in which to operate. By the time the southern landings occurred and OB West ordered German forces to retreat, changing the conditions for Dechelette again, he was ready to take advantage of the opportunity for guerrilla warfare. Over the course of the summer he had successfully united the Maquis within his region comprised of communist FTP, the non-communist AS, and the professional French soldiers of the ORA. Their effective unification mitigated his region falling to Eisenhower's lowest priority area for arms after August 1.

Eisenhower may have mis-prioritized which regions to arm, but he and his staff also dangerously underestimated the numbers of Maquis who would be pleading for weapons. He also may have been cautious about over-arming some of them at one point, but he did make the correct judgment on one big thing. He knew that for the Maquis to have any meaningful impact on Allied progress through France, a French commander had to lead them while being part and parcel of SHAEF Headquarters. Roosevelt and Churchill had visions of controlling France or aspects of its Résistance and its government in exile. The SOE and OSS had designs on controlling the Maquis with hundreds of agents and Jedburgh teams. The former is too high a level and the latter is too complicated and diffuse. But Eisenhower largely solved the dilemma when he brought General Koenig into SHAEF and treated him as one of his field commanders on par with land force commanders Generals Montgomery, Bradley, air force commander Spaatz, and naval commander Admiral Ramsay. Had he been able to do so immediately on his arrival at SHAEF in January of 1944, the Free French would have had time to make their plans Vert, Tortue, Rouge and Bibendum roll in stages, as they were needed. Instead, fearful that not much would occur, Eisenhower decided to turn them all on full steam, only to have to scramble to turn them off four short days later when he was stunned at what was occurring in France.

One may argue that the fear of leaking key information was valid enough to keep Koenig and his planners from so closely coordinating their planning with SHAEF. French communications, codes, and the BCRA were infamous for their lack of security. However, even the leak of Jedburgh information made no difference. As described in Chapter 4. William Savy went to France on the Eclaireur mission in order to scout out Jedburgh safe houses and relate the nature of the missions to General Pierre Dejessieu, the interior commander of the Free French. Some of the regional delegates and British-controlled F Section agents were made aware of SFHQ's and the BCRA's intent regarding the first Jedburgh mission, and the information was severely compromised with the arrest of Dejessieu, Eileen Nearne, and Maurice Southgate. Certainly, as the German propaganda makes clear, the Gestapo knew a great deal about the Jedburgh plan. But their understanding of what the Jedburghs were doing made no difference. They could not stop Jedburgh operations everywhere and only had consistent success in eastern France due to reasons unrelated to any specific knowledge of what occurred at Milton Hall. Indeed it seems that if Haskell or Mockler-Ferryman themselves had fallen into Nazi hands, it would have had no effect as long as the date, location, and size of the invasion force for D-Day remained secret. Therefore, taking risks to share information with the Free French could have paid off, had Roosevelt and Churchill not been so upset with de Gaulle for asserting the sovereignty he was known to have by almost all the French in North Africa, nearly every resistance movement, General Donovan and his OSS analysts, General Eisenhower, British Foreign Minister Anthony Eden, and American Assistant Secretary of War John J. McCloy and Secretary of War Henry Stimson.

Did the FDR-de Gaulle argument prevent the pre-D-Day deployment of the Jedburghs or was deploying before D-Day never the intention? The record is mixed. The SOE and OSS histories and all their pre-D-Day planning documents seem consistent in stating that the Jedburghs were to be a reserve for after D-Day. However, Eisenhower's directives to the SOE and OSS make it appear that there was some consideration of sending them in before D-Day. SHAEF directed that they be ready by April 1, even when D-Day was originally scheduled for May. Later, as D-Day neared, General

Smith was directed not to deploy them until D-Day minus ten, and then later directed that they not be sent in until D-Day minus one at the earliest. If no one intended to deploy them until after D-Day, why would SHAEF have to tell them not to do so? Adding to the confusion, there were Jeds who were told they would be in France before D-Day. That belief seems most evident with the French, and the BCRA recruiters may have sincerely believed it at the time; but since the Free French were locked out of planning until the end of May, they were making promises they could not keep. Therefore, the Jedburgh belief that they were to be in France before D-Day may simply have been the result of exuberant recruiters saying something they believed would attract the kind of men they wanted. Soldiers being soldiers, that promise to a few became rumor, which then became their reality.

The availability and the relatively late decision to use Special Air Service missions in France also caught the Jedburgh planners by surprise. The decision to insert Jedburgh teams along with the SAS, even though the missions of the two groups were markedly different, was also costly. Not only were there procedural issues that caused confusion, but the SAS mission was to strike at enemy targets while the Jedburghs had to rein in the local Maquis' desire for immediate action, and this was harmful to the Jedburgh mission. The Jedburghs had been instructed to deploy, assess the capabilities of local groups, get arms to them, train them, and then at the appropriate time take manageable numbers into hit-and-run actions against carefully selected enemy targets. The SAS wished to do its operations immediately and was supplied out of airlift sortie allocations separate from the ones for the Jedburgh teams. Therefore, when Eisenhower ordered the Maquis to cease guerrilla warfare and restricted air drops, the SAS continued to get their weapons, making the Jedburghs, working in concert with the nearby Maquis, look impotent and illegitimate. While the Maquis in some regions were then forced to wait due to lack of weapons or a too persuasive Jedburgh officer telling them to, the SAS continued on their merry way making mayhem. The swelling of Camp Dingson with hundreds of Maquis and their subsequent dispersal due to German attacks on June 18 was something Team George did not recover from until the beginning of August.

Team Frederick only avoided a tragic fate due to the help of some local Maquis and their decision to disperse before the 2nd Fallschirmjäger arrived in strength to hunt them. Moreover, one can look at the map of France noting where the SAS were and then noting where the German reprisals were, and it is no coincidence that where there was an SAS mission, reprisals on French civilians often occurred as an indirect result. If Jeds had been sent in on their own, they could have called in SAS teams to do missions beyond the ability of the local Maquis while being cognizant of local concerns. Team Hugh's decision to disobey its orders and split from the Bulbasket mission proved wise in light of the fact that the Germans mauled Bulbasket.

Of the 265 Jedburghs deployed to France, 13 were killed in combat, 2 died when their parachutes failed to open, 1 was killed by accident from a maquisard's unintended discharge of his weapon, and 2 subsequently died of combat wounds. Another 13 were wounded in combat but recovered, while 6 were severely injured in their parachute jumps; 2 of 3 Jedburghs survived being taken prisoner. Despite this, the casualty rate was far lower than many expected. When Bernard Knox of Team Giles checked out his equipment prior to leaving for France in July, he was shocked when told he need not sign for his gear. Assuming he would be killed in France, the supply officer did not expect to get it back.[5] But as it turned out, 9 out of every 10 Jeds returned.

How was this mixed and complicated record thought of for the insurgencies and guerrilla wars after World War II? Many of those who survived France became an influential force in the Cold War world. But there was no immediate attempt for a serious evaluation of the Jedburgh operations in France as Germany and Japan still remained undefeated. After the Jedburgh missions were ended in France and Holland, many of the Jeds volunteered for other operations as the war had another year to go before it was over. American Lieutenant Colonel Hod Fuller and French Lieutenant Paul Aussaresses deployed on Special Allied Airborne Reconnaissance Force (SAARF) teams attempting to ensure that the Germans did not mistreat POWs in captivity during the waning days of the war. William Colby of Team Bruce commanded an Operational Group to Norway, Bernard Knox went on an OSS mission to Italy, and Tommy MacPherson also served in an SOE mission there. Several served in China or Indo-China, twelve of whom were killed. Michel de Bourbon-Parme, the French Jed on Team Quinine, was taken prisoner by communist insurgents in Indo-China and held for nearly a year. His third escape attempt finally succeeded.[6] Team George's American Captain Paul Cyr took in a Chinese Commando unit on Mission Hound and blew up the Yellow River Bridge while a Japanese troop train passed over it on the same day Nagasaki was destroyed on August 9, 1945.[7] But the coalition nature of these missions evaporated as all but the SAARF missions went back to being unilateral. Allied unconventional warfare faded away until recently when the International Security Assistance Force brought them back to conduct various missions in Afghanistan, and the North Atlantic Treaty Organization established a Special Operations Head-quarters at Mons, Belgium, in 2010.[8]

After operations wound down in France, the British ran Jedburgh teams into Austria with some anti-Nazi Germans and Austrians, but despite their perceived success in Western Europe, small Allied teams were not employed again during the Second World War. The coalition politics that brought them into being had changed significantly by late 1944, and the senior SOE, OSS, and BCRA (which by 1945 became the Direction générale des serv-ices spéciales or DGSS) leaders seemed eager for fewer complications. In October, President Roosevelt finally recognized the Gaullist Résistance as the provisional government of France. But political recognition did not increase Franco-American understanding when fighting the Japanese in southeast Asia in 1945. Here American policy remained similar to what it had been in France. Specifically, this meant working with whoever could defeat the Japanese. Consequently, the OSS supported Ho Chi Minh's insurgents in order to win, while the French fought both the Japanese and Ho Chi Minh in an attempt to re-establish control of their colony.[9] The former French and American Jedburghs then worked at cross purposes, and Americans Aaron Bank and Lucien Conein fell out of favor with their French colleagues who were determined to wrest control of their colony back from the American-supported Ho Chi Minh. American OSS officers and the Viet Minh insurgents who would became bitter adversaries in the

1960s and 1970s literally stood together with Ho Chi Minh when he declared independence from Japan *and* France, on August 13, 1945.[10] Such declarations seemed fine with the United States, but France had other political aims with their colonies and worked hard, if unsuccessfully, to maintain its authority over Vietnam and later Algeria. Its efforts in those two conflicts kept former French Jedburghs employed at those tasks and using the lessons they had learned in conducting their own guerrilla warfare. Paul Aussaresses of Team Chrysler served as the chief of intelligence officer in Algeria and in that capacity tortured and murdered to get the information he needed.[11]

France's failed efforts in southeast Asia were followed by American attempts as well. In a telling way, those efforts were often run by former Jedburghs and explained to the public by those who had learned this craft only at the tactical end as Jedburghs. William Colby and Lucien Conein ran Central Intelligence Agency efforts in Vietnam and got results similar to those of the French, but for different reasons. Team James member, John Singlaub, now commander of Military Assistance Command, Vietnam Studies and Observations Group (MACVSOG), picked up the baton from the Central Intelligence Agency and ran a counterinsurgency against the communist North Vietnamese in the 1960s.[12] President Kennedy, who was enthusiastic about unconventional warfare, sought not only to defend against what communist movements were doing abroad but to conduct an insurgency of his own against Ho Chi Minh's communist North Vietnam. In a 1962 interview granted to journalist and former Jedburgh, Stewart Alsop, President Kennedy stated that the way the world was at that time made it necessary for the United States to have choices in how it could respond to aggression abroad. Finding himself in a situation similar to Churchill's dire straits in 1940 when he grasped for options to go on the offensive and created the Special Operations Executive, Kennedy sought more options than only nuclear weapons and told Alsop that he needed to develop choices. Reacting to how the communists were conducting their approach to the problem, Kennedy was heavily influenced by Chinese leader Mao Tse-Tung. "Guerrillas are like fish, and the people are the water in which the fish swim," Kennedy said quoting Mao. Kennedy went on to tell this former Jedburgh that "the best way—perhaps in the long run the only way—to deal with the internal Communist-guerrilla threat, is to 'control the temperature of the water,'" emphasizing in the interview that this meant a political effort.[13] Such was the case in World War II France too, but as Kennedy's predecessor, the former supreme allied commander, President Eisenhower, could have pointed out to his successor President Kennedy, the French did their own controlling of France's water temperature, while the equivalent national political will for North Vietnam was not there.[14]

Ultimately, American efforts against North Vietnam failed for the same reasons the French efforts did in Indo-China. As Richard Shultz points out, there was little popular support for an insurgency against the Ho Chi Minh regime, but President Kennedy, buttressed by his faith in unconventional warfare, sought to use it against the communists everywhere. He failed to think through the conditions required to make it work—specifically, the internal political will, unity, and effective leadership that General de Gaulle provided for France in 1944. The Kennedy-sponsored insurgency against North Vietnam started under former Jedburgh William Colby as a Central Intelligence Agency (CIA) effort. Kennedy believed the CIA did not have the resources to do pursue this with the vigor he wished so he gave the mission to the Defense Department. The army and the theater commanders then created MACVSOG and the army's relatively young Special Forces ran it. Another former Jedburgh, Colonel John Singlaub, when asked what he thought of his efforts to oversee the insurgency against Ho Chi Minh, admitted that by the time he took command of MACVSOG in 1966 the insurgency against North Vietnam was doomed. Indeed, he thought it was doomed long before his arrival due to the agreements made in 1954 that drew the dividing line between North and South Vietnam and allowed for those who wished to leave the communist North to do so. All the Vietnamese who did not wish to live in the North went elsewhere, deflating nearly all native political opposition to Ho Chi Minh's version of nationalism. All Colonel Singlaub could do was assume that the enemy had turned the saboteurs and agents he inserted into North Vietnam and then "triple turn" them. In other words, four years later, Kennedy's dreams of an insurgency were reduced to attempting to trick North Vietnam into thinking that the

United States did not know that North Vietnam knew of its operations and to feed disinformation back to "his" agents behind enemy lines.[15] Kennedy could not control the temperature of the water in which he sent fish to swim, and so Singlaub tried that tack instead of completely quitting and cutting bait.

For Eisenhower, who grasped the issues better than most, he knew he did not control the temperature of the water; de Gaulle did, and therefore controlling the French Résistance was a matter of bringing the French into SHAEF and then letting them run it while supporting their efforts with air sorties, arms, money, and training. The BCRA, with the Bloc Planning effort, organized the sabotage plans in France and worked with the SOE and OSS to arm, train, and equip their agents before D-Day, and that effort is what succeeded in supporting the initial invasion in Normandy. French men and women comprised the vast majority of "agents" sent into France by the SOE as well as the BCRA. But more important, the French Résistance was not a creation of the British SOE or the American OSS. It sprang from France itself, reflecting French traditions of political action and French notions of the state; it sought French political aims that expressed French will. Eisenhower may not have understood all of this clearly in 1944, as he never expressed it in those terms; but he recognized that General de Gaulle was France's single leader. And Eisenhower stubbornly insisted on working with General Koenig to make him a subordinate commander when Roosevelt, Churchill, Gubbins, Mockler-Ferryman, and Donovan protested, and his insistence demonstrates that he understood the fundamentals of the situation more clearly than anyone.

The Résistance's greatest achievement was the political overthrow of Vichy and the politically unified effort it pulled together to resist Germany and then govern postwar France.[16] It succeeded in offering an alternative to the French people increasingly alienated from Pétain's feckless government and the German occupation. There lies the difference between a failed insurgency and a successful revolution. De Gaulle offered an alternative that appealed to enough of the French population, weary of war and occupation, for him to successfully avoid a great deal of the chaos he feared as much as Pétain had. While terming what de Gaulle achieved as a revolution may be dubious since its immediate result was the postwar Fourth Republic that was very similar to the prewar Third Republic, his actions generally succeeded in avoiding the worst aspects of chaos an insurgency often brings when it works at dissolving the fabric of institutions, authority, and society to bring down a government. De Gaulle successfully avoided these problems when he brought the bands of FFI into the regular French Army and convinced those who maintained weapons supplied by the Allies to keep them discreetly in their homes or surrender them to the government.

Therefore, where the Jedburghs succeeded, they did so because the Résistance and de Gaulle's provisional government put in place the element necessary for success—national political will. General Eisenhower then placed that national political will, in the form of General Koenig and the Free French, within his coalition. The military conditions produced by the combat between the Germans and Allies and the ability to secure drop zones, reliable communications, and the reliability of re-supply sorties all were crucial. But they were not the hardest things to achieve. General Eisenhower could not have arranged for French political will to be parachuted into France. But he did not have to, as it was already there. Nothing the British SOE or the American OSS could do would achieve what the Résistance succeeded in achieving. In this light, Roosevelt's and Churchill's persistent undercutting of de Gaulle in an effort to control France seems increasingly harmful to Allied objectives. But then it is apparent that they, perhaps understandably, were not as concerned with France as the French were. General Koenig's intermittent ability to control the Maquis then is a testament to him, his planners, staff, and Jedburghs, and the myriad movements all determining for themselves to submit to his authority. Therefore, the Allied ability to control the French Résistance did not come about because of Jedburgh teams, as the Special Operations Executive originally wished, but because Eisenhower made Koenig subordinate to his Allied Command. That act was not something the Special Operations Executive Colonel Peter Wilkinson foresaw when he first developed the Jedburgh plan in 1942, but it was the single greatest accomplishment of Eisenhower's guerrilla war.

APPENDIX 1

French Resistance Leaders

Name	Codename(s)	Position(s)	Operational Dates	Notes
National Military Leadership				
Pierre Dejussieu	Pontcorral	National Military Delegate	Late 1943 - 1 May 1944	Germans arrested him on 1 May 1944; survived the war in Buchenwald Prison Camp
Jacques Delmas	Chaban, Arc	National Military Delegate	Aug 15 1944	Involved in the Liberation of Paris, but too late to France for a roll elsewhere
Resistance Region A				
Jean Pierre Noel Cabouat	Cardioide, Courbe	Assistant DMR	Mar 1944 to Liberation	
Pierre Marie Deshayes	Gramme, Mussel, Rod	Air Operations	Dec 1942 to Liberation	
Guy Chaumet	Cissoide, Mariotte	DMR	Apr 44 to Liberation	Served in Region B prior to Region A
Resistance Region B				
Christophe Gaillard	Triangle	DMR	Jul 44 - Nov 44	Served in Region R1 and R2 from Sept 43 to July 44
Claude Gros	Adiabatique	Air Operations	Jun 44 to Liberation	
Resistance Region C				
Gilbert Hirsh-Ollendorf	Grandval, Planete	DMR	Mar 44 to Liberation	Rose through the ranks in the interior resistance

Name	Codename(s)	Position(s)	Operational Dates	Notes
Michel Andre Pichard	Gauss, Bel, Pic, Oyster, Generatrice	Air Operations	Summer 43 to Mar 44, Mar 44 to early June, 12 August to Liberation	Prior service was head of Northern Zone
Resistance Region D				
J. G. M. D. d'Auerstaett	Ovale	DMR	5 May 44 to Liberation	
Pierre Hanneton	Ligne	Asst DMR	May 44 to Liberation	
Resistance Region M				
Maurice Louis Barthelemy	Hauteur	Asst DMR then DMR	3 May 44 - 11 August	
Jean Francois Clouet des Pesruches	Galile, Orbite	DMR	Aug 43 - May 44, 13 Aug - Sept	May 44 to Aug 44 in the UK sharing what he'd learned of Brittany's situation
Jean-Baptiste Allard	Indou	Radio operator	Sep 43 to Liberation	
Resistance Region P				
Pierre Sonneville	Equilateral	DMR	Apr 44 to Liberation	
Georges Palaud	Artilleur	2nd in Command	9 Dec 43 to March 44	Arrested and tortured in March 1944 but survived the war
Jacques M. G. L. Guerin	Ampere	Air Operations	Aug 43 to Oct 43	Arrested Oct 1943 and survived the war in prison
Colonel Fernand G. Viat	Diagramme	Commander Verviene/ Isaac Mission	Aug 44 to Liberation	Commander of Jed Team Isaac and Verviene Mission but arrived later
Resistance Region R1				
Christophe Gaillard	Triangle	DMR	Jul 44 - Nov 44	Served in Region B and R2 from Sept 43 to July 44

Name	Codename(s)	Position(s)	Operational Dates	Notes
Lucien Cambas	Trapeze	DMR	Feb to June 1944	Sept 43 Assistant to Chief of Southern Zone
Maurice Jean Marie Bourges-Maunoury	Polygone	DMR then DM for Southern Zone	Sep 43 to Jan 44	May to 7 Jun 1944 in the UK, Returned to southern France on 7 June 1944
Resistance Region R2				
Paul Pierre Michel Leistenschneider	Carre, Dragon	DMR	Oct 43 to Liberation	Moved to R1 when R2 was liberated
Louis Burdet	Circonference	military organizer	Jan 44 - arrested June 44	
Eugene Bornier	Sol, Cure, Sunfish	air operations	Jan 44 to Liberation	Was in R2 from April to Liberation
Resistance Region R3				
Lucien Cambas	Trapeze	DMR	June 1944 to Liberation	Previously was in R1
Resistance Region R4				
Henri Guillermin	Pacha, Alain	DMR	Mar 44 to Liberation	Started out in the resistance group Combat
Bernard Schlumberger	Droite	DMR	Mar 44 to Liberation	British records indicate he worked in R3 as well
Resistance Region R5				
Eugene Deschelette	Ellipse	DMR	Jan 44 to Liberation	
Georges Heritier	Croc	Assistant DMR	Jan 44 to Apr 44, Jun 44 to Liberation	Arrested in April 1944 but escaped in June
Gerard Hennebert	Baron	Air Operations, DMR?	Jan to Mar 44, Apr 44 to Liberation	British records indicate he became DMR in September

Name	Codename(s)	Position(s)	Operational Dates	Notes
		Resistance Region R6		
Pierre Paul Ulmer	Depute	DMR	Jun 44 to Liberation	Was in R1 prior running drop zones and air operations
Guy Frederic Lorenz Vivier	Isotherme	Southern Zone	9 Jun 44 to Liberation	served as assistant to Bourges-Maunoury
Jean Paul Vaucheret	Pectorale	Mission Leader, Chief of Staff Lyon FFI	13 Jun 44 to Liberation	R1 and R6

APPENDIX 2

Jedburgh Teams

Resistance Region	TEAM NAME	LAST NAME	First	Rank	Nationality	Code Name	Area of Operations	Deployment Date
R1	**ALAN**						Saone et Loire	8/12/44
		Toussaint	Robert	Lt	French	ARIEGE		
		Cannicott	Stanley M.	Capt	British	PEMBROKE		
		Clause	Robert	S/Lt	French	KRONER		
C3	**ALASTAIR**						Epinal	8/27/44
		Brown	Oliver H.	Maj	British	KENT		
		Karriere	Rene	Lt	French	DONEGALL		
		Smith	G. N.	Sgt	British	LINCOLN		
P2	**ALEC**						Loire et Cher	8/9/44
		Thomson	George C.	1Lt	American	CROMARTY		
		Bordes	A.	Lt	French	OXFORD		
		White	John A.	SSgt	American	COLORADO		
R5	**ALEXANDER**						Creuse	8/12/44
		de la Tousche	Rene	LT	French	LEIX		
		Alsop	Stewart J. O.	1Lt	American	RONA		
		Franklin	Norman R.	1Sgt	American	CORK		

Resistance Region	TEAM NAME	LAST NAME	First	Rank	Nationality	Code Name	Area of Operations	Deployment Date
D2	ALFRED						Besancon-Doubs	8/24/44
		MacDougall	L. D.	Capt	British	ARGYLL		
		Herenguel	Jean-Pierre	Lt	French	AUDE		
		Key	A. W.	Sgt	British	WAMPUM		
R5	AMMONIA						Sarlat-Dordogne	6/10/44
		Austin	Benton	Capt	American	GASPARD		
			McDonald					
		LeCompte	Raymond	Capt	French	LUDOVIC		
		Berlin	Jacob B.	Sgt	American	MARCIAL	Haute Vienne	7/11/44
R5	ANDY							
		Parkinson	R. A.	Major	British	FIFE		
		Vermeulen	G.	Major	French	CARLOW		
		Loosmore	R.	Sgt	British	LUNDY		
D1	ANTHONY						Saone et Loire	8/14/44
		Starring	Mason	1Lt	American	NEBRASKA		
		Stasse	Maurice	Capt	French	PERTH		
		Bradner	John L.	TSgt	American	PFENNIG		
C3	ARCHIBALD						Moselle	8/25/44
		du P Denning	Arthur	Maj	British	CUMBERLAND		
		Costes	Francois	Lt	French	MONTGOMERY		
		Pierre	Roger L.	MSgt	American	SEN		
C1	ARNOLD						Marne	8/24/44
		de Carville	M.	Capt	French	SUSSEX		
		Monahan	J. F. H.	Lt	British	LONDONDERRY		
		de Ville	A.	Sgt	British	ESCUDO		

Resistance Region	TEAM NAME	LAST NAME	First	Rank	Nationality	Code Name	Area of Operations	Deployment Date
D1	**ARTHUR**						Cotes D'Or	8/18/44
		Mynatt	Cecil F., Jr	Capt	American	CONNECTICUT		
		Humblet	Xavier	S/Lt	French	SMABRERE		
		Bacik	Albert V.	TSgt	American	MILLIEME		
P3	**AUBREY**						Seine et Marne	8/11/44
		Marchant	Godfrey	Capt	British	RUTLAND		
		Chaigneau	A.	Lt	French	KILDARE		
		Hooker	Ivar	Sgt	British	THALER		
C1	**AUGUSTUS**						Aisne	8/15/1944
		Bonsall	John H.	Major	American	ARIZONA		
		Delwiche	J.	Capt	French	HERAULT		
		Cote	Roger E.	TSgt	American	INDIANA		
D1 or D2	**BASIL**						Jura/Doubs	8/25/44
		Riviere	R.	Capt	French	AMBLEVE		
		Carew	T. A.	Capt	British	SUTHERLAND		
		Stoyka	John L.	TSgt	American	ORE		
C1	**BENJAMIN**						Autun	8/20/44
		O'Brien-Tear	Jim	Major	British	STIRLING		
		Moniez	Paul	Lt	French	ULSTER		
		Kaminski	H.	S/Lt	French	SERRE		
C1	**BERNARD**						Autun	8/20/1944
		de W. Waller	J.	Capt	British	TIPPERARY		
		Nasica	Etienne	Capt	French	ARGENS		
		Bassett	C. M.	Sgt	British	LANCASHIRE		

Resistance Region	TEAM NAME	LAST NAME	First	Rank	Nationality	Code Name	Area of Operations	Deployment Date
D2	BRIAN	Johnstone	F.P.C.	Major	British	ILLINOIS	Nancy	8/28/44
		Cretin	Roger	Capt	French	ORKNEY		
		Smith	N. A.	Sgt	British	LIRA		
P3	BRUCE	Colby	William E.	Major	American	BERKSHIRE	Yonne	8/14/44
		LeLong	Camille M.	Lt	French	GALWAY		
		Villebois	R	S/Lt	French	PIASTRE		
D1	BUNNY	Radice	J.F.D.	Capt	British	PESO	Haute-Marne	8/19/1944
		Geminel	Maurice	Lt	French	YEN		
		Chambers	J.	Sgt	British	DRACHMA		
R4	BUGATTI	Fuller	Horace W.	Major	American	KANSUL	Haute-Pyrenees	6/21/1944
		de la Roche	Guy	Capt	French	HOPEI		
		Sicaud	Martial	S/Lt	French	CHEKIANG		
P3	CECIL	Nielson					Aube	8/27/1944
		Nielson	D.J.	Major	British	DELAWARE		
		Keser	Alfred	Capt	French	LYS		
		Wilde	R.	Sgt	British	CENTAVO		
D2	CEDRIC	Bazata	Douglas d W.	Capt	American	VESDRE	Haute-Saone	8/28/1944
		Lesne	Louis	Capt	French	DENDRE		
		Floyd	Richard C.	TSgt	American	GULDER		

Resistance Region	TEAM NAME	LAST NAME	First	Rank	Nationality	Code Name	Area of Operations	Deployment Date
R1	CHLOROFORM	Martin	Jacques	Capt	French	JOSHUA	Drome	6/30/1944
		McIntosh	Henry D.	1Lt	American	LIONEL		
		Sassi	Jean	CCH	French	LATIMER		
R3	CHRYSLER	Sell	Cyril H.	Capt	British	ELIE	Ariege	8/17/1944
		Aussaresses	Paul	Capt	French	BAZIN		
		Chatten	Ronald E.	Sgt	British	ARTUS		
R2	CINNAMON	Harcourt	R.	Capt	British	LOUIS	Var	8/14/1944
		Lespinasse-Fonsegrive		Capt	French	ORTHON		
		Morineau	Jacques	Lt	French	LUC		
R2	CITROEN	Smallwood	J. E. Saint C.	Capt	British	ANNE	Vaucluse	8/14/1944
		Bloch	Pierre	Capt	French	LAURENT		
		Bailey	F. A.	Sgt	British	RETIF		
R3	COLLODION/ LOCH	Hall	H.	Capt	British	AUGUSTINE	Aveyron	8/7/1944
		Marsaudon	Henri	Lt	French	BENOIT		
		Baumgold	Theodore	Sgt	American	JULES		
M3	DANIEL	Bennett	K. D.	Capt	British	APOTRE	Cotes du Nord	8/6/1944
		de Schonen	Albert P.	Lt	French	ARGENTIER		
		Brierley	Ron	Sgt	British	FLORIN		

Resistance Region	TEAM NAME	LAST NAME	First	Rank	Nationality	Code Name	Area of Operations	Deployment Date
D1	DESMOND	Pietsch, Jr.	William H.	Capt	American	SKERRY	Cote-d'Or	9/5/1944
		Maunoury	Gilles	Capt	French	SHETLAND		
		Baird	Robert R.	MSgt	American	HAMPSHIRE		
R1	DODGE	Manierre, Jr.	Cyrus E.	Major	American	RUPERT	Drome	6/25/1944
		du Rocher	L. T.	Sgt	Canadian	OSWALD		
M3	DOUGLAS	Rubinstein	Richard	Capt	British	AUGURE	Morbihan, Brittany	8/5/44
		Roblot	Jean	Lt	French	ANACHORERE		
		Raven	J.D.	Sgt	British	HALF CROWN		
R1 or D1	DOUGLAS II	Rubinstein	Richard A.	Capt	British	AUGURE	Aisne/Doubs/Jura	9/15/44
		Roblot	Jean	Capt	French	ANACHORERE		
		Van Hart	John T.	TSgt	American	HALF CROWN		
R1	EPHEDRINE	Swank	Lawrence E.	1Lt	American	GANTOR	Savoie	8/13/1944
		Donnart	Louis	LT	French	JULIEN		
		Desplechin	R.	Lt	French	LEON		
M3	FELIX	Souquat	C. M.	Maj	French	CARNAVON	Cotes du Nord	8/7/1944
		Marchant	J.J.	Capt	British	SOMERSET		
		Calvin	P. M.	Sgt	British	MIDDLESEX		

Resistance Region	TEAM NAME	LAST NAME	First	Rank	Nationality	Code Name	Area of Operations	Deployment Date
M3	FRANCIS	Ogden-Smith	C. M.	Major	British	DORSET	Finistere	7/9/1944
		Leborgne	Guy	Lt	French	DURANCE		
		Dallow	A. J.	Sgt	British	GROAT		
D2	FRANK	Isaac	I.	Capt	British	WESTMORELAND	Jura/Doubs	9/27/1944
		Martelli	A.	Lt	French	DUMBARTON		
		Henney	T.	Sgt	British	CHESHIRE		
M3	FREDERICK	Wise	A. W.	Major	British	KINROS	Guincamp in Brittany	6/9/1944
		Bloch-Auroch	Paul	S/Lt	French	VIRE		
		Kehoe	Robert R.	MSgt	American	PESETA		
M3	GAVIN	Carbuccia	Joseph Jean	Major	French	SHILLING	Northern part of Ille et Vilaine	7/12/1944
		Dreux	William B.	Capt	American	SIXPENCE		
		Valentini	Paul	S/Lt	French	HALFPENNEY		
M3, M2, B2	GEORGE	Ragueneau	Philippe	Capt	French	SAVE	Redan area in Brittany	6/9/1944
		Cyr	Paul	Capt	American	WIGTON		
		Gay	Pierre	Sgt	French	RUPEE		
B1	GEORGE II	Ragueneau	Philippe	Capt	French	SAVE	Bordeaux	9/4/1944

Resistance Region	TEAM NAME	LAST NAME	First	Rank	Nationality	Code Name	Area of Operations	Deployment Date
M3	GERALD	Cyr	Paul	Capt	American	WIGTON	Morbihan, Brittany	7/18/44
		Gay	Pierre	Sgt	French	RUPPE		
M3	GILBERT	Knerly	Stephen	Capt	American	NORFOLK	Finistere	7/10/1944
		l'Herbette	Claude	Lt	French	SUFFOLK		
		Friele, Jr	Berent E.	1Sgt	American	SELKIRK		
M3	GILES	Blathwayt	C. G.	Capt	British	Surrey		
		Charron de la Carriere	P.	Lt	French	Ardeche		
		Wood	N.	Sgt	British	Doubloon	Finistere area	7/7/1944
		Knox	Bernard M. W.	Capt	American	KENTUCKY		
		Grall	Paul	Capt	French	LOIRE		
		Tack	Gordon H.	Sgt	British	TICKIE		
D2	GODFREY	Forbes	Ian	1LT	American	RHODE ISLAND	Saone et Loire	9/12/1944
		Laval	Pierre	Lt	French	ROSCOMMON		
		Hanson	Frank A.	Sgt	American	ROXBURGH		
R2	GRAHM	Crosby	M. G. M.	Major	British	HUGE	Basses Alpes	8/9/1944
		Gavet	Pierre	Capt	French	CRISPIN		
		Adams	William	1Sgt	American	DESIRE		

Resistance Region	TEAM NAME	LAST NAME	First	Rank	Nationality	Code Name	Area of Operations	Deployment Date
D2	GREGORY	Bennett	K. D.	Capt	British	APOTRE	Jura/Doubs	9/5/1944
		de Schonen	Albert	Capt	French	ARGENTIER		
		Brierley	Ron	Sgt	British	FLORIN		
M3	GUY						Southern part of Ille et Vilaine	7/12/1944
		Duron	Andre	Capt	French	DRONNE		
		Trofimov	A. A.	Capt	British	GIRONDE		
		Groult	Roger	S/Lt	French	DORDOGNE		
R5	HAMISH	Anstett	Robert M.	1Lt	American	ALABAMA	Chatellerault area of Indre	6/12/44–9/12/44
		Schmitt	Rene	Lt	French	LOUISIANA		
		Watters	Lee J.	Sgt	American	KANSAS		
M2	HAROLD	Whitty	V. E.	Major	British	ROSS	Vendee	7/15/44
		Jolleit	Pierre	Lt	French	TYRONE		
		Verlander	Harry	Sgt	British	SLIGO		
P3	HARRY	Guthrie	D. D.	Capt	British	DENBY	NW of Auton/ Morvan Mts	6/6/44–9/21/44
		Rousset	Pierre	Lt	French	GAPEAU		
		Couture	Rene	2CL	French	CINTIME		
D2	HENRY	Moore	Raymond E.	1Lt	American	NEW MEXICO	Jura/Doubs	9/10/1944

Resistance Region	TEAM NAME	LAST NAME	First	Rank	Nationality	Code Name	Area of Operations	Deployment Date
M3	HILARY	Jean-Moncler	Stephane	Capt	French	ANGLESEY		
		Rocca	Vincent M.	TSgt	American	WEST VIRGINIA	Finistere	7/17/44
M3	HORACE	Mautaint	Edgar	Lt	French	CHARENTE		
		Chadbourne, Jr.	Philip H.	1Lt	American	NEVADA		
		Hervouet	Roger	S/Lt	French	KOPEK	Finistere	7/17/44
R5	HUGH	Summers	John W.	Major	American	WYOMING		
		Leclercq	Georges	Lt	French	SOMME		
		Zielski, Jr.	William F.	T/3	American	DIME	Chateauroux in Indre	6/5/44– 9/22/44
		L'Helgouach	Louis	Capt	French	FRANC		
		Crawshay	William R. (Sir)	Capt	British	CROWN		
R5	IAN	Meyer	Rene	CC	French	YONNE	South of Poitiers, Vienne	6/20/44– 9/17/44
		Gildee, Jr.	John J.	Major	American	OKLAHOMA		
		Desfarges	Alex	Lt	French	MAINE		
		Bourgoin	Lucien J.	Sgt	American	MAYO		
D1	ISAAC	Hutchision	J. R. H.	Lt Col	British			
		Viat	F. G.	Lt Col	French		Cotes D'Or	7/6/1944
		Sharpe	J.	Sgt	British			

Resistance Region	TEAM NAME	LAST NAME	First	Rank	Nationality	Code Name	Area of Operations	Deployment Date
P2 and R6	IVOR						St Amand, Cher	8/6/44
		Cox	J. H.	Capt	British	MONMOUTH		
		Colin	Robert	Lt	French	SELUNE		
		Goddard	Lewis F.	1Sgt	American	OREGON		
C3	JACOB						Vosges	8/12/44
		Gough	Victor A.	Capt	British	ARRAN		
		Boissarie	Maurice	Lt	French	CONNAUGHT		
		Seymour	Ken	Sgt	British	SKYE		
R5	JAMES						Correze	8/11/1944
		Singlaub	John K.	1LT	American	MISSISSIPPI		
		le Bel de Penguilly	Jacques	Lt	French	MICHIGAN		
		Denneau	Anthony J.	TSgt	American	MASSACHUSETTS		
R6	JEREMY						Haute Loire	8/25/1944
		Hallowes	George M.	Capt	British	AIMABLE		
		Giese	Henri	Capt	French	FONTCROISE		
		Leney	R. A.	Sgt	British	FERNE		
D2	JIM						Jura	9/11/1944
		Donovan	Philip W.	Capt	American	PENNSYLVANIA		
		de Francesco	Jose A.	Lt	French	LEITRIM		
		Henely	Michael F.	TSgt	American	WEXFORD		
R4	JOHN						Tarn et Garonne	8/16/1944
		Stern	D. L.	Capt	British	BEAU		
		de Galbert	Maurice	ASP	French	LUCIDE		
		Gibbs	D.	Sgt	British	SILENCIEUX		

Resistance Region	TEAM NAME	LAST NAME	First	Rank	Nationality	Code Name	Area of Operations	Deployment Date
R1	JUDE	Evans	W. L. O.	Capt	British	GLAMORGAN	Loire	8/15/1944
		Larrieu	Jean	Capt	French	RENCE		
		Holdham	A. E.	Sgt	British	GUINEA		
R5	JULIAN	Clutton	A. H.	Major	South African	STAFFORD	Indre et Loire	8/11/1944
		Vermot	Marcel	Lt	French	VERMONT		
		Menzies	T. S.	CQMS	British	ESSEX		
R5	JULIAN II	Souquat	C. M.	Capt	French	CARNAVON	Northern Indre and Cher Valley	8/12/1944
		Scherrer		S/Lt	French			
		Meyer	Rene	S/Lt	French	YONNE		
R5	LEE	Brown III	Charles E.	Capt	American	PICE	Haute Vienne	8/10/1944
		Angoulvent	Paul	Lt	French	SOUS		
		Pirat	Maurice	S/Lt	French	REIS		
R4	MARK	Thevenet	Joannes	Lt	French	SYMPATHIQUE	Tarn et Garonne	8/16/1944
		Conein	Lucien E.	1Lt	American	INTREPIDE		
		Carpenter	James J.	Sgt	American	LESTER		
R4	MARTIN	Mellows	T. A.	Capt	British	BLASE	Haute Garonne	8/16/1944

Resistance Region	TEAM NAME	LAST NAME	First	Rank	Nationality	Code Name	Area of Operations	Deployment Date
R1	MASQUE	Redonnet	Georges	Lt	French	SUBTANTIF	Isere	8/27/1944
		Carey	N. E. S.	Sgt	British	PLACIDE		
		Guillot	Nelson E.	Capt	American	HARMONIEUX		
		Bouvery	Jacques	Lt	French	SUCCULENT		
		Poche, Jr	Francis M.	Sgt	American	IDEAL		
D1	MAURICE	Carman, Jr.	Charles M.	Capt	American	UTAH	Autun	8/4/1944
		Dumesnil	Hubert	Lt	French	VIRGINIA		
		Cole	Francis J.	TSgt	American	GEORGIA		
R4	MILES	Allen	Everett T.	Capt	American	LIBRE	Gers	8/17/1944
		Esteve	Rene	ASP	French	LUMINEUX		
		Gruen	Arthur	Sgt	American	FIDELE		
R3	MINARET	Hartley-Sharpe	L. C. M.	Major	British	EDMOND	Gard	7/10/1944
		Cros	P.	Capt	French			
		Ellis	John W.	Sgt	British	ARSENE		
R1	MONOCLE	Fiardo	J.	Capt	French	IMMENSE	Drome	8/14/1944
		Foster	Ray H.	1Lt	American	SOLIDE		
		Anderson	Robert J.	Sgt	American	RAIEUX		
D2	NICOLAS	Maude	J. C. C.	Capt	British	LEICESTER	Besancon	9/11/1944

Resistance Region	TEAM NAME	LAST NAME	First	Rank	Nationality	Code Name	Area of Operations	Deployment Date
D1	NORMAN	Penin	Henri	Lt	French	BREAKNECK		
		Whittle	M. A.	Sgt	British	NORTHUMBERLAND	Haute Saone	9/5/1944
R2	NOVOCAINE	Dillow	Konrad C.	Lt	American	MINNESOTA		
		Lautier	Marc	Lt	French	WASHINGTON		
		LaJeunesse	Lucien E.	1SG	American	TENNESSEE	Haute Alps	8/7/1944
		Gennerich	Charles J.	1Lt	American	MATHIEU		
		Pronost	Jean Yves	Lt	French	HARVE		
		Thompson	William T.	Sgt	American	GILLES		
R3	PACKARD	Bank	Aaron	Capt	American	CHECHWAN		
		Denis	Henri	Capt	French	FUKIEN	Lozere	8/1/1944
		Montfort	F.	Lt	British	FORMOSA		
D1	PAUL	Hood	E. H. M.	Major	British	SHROPSHIRE	Jura? Or Cote d'Or?	8/19/1944
		Vallee	Michel	Lt	French	DURTHE		
		Brown	Kenneth.J.W.	Sgt	British	LIMERICK		
C3	PHILLIP (RUPERT)	Liberos	C. J.	Capt	French	Kintyre	Meurthe et Moselle	9/1/1944
		Lucas	R. A. Lucas	Lt	American	Caithness		
		Gergat	G.	Sgt	American	Leinster		

Resistance Region	TEAM NAME	LAST NAME	First	Rank	Nationality	Code Name	Area of Operations	Deployment Date
B2	QUENTIN						Charente Inferieur	9/28/1944
		Fenton	R. S.	Capt	American	CORNWALL		
		Raux	Jean	Lt	French	WICKLOW		
		Rawson	D.	Sgt	British	MERIONETH		
R4 and R5	QUININE						Lot	6/9/1944
		MacPherson	R. Tommy	Major	British	ANSELME		
		de Bourbon de Parme	Michel	ASP	French	ARISTIDE		
		Brown	O. A.	Sgt	British	FELICIEN		
B2	RAYMOND						Vendee	8/28/1944
		DeHosses	R.	Capt	French	WATERFORD		
		Cadilhac	H.	Lt	French	GLOUCESTER		
		Adams	W.	Sgt	British	KINCARDINE		
D2	RODERICK						Doubs	9/1/1944
		Preziosi	Jean	Capt	French	NAIRN		
		Boggs	William C.	Lt	American	NEW HAMPSHIRE		
		Mersereau	Charles	Sgt	American	STRONSAY		
M3	RONALD						Finistere	8/6/1944
		Trumps	Shirly Ray	1Lt	American	BOURSIER		
		Desseilligny	Georges	Lt	French	BOUTTON		
		Esch	Elmer B.	TSgt	American	POUND		

Resistance Region	TEAM NAME	LAST NAME	First	Rank	Nationality	Code Name	Area of Operations	Deployment Date
R2	SCEPTRE	Hanna, Jr.	Walter C.	1Lt	American	VAILLANT	Alpes Maritimes	6/14/1944
		Franceschi	Francois	Lt	French	INTENSE		
		Palmer	Howard V.	MSgt	American	DEVOUX		
R1	SCION	Grenfell	O. P.	Major	British	SCINTILLATING	Seres	8/31/1944
		Gruppo	Roger	Lt	French	VIF		
		Cain	T.	Sgt	British	VIBRANT		
B2	SIMON	Coomber	A. W. C.	Capt	British	COUSTARD	Deux Sevres	9/28/1944
		Fouere	Maurice	Capt	French	FERNARD		
		Somers	C.	Sgt	British	STEPHANE		
D1	STANLEY	Craster	Oswin E.	Capt	British	YORKSHIRE	Haute Marne	9/1/1944
		Cantais	Robert	Lt	French	MEATH		
		Grinham	E. Jack	Sgt	British	WORCHESTERSHIRE		
R1/R2	TIMOTHY	Moutte	L.	Capt	French	NESQUE	Aisne/Jura	9/11/1944
		Mundinger	Robert G.	1Lt	American	MARCELIN		
		Heyns	Robert E.	1Lt	American	DYLE		
		Spears	Donald	1Sgt	American	ESCAUT		
M2	TONY	Montgomery	Robert K.	Major	American	DOLLAR	Finistere	8/18/1944

Resistance Region	TEAM NAME	LAST NAME	First	Rank	Nationality	Code Name	Area of Operations	Deployment Date
R1	VEGANIN	Paris	Lucien	Lt	French	ECY		
		McGowan	John E.	Tsgt	American	QUARTER	Sere	6/10/1944
		Marten	H. Neil	Major	British	CUTHBERT		
		Vuchot	Gaston	Capt	French	DEREK		
		Gardner	D.	Sgt	British	ERNEST		
R1	WILLYS	Montague	John C.	Capt	British	HONAN	Ardeche	6/29/1944
		Marchal	G.	Capt	French	SIMON		
		Cornick	T.	Sgt	British	CHANSI		

NOTES

Prologue: Eisenhower's Dilemma

Epigraph: Alfred D. Chandler Jr., ed., *The Papers of Dwight David Eisenhower, The War Years: II* (Baltimore: Johns Hopkins University Press, 1970), p. 679.

1. Horst Boog, Gerhard Krebs, and Detlef Vogel, *The Strategic Air War in Europe and the War in the West and East Asia 1943–1944/5* (Oxford: Clarendon Press, 2006). The number of divisions comes from their chart on page 474, the number of aircraft comes from their estimate in footnote 109 on page 528. The number of submarines is based on the number given in German message traffic on 5 August 1944, and decrypted by the British. See HW 1/3158, page 11 at the British National Archives, Kew, UK.

2. Albert Camus and Jacqueline Lévi-Valensi, *Camus at Combat: Writing 1944–1947*, trans. Arthur Goldhammer (Princeton, NJ: Princeton University Press, 2006), p. 3. Lévi-Valensi cannot be certain that Camus penned these words, but available evidence points to him as their author.

3. John Sweets, *The Politics of the Resistance in France, 1940–44: A History of the Mouvements Unis de la Resistance* (De Kalb: Northern Illinois University Press, 1976).

4. Charles L. Robertson, *When Roosevelt Planned to Govern France* (Amherst: University of Massachusetts Press, 2011), pp. 189–99.

5. Arthur Layton Funk, *Charles de Gaulle: The Crucial Years, 1943–44* (Norman: University of Oklahoma Press, 1959).

6. Michel de Bourbon-Parme, interview with author, 22 September 2007.

7. Stewart Alsop and Thomas Wardell Braden, *Sub Rosa; the O.-S.-S. and American Espionage* (New York: Reynal and Hitchcock, 1946).

8. William B. Dreux, *No Bridges Blown* (Notre Dame: University of Notre Dame Press, 1971).

9. Colonel Sir James Hutchison, *That Drug Danger* (Montrose, Scotland, UK: Standard Press, 1977).

10. M. G. M. "Bing" Crosby, *Irregular Soldier* (Guernsey: Guernsey Press, 1993).

11. Paul Aussaresses, *Pour La France: Services Spéciaux 1942–1954* ([Monaco]: Rocher, 2001); Paul Aussaresses, *The Battle of the Casbah* (New York: Enigma, 2002). In the second book, the former Jedburgh relates his experiences as the head of intelligence for his battalion during the Battle of Algiers. His complete honesty of his actions

shocked the French public and provoked the government to try him for various war crimes. He has since been amnestied and his rank reinstated. He passed away in 2013. Colonel Jean Sassi avec Jean-Louis Tremblais, *Operations Speciales 20 Ans de Guerres Secretes* (Paris: Nimrod, 2009).

12. European Theater of Operations United States Army Historical Division, *The French Forces of the Interior: Their Organization and Their Participation in the Liberation of France, 1944* (Washington, DC: Library of Congress, Photoduplication Service, 1945), microfilm. The British have their own copy which can be found in the British National Archives, Kew, UK, HS 7/127—HS 7/133. The French maintain their copy within Colonel Henri Ziegler's papers 1 K 374 at Service d'Historique de la Defense, Château de Vincennes, Paris.

13. European Theater of Operations United States Army Historical Division, *The French Forces of the Interior: Their Organization and Their Participation in the Liberation of France, 1944*, pp. 1585–99.

14. Evelyn Waugh, *The Sword of Honour Trilogy; the Final Version of the Novels: Men at Arms, 1952; Officers and Gentlemen, 1955; Unconditional Surrender, 1961* (New York: Alfred A. Knopf, 1994), p. 624.

15. Waugh, *Men at Arms, 1952*, p. 87.

Chapter 1: Guerrilla Warfare and the Design of the Jedburghs

1. Herodotus, *The Histories*, ed. David Campbell; introduction by Rosalind Thomas; trans. George Rawlinson (London: Everyman's Library, 1997), p. 353.

2. See Charles E. Callwell, *Small Wars: Their Principles and Practice*, 3rd ed. (Lincoln: University of Nebraska Press, 1996), T. E. Lawrence, *Seven Pillars of Wisdom: A Triumph* (New York: Penguin Books, 1962). Both works were very influential on British thinking of their empire and the warfare needed to maintain it.

3. Michael Korda, *Hero: The Life and Legend of Lawrence of Arabia* (New York: Harper Collins, 2011).

4. Lawrence, *Seven Pillars of Wisdom*, p. 10.

5. David Stafford, *Churchill and Secret Service* (Woodstock, NY: Overlook Press, 1998). See various passages.

6. Basil H. Liddell Hart, *Strategy*, 2nd rev. ed. (New York: Meridian, 1991), p. 365.

7. Winston Churchill, *We Shall Fight on the Beaches…Speech to the House of Commons, 4 June 1940*; http://www.winstonchurchill.org/i4a/pages/index.cfm?pageid=393.

8. William Mackenzie, *The Secret History of S. O. E.: Special Operations Executive 1940–1945* (London: St. Ermin's Press, 2002), pp. 51–55.

9. Stafford, *Churchill and Secret Service*, p. 189.

10. Peter Wilkinson and Joan Bright Astley Wilkinson, *Gubbins and SOE* (London: Pen & Sword Paperback, 1997), p. 26.

11. Stafford, *Churchill and Secret Service*, p. 139.

12. Peter Wilkinson and Joan Bright Astley, *Gubbins and SOE* (London: Leo Cooper, 1993), pp. 38–45.

13. Peter Wilkinson, *Foreign Fields: The Story of an SOE Operative* (London: I. B. Tauris, 1997), pp. 97–99.

14. Paul Kesaris et al., *Map Room Messages of President Roosevelt, 1939–1945* microform, *The Presidential Documents Series* (Frederick, MD: University Publications of America, 1981), Reel 1, Frames 74–76.

15. Charles de Gaulle, *The Complete War Memoirs of Charles De Gaulle* (New York: Carroll & Graf, 1998), pp. 53–55. De Gaulle quotes French Army Commander in Chief General Weygand as hoping the Germans would only leave him the "forces necessary to maintain order."

16. Mackenzie, *The Secret History of S. O. E.*, pp. 3–71, and Ben Pimlott, "Dalton, (Edward) Hugh Neale, Baron Dalton (1887–1962)," in *Oxford Dictionary of National Biography*, ed. H. C. G. Matthew and Brian Harrison (Oxford: Oxford University Press, 2004), http://www.oxforddnb.com.www2.lib.ku.edu:2048/view/article/32697.

17. Wilkinson and Astley, *Gubbins and SOE*, pp. 69–74.

18. Mackenzie, *The Secret History of S. O. E.*, p. 734.

19. David Stafford, *Britain and European Resistance, 1940–1945: A Survey of the Special Operations Executive, with Documents* (Toronto: University of Toronto Press, 1980), p. 118.

20. Mackenzie, *The Secret History of S. O. E.*, p. 512.

21. Wilkinson, *Foreign Fields: The Story of an SOE Operative*, p. 103.

22. Alan Brooke, Daniel Todman, and Alex Danchev, *War Diaries, 1939–1945: Field Marshal Lord Alanbrooke* (Berkeley: University of California Press, 2001), p. 680.

23. Alex Danchev, "Biffing: The Saga of the Second Front," in Theodore A. Wilson and Eisenhower Foundation (Abilene, Kansas), *D-Day, 1944, Modern War Studies* (Lawrence: Published for the Eisenhower Foundation, Abilene, by the University Press of Kansas, 1994), pp. 24–40. For a detailed work on the relations and conduct of the Allied planning staffs, see Mark A. Stoler, *Allies and Adversaries: The Joint Chiefs of Staff, the Grand Alliance, and U.S. Strategy in World War II* (Chapel Hill: University of North Carolina Press, 2000).

24. Wilkinson, *Foreign Fields*, p. 127.

25. H. R. Kedward, *In Search of the Maquis: Rural Resistance in Southern France, 1942–1944* (New York: Oxford University Press, 1993) pp. 73–160.

26. Wilkinson, *Foreign Fields*, p. 128.

27. Wilkinson, *Foreign Fields*, p. 128.

28. Richard Harris Smith, *OSS: The Secret History of America's First Central Intelligence Agency* (Guildfort, CT: First Lyons Press, 2005), pp. 150–51.

29. "Jedburgh Operations," 30 March 1943, Policy and Planning Jedburgh for OVERLORD, HS 8/288, British National Archives, Kew, UK.

30. "Review of SPARTAN," 6 April 1943, HS 8/288, British National Archives, Kew, UK.

31. "History of the Jedburgh in Europe," HS 7/17, British National Archives, Kew, UK, p. 9.

32. "History of the Jedburgh in Europe," HS 7/17, British National Archives, Kew, UK, pp. 5–6.

33. "History of the Jedburgh in Europe," HS 7/17, British National Archives, Kew, UK, p. 8.

34. William Casey, *The Secret War against Hitler* (Washington, DC: Regnery Gateway, 1988), pp. 34–37; Nelson MacPherson, *American Intelligence in War-Time London: The Story of the OSS* (Portland, OR: Frank Cass, 2003), pp. 45 and 46.

35. Nelson D. Lankford, ed., *OSS Against the Reich: The World War II Diaries of Colonel David K. E. Bruce* (Kent, OH: Kent State University Press, 1991), pp. 6–15.

36. R. Harris Smith, *OSS: The Secret History of America's First Central Intelligence Agency* (Berkeley: University of California Press, 1972), p. 164.

37. Anthony Cave Brown, *The Last Hero: Wild Bill Donovan* (New York: Times Books, 1982), p. 174. Assistance for this evidence was crystallized by 2nd Lieutenant Caleb Egli during research for a cadet paper at the United States Air Force Academy.

38. Franklin O. Canfield, "Memoirs of a Long and Eventful Life," in *Canfield Files,* Colin Beavan Papers, New York, NY, p. 27.

Chapter 2: Enter the Americans

1. Biennial Reports of the Chief of Staff of the United States Army, 1 July 1939–30 June 1945, http://www.ibiblio.org/hyperwar/USA/COS-Biennial/COS-Biennial-1 .html#page21, accessed 4 January 2014.

2. John Grenier, *The First Way of War: American War Making on the Frontier, 1607–1814* (New York: Cambridge University Press, 2005). In 2007, the Society of Military History named this work a co-winner of its Annual Book of the Year Award. Such accolades by professional military historians indicate the subject may now be more accepted and appreciated than before.

3. David Reynolds, *In Command of History: Churchill Fighting and Writing the Second World War* (New York: Allen Lane, 2004), p. 324.

4. Edwin "Ned" Putzell, interview with author, 9 June 2002. Putzell served as William J. Donovan's executive officer at OSS throughout the war.

5. William J. Casey, *The Secret War against Hitler* (New York: Regnery Gateway, 1988).

6. William J. Donovan and Edgar Mowrer, *Fifth Column Lessons for America,* with an introduction by Frank Knox (Washington, DC: American Council on Public Affairs, 1941). The term "fifth column" comes from General Emile Mola's radio broadcast in the Spanish Civil War. He had four columns of troops marching on Madrid and spoke of a "fifth column" in Madrid ready to rise to support him. The term then became synonymous with enemy groups inside one's borders. See David Stafford's *Churchill and the Secret Service,* p. 175.

7. Joseph E. Persico, *Roosevelt's Secret War: FDR and World War II Espionage* (New York: Random House, 2001), pp. 110–18.

8. Douglas Waller, *Wild Bill Donovan: The Spymaster Who Created the OSS and Modern American Espionage* (New York: Free Press, 2011), p. 69. Ian Fleming, who went on to write the wildly successful James Bond novels, may have based his character "M" on Admiral Godfrey.

9. Michel de bourbon-Parme, interview, 22 September 2007.

10. John K. Singlaub and Malcolm McConnell, *Hazardous Duty: An American Soldier in the Twentieth Century* (New York: Summit Books, 1991), pp. 29–31.

11. Michel de Bourbon-Parme, interview, 22 September 2007.

12. Keith B. Bickel, *Mars Learning: The Marine Corps Development of Small Wars Doctrine, 1915–1940* (Boulder, CO: Westview Press, 2001), pp. 1–6.

13. United States Marine Corps, *Small Wars Manual, FMFRP; 12–15* ([Washington, DC]: The Corps, 1997), p. 1.

14. United State Marine Corps, *Small Wars Manual*, pp. 1–4.

15. *OSS/London: Special Operations Branch and Secret Intelligence Branch War Diaries* (Frederick, MD: University Publications of America, 1985), microfilm, Frames 2 and 14–19.

16. Paul van der Stricht Papers, letter to Arthur L. Funk, 8 July 1968, and William Casey book manuscript, p. 5, Folder 1, Paul van der Stricht Papers, Hoover Institute, Stanford, CA.

17. Mockler-Ferryman, Brigadier Eric E. (1896–1978), Personal Papers, Liddell Hart Centre for Military Archives, King's College London, UK. The file consists of a partial biographical manuscript and speeches given about his wartime activities.

18. Rick Atkinson, *An Army at Dawn: The War in North Africa, 1942–1943* (New York: Henry Holt, 2002), p. 389.

19. Mockler-Ferryman Papers, "Supplies to Resistance Groups," unnumbered page, Liddell Hart Centre for Military Archives, London, UK. Fredendall was promoted and sent to a training command in the United States.

20. Personnel File, 1943–1945, Mockler-Ferryman, E. E. HS 9/510/1, British National Archives, Kew, UK.

21. Mockler-Ferryman Papers, Liddell Hart Centre for Military Archives, London, UK. These comments regarding his job description were written after the war by Mockler-Ferryman; the ellipsis indicates the end of the page and the next page was not in the collection. Unfortunately, little else is in the collection to illuminate any direct collaboration SOE may have had with the Strategic Bombing campaign.

22. Military Record and Report of Separation Certificate of Service, 30 November 1946, Papers of Joseph F. Haskell, Private Collection.

23. Casey book manuscript, p. 5, Paul van der Stricht Papers, Hoover, Stanford, CA; "Report by F/O Pearl Cornioley (Witherington)," 23 November 1944, HS 6/587, British National Archives, Kew, UK.

24. R. Harris Smith, *OSS: The Secret History of America's First Central Intelligence Agency* (Berkeley: University of California Press, 1972), pp. 94–95.

25. Casey book manuscript, p. 6, Paul van der Stricht Papers, Hoover, Stanford, CA; interview with Julia Paine, daughter of Joseph F. Haskell, 14 July 2007.

26. SOE/OSS Activities, Supreme Headquarters, Allied Expeditionary Force, Office of Secretary, General Staff: Records, 1943–1945, 10, Reel 5, Frames 1120–1121, Dwight D. Eisenhower Presidential Library, Abilene, KS.

27. M. R. D. Foot, *SOE in France: An Account of the Work of the British Special Operations Executive in France, 1940–1944*, rev. ed. (London: Whitehall History Publications in association with Portland, OR: Frank Cass, 2004), p. 190.

28. "Jedburgh Procedure," 12 October 1943, Policy and Planning Jedburghs for Overlord, HS 8/288, British National Archives, Kew, UK.

29. Marcel Ruby, *F Section: The Buckmaster Networks* (London: Lee Cooper, 1988), p. 63.

30. Leo Marks, *Between Silk and Cyanide: A Codemaker's War, 1941–1945* (London: Free Press, 1999), pp. 486–87.

31. Foot, *SOE in France*, p. 162.
32. Foot, *SOE in France*, pp. 83–86.
33. William Thompson, interview, 14 January 1999; Foot, *SOE in France*, p. 102.
34. Foot, *SOE in France*, pp. 75–89.
35. Foot, *SOE in France*, p. 87.
36. Foot, *SOE in France*, p. 61.
37. AIR 20-2903 Special Duty Units in Mediterranean and UK Operations, British National Archives, Kew, UK.

Chapter 3: Recreating France and the Rise of the Résistance

1. See Thomas Childers, *The Nazi Voter: The Social Foundations of Fascism in Germany, 1919–1933* (Chapel Hill: University of North Carolina Press, 1983), for a detailed description of Hitler's successful use of Germany's electoral process to seize power.
2. See Williamson Murray and Allan Reed Millett, *A War to Be Won: Fighting the Second World War* (Cambridge, MA: Belknap Press, 2000), pp. 22–23, for a summation of recent scholarship on the Wehrmacht's and Germany's adoption of their new doctrines during the 1930s.
3. Robert A. Doughty, *The Breaking Point: Sedan and the Fall of France, 1940* (Hamden, CT: Archon Books, 1990), p. 321.
4. Kesaris et al., *Map Room Messages of President Roosevelt, 1939–1945*, microform, Frame 74, Franklin D. Roosevelt Presidential Library and Museum, Hyde Park, NY.
5. Murray and Millett, *A War to Be Won*, pp. 79–81.
6. James C. Humes, *The Wit and Wisdom of Winston Churchill* (New York: Harper Perennial, 1995), p. 212.
7. Julian Jackson, *France: The Dark Years, 1940–1944* (New York: Oxford University Press, 2001), pp. 119–20.
8. Robert O. Paxton, *Vichy France: Old Guard and New Order 1940–1944* (New York: Columbia University Press, 2001), p. 14.
9. Jean Lacouture, *De Gaulle*, trans. Francis K. Price ([New York]: New American Library, 1966), p. 78.
10. Lacouture, *De Gaulle*, p. 79.
11. Arthur Layton Funk, *Charles de Gaulle: The Crucial Years, 1943–1944* (Norman: University of Oklahoma Press, 1959), pp. 10–12.
12. Jean-Louis Crémieux-Brilhac, *La France Libre: de L'appel du 18 Juin á la Libération, Tome I*, 2 vols. ([Paris]: Gallimard, 2001), p. 127.
13. François Kersaudy, *Churchill and De Gaulle* (London: Collins, 1981), p. 83.
14. Kersaudy, *Churchill and De Gaulle*, p. 85.
15. Jackson, *France: The Dark Years*, p. 406.
16. Laurent Douzou, *La Désobéissance: Histoire d'un Mouvement et d'un Journal Clandestins, Libération-Sud, 1940–1944* (Paris: O. Jacob, 1995), pp. 70–75; and Albert Camus, Jacqueline Lévi-Valensi, and Arthur Goldhammer, *Camus at Combat: Writing 1944–1947* (Princeton, NJ: Princeton University Press, 2006), p. vii.
17. Paxton, *Vichy France*, pp. 92–135.
18. Horst Boog, Gerhard Krebs, and Detlef Vogel, *The Strategic Air War in Europe and the War in the West and East Asia 1943–1944/5* (New York: Oxford University Press, 2006), p. 465.

19. "Ligne de démarcation" by François Marcot in François Marcot, Bruno Leroux, and Christine Levisse-Touzée, *Dictionnaire Historique de la Résistance: Résistance Intérieure et France Libre, Bouquins* (Paris: Laffont, 2006), pp. 262–63.

20. Thomas Johnston Laub, "The Politics of Occupation: The German Military Administration in France, 1940–1944" (Dissertation, University of Virginia, 2003), pp. 71–77.

21. Laub, "The Politics of Occupation," pp. 82–119.

22. Peter Lieb, *Konventioneller Krieg Oder Ns-Weltanschauungskrieg?: Kriegführung Und Partisanenbekämpfung in Frankreich 1943–44*, 1st ed. (München: R. Oldenbourg Verlag, 2007), p. 3.

23. Christian Pineau, *La Simple Verité*, pp. 99–100, quoted in John F. Sweets, *The Politics of Resistance in France, 1940–1944: A History of the Mouvements Unis de la Résistance* (Dekalb: Northern Illinois University Press, 1976), p. 21.

24. Pineau, *La Simple Verité*, p. 22.

25. Douzou, *La Désobéissance*, pp. 36–44.

26. Jackson, *France: The Dark Years*, p. 407.

27. Sweets, *The Politics of Resistance in France*, p. 46.

28. Hans Umbreit, "Les Allemands Face À Lutte Armée," in *La Résistance Et Les Français: Lutte Armée Et Maquis*, ed. François Marcot, Janine Ponty, Marcel Vigreux et Serge Wolikow (Beçanson et Paris, France: Annales littéraires de l'Université de Franche-Comté, 1996), p. 201.

29. Laub, "The Politics of Occupation," p. 169.

30. Joel Colton, *Léon Blum: Humanist in Politics* (Durham, NC: Duke University Press, 1987), pp. 103–4.

31. Sweets, *The Politics of Resistance in France*, pp. 116–20.

32. Sweets, *The Politics of Resistance in France*, pp. 120–21. The FN's FTP should not be confused with the Résistance movement Franc-Tireurs, largely affiliated with a centrist ideology.

33. Jackson, *France: The Dark Years*, pp. 423–25.

34. Henry Rousso, *The Vichy Syndrome: History and Memory in France since 1944* (Cambridge, MA: Harvard University Press, 1991), pp. 4–26.

35. Philippe Buton, *Les Lendemains Qui Déchantent: Le Parti Communiste Français À La Libération* ([Paris, France]: Presses de la Fondation nationale des sciences politiques, 1993), pp. 15–17.

36. H. R. Kedward, *In Search of the Maquis: Rural Resistance in Southern France, 1942–1944* (New York: Oxford University Press, 1993), p. 40.

37. Jackson, *France: The Dark Years*, p. 437.

38. Sweets, *The Politics of Resistance in France*, p. 39.

39. Pierre Guillain de Bénouville, *The Unknown Warriors, a Personal Account of the French Resistance*, trans. Lawrence G. Blochman (New York: Simon and Schuster, 1949), p. 363.

40. "Appendix B – Strength of French National Army (including FFI)," SHAEF MF/GBI/OI/180, 18 Nov. 1944, 381 France: French Participation in OVERLORD, SGS Records, 1943–1945, Dwight D. Eisenhower Presidential Library, Abilene, KS. A formulation of numbers is discussed further in the conclusion.

41. Daniel Cordier, *Jean Moulin: La République Des Catacombes, Suite Des Temps* ([Paris]: Gallimard, 1999), pp. 52–62.

42. Cordier, *Jean Moulin*, pp. 71–80.

43. William Mackenzie, *The Secret History of S. O. E.: Special Operations Executive 1940–1945* (London: St. Ermins Press, 2002), p. 274.

44. Rick Atkinson, *An Army at Dawn: The War in North Africa, 1942–1943* (New York: Henry Holt, 2002), pp. 62, 94–95.

45. Philippe Burrin, *La France á L'heure Allemande: 1940–1944* (Paris: Seuil, 1995), p. 168.

46. John F. Sweets, *Choices in Vichy France: The French under Nazi Occupation* (New York: Oxford University Press, 1986), p. 157.

47. Funk, *Charles De Gaulle: The Crucial Years*, p. 44.

48. Raoul Aglion, *Roosevelt and De Gaulle: Allies in Conflict: A Personal Memoir* (New York: Free Press, 1988), pp. 148–49.

49. *Libération-Sud, Combat, L'Insurgé* and the regional *L'Humanite* newspapers are replete with their increasing disgust with the United States on this issue. They can be found on microfilm at the Center for Research Libraries, in the "Périodiques clandestins, 1939–1945," Chicago, IL. General Donovan, as described below, related this to the president with no result.

50. Murray and Millett, *A War to Be Won*, p. 299.

51. Funk, *Charles De Gaulle: The Crucial Years*, p. 48.

52. Funk, *Charles De Gaulle*, p. 73.

53. André Dewavrin, *Colonel Passy: Memoires du Chef Des Services Secrets de la France Libre* (Paris: Editions Odile Jacob, 2000), p. 492.

54. Charles de Gaulle, *The Complete War Memoirs of Charles De Gaulle* (New York: Carroll and Graf, 1998), p. 305.

55. Dewavrin, *Colonel Passy*, pp. 516–17.

56. Daniel Cordier, *Jean Moulin: La République des Catacombes* (Paris: Gallimard, 1999), p. 387, and Jackson, *France: The Dark Years*, pp. 455–56.

57. Novick, *The Resistance Versus Vichy: The Purge of Collaborators in Liberated France*, p. 48. For Sweets's description of the creation of the CFLN, see Sweets, *The Politics of Resistance in France*, pp. 78–80.

58. Crémieux-Brilhac, *La France Libre: de L'appel du 18 Juin á la Libération, Tome I*, p. 868, as quoted from PM Minute to Lord Selborne, PREM 3/184/6 at the British National Archives.

59. Roosevelt, Franklin D. (1) [Sept. 1943—April 1945], Dwight D. Eisenhower: Papers, Pre-Presidential, 1916–52, Box 100, Dwight D. Eisenhower Presidential Library, Abilene, KS.

60. United States Army. European Theater of Operations, *The French Forces of the Interior* (Washington, DC: Library of Congress, Photoduplication Service, 1977), microfilm, Part 1, Chapter 1, pp. 73–79.

61. Jean-Louis Crémieux-Brilhac, "Le Bloc Planning Et L'insurrection Nationale," *Espoir* 139 (2004): 40–41.

Chapter 4: North African Rehearsal

1. Michel Vigneras, *United States Army in World War II, Special Studies: Rearming the French*, ed. Kent Roberts Greenfield (Washington, DC: Office of the Chief of Military History, Department of the Army, 1957), pp. 8–16.

2. Rick Atkinson, *An Army at Dawn: The War in North Africa, 1942–1943* (New York: Henry Holt, 2002), pp. 113–15.

3. Dwight D. Eisenhower, Alfred Dupont Chandler, and Louis Galambos, *The Papers of Dwight David Eisenhower* (Baltimore: Johns Hopkins University Press, 1970), Vol. 2, pp. 677, 680.

4. Letter from Darlan to Eisenhower, November 21, 1942, Butcher Diary, November 30, 1942–January 7, 1943, Pre-Presidential Papers, 19, Dwight D. Eisenhower Presidential Library, Abilene, KS. After seeing the letter at some unknown time, Churchill told Eisenhower that it was both "pathetic and dignified."

5. Mario Faivre, *Nous Avon Tue Darlan, Algiers 1942* (Paris: La Table Ronde, 1975), Ray Argyle, *The Paris Game: Charles de Gaulle, the Liberation of Paris, and the Gamble that Won France* (Ontario, Canada: Dundurn Press, 2014), p. 177, and de Francesco interview with author, 3 March 1999.

6. Atkinson, *An Army at Dawn*, p. 253.

7. Butcher Diary, 30 November 1942–7 January 1943, entry for 26 December 1942 and p. a-113, Eisenhower Presidential Library, Abilene, KS.

8. De Francesco interview with author, 3 March 1999.

9. Butcher Diary, 30 November 1942–7 January 1943, translation done by Eisenhower's staff and the messages appended to the diary on page a-132.

10. Butcher Diary, 4 January 1943, pp. a-138 and a-139.

11. Dwight D. Eisenhower, Papers, Pre-Presidential, 1916-52, Principal File, Box 100, FDR Correspondence, Dwight D. Eisenhower Presidential Library, Abilene, KS; Message from AGWAR, 8 July 1943, No. 2016, Dwight D. Eisenhower Presidential Library, Abilene, KS.

12. Dwight D. Eisenhower, Papers, Pre-Presidential, 1916–1951, Principal File, Box 34, Charles De Gaulle Folder, Dwight D. Eisenhower Presidential Library, Abilene, KS.

13. Paul Kesaris, United States Office of Strategic Services, and United States Dept. of State, *Germany and Its Occupied Territories during World War II. Microfilm, O.S.S./State Department Intelligence and Research Reports; Pt. 4* (Washington: University Publications of America, 1977), Reel 8, "Survey of French Underground Movements," 28 January 1944.

14. See Julian Jackson's work *France: The Dark Years* for a synthetic account of France during the war. The list of scholars who agree on this point begins with Sweets, Paxton, Michel, Kedward, Funk, and Novick, whose works are all listed in the bibliography.

15. Raoul Aglion, *Roosevelt and De Gaulle: Allies in Conflict: A Personal Memoir* (New York: Free Press, 1988), pp. 184–87.

16. David G. Haglund, "Roosevelt as 'Friend of France—but Which One?" *Diplomatic History* 31, no. 5 (2007): 895–98. Haglund attributes FDR's anti-Imperialism as the source of his zeal to ensure de Gaulle remained unrecognized.

17. Franklin D. Roosevelt and William C. Bullitt, *For the President, Personal and Secret; Correspondence between Franklin D. Roosevelt and William C. Bullitt* (Boston: Houghton Mifflin, 1972), p. 581.

18. Letter to General Eisenhower from General De Gaulle, 28 December 1943, De Gaulle, Charles (Personal Correspondence), Dwight D. Eisenhower, Papers, Pre-Presidential, 1916–52, 34, Dwight D. Eisenhower Presidential Library, Abilene, KS.

19. Charles de Gaulle, *The Complete War Memoirs of Charles De Gaulle* (New York: Carroll and Graf, 1998), p. 545.

20. France: French Participation in Overlord, Supreme Headquarters, Allied Expeditionary Force, Office of the Secretary, General Staff, 1943–1945, Series II Country File: Box 6, Reel 52, 381, Dwight D. Eisenhower Presidential Library, Abilene, KS, microfilm.

21. France: French Participation in Overlord, Supreme Headquarters, Allied Expeditionary Force, Office of Secretary, General Staff, 1943–45, Series II, Box 6, Roll 52, Frame 1242, Dwight D. Eisenhower Presidential Library, Abilene, KS.

22. France: French Participation in Overlord, Supreme Headquarters, Allied Expeditionary Force, Office of Secretary, General Staff, 1943–45, Series II, Box 6, Roll 52, Frame 240, Dwight D. Eisenhower Presidential Library, Abilene, KS.

23. Paul Kesaris, ed., *Map Room Messages of President Roosevelt, 1939–1945 Microform* (Frederick, MD: University Publications of America, 1981), 9 microfilm reels, Reel 3, Frame 852.

24. Paragraph 8, Directive to Supreme Allied Commander, Expeditionary Force, CAB 79/70, British National Archives, Kew, UK.

25. De Gaulle, *The Complete War Memoirs of Charles De Gaulle*, p. 546.

26. Dwight D. Eisenhower and Robert H. Ferrell, *The Eisenhower Diaries* (New York: Norton, 1981). p. 118.

27. "Jedburghs," 20 Dec 1943, HS 8/288, British National Archives, Kew, UK.

28. Dwight D. Eisenhower, Supreme Headquarters, Allied Expeditionary Force and Chief of Staff, Supreme Allied Command, Office of G-3: Records, 1943–1946 (Harold R. Bull), Box 1, Reel 2, Frame 1238, Dwight D. Eisenhower Presidential Library, Abilene, KS.

29. Vigneras, *United States Army in World War II*, p. 300.

30. After action, Jedburgh team reports universally complained of the lack of weapons due to the greater than expected number of Maquis. See OSS/London War Dairy Vol. 8, microfilm, NARA (National Archives and Records Administration), College Park, MD.

31. See H. R. Kedward, *In Search of the Maquis: Rural Resistance in Southern France, 1942–1944* (Oxford: Oxford University Press, 1993); Laurent Douzou, *La Désobéissance: Histoire D'un Mouvement et d'un Journal Clandestins, Libération-Sud, 1940–1944* (Paris: O. Jacob, 1995); Peter Novick, *The Resistance versus Vichy: The Purge of Collaborators in Liberated France* (London: Chatto & Windus, 1968).

32. Kedward, *In Search of the Maquis*, pp. 73–115.

33. David Stafford, *Churchill and the Secret Service* (Woodstock, NY: Overlook Press, 1998), pp. 300–302.

34. William Mackenzie, *The Secret History of S. O. E.: Special Operations Executive 1940–1945* (London: St. Ermin's Press, 2002), p. 284. It is unclear when de Gaulle discovered that F Section and SIS were running operations in France without his approval or knowledge, but on 6 November 1941, he "berated" the SOE officer responsible. But while he knew about it, he could not shut it down, at least not until late in 1944.

35. See Mackenzie, *The Secret History of S. O. E.*, for the details of how the agreements came to be. See BNA HS 8/1000 and HS 8/1001, British National Archives, Kew,

UK, as they are used to gain the fuller appreciation on the process and method described.

36. Mackenzie, *The Secret History of S. O. E.*, pp. 257–61.

37. James Hutchison, *That Drug Danger* (Montrose, Scotland: Standard Press, 1977), p. 91.

38. Undated, "Jedburghs," BCRA Planning Documents, 3 AJ 2 462, Archive National, Paris, France.

39. Copie de Telegrame—Depart, 11.1.1944 No. 57, BCRA Planning Documents, 3 AJ 2 462, Archives National, Paris, France.

40. "Compte Rendu Sur La Situation Du Plan J Au 20 Janvier 1944, BCRA Planning Documents, 3 AJ 2 462, Archives National, Paris, France, pp. 1–4.

41. Anne-Aurore Inquimbert, *Les Equipes Jedburgh (juin 1944–décember 1944) Le rôle des services spéciaux allies dans le contrôle de la Résistance intérieure française* (Service historique de la Défense, Lavauzelle, 2006), p. 84.

42. Compte Rendu Sur La Situation Du Plan J au 20 Janvier 1944, BCRA Planning Documents, 3 AJ 2 462, Archives National, Paris, France, pp. 3–4.

43. Eclaireur Team, Jedburgh Team Reports, HS 6/504, British National Archives, Kew, UK, p. 1.

44. Letter to William Casey, 23 December 1977. Paul Van Der Stricht Papers, 1990, Paul Van der Stricht, 1943–1977, Folder 1, Hoover Institution Archives, Stanford, CA.

45. HS 9/1318-3, British National Archives, Kew, UK.

46. M. R. D. Foot, *SOE in France: An Account of the Work of the British Special Operations Executive in France, 1940–1944* (London: Whitehall History Publications in association with Portland, OR: Frank Cass, 2004), pp. 369–70.

47. Eclaireur Team, HS 6/504, British National Archives, Kew, UK.

48. Inmate Identification Card, 20 August 1944 and train manifest, 10 August 1944; ITS Digital Collection, United States Holocaust Memorial and Museum, Washington, DC.

49. Sarah Helm, *A Life in Secrets: Vera Atkins and the Missing Agents of WWII* (London: Abacus, 2006), pp. 101–3.

50. Foot, *SOE in France*, p. 329.

51. "Plan 'J' 23 Mars 1944," BCRA Planning Documents, 3 AJ 2 462, Archives National, Paris, France, p. 11.

52. United States War Department, Strategic Services Unit, History Project, Vol. 1, *The War Report of the OSS* (Office of Strategic Services), with a new introduction by Kermit Roosevelt (New York: Walker, 1976), p. 210.

53. FOIA Request to CIA, Ref F-2007-01590, Letter from Fuller to E. C. Huntington Jr., 19 May, 1943. In possession of author.

54. FOIA Request to CIA, Ref F-2007-01590, Letter from James Roosevelt to William J. Donovan, 26 July 26 1943.

55. "The Jedburgher," Christmas issue, 1989. Courtesy of Steven Kippax. In possession of author.

56. William Thompson, interview, 14 January 1999.

57. Thompson interview; and William B. Dreux, *No Bridges Blown* (Notre Dame, IN: University of Notre Dame Press, 1971), pp. 11–19.

58. Wyman W. Irwin, "A Special Force: Origin and Development of the Jedburgh Project in Support of Operation OVERLORD" (MMAS Thesis, U. S. Army Command and General Staff College, Fort Leavenworth, KS, 1991), 119–21; and Nigel West, *Secret War: The Story of SOE, Britain's Wartime Sabotage Organisation* (London: Houghton and Stoughton, 1992), p. 268.

59. Crawshay, William Robert, 24 March 1992, Sound, 12521, Imperial War Museum, London, UK.

60. OSS/SO London, microfilm, Vol. 12, 42–43, NARA (National Archives and Records Administration), College Park, MD.

61. Irwin, "A Special Force," p. 124; and Thompson interview.

62. Irwin, "A Special Force," p. 124; and Joseph de Francesco, telephone conversation with author, 3 March 1999. My conversations with French Jedburghs Paul Moniez and Paul Aussaresses reinforce the lack of arguments within the Jedburghs regarding politics. When they argued, it tended to be more about proper tactics, procedures, or personal issues.

63. Michel de Bourbon-Parme, interview, 22 September 2007.

64. Dreux, *No Bridges Blown*, pp. 58–59; and Thompson interview. Michel de Bourbon-Parme recalls that 8th Air Force Commander, General James Doolittle, got the same treatment when he promised to drop them right on target. The Jedburghs didn't care for such boasting. For Spooner's difficulties, see his SOE Personnel File, HS 9/1400/1, British National Archives, Kew, UK.

65. Thompson interview; de Francesco telephone conversation; Daphne Friele, telephone conversation with author, 2 March 1999; and Mamie Gauthier, telephone conversation with author, 6 March 1999.

66. Paul Moniez, interview, 17 September 2007.

67. "Role of the Jedburghs"—Summary of Speech by E. E. Mockler-Ferryman to Jedburgh students on 24 February 1944, 10 March 1944, Policy and Planning Jedburghs for Overlord, HS 8/288, National Archives, Kew, UK.

68. Stewart Alsop and Thomas Wardell Braden, *Sub Rosa; the O.-S.-S. and American Espionage* (New York: Reynal and Hitchcock, 1946), p. 144.

69. Jean-Louis Crémieux-Brilhac, *La France Libre: de l'appel du 18 Juin à la Libération*, 2 vols. (Paris: Gallimard, 2001), Vol. 2, p. 1142.

70. Mackenzie, *The Secret History of S. O. E.*, pp. 611–13.

71. Ben Parnell, *Carpetbaggers: America's Secret War in Europe* (Austin, TX: Eakin Press, 1987), p. 2; and OSS/SO London microfilm, Vol. 12, p. 137–38, NARA (National Archives and Records Administration), College Park, MD. A "moon period" is the days just before and after a full moon when there was sufficient illumination for night parachute drops.

72. OSS/SO London microfilm, Vol. 11, p. 9, NARA (National Archives and Records Administration), College Park, MD.

73. Bernard V. Moore, II. "The Secret Air War over France": USAAF Special Operations Units in the French Campaign of 1944" (MA Thesis, Air University, School of Advanced Airpower Studies, Maxwell AFB, AL, 1992), pp. 26–35.

74. Parnell, *Carpetbaggers*, p. 12.

75. Parnell, *Carpetbaggers*, pp. 15–28.

76. OSS/SO London microfilm. Vol. 6, p. 84, NARA (National Archives and Records Administration), College Park, MD.

77. Foot, *SOE in France*, p. 475.

78. SHAEF SGS microfilm, Reel 12, Frame 645, Dwight D. Eisenhower Presidential Library, Abilene, KS.

79. Anthony Cave Brown, *Bodyguard of Lies* (New York: Harper and Row, 1975), p. 525.

80. SHAEF SGS microfilm, Reel 52, Frame 1030, Dwight D. Eisenhower Presidential Library, Abilene, KS.

81. SHAEF SGS microfilm, Reel 52, Frame 1063, Dwight D. Eisenhower Presidential Library, Abilene, KS.

82. SHAEF SGS microfilm, Reel 12, Frames 588–616, Dwight D. Eisenhower Presidential Library, Abilene, KS.

83. Foot, *SOE in France*, p. 473.

84. Mackenzie, *The Secret History of S. O. E.*, p. 613.

Chapter 5: The Politics Running into D-Day

1. Paul Kesaris, *Map Room Messages of President Roosevelt, 1939–1945*, microform, Reel 4, Frame 517, Franklin D. Roosevelt Presidential Library and Museum, Hyde Park, NY.

2. "Memorandum for the President from Director, OSS, 3 April 1944," Roosevelt, *President Franklin D. Roosevelt's Office Files, 1933–1945, Part 1: "Safe and Confidential Files*. Reel 4, Franklin D. Roosevelt Presidential Library and Museum, Hyde Park, NY.

3. Peter Lieb, *Konventioneller Krieg oder NS-Weltanschauungskrieg? Kriegführung und Partisanenbekämpfung in Frankreich 1943–44*, pp. 323–25.

4. Eisenhower, Supreme Headquarters, Allied Expeditionary Force, Office of the Secretary, General Staff, 1943–1945, Series II Country File: 381 France: French Participation in Overlord, Box 6, Reel 52, Frame 196, Dwight D. Eisenhower Presidential Library, Abilene, KS.

5. SHAEF, SGS, Records, 1943–1945, Reel 5, Frames 1093–1101, Dwight D. Eisenhower Presidential Library, Abilene, KS.

6. SHAEF, SGS, Records, 1943–1945, Reel 5, Frames 847–850, Dwight D. Eisenhower Presidential Library, Abilene, KS.

7. Walter B. Smith, Collection of WWII Documents, Box 24, Cable Log-out (May 1944), Dwight D. Eisenhower Presidential Library, Abilene, KS.

8. Former Jedburgh Jack Poche, email to author, 13 April 2007, and the SHAEF item quoted in n. 5 above contrasted with OSS London War Diary, Roll 8, Book I, p. ii, NARA (National Archives and Records Administration), College Park, MD, where it states, "they will be dropped by parachute at pre-arranged spots behind enemy lines in France, Belgium, and Holland on and after D-Day." Written after D-Day, it contrasts with Jedburgh memories of their intended use as well as SHAEF documents.

9. Historical Division, *The French Forces of the Interior: Their Organization and Their Participation in the Liberation of France, 1944*, pp. 73–86, File no. 8-3 Fr, acc.

No. 419–1 Center for Military History, Carlisle Barracks, PA. This same document was found in the 1 K 374 1, French Army Archives, Vincennes, Paris, France—in French, of course.

10. Alex Danchev and Daniel Todman, *War Diaries, 1939–1945: Field Marshal Lord Alanbrooke* (Berkeley: University of California Press, 2001), p. 546.

11. Message, 9 May 1944, in Smith, Walter Bedell: Collection of WWII Documents, 1941–1945, Box 24, Cable Log-Out (May 1944), Dwight D. Eisenhower Presidential Library, Abilene, KS.

12. SHAEF SGS Records, 381 France: French Participation in OVERLORD, Box 6, Reel 52, Frame 217, Dwight D. Eisenhower Presidential Library, Abilene, KS.

13. "Folder 3, Butcher Dairy, Pre-Presidential Papers, 22 April 1944 p. 1219, Dwight D. Eisenhower Presidential Library, Abilene, KS.

14. Folder 011—French National Committee, Map Room Files, Special Files, Franklin D. Roosevelt Presidential Library and Museum, Hyde Park, NY. The comment about the absence of a thank you regarding American efforts drew a "!!" in the margins from FDR.

15. Eisenhower, Supreme Headquarters, Allied Expeditionary Force, Office of the Secretary, General Staff, 1943–1945, Series II Country File: 381 France: French Participation in Overlord, Reel 52, Frames 99–103, Dwight D. Eisenhower Presidential Library, Abilene, KS; and Jean-Louis Crémieux-Brilhac, *La France Libre: De L'appel Du 18 Juin à la Libération*, 2 vols. (Paris: Gallimard, 2001), pp. 834–41.

16. OVERLORD Joint Administrative Plan for Operation OVERLORD—Joint Operation Plan for U. S. Forces—Operation OVERLORD, SHAEF SGS Records, Dwight D. Eisenhower Presidential Library, Abilene, KS.

17. "SHAEF 17240/17/Ops 8 May 1944, Directions to BBC," HS 6/610, British National Archives, Kew, UK.

18. Paul Aussaresses, *Pour La France: Services Spéciaux 1942–1954* (Monaco: Rocher, 2001), p. 116.

19. Paul Aussaresses, interview, 25 September 2007.

20. Bourbon-Parme, interview, 22 September 2007.

21. Message 11 May 1944 in Smith, Walter Bedell: Collection of WWII Documents, 1941–1945, Box 24, Cable Log-Out (May 1944), Dwight D. Eisenhower Presidential Library, Abilene, KS.

22. Jean-Louis Crémieux-Brilhac, interview, 20 September 2007. M. Crémieux-Brilhac served in London in the France Libre interior ministry during the war.

23. Crémieux-Brilhac, *La France Libre*, pp. 1148–52.

24. "Conference Meeting Minutes," 20 May 1944, HS 6/607, British National Archives, Kew, UK.

25. "ISAAC Mission," HS 6/366, British National Archives, Kew, UK.

26. Paul Kesaris, *Map Room Messages of President Roosevelt, 1939–1945*, microform, Reel 4, Frame 602, Franklin D. Roosevelt Presidential Library and Museum, Hyde Park, NY.

27. April Report dated, 7 May and May Report dated 10 June, SOE/SO Monthly Reports, SHAEF, SGS Records, Dwight D. Eisenhower Presidential Library, Abilene, KS.

28. Order No. 3, Order No. 4, "Ordres d'EMFFI," 3 AG 2 473. Archives National, Paris, France.

29. To General Koenig, 31 May 1944, Folder 2 of 2, Frame 862, Command and Control of French Forces of the Interior, SHAEF SGS Records, Dwight D. Eisenhower Presidential Library, Abilene, KS.

30. Untitled Memo, 30 May 1944, HS 6/610, British National Archives, Kew, UK.

31. Anthony Cave Brown, *The Last Hero: Wild Bill Donovan: The Biography and Political Experience of Major General William J. Donovan, Founder of the OSS and "Father" of the CIA, from His Personal and Secret Papers and the Diaries of Ruth Donovan* (New York: Times Books, 1982), p. 550.

32. Butcher Dairy, 1 June—27 June 1944 (1), Butcher Diary, Pre-Presidential Papers, 1916–1952, Box 168, Dwight D. Eisenhower Presidential Library, Abilene, KS.

33. Orders No. 5 and No. 6, Ordres d'EMFFI, 3 AG 2 473, Archives National, Paris, France.

34. Crémieux-Brilhac, *La France Libre*, pp. 1221–22.

35. Dwight D. Eisenhower and Robert H. Ferrell, *The Eisenhower Diaries* (New York: Norton, 1981), pp. 113–18.

36. Williamson Murray and Allan Reed Millett, *A War to Be Won: Fighting the Second World War* (Cambridge, MA: Belknap Press, 2000), pp. 420–21.

37. "Memorandum of Record: SAC Meeting Minutes 4 June, 1944," Supreme Headquarters, Allied Expeditionary Force, and Chief of Staff, Supreme Allied Command, Office of G-3 (Harold R. Bull): Records, 1943–46, microfilm, Reel 2, Frames 788–789, Dwight D. Eisenhower Presidential Library, Abilene, KS.

38. Butcher Dairy, 1 June–27 June 1944 (1), entry for 4 June, p. 1327; Papers, Pre-Presidential, 1916–1952, Dwight D. Eisenhower Presidential Library, Abilene, KS.

39. François Kersaudy, *Churchill and De Gaulle* (London: Collins, 1981), pp. 339–43. Kersaudy provides an amazingly well-woven reconstruction of the meeting from over seven different diaries and official records.

40. Butcher Dairy, 1 June–27 June 1944 (1), p. 1343, Dwight D. Eisenhower Presidential Library, Abilene, KS.

41. Charles de Gaulle, *The Complete War Memoirs of Charles De Gaulle* (New York: Carroll and Graf, 1998), pp. 558–59.

42. "Memorandum of Record: SAC Meeting Minutes, 4 June, 1944, Dwight D. Eisenhower Presidential Library, Abilene, KS, p. 3.

43. Butcher Dairy, 1 June–27 June 1944 (1), p. 1343, Dwight D. Eisenhower Presidential Library, Abilene, KS.

44. Butcher Diary, 1 June–27 June 1944 (1), p. 1334, Dwight D. Eisenhower Presidential Library, Abilene, KS.

45. DR/1654, 2 June 1944, "Directions to BBC," HS 6/610, British National Archives, Kew, UK.

46. DR/1654, 2 June 1944, "Directions to BBC," HS 6/610, "List B," p. 1, British National Archives, Kew, UK.

47. Pages 3 and 4, "SOE/SO Monthly Report," 10 June 1944, 319.1/10 Monthly SOE/SO Reports, SHAEF SGS Records, Dwight D. Eisenhower Presidential Library, Abilene, KS.

48. 31 May 1944, untitled memorandum From DR/S to DR/US, HS 6/610, British National Archives, Kew, UK.

Chapter 6: The Struggle for Control

1. HW 1/2937, British National Archives, Kew, UK. This source and all others below from the HW series in the British National Archives are decoded messages of German radio traffic. Many of these "Special Messages," as Churchill and the head of the British SIS Stewart Menzies, called them, are now available to researchers and provide a very valuable resource on Wehrmacht operations, since many of the German documents were destroyed during the war.
2. 22 April 1944, Bandenbekampfung, Enthalt: Befehle; Strafverfahren gegen Terroristen; Bekampfung der Widerstandsbewegung, RW 35/551, Bundesarchiv-Militärchiv, Freiburg im Breisgau, Germany.
3. HS 6/601, National Archives, Kew, UK.
4. For a discussion of the application of civil power in France see Charles-Louis Foulon, *Le Pouvoir en Province à la Liberation: Les Commissaires de la République, 1943–1946, Travaux et Recherches de Science Politique; 32* (Paris: Fondation Nationale des Sciences Politiques, 1975).
5. RH 19 IV/64 Karte—2, Bundesarchiv-Militärchiv, Freiburg im Breisgau, Germany.
6. G-3, OVERLORD Joint administrative Plan for Operation OVERLORD—Joint Operation Plan for U. S. Forces—Operation OVERLORD [52–573], 8 May 1944 (Revised), Supreme Headquarters, Allied Expeditionary Force, Office of Secretary, General Staff: Records, 1943–45, microfilm, 381/3, Dwight D. Eisenhower Presidential Library, Abilene, KS.
7. Ordre No. 1 de General Koenig à DMN, DMZ, DMRs et MASSINGHAM, 3 AG 2 473, Archives National, Paris, France.
8. HS 6/526, pp. 1–2, National Archives, Kew, UK. All the French Jedburghs and agents used false names to protect their families from German or Vichy punishment should they be arrested. Few knew their real names; in fact, the British and American Jedburghs did not learn their French partners' real names until long after the war.
9. Joe de Francesco, interview, 3 March 1999.
10. Letter from Lady Crawshay, 28 July 1998.
11. Crawshay, William Robert, 12521/3, Sound Archive, Imperial War Museum, London, UK.
12. Crawshay, William Robert, 12521/3, Sound Archive, Imperial War Museum, London, UK, and HS 9/371/2, Crawshay PF, National Archives, Kew, UK.
13. Michel Jouanneau, *L'organisation de la Résistance dans l'Indre: Juin 1940–Juin 1944* (Versailles, France: Le Impremerie Aubert S. A., 1975), pp. 25–29.
14. Alistair Cole and Peter Campbell, *French Electoral Systems and Elections since 1789* (Aldershot, Hants., England, 1989), p. 69.
15. M. R. D. Foot, *SOE in France: An Account of the Work of the British Special Operations Executive in France, 1940–1944* (London, UK: Her Majesty's Stationery Office, 1966), pp. 147–48.
16. HS 6/526, pp. 1–2 of the French version of the report. British National Archives, Kew, UK.

17. OSS London Microfilm, Reel 8, book 4, HUGH's radio messages, pp. 21–22, NARA (National Archives and Records Administration), College Park, MD.
18. "Telegrams à ELLIPSE," 10 Juin 1944, 3 AG 2 562, Archives National, Paris, France.
19. Michel Pichard, *L'Espoir des Ténèbres: Parachutages sous l'Occupation* (Paris: Editeur, 1990), p. 254.
20. Mission Report of Drop—Fish Crew- 0629, 13 June 1944, Carpetbagger Archive, http://home.comcast.net/~801492bg.historian/Index.html. This website was run by the son of a former Carpetbagger. Over the last twenty years, Mr. Tom Ensminger, Lt. Col. J. W. Bradbury, USAF (Ret.), and many others have taken documents from the national archives regarding Carpetbagger operations and placed them on the website. Mr. Ensminger, who passed away 3 May 2012, will be deeply missed, as his work supporting Carpetbagger history was a marvel. The collection was donated to the Special Collections, US Air Force Academy Library, and they are currently working to make it available again to researchers and the public.
21. OSS London Microfilm, Reel 8, Book IV, pp. 22 and 46, NARA (National Archives and Records Administration), College Park, MD.
22. (Witherington), Pearl Cornioley, Report by F/O Pearl Cornioley (nee Witherington), 23 November 1944, HS 6/587, British National Archives, Kew, UK.
23. OSS London Microfilm, Reel 8, Target 1, Vol. V, Book I, p. 52, NARA (National Archives and Records Administration), College Park, MD. The term "Boche" is a pejorative often used by World War II soldiers, especially the French, referring to the Germans.
24. HS 6/526, British National Archives, Kew, UK, p. 4.
25. HS 6/526, National Archives, Kew, UK, p. 4, and Crawshay sound file 12521, reel 2, Imperial War Museum, London, UK.
26. "Biographical file, George Hertier, HS 8/1001, National Archives, Kew, UK.
27. Crawshay sound file 12521, reel 2, IWM, London, UK.
28. HS 6/526, British National Archives, Kew, UK, pp. 4 and 5.
29. "Telegrams de ELLIPSE" 10 Feb 44, 3 AG 2 561, Archives National, Paris, France.
30. HS 6/526, p. 6, British National Archives, Kew, UK.
31. "Telegrams à ELLIPSE," 25 Juin 1944, 3 AG 2 562, Archives National, Paris, France.
32. "Team ISAAC," HS 6/366, British National Archives, Kew, UK, p. 1.
33. James Hutchison, *That Drug Danger* (Montrose, Scotland: Standard Press, 1977), p. 104.
34. "Order No. 3," Odres des EMFFI, 3 AG 2 473, Archives National, Paris, France, p. 2.
35. Hutchison, *That Drug Danger*, pp. 107–8.
36. Henri Noguères, Marcel Degliame-Fouché, and Jean Louis Vigier, *Histoire de la Résistance en France, de 1940 à 1945*, 5 vols. (Paris: R. Laffont, 1981), pp. 86–89.
37. Noguères et al., *Histoire de la* Résistance, p. 89.
38. HS 6/522, Team Harry, p. 1 and Team Isaac, HS 6/366, p. 3, National Archives, Kew, UK.
39. Julian Jackson, *France: The Dark Years, 1940–1944* (Oxford: Oxford University Press, 2001), p. 549.
40. "Telegram de ISAAC, 21.6.44," Fond Ziegler 1 K 374/9, Service d'Historique de la Defense, Château de Vincennes, Paris.
41. "Team Isaac," HS 6/366, British National Archives, Kew, UK, pp. 6–7.
42. "Team Harry," HS 6/522, British National Archives, Kew, UK, p. 3.

43. "Team Harry," HS 6/522, British National Archives, Kew, UK, p. 4, and OSS London Microfilm, Air Operations, Reel 9, Frame 0928, NARA (National Archives and Records Administration), College Park, MD.

44. "Team Harry," HS 6/522, British National Archives, Kew, UK, p. 4.

45. "Maps of French Resistance," Audiovisual Collection, Map Room Files, SPECIAL FILES, Papers of Roosevelt, Franklin D.: Papers as President, Franklin D. Roosevelt Presidential Library and Museum, Hyde Park, NY.

46. Telegram Winant to Hull, 8 June 1944, Box 11, Franklin D. Roosevelt-John D. Winant, 1944, MAP ROOM FILES, Franklin D. Roosevelt Presidential Library and Museum, Hyde Park, NY.

47. "OPNAV to ALUSNA London, 13.6.44," Box 11, Franklin D. Roosevelt-John D. Winant, 1944, MAP ROOM FILES, Franklin D. Roosevelt Presidential Library and Museum, Hyde Park, NY.

48. Henry L. Stimson et al., *The Henry Lewis Stimson Diaries in the Yale University Library* (New Haven, CT: Yale University Library, 1973), microfilm. See entries for 14 and 16 June 1944.

49. Stimson diary, entry for 15 June 1944. Donovan often sent raw intelligence to FDR and reports he had received from his own field offices. He simply attached a cover note and passed them along to the president's secretary Grace Tully who placed them at the president's disposal in the Map Room adjacent to the Oval Office. The president could then read about Jedburgh team operations; for instance, he knew the location of Hugh and Hamish in central France, their tactical difficulties, and other very detailed issues regarding the status of Allied Special Operations and the Maquis. The two divisions were probably the 2nd SS "Das Reich" Panzer Division and the 11th Panzer Division, discussed below. Seeing, interpreting, and judging raw intelligence was evidently what FDR wanted to do. However, it is not a practice presidents continue today.

50. OSS Washington Director's Office Administrative Files, 1941–1945 (M1642), United States Air Force Academy Cadet Library, Colorado Springs, CO, Reel 23, Frames 902–905.

51. Thomas Alan Schwartz, *America's Germany: John J. McCloy and the Federal Republic of Germany* (Cambridge, MA: Harvard University Press, 1991), p. 19.

52. "Command of the Organisation of the French Forces of the Interior," 9 June 1944, Box 2, 322 FFI Command and Control of the French Forces of the Interior, SHAEF SGS Records, Dwight D. Eisenhower Presidential Library, Abilene, KS.

53. "SHAEF/17245/6/5/2/Ops(A), Directive to the Commanding General French Forces of the Interior," 17 June 1944, Box 2, 322 FFI Command and Control of the French Forces of the Interior, SHAEF SGS Records, Dwight D. Eisenhower Presidential Library, Abilene, KS.

54. "Brief of Tenth Monthly Progress Report to SHAEF from SFHQ," 14 July 1944, Appendix B, Box 2, 319.1/10 Monthly SOE/SO Reports. SHAEF SGS Records, Dwight D. Eisenhower Presidential Library, Abilene, KS.

55. Paul Durand, *La S.N.C.F. Pendant La Guerre, Sa Résistance à L'occupant* (Paris: Presses universitaires de France, 1968), p. 445.

56. "Brief of Tenth Monthly Progress Report to SHAEF from SFHQ," 14 July 1944, Appendix B, Box 2, 319.1/10 Monthly SOE/SO Reports. SHAEF SGS Records, Dwight D. Eisenhower Presidential Library, Abilene, KS, p. 1.

57. OSS London Microfilm, Roll 10, Vol. 13, book II, Miscellaneous, pp. 15–38, NARA (National Archives and Records Administration), College Park, MD.

58. OSS London Microfilm, Roll 10, Vol. 13, pp. 251, 1085–86, NARA (National Archives and Records Administration), College Park, MD.

59. OSS London Microfilm, Roll 10, Vol. 13, p. 25, NARA (National Archives and Records Administration), College Park, MD.

60. "JOCKEY Report," January 1945, HS 6/568, British National Archives, Kew, UK, p. 1.

61. "Biography," 1945, Biographies of French Agents, HS 8/1001, National Archives, Kew, UK.

62. All the Allied officers had to fight this rumor. Specifically for the Vercors, see EUCALYPTUS Mission Report in OSS/London Microfilm, Roll 7, Vol. 3, Frame 1449, NARA (National Archives and Records Administration), College Park, MD.

63. "Report of Team VEGANIN & DODGE," undated, HS 6/501, British National Archives, Kew, UK.

64. "Report of Team VEGANIN & DODGE," HS 6/501, p. 12.

65. "Report of Team VEGANIN & DODGE," HS 6/501, p. 8.

66. "Report of Team VEGANIN & DODGE," HS 6/501, p. 8. Counter to this are Manierre's kind words regarding Bozambo in his statement after returning from the LuftStalag in May, 1945.

67. "Report of Team VEGANIN & DODGE," HS 6/501, pp. 7–8.

68. "Report of Team VEGANIN & DODGE," HS 6/501, pp. 7–8.

69. "Report of Team DODGE," HS 6/501, British National Archives, Kew, UK, p. 3.

70. "Report of Team DODGE," HS 6/501, p. 6.

71. Cyrus Manierre and Carter Manierre, "Pop's War" (unpublished memoir, 2002), p. 75. In possession of author.

72. "EMFFI Operation Order No. 35," 10 August 1944, Ordres d'Etat Major Forces Française l'Interieur, 3 AG 2 473, Archives National, Paris, France, p. 2.

73. Mission Report 0677-Stinchcomb-21 June 1944. Carpetbagger Archives.

74. OSS/London Microfilm, Roll 8, Vol. 4, Book I, p. 59 and Book II, p. 299.

75. OSS/London Microfilm, Roll 8, Vol. 4, Book II, p. 307.

76. OSS/London Microfilm, Roll 8, Vol, 4, Book II, p. 308.

77. OSS/London Microfilm, Roll 8, Vol, 4, Book II, pp. 308–10, and Gauthier, interview, 6 March 1999.

78. OSS/London Microfilm, Roll 8, Vol 4, Book II, p. 302, 311–12. Indeed, it is clear that the Vichy had little authority at all even before Team Ian arrived. For a discussion on the Vichy's authority in France after the Allied invasion of North Africa, see John F. Sweets, *Choices in Vichy France: The French under Nazi Occupation* (New York: Oxford University Press, 1986) or H. R. Kedward, *In Search of the Maquis: Rural Resistance in Southern France, 1942–1944* (New York: Oxford University Press, 1993). Kedward, *In Search of the Maquis*, has several detailed discussions on localities

in southern France and how the Maquis groups worked to assert local authority from Vichy.

79. OSS/London Microfilm, Roll 8, Vol. 4, Book II, pp. 313–15.

80. OSS/London Microfilm, Roll 8, Vol. 4, Book II, pp. 315–16.

81. Gauthier interview and "Combat de PLEUVILLE, 2 Aout 1944" found in HS 5/527, BNA, Kew, UK. Mamie Gauthier related to me what French Jedburgh Desfarges had described to her in 1994 during her visit to the village where her brother was killed. Her description is largely similar to the report in the SOE records of the event Desfarges wrote in 1944.

82. Gauthier, telephone conversation; and OSS/London Microfilm, Roll 8, Book II, 302, 316–17. The Pleuville church stone floor still retains Bourgoin's and Mondinaud's bloodstains.

83. Max Hastings, *Das Reich: Resistance and the March of the 2nd SS Panzer Division through France, June 1944* (London: M. Joseph, 1981), p. 240.

84. Peter Lieb, *Konventioneller Krieg Oder NS-Weltanschauungskrieg?: Kriegführung und Partisanenbekämpfung in Frankreich 1943/44, Quellen Und Darstellungen Zur Zeitgeschichte; Bd. 69* (München: Oldenbourg, 2007), pp. 360 and 364.

85. Bourbon-Parme, interview, 22 September 2007.

86. Hastings, *Das Reich*, p. 138; HS 8/1001 Biographies, and HS 9/1325/4, National Archives, Kew, UK.

87. "REPORT of AMMONIA," Box 2, Entry 99, RG 226, National Archives and Records Administration II, National Archives, College Park, MD.

88. Fonds du Colonel Zeigler, 1 K 374, de R4 Telegrams, Vincennes, France, Telegrams 2 et 4 Juni 44.

89. Lieb, *Konventioneller*, pp. 357–86.

90. Bruno Leroux, "10 juin 1944: le massacre d'Oradour-sur-Glane" *Dictionnaire Historique de la Resistance* (Paris: Laffont, 2006), p. 634.

91. William J. Donovan and OSS Washington Office, *OSS Washington Director's Office Administrative Files, 1941–1945 (M1642)* (Washington, DC: United States Government, 1998), microfilm. Reel 50, Frames 450–58.

92. Robert Lester et al., *President Franklin D. Roosevelt's Office Files, 1933–1945* (Bethesda, MD: University Publications of America, 1990), microfilm reels,. Part 4, Reel 27, Frames 1–36.

93. 7/6/1944, FDR: Day by Day—The Pare Lorentz Chronology, Grace Tully's Appointment Book, Franklin D. Roosevelt Presidential Library and Museum, Hyde Park, NY.

94. 7/6/1944, FDR: Day by Day—The Pare Lorentz Chronology, Grace Tully's Appointment Book, Franklin D. Roosevelt Presidential Library and Museum, Hyde Park, NY, and Harold Callenders Special to the New York Times. "De Gaulle Power Not Parley Issue; Question of Recognition as Government Will Not Come Up," New York Times (1857—Current file), 8 July 8 1944, http://www.proquest.com .www2.lib.ku.edu:2048/accessed March 18, 2008).

95. Charles de Gaulle, *The Complete War Memoirs of Charles De Gaulle* (New York: Carroll and Graf, 1998), p. 574.

96. De Gaulle, *The Complete War Memoirs*, p. 573.

97. Jackson, *France: The Dark Years*, pp. 518–19.
98. "'Administration' française," *Libération*, 17 Julliet 1944, p. 2. Courtesy of the Center for Research Libraries, Chicago, IL.

Chapter 7: The Free French Battle for Brittany and Eisenhower Battles for the Free French

1. RH 24-25-75, Bundesarchiv-Militärchiv, Freiburg im Breisgau, Germany, and Horst, Boog, Gerhard Krebs, and Detlef Vogel, *The Strategic Air War in Europe and the War in the West and East Asia 1943–1944/5* (New York: Oxford University Press, 2006), p. 517.
2. Peter Lieb, *Konventioneller Krieg oder NS-Weltanschauungskrieg? Kriegführung und Partisanenbekämpfung in Frankreich 1943/44*, Quellen und Darstellungen zur Zeitgeschichte; Bd. 69 (München: Oldenbourg, 2007), p. 525. The infamous Geheim Staatspolizei, often referred to as the Gestapo, had by this time subsumed this into their organization and so the Jedburghs often refer to the region's Kommandeur der Sicherheitspolizei und des Sicherheitsdienst (KdS), or headquarters of the secret police, its agents and soldiers as the Gestapo.
3. Lieb, *Konventioneller*, pp. 65 and 536.
4. "OKW Nr. 002143/44 g.K./WFSt/Qu. (Verw.1) Bekämpfung von Terroristen-Gerichtsbarkeit" 4.3.44, RW 35-551, Bundesarchiv-Militärchiv, Freiburg im Breisgau, Germany.
5. "Kriegsgliederungen 44. Juni," 24/25-256, Bundesarchiv-Militärchiv, Freiburg im Breisgau, Germany.
6. Anlage 4 zum, K. T. B. 6.6.44–30.6.44, XXV AK., RH 24-25/76, Bundesarchiv-Militärchiv, Freiburg im Breisgau, Germany.
7. Robert Kehoe, "Jed Team Frederick, 1944: An Allied Team with the French Resistance," *Studies in Intelligence* (Winter 1998–1999): 12.
8. For the Brittany command structure, see ETOUSA FFI History, "Region M Command Structure" p. 636, File no. 8-3 Fr, acc. No 419-1, Center for Military History, Carlisle Barracks, PA. For decoding the DMR's I used Henri Noguères, Marcel Degliame-Fouché, and Jean Louis Vigier, *Histoire de la Résistance en France, de 1940 Á 1945*, 5 vols., vol. V (Paris: R. Laffont, 1967), pp. 922 and 892.
9. Team George Report in John Mendelsohn, ed., *Covert Warfare Intelligence, Counterintelligence, and Military Deception during the World War II Era*, 18 vols. (New York: Garland, 1989), Vol. 3, pp. 157–58.
10. Team George Report in Mendelsohn, *Covert Warfare Intelligence*, pp. 43 and 158–60.
11. Team George Report in Mendelsohn, *Covert Warfare Intelligence*, pp. 161–62.
12. Team George Report in Mendelsohn, *Covert Warfare Intelligence*, p. 164.
13. Team George Report in Mendelsohn, *Covert Warfare Intelligence*, pp. 164–65.
14. "Fernspuch: Ia/Ia Feld-Kdtr. Vannes Oberstlt. Maser," 11–20 Juni, 1944, K. T. B. RH 24-25/74, Bundesarchiv-Militärchiv, Freiburg im Breisgau, Germany. The log books also note the presence of women among the Maquis.
15. Team George Report in Mendelsohn, *Covert Warfare Intelligence*, pp. 169–70.
16. Team George Report in Mendelsohn, *Covert Warfare Intelligence*, pp. 171–73.

17. Operations Order No. 10, 16 June, Ordres d'EMFFI, 3 AG 2 473, Archives National, Paris, France.
18. Team George Report in Mendelsohn, pp. 45 and 177.
19. Team George Report in Mendelsohn, *Covert Warfare Intelligence*, pp. 179–83.
20. Order No. 6, 2 June 1944, Team Frederick, 3 AG 2 463, Archives National, Paris, France.
21. Kehoe, "Jed Team Frederick, 1944," p. 14.
22. "Report on Team Frederick (By Major Wise)," undated, Frederick Team, HS 6/509, National Archives, Kew, UK, pp. 1–2.
23. United States, Office of Strategic Services, *OSS/London: Special Operations Branch and Secret Intelligence Branch War Diaries, 1944* (microfilm) (Frederick, MD: University Publications of America, 1985), Reel 8, Vol. IV, Book I, p. 36.
24. HS 6/509, p. 2, British National Archives, Kew, UK.
25. Kehoe, "Jed Team Frederick, 1944," pp. 15–16.
26. K. T. B. 6.6.44–7.6.44, RH 26-266, BA-MA, Bundesarchiv-Militärchiv, Freiburg im Breisgau, Germany.
27. Kehoe, "Jed Team Frederick, 1944," p. 17.
28. Kehoe, "Jed Team Frederick, 1944," p. 18.
29. Noguères, Degliame-Fouché, and Vigier, *Histoire de la Résistance en France, de 1940 á 1945.* p. 78.
30. HS 6/509, pp. 3–4, British National Archives, Kew, UK.
31. Kehoe, "Jed Team Frederick," pp. 20–21.
32. Ic Nr. 4203/44, 21.6.1944, RH 19 IV, 133, Fiche 1, Bundesarchiv-Militärchiv, Freiburg im Breisgau, Germany.
33. Report of Major Wise, pp. 3–4, British National Archives, Kew, UK.
34. Report of Team Giles, OSS London Microfilm, Roll 8, Target 1, Vol. 4, Book II, p. 324.
35. "NOTE POUR M. LE COLONEL VERNON CHEF DE L'E.M.F.F.I" 14.6.1944, No. S 365 de CDT Lejeune, BCRA Correspondence; "Operations Order no. 14," pp. 1–4; and "Troops in Finistere, ANNEX C," all found in 3 AG 2 462, Archives National, Paris, France.
36. Report of Team Giles, OSS London Microfilm, Roll 8, Target 1, Vol. 4, Book II, p. 324.
37. Bernard Knox, interview, 8 June 2001.
38. Report of Team Giles, OSS London Microfilm, Roll 8, Target 1, Vol. 4, Book II, pp. 338–39, and Knox, letter in author's possession. Napolean's Hat is the name of a rock formation off the coast of France near the town of Perros-Guirec.
39. "Frederick, June Moon through August non-Moon," HS 8/148, British National Archives, Kew, UK.
40. Report of Team Giles, OSS London Microfilm, Roll 8, Target 1, Vol. 4, Book II, pp. 339 and 623; Joseph de Francesco telephone conversation; Bernard Knox to author, 2 April 2 1999; Knox interview, June 2001.
41. OSS London Microfilm, Roll 8, Target 1, Vol. 4, Part I, p. 327, and Part II, pp. 340–41.
42. OSS London Microfilm, Roll 8, Target 1, Vol. 4, Part I, p. 327, and Part II, pp. 340–41.
43. OSS London Microfilm, Roll 8, Target 1, Vol. 4, Part I, p. 327, and Part II, pp. 327 and 342.

44. OSS London Microfilm, Roll 8, Target 1, Vol. 4, Part I, p. 327, and Part II, pp. 342–43, and Noguères, Degliame-Fouché, and Vigier, *Histoire de la Résistance en France, de 1940 á 1945*, p. 285.

45. OSS London Microfilm, Roll 8, Target 1, Vol. 4, Part I p. 327, and Part II, pp. 328–29 and 343–44.

46. OSS London Microfilm, Roll 8, Target 1, Vol. 4, Part I, p. 327, and Part II, pp. 344–45.

47. OSS London Microfilm, Roll 8, Target 1, Vol. 4, Part I, p. 327, and Part II, p. 345.

48. "Report of Captain Le Zachmeur" pp. 1–4. HS 6/507, British National Archives, Kew, UK.

49. Knox interview.

50. PF HS 9/1377/2, British National Archives, Kew, UK. The Ogden Smith company no longer exists, but their equipment, rods, reels, and tackle still command a great following and high prices.

51. "Report of Capitaine Le Zachmuer on the Death of Major Ogden-Smith 91977 R. A. and Maurice Myodon S. A.S." and "Team FRANCIS: Report of Sergeant Dallow, A. 14403727," both undated but probably written during August or September of 1944. Found in *The French Forces of the Interior*, Washington, DC, Library of Congress, Photoduplication Service, 1977, microfilm, pp. 888–902.

52. Peter Wilkinson and Joan Bright Astley Wilkinson, *Gubbins and SOE* (London: Pen & Sword Paperback, 1997), pp. 168–69; HS 9/1377/2, National Archives, Kew, UK.

53. "Designation of the Commander of the French Forces of the Interior," 23 June 1944, Command and Control of French Forces of Interior, SHAEF SGS, Dwight D. Eisenhower Presidential Library, Abilene, KS.

54. "AGWAR FROM MARSHALL to ETOUSA." SHAEF SGS, Dwight D. Eisenhower Presidential Library, Abilene, KS.

55. Today such duties are referred to as Administrative Control and Operational Command.

56. "Integration with the French," 2.6.44, HS 6/607, British National Archives, Kew, UK.

57. SHAEF/17945/6/5/Ops," 12.6.44, HS 6/607, British National Archives, Kew, UK.

58. "No. D478/FILA, Subject – F. F. I. Hq. 5 July 1944," Command and Control of the French Forces of the Interior, SHAEF SGS, Dwight D. Eisenhower Presidential Library, Abilene, KS.

59. "Notes of Decisions Made at a Meeting Held at SHAEF on 10th JULY, 1944," Command and Control of French Forces of the Interior, SHAEF SGS, Dwight D. Eisenhower Presidential Library, Abilene, KS.

60. "Eric Edward Mockler-Ferryman – born 27.06.1896," HS 9/510/1, British National Archives, Kew, UK.

61. Neither Foot's [M. R. D. Foot, *SOE in France: An Account of the Work of the British Special Operations Executive in France, 1940–1944* (London, UK: Her Majesty's Stationery Office, 1966)] nor Mackenzie's [William Mackenzie, *The Secret History of S. O. E.: Special Operations Executive 1940–1945* (London, UK: St. Ermins Press, 2002)] work mentions this, nor does Redman's name appear in either book. This is understandable since both authors were concerned with the SOE, and Redman was not in that organization.

62. British Army Registry, HMSO, National Archives, Kew, UK.

63. "Eisenhower from Donovan, OSS," August 2, 1944, Officer of the Director's Files, Microfilm, Roll 81, Frame 14, United States Air Force Academy, CO.

64. "Eisenhower from Donovan, OSS," August 2, 1944, Officer of the Director's Files, Microfilm, Roll 81, Frames 36 and 39, United States Air Force Academy, CO.

65. Fichier 2, Carton 8, Fonds Ziegler, 1 K 374, Service d'Historique de la Defense, Château de Vincennes, Paris, France.

66. "SITUATION OF *RÉSISTANCE* IN BRITTANY AS AT JULY 29, 1944," Folder 12, Box 329, Entry 190, RG 226, National Archives and Records Administration, College Park, MD.

67. "FFI/214," 21st July 1944, Jedburgh Documents, 3 AG 2 462, Archive National, Paris, France.

68. "Journal des Marches & Operations du Commandement des F. F. I. en Bretagne," United States Army, European Theater of Operations, *The French Forces of the Interior* (Washington, DC: Library of Congress, Photoduplication Service, 1977), microfilm, pp. 769–73.

69. OSS London Microfilm, Reel 8, Target 2, Vol. 4, Book II, pp. 346–48.

70. OSS London Microfilm, Reel 8, Target 2, Vol. 4, Book II, pp. 346–50.

71. United States, Office of Strategic Services, *OSS/London: Special Operations Branch and Secret Intelligence Branch War Diaries, 1944*, microfilm, p. 331.

72. United States, Office of Strategic Services, *OSS/London: Special Operations Branch and Secret Intelligence Branch War Diaries, 1944*, microfilm, p. 330.

73. United States, Office of Strategic Services, *OSS/London: Special Operations Branch and Secret Intelligence Branch War Diaries, 1944*, microfilm, p. 350.

74. Kehoe, "Jed Team Frederick, 1944," pp. 34–35.

75. United States, Office of Strategic Services, *OSS/London: Special Operations Branch and Secret Intelligence Branch War Diaries, 1944*, microfilm, pp. 333 and 351–52.

76. United States, Office of Strategic Services., *OSS/London: Special Operations Branch and Secret Intelligence Branch War Diaries, 1944* (microfilm), p. 366.

77. United States, Office of Strategic Services., *OSS/London: Special Operations Branch and Secret Intelligence Branch War Diaries, 1944* (microfilm), p. 377.

78. United States, Office of Strategic Services, *OSS/London: Special Operations Branch and Secret Intelligence Branch War Diaries, 1944* (microfilm), pp. 336 and 353; Claude E. Boillot, U. S. Representative, Suez Canal Company (Compagnie Universelle du Canal Maritime de Suez), 1952–78, Papers, 1924–1984, Dwight D. Eisenhower Presidential Library; and Foot, *SOE in France*, pp. 407–8.

79. HS 6/515, British National Archives, Kew, UK. This is the SOE version of the OSS copy of the report used above for all my sourcing regarding Team Giles. The difference between the two reports is only in their format. However, in January of 1945, Captain Grall read the final version of what he and Knox had written. He was disappointed with the translation into English and some of the re-crafting of the report by the SOE translator and Knox after Grall departed the UK. He believed the translation made it appear to the reader that Knox had been the team's leader. He did not agree with that, and amicably wished to emphasize that their team's good relationship was one of cooperation. Furthermore, Knox's views on the Aloes mission was not Grall's and he provided more context on what Eon, Dewavrin, and

the mission was attempting to do. In sum, he thought Aloes performed well in the operations against the German fortifications around Brest. Furthermore, he wished to go on another mission with Knox and Tack. Giles was placed on reserve for a second mission in the east of France but was not deployed.

80. United States Army, European Theater of Operations, *The French Forces of the Interior* (Washington, DC: Library of Congress, Photoduplication Service, 1977), microfilm, p. 867.

81. United States, Office of Strategic Services, *OSS/London: Special Operations Branch and Secret Intelligence Branch War Diaries, 1944*, microfilm, pp. 186–88; and "Jedburghs," 22 July 1944, 3 AG 462, Archives National, Paris, France. Note next to George's status says, "may be Gestapo-controlled."

82. United States, Office of Strategic Services, *OSS/London: Special Operations Branch and Secret Intelligence Branch War Diaries, 1944*, microfilm, pp. 188–203.

83. United States, Office of Strategic Services, *OSS/London: Special Operations Branch and Secret Intelligence Branch War Diaries, 1944*, microfilm, p. 209.

84. United States, Office of Strategic Services, *OSS/London: Special Operations Branch and Secret Intelligence Branch War Diaries, 1944*, microfilm, p. 217.

85. M. R. D. Foot, *SOE in France: An Account of the Work of the British Special Operations Executive in France, 1940–1944* (London, UK: Her Majesty's Stationery Office, 1966), p. 403.

86. "Additif du Capitaine LEBEL, Paul" 3 Janvier 1945, HS 6/515, British National Archives, Kew, UK.

87. Knox, interview.

88. Knox letter to the author, and Foot, *SOE in France*, p. 403.

89. Operations, *The French Forces of the Interior*. Annex 1. "Situation as to the *Résistance* in Brittany as of 29 July 1944," p. 666; and "Arms Deliveries, July 44," Eleventh Monthly SFHQ Report, Monthly SOE/SO Reports, SHAEF SGS Records, 1943–1945, Dwight D. Eisenhower Presidential Library, Abilene, KS.

90. Luc Capdevila, *Les Bretons au lendemain de l'Occupation: Imaginaire et comportement d'une sortie de guerre 1944–1945* (Rennes, France: Presses Universitaires de Rennes, 1999), pp. 23–24.

91. Knox, letter to author.

92. Kehoe, "Jed Team Frederick, 1944," p. 34; Robert Kehoe, "Jed Team Frederick, 1944: An Allied Team with the French Resistance," *Studies in Intelligence* (Winter 1998–1999).

Chapter 8: Setting the Trap

1. "2nd SS Panzer Division, formerly 7th Army Reserve now designated Army H Group Reserve," 22 June 1944, Signals intelligence passed to the Prime Minister, HW 1/3003, British National Archives, Kew, UK; and Max Hastings, *Das Reich: Resistance and the March of the 2nd SS Panzer Division through France, June 1944* (London: M. Joseph, 1981), p. 210.

2. Hastings, *Das Reich*, p. 127.

3. Martin Blumenson and Center of Military History, *Breakout and Pursuit, CMH Pub; 7–5* (Washington, DC: Center of Military History, US Army, 2005), p. 344.

4. "SHAEF 2FI/IFT," 6 June 1944, Supreme Headquarters, Allied Expeditionary Force, Office of Secretary, General Staff: Records, 1943–45, microfilm, 311.5, Vol. I, Code Names and Code Words, Dwight D. Eisenhower Presidential Library, Abilene, KS, and Robert Le Blanc, telephone conversation, 22 January 2008. Robert Le Blanc served under Lt. Col. Powell in SF Detachment 11 with the US 3rd Army.

5. Jeffrey J. Clarke, Robert Ross Smith, and Center of Military History, *Riviera to the Rhine*, World War II 50th anniversary commemorative ed., *Cmh Pub; 7–10* (Washington, DC: Center of Military History, US Government Printing Office, 1993), p. 21.

6. "PM to Harry Hopkins," 6 August 1944, Map Room Files, to and from Harry Hopkins, Franklin D. Roosevelt Presidential Library and Museum, Hyde Park, NY.

7. "Number 36 Personal and Top Secret, for the Prime Minister from Mr. Harry Hopkins," 7 August 1944, Map Room Files, to and from Harry Hopkins, Franklin D. Roosevelt Presidential Library and Museum, Hyde Park, NY.

8. Arthur Layton Funk, *Hidden Ally: The French Resistance, Special Operations, and the Landings in Southern France, 1944*, Contributions in Military Studies, No. 122 (New York: Greenwood Press, 1992), pp. 38–39.

9. 370.64 France Vol. II, French Resistance Groups, Dwight D. Eisenhower Presidential Library, Abilene, KS.

10. "Monthly Progress Report. Summary of Resistance Activities 6 July–6 August," 14 August 1944, Monthly SOE/SO Reports, SHAEF SGS Records, Series II, 319.1/10, Dwight D. Eisenhower Presidential Library, Abilene, KS.

11. "Butcher's Diary," 17 July 1944, Dwight D. Eisenhower: Papers, Pre-Presidential, 1916–52, July 17–August 30, 1944 (1), Dwight D. Eisenhower Presidential Library, Abilene, KS.

12. "Use of Jedburghs," 28 July 1944, BCRA Documents—Jedburghs, 3 AG 2 462, Archives National, Paris, France.

13. Laub, Thomas. "The Politics of Occupation: The German Military Administration in France, 1940–1944" pp. 282–86.

14. "Ausserhalb des Gesetzes!" copie des *Pariser Zeitung*, RW 35/551, Bundesarchiv-Militärchiv, Freiburg im Breisgau.

15. Dossiers 1, GB Cabinet du Koenig, 8 P 1, Service d'Historique de la Defense, Château de Vincennes, Paris, France.

16. "Ordinance," 9 June 1944, Command and Control of French Forces of the Interior, Supreme Headquarters, Allied Expeditionary Force, Office of Secretary, General Staff: Records, 1943–45, 322, Dwight D. Eisenhower Presidential Library, Abilene, KS.

17. "Brassards," 28 June 1944, Resistance after D Day, HS 6/377, British National Archives, Kew, UK.

18. "K. T. B.," Juni 1944, OB West Ic, RH 19 IV/133, Bundesarchiv-Militärchiv, Freiburg im Breisgau.

19. "Commandement Supérieur Des Forces Françaises en Grande Bretagne," 1944, GB Cabinet du Gen Koenig, Dossiers 1, 8 P 1, Service d'Historique de la Defense, Château de Vincennes, Paris, France.

20. "French Forces of the Interior," 22 July 1944, Command and Control of French Forces of the Interior, Supreme Headquarters, Allied Expeditionary Force, Office of

Secretary, General Staff: Records, 1943–45, 322, Dwight D. Eisenhower Presidential Library, Abilene, KS. The German Organisation Todt was constituted of many Eastern Europeans pressed into service in order to build France's coastal defenses. The German government broadcast that many of these people were now bona fide members of their armed forces and should be viewed as legal combatants.

21. "EMFFI Operation Order No. 18, Amendment No. 2 Operation BUICK," 28 July 1944, EMFFI Ordres, 3 AG 2 473, Archives National, Paris, France.

22. United States, Office of Strategic Services, *OSS/London: Special Operations Branch and Secret Intelligence Branch War Diaries, 1944*, microfilm, Roll 10, Target 6, Vol. 13, Book II, p. 65.

23. "Operations Order No. 21, 31 July 1944" 3 AG 2 473, Archives National, Paris, France.

24. "Supplies to Resistance Groups," 31 July 1944, France, Vol. II French Resistance Groups (Guerilla Warfare) SHAEF SGS Records, Dwight D. Eisenhower Presidential Library, Abilene, KS.

25. "SPOC Jedburgh Planning document," 3 AG 2 462, Archives National, Paris, France.

26. FWD-12522, 1 August 44, 370.64, France, Vol. II, French Resistance Groups (Guerrilla Warfare), SHAEF, Office of Secretary, General Staff Records, 1943–1945, Dwight D. Eisenhower Presidential Library, Abilene, KS.

27. 2 August 1944, 3 AG 2 462, Archives National, Paris, France. From the nomenclature of the teams it is clear that male first names are being used by London while Algiers is using automobile names or chemicals. "Team Joseph" never came to fruition.

28. FX-78011, 2 August 1944, France, Vol. II, French Resistance Groups (Guerrilla Warfare), SHAEF, Office of Secretary, General Staff Records, 1943–1945, Dwight D. Eisenhower Presidential Library, Abilene, KS.

29. United States, Office of Strategic Services, *OSS/London: Special Operations Branch and Secret Intelligence Branch War Diaries, 1944*, microfilm, Roll 8, Target 2, Vol. 4, Book II, p. 267.

30. "Operations Order No. 28," 3 August, 1944, EMFFI Ordres, 3 AG 2 473, Archives National, Paris, France.

31. United States, Office of Strategic Services, *OSS/London: Special Operations Branch and Secret Intelligence Branch War Diaries, 1944*, microfilm, Roll 8, Target 2, Vol. 4, Book II, p. 271.

32. United States, Office of Strategic Services, *OSS/London: Special Operations Branch and Secret Intelligence Branch War Diaries, 1944*, microfilm, Roll 8, Target 2, Vol. 4, Book II, p. 271.

33. Team Report of Ivor, HS 6/528, British National Archives, Kew, UK.

34. Team Report of Ivor, HS 6/528, British National Archives, Kew, UK. Loosmore's messages in Vernon's papers in SHD, Vincennes, are from Ivor but read that they are from Andy. The pencil markings on the original message question how this could be.

35. Note from Bourne-Patterson, 10 August 1944, Laisse 1, 3 AG 2 462, Archives National, Paris, France.

36. United States, Office of Strategic Services, *OSS/London: Special Operations Branch and Secret Intelligence Branch War Diaries, 1944*, microfilm, "ALEC Team Report," Roll 8, Target 4, Vol. 4, Book IV, p. 680.

37. United States, Office of Strategic Services, *OSS/London: Special Operations Branch and Secret Intelligence Branch War Diaries, 1944*, microfilm, "ALEC Team Report," Roll 8, Target 4, Vol. 4, Book IV, p. 813, and Dick Franklin, "Jedburg" (unpublished memoir, 2004), p. 209; telephone Franklin interview 23 May 2008.

38. "Position in Zone Sud and Need for Arms," undated (likely 15 to 25 June), Appendix A, HS 6/377, National Archives, Kew, UK.

39. B-17s could only carry 10 containers while the B-24 Liberator carried 15.

40. SHAEF 17240/23/Ops, 15 August 1944, 370.64 France, Vol. II, French Resistance Groups (Guerilla Warfare), SHAEF SGS Records, Dwight D. Eisenhower Presidential Library, Abilene, KS.

41. SHAEF 17240/23/Ops, 15 August 1944, 370.64 France, Vol. II, French Resistance Groups (Guerilla Warfare), SHAEF SGS Records, Dwight D. Eisenhower Presidential Library, Abilene, KS.

42. "To C.D." 27 July 1944, HS 9/510/1, British National Archives, Kew, UK.

43. "EMFFI Operation Order No. 30," 6 August 1944, Ordres d'Etat Major Forces Française l'Interieur, 3 AG 2 473, Archives National, Paris, France.

44. "Order No. 31" 6 August 1944, 3 AG 2 473, British Archives National, Paris, France.

45. Horst Boog, Gerhard Krebs, and Detlef Vogel, *The Strategic Air War in Europe and the War in the West and East Asia 1943–1944/5* (New York: Oxford University Press, 2006), p. 561.

46. Martin Blumenson and Center of Military History, *Breakout and Pursuit, CMH Pub; 7–5* (Washington, DC: Center of Military History, U.S. Army, 2005), p. 567.

47. HW 1/3173, British National Archives, Kew, UK.

48. Peter Lieb, *Konventioneller Krieg oder NS-Weltanschauungskrieg?: Kriegführung und Partisanenbekämpfung in Frankreich 1943/44*, Quellen und Darstellungen zur Zeitgeschichte; Bd. 69 (München: Oldenbourg, 2007), p. 542.

49. RH 19 IV 62 Karte, Bundesarchiv-Militärchiv, Freiburg im Breisgau; Blumenson and Center of Military History, *Breakout and Pursuit*, p. 567.

50. HS 8/1001, Biographies, British National Archives, Kew, UK.

51. "Fonds Bourgès-Maunoury—Cables December 1943 to September 1944," 1943–1944, Papiers Bourgès-Maunoury messages to London as Polygone, 1 K 375, Service historique de l'Armée de Terre, Paris, France.

52. "Fonds Bourgès-Maunoury—Cables December 1943 to September 1944," 1943–1944, Papiers Bourgès-Maunoury messages to London as POLYGONE, 1 K 375, Service historique de l'Armée de Terre, Paris, France. These are copies of some of his messages to London while in France. One can also see many of his messages in 3 AG 2 482 and 483, Archive National, Paris, France. He is persistently working to coordinate activities, warn colleagues of who was arrested, appoint replacement subordinate leaders, arranging meetings, and passing on news to London and Algiers. Many times during the summer of 1944 he sends and receives multiple messages each day using several radio operators. The amount of traffic from one person under such circumstances is impressive. For his success in the Correze in August see Louis and Marcel Barbanceys Le Moigne, *Sedentaires, Refractaires, Et Maquisards: L'armée Secrète En Haute Correze, 1942–1944* (Moulins: Les Imprimiers Reunies, 1979), p. 362.

53. "'BUGATTI Report,'" undated, Team Bugatti, HS 6/490, British National Archives, Kew, UK.

54. "Report on Mission in France," 18 September 1944, Miss A. M. Walters, COLETTE of WHEELWRIGHT Circuit, HS 6/583, British National Archives, Kew, UK.

55. Beavan Papers: Jedburgh Interviews; Thomas MacPherson, interview, June 21, 2002; Bourbon-Parme, interview, 2002.

56. "Messages de R4," "Dossier EMFFI Histoire de la Résistance," Fonds Ziegler, 1 K 374, Service historique de l'Armée de Terre, Paris, France.

57. "Team Report," undated, HS 6/498, British National Archives, Kew, UK.

58. "Team Report," undated, HS 6/549, British National Archives, Kew, UK.

59. K. T. B. Ia, 19 AOK, RH-19 IV, 133, Bundesarchiv-Militärchiv, Freiburg im Breisgau, Germany.

60. Henri Noguères, Marcel Degliame-Fouché, and Jean Louis Vigier, *Histoire de la Résistance en France, de 1940 à 1945*, I–V vols. (Paris: R. Laffont, 1981).

61. Team CHRYSLER Report, HS 6/495, British National Archives, Kew, UK.

62. John K. Singlaub, interview with author, 9 June 2001.

63. "Report of the JAMES Mission," undated, Team Report, HS 6/530, British National Archives, Kew, UK, p. 4.

64. Singlaub, interview, 9 June 2001.

65. "de ELLIPSE," 6 September 1944, ELLIPSE Telegrams, 3 AG 2 561, Archives National, Paris, France.

66. Team JAMES Report, HS 6/530, British National Archives, Kew, UK, p. 12.

67. "de ELLIPSE," 10 September 1944, ELLIPSE Telegrams, 3 AG 2 561, Archives National, Paris, France.

68. United States, Office of Strategic Services, *OSS/London: Special Operations Branch and Secret Intelligence Branch War Diaries, 1944*, microfilm, Roll 8, Target 4, Vol. 4, Book IV, p. 686.

69. 13 P 156, Service d'Historique de la Defense, Château de Vincennes, Paris, France. This is a collection of records and files provided to the French Army sometime after the war for R5. Colonel Riviere, the FFI commander for the Region under Dechelette apparently approved what was included. Guingouin, Raymond Chomel, Theogene Briant, and many of the other leaders are included in this haphazard but comprehensive file numbering nearly 200 pages. It is filled with detailed accounts of daily activity from before D-Day to when the area was liberated in late September. The sheer volume of destruction is overwhelming.

70. United States, Office of Strategic Services, *OSS/London: Special Operations Branch and Secret Intelligence Branch War Diaries, 1944*, microfilm. Roll 8, Target 4, Vol. 4, Book IV, p. 695.

71. Lieb, *Konventioneller*, pp. 454–55.

72. "Letter to R. Harris Smith," 14 April 1971, Paul van der Stricht Papers, Folder 1, Hoover Institution Archives, Stanford, CA.

73. "Brittany HQ 3rd Army After Action Report," United States Army, European Theater of Operations, *The French Forces of the Interior* (Washington, DC: Library of Congress, Photoduplication Service, 1977), microfilm, p. 724.

74. Robert Le Blanc, interview, 22 January 2008. Robert Le Blanc served as one of Powell's officers in SF Detachment 11. He was detailed out to work with different

units and would always work to keep the Corps commander up to date on what the FFI could do for him.

75. "TO WATERMARK," 31 August 1944, Laisse 479, 3 AG 2 479, Archives National, Paris, France.

76. "K. T. B. Nr. 5" 11 June 1944, GenKdo. LXXXVI A. K. Abt. Ia RH 24-86-11, Bundesarchiv-Militärchiv, Freiburg im Briesgau, Germany.

77. Fichia 4, Cables address a EMFFI London par Region R, 1 K 374 9, Service d'Historique de la Defense, Château de Vincennes, Paris, France.

78. Beavan's interview with MacPherson, June 2002.

79. "JULIAN report," HS 6/536, National Archives, Kew, UK.

80. "Ordre General d'operations," 30 Aout 1944, Region R5 departement de l'Indre Rapports, Avril 44–5 Fevier 45, 13 P 156, Service d'Historique de la Defense, Château de Vincennes, Paris, France.

81. JULIAN report, British National Archives, Kew, UK.

82. Fond R5—Indre, 13 P 156, Service d'Historique de la Defense, Château de Vincennes, Paris, France.

83. Julian's report states that no one from their team was at this meeting but says that Lt. Magill was there. The French report does not mention Magill until the following day. See p. 730 and "Exposé sur le déroulement des négociations relatives à la reddition du Généralmajor ELSTER, commandant la Marchgruppe sud" in 13 P 156, Region 5 Fond 2, Service d'Historique de la Defense, Château de Vincennes, Paris, France.

84. Lieb, *Konventioneller*, p. 459.

85. Team Julian message on 8 September 44, Colonel Ziegler's, Messages de R5, Carton 9, Fichier 4, 1 K 374, Service d'Historique de la Defense, Château de Vincennes, Paris, France.

86. Julian Report, OSS/SO London Microfilm, Roll 8, Target 4, Vol. 4, Book IV, p. 732.

87. Julian Report, OSS/SO London Microfilm, Roll 8, Target 4, Vol. 4, Book IV, p. 733.

88. IVOR, OSS/SO London Microfilm, Roll 8, Target 4, Vol. 4, Book IV, p. 656.

89. Team JULIAN Report, OSS/SO London Microfilm, Roll 8, Target 4, Vol. 4, Book IV, pp. 735–36.

90. Report of Pearl Witherington, HS 6/587, British National Archives, Kew, UK, p. 7.

91. Colin Beavan, *Operation Jedburgh: D-Day and America's First Shadow War* (New York: Viking, 2006). Beavan's main source for the whole event is his interview with Sir Tommy MacPherson in June of 2002. In his interview with Beavan, MacPherson seems to be unaware of his fellow Jedburgh colleague Arthur H. Clutton's work the day before he talked with Elster and there is no mention of Colonel Chomel at all. In Beavan's notes of his interviews, which he kindly made available to me, Cox claimed to be just a liaison and to have not taken part in the negotiations. But despite Cox telling this to Beavan and his book listing many of the sources I use above with the exception of French Army Archives in Paris, he still gives MacPherson all the weight in the story and makes it look as if Magill merely "skidded up in a jeep" just as MacPherson and Elster supposedly concluded the whole arrangement. It appears that Beavan inflated MacPherson's and Cox's conversation with Elster on June 11 in which they were merely ironing out procedures and not conducting the hard

negotiations that occurred on June 9 and 10. In fact, Beavan's notes of his conversation with John Cox reveal that "we [Cox and MacPherson] never had anything to do with telling Elster to stop. That was the resistance chap"—which must refer to Colonel Chomel. But unfortunately, the resulting description in Beavan's book on pages 285 to 291 drops Clutton, Chomel, Macon, and their staff officers completely from the negotiations. Thus the event's complex nature is completely obscured, and instead of the US forces of the 83rd Division getting all the credit, two British Jedburghs appear to have achieved a miracle.

92. Stanley P. Hirshson, *General Patton: A Soldier's Life* (New York: HarperCollins, 2002), p. 540.
93. "Regions R5 etats des pertes," 13 P 62, Service d'Historique de la Defense, Château de Vincennes, Paris, France.
94. "NOTE sur la Brigade CHARLES MARTEL," 13 P 156, Region 5 Fond 2, Service d'Historique de la Defense, Château de Vincennes, Paris, France.
95. "Report of ISAAC/VERVEINE," 1944, Team Isaac, HS 6/366, British National Archives, Kew, UK, pp. 10–11.
96. Team Isaac, HS 6/366, British National Archives, Kew, UK, p. 11.
97. Boog, Krebs, and Vogel, *The Strategic Air War in Europe and the War in the West and East Asia 1943–1944/5*, p. 661.
98. Erasmus Kloman, telephone interview, 21 August 2005.

Chapter 9: The Fog of War in Eastern France

1. See Team report of GILES HS 6/515 and LEE HS 6/538, British National Archives, Kew, UK.
2. Compare Team Giles' comments of interrogation with Team Maurice's. The latter found Germans exhausted from a long march; many of them were not frontline combat troops. Giles found prisoners unwilling to believe that Rennes had fallen and that Allied troops were that far into France.
3. Singlaub, interview with author, 9 June 2001.
4. FFI/214, 21st July 1944, Jedburgh Documents, 3 AG 2 462, Archive National, Paris, France.
5. Emails and unpublished work by Colin Burbidge, nephew of Victor Gough, 18 May 2008. In possession of author.
6. Henri Noguères, Marcel Degliame-Fouché, and Jean Louis Vigier, *Histoire de la Résistance en France, de 1940 à 1945*, 5vols. (Paris: R. Laffont, 1981), p. 545.
7. Gilbert Grandval and A. Jean Collin, *Libération de l'est de la France* (Paris: Hachette, 1974), pp. 13–20.
8. John Hislop. *Anything but a Soldier* as quoted in "Captain Victor Gough," Burbidge manuscript, in possession of the author.
9. "Report on Team JACOB," 1945, Team JACOB, HS 6/529, British National Archives, Kew, UK, p. 1.
10. United States, Office of Strategic Services, *OSS/London: Special Operations Branch and Secret Intelligence Branch War Diaries, 1944*, microfilm. Roll 8, Target 4, Volume 4, Book IV, pp. 765–66.

11. Team JACOB Report, HS 6/529, British National Archives, Kew, UK, pp. 2–3.

12. Telegram from SPOC to Haskell, 18 Aug 44, Dossier 1, 3 AG 2 462, Archives National, Paris, France.

13. Haskell to Van der Stricht, 22 Aug 44, Dossier 1, 3 AG 2 462, Archives National, Paris, France.

14. Rosell to Haskell, 22 Aug 44, Dossier 1, 3 AG 2 462, Archives National, Paris, France.

15. Rosell to Haskell, 22 Aug 44, Dossier 1, 3 AG 2 462, Archives National, Paris, France.

16. Letter from OG Alice member Francis Coleman, 10 March 1987 to Carter Manierre as quoted in Manierre and Manierre, "Pop's War" (unpublished memoir), p. 79.

17. Team Report of Dodge, HS 6/501, British National Archives, Kew, UK.

18. Manierre and Manierre, "Pop's War" (unpublished memoir), p. 79.

19. EMFFI Operation Order No. 34, 8 August 1944, Ordres d'Etat Major Forces Française l'Interieur, 3 AG 2 473, Archives National, Paris, France.

20. EMFFI Operation Order No. 34, 8 August 1944, Ordres d'Etat Major Forces Française l'Interieur, 3 AG 2 473, Archives National, Paris, France.

21. "From Major Cox to Col Haskell," 14 August 1944, 3 AG 2 462, microfilm 171/178, Archives National, Paris, France.

22. Most of these teams bounced from one operations order to the next until the last teams were sent to France in mid-September.

23. Jacques Chaban-Delmas, *Mémoires pour Demain* (Paris: Flammarion, 1997), p. 83.

24. Lt. Col. Hutchison's exasperation with SFHQ discussed in Chapters 6 and 8 demonstrated one aspect of this tension between those who believed EMFFI London needed to direct the FFI while those in France, whether French, British or American, often believed that direction should be done from within the country.

25. Horst Boog, Gerhard Krebs, and Detlef Vogel, *The Strategic Air War in Europe and the War in the West and East Asia 1943–1944/5* (New York: Oxford University Press, 2006), p. 614.

26. "Compte Rendu sur l'action deroulee le 27 Aout a Forfry," undated, Report of Spiritualist, HS 6/571, British National Archives, Kew, UK.

27. Team Aubrey Report, HS 6/483, HS 7/18 & 19 section VI, and HS 9/288, National Archives, Kew, UK; and M. R. D. Foot, *SOE in France: An Account of the Work of the British Special Operations Executive in France, 1940–1944* (London, UK: Her Majesty's Stationery Office, 1966), p. 411.

28. Gaston Costeaux and Emile Fortier, "Rapport sur l'activite de la mission 'AUGUSTE,'" WASH-COMMO-OP-74, Box 2, Folder 23, Entry 103, RG 226, National Archives and Records Administration, College Park, MD.

29. Samuel J. Lewis, *Jedburgh Team Operations in Support of 12th Army Group, August 1944* (Washington, DC: Combat Studies Institute, Command and General Staff College, United States Army, 1991).

30. Noguères, Degliame-Fouché, and Vigier, *Histoire de la Résistance en France, de 1940 á 1945*, Vol. 3, p. 107. Information on Chaumet is sparse with only a listing of his name among code names in HS 6/468, British National Archives, Kew, UK, and an entry of his personnel file in SOE records. He is not mentioned in the works of Foot,

Noguères, nor Dewavrin, but he is described briefly in Bruno Leroux's entry on Bureau d'Opérations Aériennes (BOA) in the *Dictionnaire Historique de la Résistance: Résistance Intérieure et France Libre, Bouquins* (Paris: Laffont, 2006) on page 168.

31. United States, Office of Strategic Services, *OSS/London: Special Operations Branch and Secret Intelligence Branch War Diaries, 1944*, microfilm, Reel 8, Target 6, Vol. IV, Book 4, pp. 23–24; and Gaston Costeaux, and Emile Fortier, "Rapport sur l'activite de la mission 'AUGUSTE,'" National Archives and Records Administration, College Park, MD.

32. United States, Office of Strategic Services, *OSS/London: Special Operations Branch and Secret Intelligence Branch War Diaries, 1944*, microfilm, Reel 8, Target 6, Vol. IV, Book 4, pp. 25.

33. Costeaux, Gaston, and Fortier Emile, "Rapport sur l'activite de la mission 'AUGUSTE,'" NARA II (National Archives and Records Administration), College Park, MD, pp. 6–7.

34. United States, Office of Strategic Services., *OSS/London: Special Operations Branch and Secret Intelligence Branch War Diaries, 1944*, microfilm, Reel 8, Target 6, Vol. IV, Book 4, pp. 27.

35. United States, Office of Strategic Services, *OSS/London: Special Operations Branch and Secret Intelligence Branch War Diaries, 1944*, microfilm, Reel 8, Target 6, Vol. IV, Book 4, p. 25.

36. In Zeigler's handwriting on one of the planning documents is his list of teams by region and his math in the margins with the comment: "4 par jours" noting the rate they would be deployed if the plan went as designed. The emphasis is Zeigler's. Not able to achieve that kind of pace on a regular basis, EMFFI did manage to deploy four teams on August 28.

37. Operations Order No. 34, 8 August 1944, Ordres d'Etat Major Forces Française l'Interieur, 3 AG 473, Archives National, Paris, France; with amendments 1–4.

38. "To: All Jedburgh teams for France still in England," 26 August 1944, BCRA Documents—Jedburghs, 3 AG 2 462, Archives National, Paris, France.

39. United States, Office of Strategic Services, *OSS/London: Special Operations Branch and Secret Intelligence Branch War Diaries, 1944*, microfilm, Reel 8, Target 6, Vol. IV, Book 4, p. 7.

40. All the team deployment dates were taken from HS 7/19 maps, National Archives, Kew, UK. Maurice's deployment date is listed incorrectly on the map. The argument with the crew is related in the Team's report, HS 6/542, pp. 2–3, National Archives, Kew, UK.

41. "Team MAURICE," undated, MAURICE Report, HS 6/542, p. 1, National Archives, Kew, UK.

42. François Marcot, and Angèle Baud, *La Résistance dans le Jura* (Besançon: Cêtre, 1985), p. 86.

43. Marcot and Baud, *La Résistance dans le Jura*, p. 3.

44. Marcot and Baud, *La Résistance dans le Jura*, p. 108. Marcot does not mention the DMR, Pierre Hanneton, in his book on the Jura.

45. "Telegrams de Region D," Fonds du Ziegler, 1 K 374, Carton 9, Fichier 3, SHAT (Le service historique de l'armée de terre), Vincennes, France.

46. Joe de Francesco, letter to author, 3 March 1999.
47. De Francesco, telephone conversation with author, 3 March 1999.
48. "Operations Order, 41," 20 August 1944, Ordres d'Etat Major Forces Française l'Interieur, 3 AG 2 473, Archives National, Paris, France, pp. 1–2.
49. Peter Lieb, *Konventioneller Krieg oder NS-Weltanschauungskrieg?: Kriegführung und Partisanenbekämpfung in Frankreich 1943/44*, Quellen und Darstellungen zur Zeitgeschichte; Bd. 69 (München: Oldenbourg, 2007), pp. 339–50.
50. Lieb, *Konventioneller*, Amendments 1–5, 20 to 28 August 1944.
51. "Telegram de PLANETE," 3 September 1944, 1 K 374, Archives National, Paris, France.
52. "FWD-13971, FROM SHAEF FORWARD TO SHAEF MISSION TO FRENCH FOR REDMAN, 6 Sept 44," "Various," Various, France Vol. II. French Resistance Groups (Guerilla Warfare), Supreme Headquarters, Allied Expeditionary Force, Office of Secretary, General Staff: Records, 1943–45, Series II, 370.64 (alternately Reel 52, Frames 516–7), Dwight D. Eisenhower Presidential Library, Abilene, KS.
53. "FWD-13971, FROM SHAEF FORWARD TO SHAEF MISSION TO FRENCH FOR REDMAN, 6 Sept 44"; "SHAEF AEF Mission to France from Redman to SHAEF FWD" 11 September 1944.
54. John C. Warren, *USAF Historical Study 97: Airborne Operations in World War II, European Theater* (Maxwell Air Force Base, AL: Air University, 1956), p. 81.
55. 26 August 1944, Cables a EMFFI Londres par D et P, Ziegler, Papers, 1 K 374/9, SHAT (Le service historique de l'armée de terre), Vincennes, France.
56. "June and July EMFFI Monthly Reports to SHAEF," SGS Reports, Dwight D. Eisenhower Presidential Library, Abilene, KS.
57. "from ALASTAIR to EMFFI," 5 September 1944, Cables a EMFFI Londres par D et P, Ziegler Papers, 1 K 374/9, SHAT (Le service historique de l'armée de terre), Vincennes, France.
58. United States, Office of Strategic Services, *OSS/London: Special Operations Branch and Secret Intelligence Branch War Diaries, 1944*, microfilm, Reel 8, Target 5, Vol. 4, Book V.
59. Grandval and Collin, *Libération de l'est de la France*, p. 186.
60. United States, Office of Strategic Services, *OSS/London: Special Operations Branch and Secret Intelligence Branch War Diaries, 1944*, microfilm, Reel 10, Target 6, Vol. 13, Book II, p. 79.
61. Boog, Krebs, and Vogel, *The Strategic Air War in Europe*, p. 667.
62. "Means of Implementing Plans," 1 August 1944, Records of the Office of Strategic Services, Folder 12, Box 329, Entry 190, RG 226, National Archives II, College Park, MD.
63. United States, Office of Strategic Services, *OSS/London: Special Operations Branch and Secret Intelligence Branch War Diaries, 1944*, microfilm, Reel 8, Target 5, Vol. 4, Book V, p. 8.
64. Paul Moniez, interview, 11 September 2007.
65. United States, Office of Strategic Services, *OSS/London: Special Operations Branch and Secret Intelligence Branch War Diaries, 1944*, microfilm, Reel 8, Target 5, Vol. 4, Book V, p. 14.

66. United States, Office of Strategic Services, *OSS/London: Special Operations Branch and Secret Intelligence Branch War Diaries, 1944*, microfilm, Reel 8, Target 5, Vol. 4, Book V, pp. 15–16.

67. United States, Office of Strategic Services, *OSS/London: Special Operations Branch and Secret Intelligence Branch War Diaries, 1944*, microfilm, Reel 8, Target 5, Vol. 4, Book V, p. 18.

68. Paul Moniez, interview, 11 September 2007.

69. Colin Burbidge, "Captain Victor Gough," unpublished manuscript, 2008, p. 7, in possession of author.

70. Kenneth Seymour, "Team Jacob Report," HS 6/529, National Archives, Kew, UK, p. 3.

71. Statement of Wilhelm Schneider in "Murder of Parachutists in northeast France Aug–Oct 1944: Report prepared for 2 SAS Regiment," WO 218/222, as quoted in Burbidge manuscript, "Captain Victor Gough," p. 8.

72. "Team JACOB Report," HS 6/529, National Archives, Kew, UK, p. 3.

73. "Telegram de PLANETE," 3 Sept 44, 1 K 374, Archives National, Paris, France.

74. United States, Office of Strategic Services, *OSS/London: Special Operations Branch and Secret Intelligence Branch War Diaries, 1944*, microfilm, Reel 8, Target 4, Vol. 4, Book IV, p. 766.

75. "Status of Jedburghs" Amended 27 August, 1944, 3 AJ 2 462, Archives National, Paris, France.

76. United States, Office of Strategic Services, *OSS/London: Special Operations Branch and Secret Intelligence Branch War Diaries, 1944*, microfilm, Reel 8, Target 4, Vol. 4, Book IV, p. 767.

77. Jeffrey J. Clarke, Robert Ross Smith, and Center of Military History, *Riviera to the Rhine*. World War II 50th anniversary commemorative edition, *CMH Pub; 7–10* (Washington, DC: Center of Military History, US Government Printing Office, 1993), p. 260.

78. Eric A. Johnson, *Nazi Terror: The Gestapo, Jews, and Ordinary Germans* (New York: Basic Books, 2001), pp. 57–58.

79. Kenneth Seymour, "Team JACOB Report," HS 6/529, p. 4, National Archives, Kew, UK.

80. Burbidge lists the airmen as Lt. G. P. Jacoby, Sgt. Michael Pipock, Sgt. Curtis Hodges, and Sgt. Maynard Latten. The priests were Abbe Roth, Abbe Claude, and Father Pennarath. The Frenchman's name was Werner Jakob. Burbidge manuscript, "Captain Victor Gough," in possession of author.

81. Burbidge manuscript, "Captain Victor Gough," p. 13.

82. Burbidge manuscript, "Captain Victor Gough," p. 14. Quoted from Buck's sworn statement of 22 Sept 1945 from WO 218/222.

83. Burbidge manuscript, "Captain Victor Gough," pp. 18–19.

84. Colin Burbidge, "Major Eric Barkworth," unpublished manuscript, 2008, pp. 12–16. Manuscript in possession of author.

85. Team Jacob, HS 6/529, pp. 4, 6, National Archives, Kew, UK.

86. Manierre and Manierre, "Pop's War" (unpublished memoir), pp. 83–93.

Conclusion: Eisenhower's Guerrillas in History and Memory

1. "Grand Total des Armes Principales parachutes en France par R. F. et F compris Massingham-Alger Durant les annees 1941, 1942, 1943, 1944," de Charles W. Cowie, Chief of Section Statistiques, United States Army, European Theater of Operations, *The French Forces of the Interior* (Washington, DC: Library of Congress, Photoduplication Service, 1977), microfilm, Center for Military History, Carlisle Barracks, PA.

2. SHAEF G-2 Memo, "MF/GBI/OI/180," 25 November 1944, France, Vol. III, French Resistance Groups, Reel 52, Frame 396, SHAEF SGS Records, Dwight D. Eisenhower Presidential Library, Abilene, KS. These 114,000 did not include those involved in combat in western or eastern France. Therefore, the total armed by clandestine methods may be far higher. But the number also includes the FFI armed from French Armistice Army weapons brought out during the Libération or with captured German weapons.

3. OSS/SO London Microfilm, Reel 8, Target 1, Vol. 4, Book I, p. 105.

4. "Report of Captain Lake, DIGGER Circuit," 27 September 1944, HS 6/574, British National Archives, Kew, UK, p. 4. Aristide's real name was Roger Landes who directed Team Ammonia while in Bordeaux but assumed that role, as EMFFI never gave him any authority there. Hilaire's real name was George Starr, probably the most influential British subject in France at the time, who attempted to make Teams Bugatti, Quinine, Mark, Chrysler, Miles, and Martin as effective and useful as possible and integrate their actions with his and SFHQ's plans. Starr's own effectiveness may be the reason the regional military delegate (DMR) could not gain any meaningful power in the region. No historical work on the DMRs has been done to examine their effectiveness, so this is merely a guess.

5. Bernard M. W. Knox, interview, 8 June 2001. Since he survived, but did not sign for his gear, Captain Knox did not return it. His souvenirs of the war are indeed impressive and include the hat belonging to an SS colonel whom he conned into surrendering in April of 1945 in Italy.

6. Michel de Bourbon-Parme, interview, 22 September 2007.

7. Telephone interview with Donna Cyr, 30 March 1999.

8. Emails from Lieutenant General Frank Kisner, Commander, NATO Special Operations Headquarters, to the author, July 2010.

9. See Dixee R. Bartholomew-Feis, *The OSS and Ho Chi Minh: Unexpected Allies in the War against Japan* (Lawrence, KS: University of Kansas Press, 2007).

10. Bernard Fall, *Street without Joy: The French Debacle in Indochina* (Harrisburg, PA: Stackpole Books, 1994), pp. 22–27.

11. See General Paul Aussaresses, *The Battle of the Casbah: Terrorism and Counterterrorism in Algeria 1955–1957* (New York: Enigma Books, 2004).

12. See Richard H. Shultz Jr. *The Secret War against Hanoi: Kennedy's and Johnson's use of Spies, Saboteurs, and Covert Warriors in North Vietnam* (New York: Harper Collins, 1999).

13. Stewart Alsop, "Kennedy's Grand Strategy," *Saturday Evening Post* 31, no. 13 (March 1962): 11–15. The irony of how things have changed is clear. In 1962, in the

bipartisan Cold War efforts, Americans wished to "carry any burden," as President Kennedy put it, to win in Vietnam, Berlin, Cuba, and elsewhere and marshaled all political and military efforts toward that goal. Now President Obama avoids risk by using unmanned aircraft to kill enemy leaders, supports the nation that provides the enemy sanctuary, is reducing support to the Afghan government, is getting nothing from the enemy in return, and expects all this to produce a favorable result.

14. The Geneva Accords of 1954 set up a path to unify Vietnam, but neither the United States nor South Vietnam signed them. Eisenhower's former SHAEF Chief of Staff, General William Bedell Smith, who was in 1954 secretary of state, opted out of the Accords as they did not have the guarantees necessary for an honest result. When the subsequent mass immigration of Vietnamese from the north to the south occurred through 1955, most of the non-communists left North Vietnam for South Vietnam. Their absence made any future insurgency against Ho Chi Minh nearly impossible.

15. Interview with Major General John K. Singlaub, 9 June 2001.

16. Historians Peter Novick, Charles-Louis Foulon, John Sweets, and Jean-Louis Crémieux-Brilhac, among others, have all demonstrated this point in their works. Their cases are quite convincing, but readers may wish to look into them directly.

BIBLIOGRAPHY

PRIMARY SOURCES

Archival

UNITED STATES

Dwight D. Eisenhower Presidential Library, Abilene, KS
    Pre-Presidential Papers, 1916–1952
    Smith, Walter Bedell, Collection of WWII Documents, 1941–1945
    Supreme Headquarters, Allied Expeditionary Force, Office of Secretary, General
        Staff: Records, 1943–45
    Supreme Headquarters, Allied Expeditionary Force, and Chief of Staff, Supreme
        Allied Command, Office of G-3 (Harold R. Bull): Records, 1943–46, microfilm
    Wyden, Barbara Papers, 1944–1946
Franklin D. Roosevelt Presidential Library and Museum, Hyde Park, NY
    Roosevelt, Franklin D., Papers as President, Map Room File
    Pare-Lorenz Chronology
National Archives, College Park, MD
    Record Group 226
Hoover Institution, Stanford, CA
    Paul van der Stricht Papers
Center for Military History, Carlisle Barracks, PA
    File no. 8-3 France, acc. No 419-1
OSS Washington Director's Office Administrative Files, 1941–1945 (M1642), United
    States Air Force Academy Cadet Library, Colorado Springs, CO
Manuscript #53, Special Operations Collection, McDermott Library, United States Air
    Force Academy, CO. (Originally, this source was created by Mr. Tom Ensminger
    from government documents and veterans' gifts. Mr. Ensminger passed away in 2012
    and the format in which the author made these sources available has since changed.
    The documents were subsequently given to the Air Force Academy. The Special
    Collections archivists are, as of this printing, working to make them again available
    to researchers.)

UNITED KINGDOM

National Archives, Kew
    AIR Series

FO Series
HS Series
HW Series
WO Series
Imperial War Museum, London
  Sound Archive—Irregular Warfare
  Liddell Hart Centre for Military Archives, King's College London
  Mockler-Ferryman, Brig Eric (1896–1978) Papers

FRANCE
Archives National, Paris
  3 AG 2
  3 AG 3
Service d'Historique de la Defense, Château de Vincennes, Paris
  8 P 1
  1 K 237
  1 K 374
  1 K 375
  13 P 62
  13 P 63
  13 P 151
  13 P 156

GERMANY
Bundesarchiv-Militärchiv, Freiburg im Breisgau
  RH 19
  RH 24–25
  RH 24–86
  RH 26–266
  RW 20
  RW 35–551

Private Collections

Beavan, Colin, papers and interview transcripts used for *Operation Jedburgh: America's First Shadow War* (New York: Viking), 2006
  Tommy MacPherson Interview
  John Cox Interview
  Michel de Bourbon-Parme Interview
  Paul van der Stricht Interview
  Canfield, Franklin. "Memoirs of a Long and Eventful Life"
  Jacques de Penguilly Interview
Carpetbagger Archive (formerly), http://home.comcast.net/~801492bg.historian/ Index.html now residing in a reorganized collection at the United States Air Force Academy, McDermott Library
Haskell, Joseph F. Service Papers and Photographs, courtesy of Julia Haskell Paine and Janet Haskell Spalding, New York, NY

Interviews with Author

Aussaresses, Paul. Interview, 25 September 2007
Cyr, Donna. Telephone interview, 30 March 1999
De Bourbon-Parme, Michel. Interview, 22 September 2007
De Francesco, Joseph. Telephone interview, 2 March 1999
Franklin, Dick, Telephone interview, 23 May 2008
Friele, Daphne. Telephone interview, 2 March 1999
Gauthier, Mamie. Telephone interview, 6 March 1999
Kehoe, Robert. Interview, 26 August 2000
Kloman, Erasmus. Telephone interview, 21 August 2005
Knox, Bernard M. W. Interview, 8 June 2001
Le Blanc, Robert. Telephone interview, 22 January 2008
Le Long, Camille. Telephone interview, 24 July 2007
Moniez, Paul. Interview, 11 September 2007
Paine, Julia. Interview, 14 July 2007
Putzell, Edward. Interview, 8 June 2002
Singlaub, John K. Interview, 9 June 2001 and 24 January 2007
Thompson, William. Interview, 14 January 1999

Correspondence

Aussaresses, Paul. Letter to author, 2 June 1999
Brown, O. A. Letter to author, 26 June 1999
Burbidge, Colin. Emails to author, 17–31 May 2008
Crawshay, Elizabeth. Letter to author, 29 July 1998
Dechelette, Anne. Letter to author, 18 February 2009
De Francesco, Joe. Letter to author, 3 March 1999
Franklin, Dick. Numerous emails to author
Henely, Joann and Michael Henely. Numerous emails to author
La Jeunesse, Lou. Numerous emails to author, 2002 to 2003
Poche, Jack. Email to author, 13 April 2007

Unpublished Works

Burbidge, Colin. "Major Barkworth," 2008. In possession of author.
Burbidge, Colin. "Captain Victor Gough," 2008. In possession of author.
Moore, Bernard Victor. "The Secret Air War over France: USAAF Special Operations Units in the French Campaign of 1944." A Historical Case Study of the Role of Air Force Special Operations Forces in High Intensity Conflict. Thesis. School of Advanced Airpower Studies, Air University, Maxwell AFB, AL, 1992.
Irwin, Wyman W. "A Special Force: Origin and Development of the Jedburgh Project in Support of Operation OVERLORD," MMAS Thesis, U. S. Army Command and General Staff College, Fort Leavenworth, KS.

Published Works

Alsop, Stewart. *Stay of Execution: A Sort of Memoir*. Philadelphia: Lippincott, 1973.

Alsop, Stewart, and Thomas Wardell Braden. *Sub Rosa; the O.-S.-S. and American Espionage*. New York: Reynal and Hitchcock, 1946.

Aussaresses, Paul. *Pour la France: Services Spéciaux 1942–1954*. Monaco: Rocher, 2001.

Aussaresses, Paul. *The Battle of the Casbah*. New York: Enigma, 2002.

Bradley, Omar Nelson, and Herman Finkelstein Collection (Library of Congress). *A Soldier's Story*. Edited by Caleb Carr. New York: Random House, 1999. Reprint, Modern Library Paperback Edition.

Brooke, Alan, Daniel Todman, and Alex Danchev, *War Diaries, 1939–1945: Field Marshal Lord Alanbrooke*. Berkeley: University of California Press, 2001.

Bruce, David K. E. *OSS against the Reich: The World War II Dairies of Colonel David K. E. Bruce*. Edited by Nelson D. Lankford. Kent, OH: Kent State University Press, 1991.

Chaban-Delmas, Jacques. *Mémoires Pour Demain*. Paris: Flammarion, 1997.

Camus, Albert, Jacqueline Lévi-Valensi, and Arthur Goldhammer. *Camus at Combat: Writing 1944–1947*. Princeton, NJ: Princeton University Press, 2006.

Crosby, M. G. M. "Bing." *Irregular Soldier*. Guernsey: Guernsey Press, 1993.

Churchill, Winston. *The River War, an Account of the Reconquest of the Sudan*. London: Eyre and Spottiswoode, 1951.

Danchev, Alex, and Daniel Todman, eds. *War Diaries, 1939–1945: Field Marshal Lord Alanbrooke*. Berkeley: University of California Press, 2001.

Dewavrin, Andre. *Colonel Passy: Memoires du Chef des Services Secrets de la France Libre*. Paris: Editions Odile Jacob, 2000.

Donovan, William J., and Edgar Mowrer. *Fifth Column Lessons for America*, with an introduction by Frank Knox. Washington, DC: American Council on Public Affairs, 1941.

Dreux, William B. *No Bridges Blown*. Notre Dame: University of Notre Dame Press, 1971.

Dulles, Allen Welsh, Neal H. Petersen, and United States Office of Strategic Services. *From Hitler's Doorstep: The Wartime Intelligence Reports of Allen Dulles, 1942–1945*. University Park: Pennsylvania State University Press, 1996.

Eisenhower, Dwight D., Alfred D. Chandler, and Louis Galambos. *The Papers of Dwight David Eisenhower*. Baltimore, MD: Johns Hopkins University Press, 1970.

Eisenhower, Dwight D., and Robert H. Ferrell. *The Eisenhower Diaries*. New York: Norton, 1981.

Gaulle, Charles de. *The Complete War Memoirs of Charles De Gaulle*. New York: Carroll and Graf, 1998.

Grandval, Gilbert, and A. Jean Collin. *Libération de l'est de la France*. Paris: Hachette, 1974.

Guillain de Bénouville, Pierre. *The Unknown Warriors, a Personal Account of the French Resistance*. New York: Simon and Schuster, 1949.

Hutchison, James. *That Drug Danger*. Montrose, Scotland, UK: Standard Press, 1977.

Kehoe, Robert. "Jed Team Frederick, 1944: An Allied Team with the French Resistance." *Studies in Intelligence* (Winter 1998–1999).

Knox, Bernard M. W. *Essays: Ancient and Modern*. Baltimore, MD: Johns Hopkins University Press, 1989.

Koenig, Pierre. *Bir-Hakeim, 10 Juin 1942*. Paris: R. Laffont, 1971.

Lawrence, T. E. *Seven Pillars of Wisdom: A Triumph*. New York: Penguin Books, 1962.

Mendelsohn, John, ed. *Covert Warfare Intelligence, Counterintelligence, and Military Deception during the World War II Era*. 18 vols. New York: Garland, 1989. Vol. 3.

Marks, Leo. *Between Silk and Cyanide: A Codemaker's War, 1941–1945*. London: Free Press, 1999.

Marshall, George C., Larry I. Bland, and Sharon R. Ritenour. *The Papers of George Catlett Marshall*. Baltimore, MD: Johns Hopkins University Press, 1981.

Pichard, Michel. *L'Espoir des Ténèbres: Parachutages sous l'Occupation*. Paris: Editeur, 1990.

Rémy. *Mémoires d'un Agent Secret de la France Libre*. Ed. rev. et augm., avec un témoignage autographe du général de Gaulle et une postface du colonel "Passy." ed. Paris: Editions France-Empire, 1983.

Roosevelt, Franklin D., and William C. Bullitt. *For the President, Personal and Secret; Correspondence between Franklin D. Roosevelt and William C. Bullitt*. Edited by Orville H. Bullitt. Boston: Houghton Mifflin, 1972.

Sassi, Jean, with Jean-Louis Tremblais. *Operations Speciales 20 Ans de Guerres Secretes*. Paris: Nimrod, 2009.

Singlaub, John K., with Malcolm McConnell. *Hazardous Duty: An American Soldier in the Twentieth Century*. New York: Simon and Schuster, 1991.

Travers, Susan, and Wendy Holden. *Tomorrow to Be Brave*. New York: Free Press, 2001.

United States Marine Corps. *Small Wars Manual, FMFRP; 12–15*. Washington, DC: The Corps, 1997.

United States War Department, Strategic Services Unit. History Project, Vol. 1, *The War Report of the OSS* (Office of Strategic Services), with a new introduction by Kermit Roosevelt New York: Walker, 1976.

Warlimont, Walter. *Inside Hitler's Headquarters, 1939–45*. London: Weidenfeld and Nicolson, 1964.

Wilkinson, Peter. *Foreign Fields: The Story of an SOE Operative*. London: I. B. Tauris, 1997.

Wilkinson, Peter, and Joan Bright Astley Wilkinson. *Gubbins and SOE*. London: Pen & Sword Paperback, 1997.

Unpublished Memoirs

Brown, Arthur. "The Jedburghs: A Short History," undated. In author's possession.

Brown, Arthur. Some Notes on Jedburgh "QUININE," Rev. June 1999. In author's possession.

Franklin, Dick. "Jedburg," 2004. In author's possession.

Manierre, Cyrus and Carter Manierre. "Pop's War," 2002. In author's possession.

Microfilm

Donovan, William J., and OSS Washington Office. *OSS Washington Director's Office Administrative Files, 1941–1945 (M1642)*. Washington, DC: US Government Printing Office, 1998. 136 Microfilm reels. Copy at McDermott Library, United States Air Force Academy, CO.

Kesaris, Paul, editor. *Map Room Messages of President Roosevelt, 1939–1945 Microform.* Frederick, MD: University Publications of America, 1981. 9 microfilm reels.

Kesaris, Paul, editor. United States Office of Strategic Services, and United States Department of State. *Germany and Its Occupied Territories during World War II Microfilm, O.S.S./State Department Intelligence and Research Reports; Pt. 4.* Washington: University Publications of America, 1977.

Lester, Robert, Blair Hydrick, Franklin D. Roosevelt, and John Franklin Carter. *President Franklin D. Roosevelt's Office Files, 1933–1945.* Bethesda, MD: University Publications of America, 1990. Microfilm.

Roosevelt, Franklin D. *President Franklin D. Roosevelt's Office Files, 1933–1945, Part 1: "Safe" and Confidential Files.* Bethesda, MD: University Publications of America. Microfilm.

Stimson, Henry L., Herman Kahn, Bonnie B. Collier, and Pauline Goldstein. *The Henry Lewis Stimson Diaries in the Yale University Library.* New Haven, CT: Yale University Library, 1973. Microfilm.

United States Army, European Theater of Operations. *The French Forces of the Interior.* Washington, DC: Library of Congress, Photoduplication Service, 1977. Microfilm. [The paper copy, in French, is in Vincennes (Paris) at the French Army archives, and another paper copy resides in the British National Archives.]

United States, Office of Strategic Services. *OSS/London: Special Operations Branch and Secret Intelligence Branch War Diaries, 1944.* Frederick, MD: University Publications of America, 1985. Microfilm.

SECONDARY

Scholarly Journals

David G. Haglund. "Roosevelt as 'Friend of France—but Which One?" *Diplomatic History* 31, no. 5 (2007): 895–98.

Published Books

Aglan, Alya. *La Résistance Sacrifiée Le mouvement: Libération Nord.* Paris: Flammarion, 1999.

Aglion, Raoul. *Roosevelt and De Gaulle: Allies in Conflict: A Personal Memoir.* New York: Free Press, 1988.

Atkinson, Rick. *An Army at Dawn: The War in North Africa, 1942–1943.* New York: Henry Holt, 2002.

Argyle, Ray. *The Paris Game: Charles de Gaulle, the Liberation of Paris, and the Gamble that won France.* Ontario, Canada: Dundurn Press, 2014.

Baudot, Marcel. *Libération de la Bretagne.* Paris: Hachette, 1973.

Bartholomew-Feis, Dixee R. *The OSS and Ho Chi Minh: Unexpected Allies in the War against Japan.* Lawrence: University of Kansas Press, 2007.

Beaufre, André. *1940; the Fall of France, by General André Beaufre.* London: Cassell, 1967.

Beavan, Colin. *Operation Jedburgh: D-Day and America's First Shadow War.* New York: Viking, 2006.

Bickel, Keith B. *Mars Learning: The Marine Corps Development of Small Wars Doctrine, 1915–1940*. Boulder, CO: Westview Press, 2001.

Bloch, Marc. *Strange Defeat; a Statement of Evidence Written in 1940*. Translated by Gerard Hopkins. New York: Norton, 1968.

Blumenson, Martin, and Center of Military History. *Breakout and Pursuit, CMH Pub; 7–5*. Washington, DC: Center of Military History, U.S. Army, 2005.

Blumentritt, Günther, and David C. Isby. *Fighting the Invasion: The Germany Army at D-Day*. London: Greenhill Books, 2000.

Bonn, Keith E. *When the Odds Were Even: The Vosges Mountains Campaign, October 1944–January 1945*. Novato, CA: Presidio, 1994.

Bonnet, Gabriel Georges Marcel. *Les Guerres Insurrectionnelles et Révolutionnaires de L'antiquité à nos Jours*. Paris: Payot, 1958.

Boog, Horst, Gerhard Krebs, and Detlef Vogel. *The Strategic Air War in Europe and the War in the West and East Asia 1943–1944/5*. New York: Oxford University Press, 2006.

Brown, Anthony Cave. *The Last Hero: Wild Bill Donovan*. New York: Times Books, 1982.

Burrin, Philippe. La France á L'heure Allemande: 1940–1944. Paris: Seuil, 1995.

Buton, Philippe. *Les Lendemains Qui Déchantent: Le Parti Communiste Français á la Libération*. [Paris, France]: Presses de la Fondation nationale des sciences politiques, 1993.

Callwell, Charles E. *Small Wars: Their Principles and Practice*. 3rd ed. Lincoln: University of Nebraska Press, 1996.

Calvi, Fabrizio, and Olivier Schmidt. *OSS: La Guerre Secréte en France, 1942–1945: Les Services Spéciaux Américains, La Résistance et La Gestapo*. Paris: Hachette, 1990.

Capdevila, Luc. *Les Bretons au lendemain de l'Occupation: Imaginaire et comportement d'une sortie de guerre 1944–1945*. Rennes, France: Presses Universitaires, 1999.

Casey, William. *The Secret War against Hitler*. Washington, DC: Regnery Gateway, 1988.

Childers, Thomas. *The Nazi Voter: The Social Foundations of Fascism in Germany, 1919–1933*. Chapel Hill: University of North Carolina Press, 1983.

Clarke, Jeffrey J., Robert Ross Smith, and Center of Military History. *Riviera to the Rhine*. Washington, DC: US Government Printing Office, 1993.

Clausewitz, Karl von. *On War*. Edited and translated by Michael Howard, Peter Peret, and Bernard Brodie; with a commentary by Bernard Brodie. Princeton, NJ: Princeton University Press, 1989.

Cole, Alistair, and Peter Campbell. *French Electoral Systems and Elections since 1789*. Aldershot, England: Gower, 1989.

Colton, Joel. *Léon Blum: Humanist in Politics*. Durham, NC: Duke University Press, 1987.

Cookridge, E. H. *Inside S. O. E.: The Story of Special Operations in Western Europe, 1940–45*. London: Barker, 1966.

Cordier, Daniel. *Jean Moulin: La République des Catacombes, Suite des Temps*. Paris: Gallimard, 1999.

Courtois, Stéphane. *Le P C F dans la Guerre: De Gaulle, la Résistance, Staline*. Paris: Ramsay, 1980.

Crémieux-Brilhac, Jean-Louis. *La France Libre: De L'appel du 18 Juin à la Libération.* 2 vols. Paris: Gallimard, 2001.

Crémieux-Brilhac, Jean-Louis. *Les Français de l'An 40.* 2 Vols., *La Suite Des Temps.* [Paris]: Gallimard, 1990.

Doubler, Michael D. *Closing with the Enemy: How GIs Fought the War in Europe, 1944–1945, Modern War Studies.* Lawrence: University Press of Kansas, 1994.

Doughty, Robert A. *The Breaking Point: Sedan and the Fall of France, 1940.* Hamden, CT: Archon Books, 1990.

Douzou, Laurent. *La Désobéissance: Histoire d'un Mouvement et d'un Journal Clandestins, Libération-Sud, 1940–1944.* Paris: O. Jacob, 1995.

Durand, Paul. *La S.N.C.F. Pendant La Guerre, sa Résistance à l'Occupant.* Paris: Presses universitaires de France, 1968.

Fall, Bernard. *Street without Joy: The French Debacle in Indochina.* Harrisburg, PA: Stackpole Books, 1994.

Foot, M. R. D. *SOE in France: An Account of the Work of the British Special Operations Executive in France, 1940–1944.* London: Her Majesty's Stationery Office, 1966.

Footitt, Hilary, and John Simmonds. *France 1943–1945, the Politics of Liberation Series.* [Leicester]: Leicester University Press, 1988.

Foulon, Charles-Louis. *Le Pouvoir en Province à la Libération: Les Commissaires de la République, 1943–1946, Travaux et Recherches de Science Politique; 32.* Paris: Fondation Nationale des Sciences Politiques, 1975.

Funk, Arthur Layton. *Charles de Gaulle: The Crucial Years, 1943–1944.* Norman: University of Oklahoma Press, 1959.

Funk, Arthur Layton. *Hidden Ally: The French Resistance, Special Operations, and the Landings in Southern France, 1944, Contributions in Military Studies, No. 122.* New York: Greenwood Press, 1992.

Gaujac, Paul. *Special Forces in the Invasion of France.* Translated by Janice Lert. Edited by Eric Micheletti. *Special Operations Series.* Paris: Histoire et Collections, 1999.

Guéguen-Dreyfus, Georgette, and Bernard Lehoux. *Résistance Indre et Vallée du Cher. Témoignages de Résistants de l'Indre et de la Vallée du Cher; de la Creuse, Région de la Souterraine; de l'Indre-et-Loire, Lochois; du Cher-Sud, Saint-Amand, et de la Vienne, Montmorillon, Recueillis.* Paris: Editions sociales, 1970.

Grenier, John. *The First Way of War: American War Making on the Frontier, 1607–1814* New York: Cambridge University Press, 2005.

Hastings, Max. *Das Reich: Resistance and the March of the 2nd SS Panzer Division through France, June 1944.* London: M. Joseph, 1981.

Helm, Sarah. *A Life in Secrets: Vera Atkins and the Missing Agents of WWII.* London: Abacus, 2006.

Herodotus. *The Histories.* Edited by David Campbell; introduction by Rosalind Thomas. Translated by George Rawlinson. London: Everyman's Library, 1997.

Hirshson, Stanley P. *General Patton: A Soldier's Life.* New York: HarperCollins, 2002.

Humes, James C. *The Wit and Wisdom of Winston Churchill.* New York: Harper Perennial, 1995.

Irwin, Will. *The Jedburghs: The Secret History of the Allied Special Forces, France 1944.* New York: Public Affairs, 2005.

Inquimbert, Anne-Aurore. *Les Equipes Jedburgh (juin 1944–décembre 1944) Le rôle des services spéciaux alliés dans le contrôle de la Résistance intérieure française.* Lavauzelle: Service historique de la Defense, 2006.

Jackson, Julian. *France: The Dark Years, 1940–1944.* Oxford: Oxford University Press, 2001.

Johnson, Eric A. *Nazi Terror: The Gestapo, Jews, and Ordinary Germans.* New York: Basic Books, 2001.

Jouanneau, Michel. *L'organisation de la Résistance dans L'indre: Juin 1940–Juin 1944.* Versailles, France: Le Impremerie Aubert S. A., 1975.

Kedward, H. R. *In Search of the Maquis: Rural Resistance in Southern France, 1942–1944.* New York: Oxford University Press, 1993.

Kersaudy, François. *Churchill and De Gaulle.* London: Collins, 1981.

Korda, Michael. *Hero: The Life and Legend of Lawrence of Arabia.* New York: Harper Collins, 2011.

Laborie, Pierre. *L'opinion Française Sous Vichy, l'Univers Historique.* Paris: Seuil, 1990.

Lewis, Samuel J. *Jedburgh Team Operations in Support of the 12th Army Group, August 1944.* Fort Leavenworth, KS: US Army Command and General Staff College, 1991.

Lacouture, Jean. *De Gaulle.* New York: New American Library, 1966.

Le Moigne, Louis and Marcel Barbanceys. *Sedentaires, Refractaires, et Maquisards: L'armée Secrète en Haute Correze, 1942–1944.* Moulins: les Imprimiers Reunies, 1979.

Liddell Hart. B. H. *Strategy.* 2nd rev. ed. New York: Penguin, 1991.

Lieb, Peter. *Konventioneller Krieg oder NS-Weltanschauungskrieg?: Kriegführung und Partisanenbekämpfung in Frankreich 1943/44*, Quellen und Darstellungen zur Zeitgeschichte; Bd. 69. München: Oldenbourg, 2007.

Mackenzie, William. *The Secret History of S. O. E.: Special Operations Executive 1940–1945.* London, UK: St. Ermins Press, 2002.

MacPherson, Nelson. *American Intelligence in War-Time London: The Story of the OSS.* Portland, OR: Frank Cass, 2003.

Marcot, François, and Angèle Baud. *La Franche-Comté sous l'Occupation, 1940–1944.* Besançon: Cêtre, 1985.

Marcot, François, and Angèle Baud. *La Résistance dans le Jura.* Besançon: Cêtre, 1985.

Marcot, François, Bruno Leroux, and Christine Levisse-Touzé. *Dictionnaire Historique de la Résistance: Résistance Intérieure et France Libre, Bouquins.* Paris: Laffont, 2006.

Michel, Henri. *The Shadow War; European Résistance, 1939–1945.* New York: Harper and Row, 1972.

Millett, Allan Reed, and Peter Maslowski. *For the Common Defense: A Military History of the United States of America.* Rev. and expanded ed. New York: Free Press, 1994.

Mitcham, Samuel W. *Retreat to the Reich: The German Defeat in France, 1944.* Westport, CT: Praeger, 2000.

Murray, Williamson, and Allan Reed Millett. *A War to Be Won: Fighting the Second World War.* Cambridge, MA: Belknap Press of Harvard University Press, 2000.

Noguères, Henri, Marcel Degliame-Fouché, and Jean Louis Vigier. *Histoire de la Résistance en France, de 1940 à 1945*. 5 vols. Paris: R. Laffont, 1981.

Novick, Peter. *The Resistance versus Vichy: The Purge of Collaborators in Liberated France*. London: Chatto and Windus, 1968.

Parnell, Ben. *Carpetbaggers: America's Secret War in Europe*. Austin, TX: Eakin Press, 1987.

Paxton, Robert O. *Vichy France: Old Guard and New Order 1940–1944*. New York: Columbia University Press, 2001.

Persico, Joseph E. *Roosevelt's Secret War: FDR and World War II Espionage*. New York: Random House, 2001.

Porch, Douglas. *The French Secret Service: From the Dreyfus Affair to the Gulf War*. New York: Farrar, Straus and Giroux, 1995.

Price, Frank James. *Troy H. Middleton: A Biography*. Baton Rouge: Louisiana State University Press, 1974.

Reynolds, David. *In Command of History: Churchill Fighting and Writing the Second World War*. London: Allen Lane, 2004.

Robertson, Charles L. *When Roosevelt Planned to Govern France*. Amherst: University of Massachusetts Press, 2011.

Rousso, Henry. *The Vichy Syndrome: History and Memory in France since 1944*. Cambridge, MA: Harvard University Press, 1991.

Ruby, Marcel. *F Section: The Buckmaster Networks*. London: Lee Cooper, 1988.

Sassi, Jean, with Jean-Louis Tremblais. *Operations Speciales 20 Ans de Guerres Secretes*. Paris: Nimrod, 2009.

Schwartz, Thomas Alan. *America's Germany: John J. McCloy and the Federal Republic of Germany*. Cambridge, MA: Harvard University Press, 1991.

Shultz, Richard H. *The Secret War against Hanoi: Kennedy's and Johnson's Use of Spies, Saboteurs, and Covert Warriors in North Vietnam*. New York: HarperCollins, 1999.

Silvestre, Paul, and S. Silvestre. *Chronique des Maquis de l'Isére: 1943–1944*. Grenoble: Presses Universitaires de Grenoble, 1995.

Smith, Jean Edward. *FDR*. New York: Random House, 2007.

Smith, Richard Harris. *OSS: The Secret History of America's First Central Intelligence Agency*. Guildford, CT: First Lyons Press, 2005; originally published Berkeley: University of California Press, 1972.

Stafford, David. *Britain and European Resistance, 1940–1945: A Survey of the Special Operations Executive, with Documents*. Toronto: University of Toronto Press, 1980.

Stafford, David. *Churchill and the Secret Service*. Woodstock, NY: Overlook Press, 1998.

Stimpel, Hans-Martin. *Die Deutsche Fallschirmtruppe 1942–1945: Einsätze auf Kriegsschauplätzen im Osten und Westen*. Hamburg: E.S. Mittler, 2001.

Stoler, Mark A. *Allies and Adversaries: The Joint Chiefs of Staff, the Grand Alliance, and U.S. Strategy in World War II*. Chapel Hill: University of North Carolina Press, 2000.

Sweets, John F. *Choices in Vichy France: The French under Nazi Occupation*. New York: Oxford University Press, 1986.

Sweets, John F. *The Politics of Résistance in France, 1940–1944: A History of the Mouvements Unis de la Résistance*. Dekalb: Northern Illinois University Press, 1976.

Todorov, Tzvetan. *A French Tragedy: Scenes of Civil War, Summer 1944*. Translated by Mary Byrd Kelly. Edited and annotated by Richard J. Golsan. Hanover, NH: University Press of New England, 1996.

United States, Office of Strategic Services. *Assessment of Men: Selection of Personnel for the Office of Strategic Services*. New York: Rinehart, 1948.

Vergnon, Gilles. *Le Vercors: Histoire et Mémoire d'un Maquis*. Paris: Atelier, 2002.

Vigneras, Marcel. *The United States Army in World War II, Special Studies: Rearming the French*. Edited by Kent Roberts Greenfield, *United States Army in World War II*. Washington, DC: US Government Printing Office, 1957.

Waller, Douglas. *Wild Bill Donovan: The Spymaster Who Created the OSS and Modern American Espionage*. New York: Free Press, 2011.

Waugh, Evelyn. *Sword of Honour: A Final Version of the Novels, Men at Arms 1952; Officers and Gentlemen 1955; and Unconditional Surrender 1961*. London: Random House, 1994.

Nigel West. *Secret War: The Story of SOE, Britain's Wartime Sabotage Organisation*. London: Houghton and Stoughton, 1992.

White, Dorothy Shipley. *Seeds of Discord: De Gaulle, Free France, and the Allies*. Syracuse, NY: Syracuse University Press, 1964.

Williams, Heather. *Parachutes, Patriots and Partisans: The Special Operations Executive and Yugoslavia, 1941–1945*. London: Hurst, 2003.

Wilkinson, Peter and Joan Bright Astley Wilkinson, *Gubbins and SOE*. London: Pen & Sword, 1997.

Wilson, Theodore A., and Eisenhower Foundation. *D-Day, 1944, Modern War Studies*. Lawrence: Published for the Eisenhower Foundation, Abilene, KS, by the University Press of Kansas, 1994.

Young, Robert J. *In Command of France: French Foreign Policy and Military Planning, 1933–1940*. Cambridge, MA: Harvard University Press, 1978.

Colloquium Proceedings, Dissertations and Theses

Irwin, Wyman W. "A Special Force: Origin and Development of the Jedburgh Project in Support of Operation OVERLORD." MMAS Thesis, US Army Command and General Staff College, Fort Leavenworth.

Laub, Thomas Johnston. "The Politics of Occupation: The German Military Administration in France, 1940–1944." Dissertation, University of Virginia, 2003.

Moore, Bernard Victor. "The Secret Air War over France: USAAF Special Operations Units in the French Campaign of 1944," a Historical Case Study of the Role of Air Force Special Operations Forces in High Intensity Conflict. Thesis, School of Advanced Airpower Studies, Air University, Maxwell AFB, AL, 1992.

Marcot, François, Janine Ponty, Marcel Vigreux, et Serge Wilikox: *La Résistance et la Français: Lutte armée et Maquis*. Actes du colloque international de Besançon—15–17 juin 1995. Annales littéraires de l'Université de Franch-Comté diffusion Les Belles Lettres, Paris, 1996.

Newspapers and Magazines

Alsop, Stewart. "Kennedy's Grand Strategy." *Saturday Evening Post,* March 31, 1962.
Harold Callenders. Special to the *New York Times.* "De Gaulle *Power* Not Parley Issue: Question of Recognition as Government Will Not Come Up," *New York Times* (1857—Current file), July 8, 1944, http://www.proquest.com.www2.lib.ku .edu:2048/accessed March 18, 2008.
"Administration' française," *Libération,* 17 Julliet 1944, p. 2. Courtesy of the Center for Research Libraries.

Unpublished Works

Burbidge, Colin. "Major Barkworth," 2008.
Burbidge, Colin. "Captain Victor Gough," 2008.

INDEX